John Lepper worked for 17 years in the finance industry, 26 years as an economic advisor, and eight years as teacher/post-doctoral research fellow at universities in New Zealand, the UK, People's Republic of China and Australia.

LAND and MONEY

Volume I

JOHN LEPPER

KERR

Melbourne, Victoria

First published 2025
Kerr Publishing Pty Ltd
Melbourne, Victoria
ABN 64 124 219 638

Copyright © 2025 John Lepper

This book is copyright. Unless stated otherwise, all images are included in the above copyright. Apart from fair dealing for the purpose of private study, research, criticism or review, or under the Copyright Agency Ltd rules of recording, no part may be reproduced by any means.

The moral right of the author has been asserted.

ISBN 978-1-875703-54-8
ISBN 978-1-875703-61-6 (Paperback Volume 2)
ISBN 978-1-875703-55-5 (eBook Volume 1)
ISBN 978-1-875703-64-7 (eBook Volume 2)

BIC Category:	KCZ/ Economic History
BISAC Category 1:	BUS023000BUSINESS AND ECONOMICS/Economic History
BISAC Category 2:	LAW/1100000/Indigenous Law
BISAC Category 3:	LAW/055000/Land Use
BISAC Category 4:	LAW/074000/Law/Property
BISAC Category 5:	POLITICAL SCIENCE/World/Australian and Oceanian

Cover and book design: Paul Taylder, Xigrafix Media & Design
Type set in Garamond Pro 11/13

National Library of Australia PrePublication Data Service:

A catalogue record for this book is available from the National Library of Australia

This work is dedicated in loving respect and comradely esteem to the Honourable Sandra Te Hakamatua Lee who has taught me all I know about the past, present and future of colonial worlds

CONTENTS

Foreword vii

Note on Names ix

Measurements Used in this Work x

Introduction 1

CHAPTER 1
Why Colonise Australasia? 5

CHAPTER 2
Planting Non-Indigenous People, Enterprise and Society 47

CHAPTER 3
Monetisation of Australasia 81

CHAPTER 4
Marketable Land in Australasia 109

CHAPTER 5
Start of an Australasian Banking Industry 151

CHAPTER 6
Australasia and the Developing Gold Standard 179

CHAPTER 7
New Zealand Land Markets 203

Index 229

FOREWORD

Land and Money provides a detailed description of the evolution of monetary and banking systems in Australia and New Zealand from colonialist 1770s to the 1920s and their relationship to the ownership and transfer of land.

John Lepper sets his narrative of the imposition of British concepts of land ownership in the context of the different customary practices of the indigenous Australian Aboriginals and Māori of the two colonies as well as later developments such as the discovery of gold, agricultural and pastoral settlement and urbanisation. Indigenous peoples suffered from the loss of land usurped under gunfire and loss of life, succumbing to European-introduced diseases like smallpox, influenza and VD. The shared Australasian history is one of the imposition of British colonial rule and its influence in establishing the institutions that entrenched the dominance of colonial and private corporate power relations.

While Australia was chosen as a penal colony aimed initially at alleviating prison overcrowding in Britain, and New Zealand was not, the Australasian temperate climate appealed more to British colonisers than other colonies like Sierra Leone and India, where the British succumbed to tropical diseases like malaria and yellow fever. With or without treaties the Indigenous owners in Australia and New Zealand were marginalised and pushed to the periphery by British pastoralists who were favoured by land grants and banking loans under colonially-imposed institutions and governance systems. These were explicitly designed to maximise imperial benefit through the usurpation of land and the intrenchment of private property over indigenous ownership held communally. Favourable lending practices by corrupt colonial banks dependent on London banking, lent heavily on real estate secured by mortgages, entrenching settler interests and future choices and compromising the Indigenous futures.

As Lepper argues,

> "The Law of First Taker meant that since no-one owned or occupied or lived upon the land in Australia, no-one could own it. The Law of First Taker asserted that if there were no owners, then the land could not be sold or otherwise ceded by the people who roamed across it. Lawyers reasoned that it followed that lands devoid of people who could reasonably be regarded as land owners was available for the taking by any nation that wished to exercise sovereignty over it."

Land and Money as Lepper explains, is a descriptive account and draws largely on secondary sources and contemporary printed material alongside archival research, including largely unexplored banking archives demonstrating how corrupt cartel practices ruled. He delivers an opus that is detailed and comprehensively buttressed by an extensive number of sources. He makes comprehensive use of contemporary writings and secondary sources to demonstrate how land was legally defined and given meaning socially in those contexts and how the monetary systems of Australia and New Zealand, both reinforced and changed that meaning during the period under study.

The book takes a largely chronological approach, except for Chapter 12 on land companies and Chapter 13 on suburban subdivision, which illustrate how two of the largest land companies operated in Australia and New Zealand.

Like many stories of colonial rule, systems around land and money focused on the repatriation of profit back to colonial interests and to British settlers and financial interests who were in turn, shaped and constrained by colonial institutions.

This well-researched work will contribute to the growing literature on colonisation, which recognises the importance of financial processes—in the formation of colonies and empires relevant to the on-going legacy of colonially imposed institutions and governance systems—especially on indigenous groups up to the present.

It will be an important key source for researchers of Australian and New Zealand economic history and British colonialism, where debt to financial institutions has rendered us conformist and passive to changing inherently exploitative finance and property systems.

Linda Hancock
Professor of Public Policy
Deakin University

NOTE ON NAMES

In Roman times, it was reasoned that Terra Australis or Terra Australis Incognita must exist in the Southern Hemisphere to balance the land massed north of the Equator. During the Middle Ages this theoretical territory became known as The Antipodes. European observation of reality began in earnest in 1642 and 1643, when Abel Tasman named Nieuw Holland and Nieuw Zeland. Over the next generation they became Anglicised respectively as New Holland and New Zealand. New Holland appears to have been used to refer to the entire continent of Australia rather than just the eastern seaboard. James Cook claimed New South Wales for Great Britain in 1770. Matthew Flinders in his report of his circumnavigation of the continent in 1814 coined the term Australia apparently because he liked the sound of it. In 1817 Lachlan Macquarie, Governor of New South Wales, in his response to the Colonial Office on receiving copies of Flinders's charts, suggested to Lord Bathurst, Secretary of State for War and the Colonies, that the continent be called Australia. But the Admiralty did not accept the suggestion until 1824 and did not act upon it until 1830 when the name first appeared on Admiralty charts.

In the 20th century evidence for the existence of The Antipodes came to light. A submerged continent has been identified to the east and south-east of Australia. This land was named Tasmantis in 1919 by Sussmilch and David[1], Zealandia by Luyendyk[2] in 1995 and Te Riu-a-Maui in Māori. The continent is estimated to have an area of 4.9 million square km, more than half the area of Australia, and to be 1 billion years old.

In this work, "Australia" means the present Commonwealth of Australia and its dependent territories. "New Zealand" means all the islands of New Zealand and its dependencies. "Australasia" comprises the Commonwealth of Australia and New Zealand.

The long nineteenth century means the period between the signing of the Treaty of Paris at the conclusion of the American War of Independence in 1783 and Declaration of War on Germany and its Allies in 1914.

Chapter Notes

1. Sussmilch, CA and David, TW Edgeworth: "Sequence, glaciation and correlation of the Carboniferous rocks of the Hunter River District, New South Wales", *Journal and Proceedings of the Royal Society of New South Wales*, Vol. 53, 1919, pp. 248–338.
2. Luyendyk, Bruce P: "Hypothesis for Cretaceous rifting of east Gondwana caused by subducted slab capture", *Geology*, Vol 23 (4), April 1995, pp. 373–376. New Zealand earth scientists appear to be particularly eager to have Zealandia widely adopted. The New Zealand Government, by contrast, seems to be less at ease with the suggested nomenclature presumably because it does not command the resources required to administer so large a continental economic zone.

MEASUREMENTS USED IN THIS WORK

The Imperial System or Exchequer Standards was established by the Weights and Measures Act, 1824. Measurement of land area was based on a standard surveyor's chain 22 yards long composed of 100 links.

- 1 link is 7.92 inches or one-hundredth of a chain;
- A rod, pole or perch is 25 links or five and a half yards or one quarter of a chain;
- 1 perch is 1 square rod or 272.25 square feet;
- 1 furlong is 10 chains or 220 yards;
- 1 rood is 1 furlong by 1 rod or 10,890 square feet or 1,210 square yards;
- 1 acre is 1 furlong by 1 chain or 43,560 square feet or 4,840 square yards;
- 640 acres equalled 1 square mile.

Linear measurements were as follows:
- 12 inches equalled 1 foot;
- 3 feet equalled one yard;
- 220 yards equalled 1 furlong;
- 8 furlongs equalled 1 mile or 1,760 yards or 5,280 feet.

Sterling currency was denominated as follows:
- 1 penny (1d.) equalled four farthings or two half-pennies;
- 12 pence equalled 1 shilling (1s.);
- 20 shillings equalled one pound (£1);
- 21 shillings equalled 1 guinea (1gn);
- 1 Crown equalled five shillings (5s) and was sometimes called a Dollar-;
- Half-a-Crown equalled two shillings and sixpence (2/6).

INTRODUCTION

Land and Money explains why Australasia (i.e. Australia and New Zealand) was incorporated into the British Empire, how that inclusion was accomplished and the various consequences that resulted.

The book deals principally with events during the long nineteenth century from the time that the United States was recognised as an independent nation by the Treaty of Paris in 1783 until the outbreak of World War I in 1914. It joins a growing literature on colonisation which recognises the importance of financial processes in the formation of colonies and empires[1] and builds upon the foundations laid by Bedford, Butlin and Sheppard and Whitwell. I am also deeply indebted to the work of Boast on the history of land law in New Zealand.

But the book takes further the work of these illustrious forebears *Land and Money* explores how colonial land affected colonial money and how the nature of colonial money influenced the nature of colonial land. The close interaction between land and money in the Australasian colonies meant that, over time, land came to mean a legally-defined title to a "piece" of space and money was no more than a form of debt. By the start of World War I, a piece of land was valued in terms of a known amount of debt that it could extinguish and a given amount of money gave access to a piece of land. By 1914, it had become possible for a large proportion of the colonial population to acquire capital gains by borrowing from banks to acquire title to landed estates.

I adopt a descriptive approach to telling this history. At each stage, I strive to imagine myself as an active maker of choices so that I can describe the actual risks and prospective rewards that were encountered by people at the time. This involves my trying to understand the information that was available to makers of choices. It also requires that the constraints emanating from the beliefs, rules and norms of society are outlined. At no time have I knowingly chosen a particular philosophical approach to this history. Rather, I have presented the colonisation of Australasia as a series of unforeseen accidents by which outcomes of past choices are moulded into the foundations of future actions and behaviours.

The book is largely set out in a chronological order starting in the 1770s and ending in the 1920s. But the chronology is not strictly adhered to throughout. During some past periods little occurred to affect the future that was to come. Such periods are glossed over. A reader in search of an encyclopaedic chronology will not find it in *Land and*

Money. Nevertheless, I have taken great pains to offer precise dates in circumstances when the order of events is of importance to help explain what happened.

This general chronological approach is abandoned in two Chapters. Chapter 12 on land companies and Chapter 13 on suburban subdivision do not adhere to the main chronology adopted in the rest of the book. Rather, these chapters discuss illustrative examples of how two of the largest land companies operated in Australia and New Zealand and how three areas close to the centres of Auckland, Melbourne and Sydney were made available for suburban development. Together, these chapters serve to illustrate how far the enterprise of land development reached in Australasian societies.

Land and Money argues that the main reasons for the colonisation of Australasia was to facilitate the activities of British and some colonial investment companies. Such institutions envisaged the future profit that could be earned form the actions involved in colonisation. They organised the expropriation of land held communally within tribal societies and the use of that land to yield produce for the rest of the world. For the most part, such activities originated in Great Britain. This cause provided the impetus for colonisation of new territory and financial innovation that continued throughout the long nineteenth century. Occasionally other reasons for empire building supervened on business and official thinking. For example, the colony of New South Wales was founded as a substitute home for felons transported by the English penal system. Global strategy was one reason for colonising New Zealand which, it was believed, could assist in safeguarding Sydney from the potential depredations of other colonial powers. But in the long run the colonising processes that shaped Australasia were determined by the imperatives of the London capital market.

For that to be possible, it was necessary to set out the rules of the "colonising game". This was done by a series of legal innovations imposed on colonial society by the Crown and its colonial offshoot, the Settler-Crown. These included defining the meaning of "land" and its ownership, providing rules for its sale and purchase and making illegitimate some forms of ownership. In both Australia and New Zealand the Crown (and the Settler-Crown) was given free rein. This meant that Aboriginal Peoples were assumed to have no ownership over any Australian land and Māori were subjected to inexorable legal expropriation. In their different ways these innovations ensured that colonists were offered a ready supply of land which facilitated the expansion of their speculations.

At the same time, despite a rhetorical allegiance to the rules of the gold standard, colonial banks created credit by means of granting overdrafts to customers who used the money to purchase or settle land. Colonial banks paid scant regard to the dictates of the UK Treasury which believed that banks should not lend against the security of landed estates. By the time all banks were permitted by the Privy Council to undertake such lending most colonial banks were lending heavily on real estate secured by mortgages. Consequently, banks made it possible for colonists to make capital gains on landed investments with minimal financial inputs; a pattern that still persists.

Banks when lending against the security of real estate run the risk that they will not be repaid or that their customers will not be able to meet regular payments of interest on the loans. They also must plan for the risk that banks will not be able to attract sufficient new deposits to continue in business. For these reasons, banks must hold reserves which can quickly be turned into cash. In the gold standard such reserves are gold. Both Australia and New Zealand were significant gold producers so banks could always obtain gold in exchange for their own banknotes. Bank lending continued without serious interruption until the 1890s. This raised land prices and encouraged more speculation. Indeed, speculation in landed estates became normal and was actively encouraged by politicians of all persuasions, many of whom were closely associated with banking companies. Again, a pattern of behaviour which continues to the present.

The accumulation of capital gains from buying colonial landed estates with borrowed money had a number of far-reaching results. First, the practice spread widely in colonial society which meant that many people aspired to become worthy of being lent, otherwise known as becoming credit-worthy. Second, no government could expect to be elected if it promised to enforce "austerity". In particular, this meant that wealth tax was never popular and more often than not a source of government defeat. Third, in order to ensure the continuation of capital gains, a ready supply of land had to be made available for sale. Fourth, speculation in land took on new guises as settlement took shape and native land came into the hands of non-indigenous colonists. I call the result a state of Prosperous Servitude.

Writing *Land and Money* has taken many years. During that time, I have benefitted from help and encouragement from many people, some of whom I have forgotten. To them I offer my abject apologies. My greatest debt is to, my wife, the Honourable Phillida Bunkle who read and argued with me over every word so clarifying and enlivening my text. I am particularly grateful to Professor Linda Hancock who pressed me to extend the history to events in the Australian colonies amid unceasing encouragement. I thank Professor Sue Middleton who lent me unpublished material on Hon. Algernon Tollemache. I thank Felicity Day, Cliff Fell, Kate Lepper, Shona Macfarlane, Dr Maurice Ormsby and Dr Petrus Simons all of whom read early drafts, made perceptive comments and saved me from many errors. I also thank the Australia and New Zealand Bank and the Bank of New Zealand for granting access to relevant archives. Finally, I acknowledge the courteous and knowledgeable assistance I have been afforded by the Alexander Turnbull Library, Archives New Zealand, the Auckland Central Library, the General Assembly Library, the Nelson Public Library, the Porirua City Library and the Waiheke Library. Any errors of fact, understanding or interpretation that remain in the text are my responsibility for which I unreservedly apologise.

Nelson,
February 2024

Chapter Notes

1   A notable recent contribution is Catherine Comyn: "The Financial Colonisation of Aotearoa", Auckland, Economic and Social Research Aotearoa, 2022.

CHAPTER 1

WHY COLONISE AUSTRALASIA?

This Chapter explores why Great Britain colonised overseas territories. To a large extent colonisation was the result of a grand bargain between the sovereign and the ruling class. In it, the sovereign pledged to provide order and good conduct by extending the sovereign's peace to new territories. Peace meant "law and order" plus conformity to authority. In return the aristocracy promised to share the spoils of colonisation with the sovereign. Altruism had no part to play. In addition, the role of Manifest Destiny in the form of the spread of British colonisation and the importance of "Kith and Kin" were only of sporadic importance during the long nineteenth century. The growing impulse of British capitalists increasingly pushed the British Government towards the acquisition of new territories and drove the British Empire to make land exchangeable for money and money exchangeable for land.

Grand Bargain

For centuries, English gentry and the adventurers they sponsored planted themselves in other people's lands. King Henry II started this tendency. Encouraged by *Laudabiliter*[1] to subdue the Irish, he declared himself Lord of Ireland in 1171. A papal invitation coupled with the Divine Right of kings was more than sufficient to deter other Christian sovereigns from interfering in England's Irish adventures for the next 400 years. Henry demanded an annual tribute of one hide for every 10 head of cattle so setting an important precedent. From its beginnings, English colonisation involved a Grand Bargain; the sovereign extended territory covered by the King's Peace[2] and, in return, claimed a share of the produce of the land as spoils of conquest.

The general form of the Grand Bargain survived until it was unilaterally cancelled by the revolt of American colonists in the late 18th century. Queen Mary, Queen Elizabeth I and the Stuart kings granted Royal Charters, which were ornately expressed monopolies, to associations of gentlemen who, in return, pledged to provide the sovereign with a share (usually one-fifth) of any valuable minerals extracted. Charters became more complex to define the geographical extent and internal governance of colonies. Later, Sovereigns taxed trade between their colonies and between the rest of the world and their colonies in an ultimately unsuccessful attempt to ensure that colonial exports and imports were carried in English or British-flagged vessels[3] so as to profitably tie all colonial trade to England or Great Britain. Relationships between the sovereign[4] and the upper class were carefully managed within the confines set out in Magna Carta, the great charters and by other laws and conventions which included the Grand Bargain. But among all the fine words, relationships with indigenous peoples were largely ignored. First the Irish and later the American nations were distressed by the presence of foreign usurpers, to whom, ultimately, they offered violent insurrection. Monarchs mounted military expeditions to quell riot and rebellion to reimpose the King's Peace and the Grand Bargain. Maintaining the King's Peace in the colonies eventually proved beyond the capacities of a sovereign and could only be maintained by an effective Royal Navy and a centralised administration. Both became a permanent and significant drain on the Exchequer. During the 17th and 18th centuries, as part of this process, England concluded treaties[5] with indigenous peoples which usually involved three elements. First, the English sovereign asserted ownership of the land; second, land designated as European plantations and the settlers residing on them were segregated from land reserved for occupation by indigenous peoples; and, third, proprietorship over those reserves was guaranteed to indigenous peoples. In the Colony of Virginia this involved building a barrier between the plantations and the reserves and the use of Pass Laws to restrict access to the plantation areas by indigenous peoples. Nevertheless, conflicts persisted between colonists and indigenous peoples. Upper class settlers were generally ambitious and sought to subjugate ever more land. But with only their own class as fellow residents they were impelled to import slaves and indentured workers from Africa and Great Britain to work their plantations. By direct contrast, indigenous peoples sought to control, through negotiation of a series of treaties, the cultural disturbances that settlement brought.

Colonisation is a never-ending tussle between colonisers and colonised.[6] Like separating a limpet from its rock, colonising powers prise the salient features of indigenous societies away from the time-honoured native processes of management and ownership. With colonisation indigenous people lose control of the valuable attributes of their lands including minerals or fertile land, an inventive population, advanced technology, benign climates or strategic locations. Colonisation also separates indigenous people from the very relationships which comprise the society that raised them and, before colonisation, by means of which they expected to make their future lives. In extreme cases, as in Van Diemen's Land (Tasmania), colonisers deliberately set about exterminating the colonised.[7] Elsewhere, other no less determined measures, like large-scale, systematic alienation of land held, or destruction of flora and fauna enjoyed by the indigenous community, ensured that traditional ways of life were made non-viable in, or irrelevant to, the future of the colony[8].

During the 17th and much of the 18th centuries British colonies were administered in London as if they were personal possessions of the sovereign by the King and the Privy Council.[9] The conflicts between colonists and native peoples, between the sovereign and the colonists and between different colonies were too deep-seated to be adequately managed by the very personal system of colonial administration which developed in the 18th century. Until it was possible to install representative government among colonists, the quality of colonial administration was largely determined by the talents (or otherwise) of the person appointed colonial governor. The history of the British Empire shows that searches for the ideal colonial governor, like for the complete centre-forward, last an eternity but are doomed to ultimate failure. Increasingly, the Grand Bargain was upheld by local, short-term expedients. Colonial governors were forced by the "tyranny of distance"[10] from London to operate according to their own beliefs and prejudices. They often made arbitrary and inconsistent decisions which alienated settlers and indigenous peoples alike. They regularly tested the patience and attracted the ire of successive Secretaries of State. Many deliberately misled the British Government and neglected to obey direct orders. Yet, despite these shortcomings, it was not until 1837 that the British Colonial Department published the rules for colonial administration. [11]

But colonisation is a two-way process. While colonialisation disrupts a colonised society, it simultaneously changes the colonising society in many ways ranging from diet to working habits. When a country takes the colonising choice, however reluctantly, it makes an open-ended commitment to maintain control of its foreign territories. Many of the actions required to sustain this commitment are unforeseeable at the time that the decision to colonise is taken. They may eventually prove to be exceedingly distasteful to middle-class sensibilities. Of necessity, colonial powers became progressively enmeshed[12] in the fortunes of their colonies. The expense of people and treasure involved is one, albeit partial, measure of the "fatal necessity"[13] ultimately faced by all governments which would exercise, and by those who are subject to, colonial powers. Once begun, the colonising process consisted of a constant struggle for autonomy between would-be colonisers and those whom they would colonise. All affected parties were destined to find themselves devoting a wide variety of energies and resources to the tussle that could otherwise be used to benefit their respective populations. Why then did colonisation remain at the centre of British foreign policy for so long?[14]

An early attempt to answer this question was provided by John Seeley[15] who stated:

> "I am concerned always with a single problem only, that of causation. My question always is, How came this enterprise to be undertaken, how came it to succeed?"[16]

Seeley, emphasised the importance of colonisation as an outlet for the normal occupations and motivations of residents of the colonising power. He rejected the view that colonisation had a religious purpose and argued that colonisation usually resulted from rapacious materialism. He thought that states are held together by reason of community of race (or nationality), community of religion and community of interest. A colony is, therefore, an extension or:

> "… augmentation of the national estate. They are lands for the landless, prosperity and wealth for those in straightened circumstances."[17]

In addition, Seeley emphasised the importance of "native races" not being in a position to withstand the "peaceful competition, much less the power of the immigrants"[18].

Unfortunately, Seeley did not identify the components of possible causal explanations of the colonisation of Australasia sufficiently clearly to allow proper examination of the processes which governed its development.[19] It is to this task I now turn.

1. "Manifest Destiny"[20]

Contrary to the opinion of Seeley, some English christians, especially unitarians and evangelical anglicans, held that it was the duty of "civilised nations" to "civilise" backward peoples thus bringing them into enlightenment so that, in due time, they could join the concert of nations as fully functioning independent, civilised states. As colonists, they would spread civilising influences about them[21] like a beacon. Similar sentiments motivated missionaries of many doctrinal persuasions in many parts of the world. In Australasia, in the late 18th century, there were at least two variants of this basic doctrine.

On 10 August 1768, the Earl of Morton, President of the Royal Society[22], wrote "in haste" to Captain Cook[23], Mr Joseph Banks, Doctor Solander and the other gentlemen on HMS *Endeavour* to offer hints about dealing with primitive peoples they may encounter. His suggestions have become known as Morton's Hints.[24] He urged "utmost patience and forbearance" when dealing with "Natives". In accordance with the Instructions Cook received from the Lords of the Admiralty, Morton also warned against annexation of territory without agreement from the resident people who he called "… the legal proprietors of the several Regions they inhabit." Morton's letter was dated a week before Cook departed Plymouth for Madeira on 17 August 1768. Morton died before Cook departed. Strikingly, he wrote: "… have it still in view that shedding the blood of these people is a crime of the highest nature:—They are human creatures, the work of the same Omnipotent Author, equally under his care with the most polished European, perhaps being less offensive more entitled to his favour."

The second train of thought was the idea that trade (or "traffick" as it was then known) was the key that would unlock the benefits of colonisation without the need for violent confrontation.[25] Trade was regarded as powerful a tool as religion in establishing British sovereignty over foreign territories because it meant that eventually indigenous peoples accepted trade as a model of good conduct.[26] That was something the British understood and respected.

British commerce was the materialistic twin of christianity in the acquisition of the British Empire, as if commercial resourcefulness Great Britain had earned the right to colonise New South Wales and New Zealand. But trade was not charity as christianity purported to be. Cook tried to encourage "traffick" with the people he encountered. Especially in Tahiti and less so in New Zealand Cook and his party encountered active interest in trade and socialising among Polynesian people.[27] But there were limits. Attempts to interest some of the Aboriginal people of New Holland in baubles, nails and mirrors were unsuccessful.[28] To Cook, this lack of interest signified that New Holland[29] was populated by a people who were virtually "in a pure state of nature"[30]. This lack of interest should have immunised indigenous peoples of New South Wales to the temptations posed by British trade goods.

But none of this discussion explained why colonisation was desirable in the first place. British ideas of sovereignty were a complex, mystical manifold of legal concepts and historical precedents which were often misunderstood, even by British subjects[31] let alone by Aboriginal peoples with whom non-indigenous people[32] could not communicate. Absence of shared understanding raised the ethical question of how and with what justification Great Britain could first obtain and then exercise legal sovereignty over Australia. In practice, the British Government could achieve these ends because no other nation and no adverse circumstances prevented it while influential lawyers of the day, such as Sir William Blackstone,[33] argued that it had a natural right so to do. By 1765, when Blackstone published Volume I of his highly influential commentaries on the Common Law, British lawyers had identified three legally justifiable methods of exercising the sovereign's prerogative[34] over another territory; namely, purchase, conquest and cession by gift or treaty.

But these theoretical legal niceties were of little or no assistance in guiding those making choices in London about Australasia. Since the late 1620s a doctrine composed by John Winthrop, a Puritan clergyman, became widely accepted. It taught that only someone who altered the natural state of the land could be regarded as the land's owner. Aboriginal peoples occupied the land but did not subjugate it. To the British that meant that indigenous peoples did not own the land that they occupied. British Government officials accepted without question that, in New South Wales:

- No-one owned the land, so it could not be purchased. By the same token it could not be stolen;
- There was no military power to conquer; and
- There was no polity with whom cession of land by purchase or lease could be negotiated or otherwise arranged.

So, officials came to believe that if, for example, New South Wales was to replace the American colonies as a place of mass incarceration, British occupancy of the territory would face no legal impediment and only minor military inconvenience.

In the late 18th Century official ignorance about the continent of Australia and its peoples was almost total. Only travellers' tales[35] from parts of the western, northern and eastern seaboards were available to inform policy-making. Descriptions of Aboriginal Peoples were confined to their lack of permanent abodes, the simplicity of their weapons, their nudity and their lack of a language which was recognisable to European visitors.[36] Virtually nothing was known about the interior of the country. Little except cursory observation was made about the languages, the social organisation, the beliefs or the ways of life of the inhabitants. Nevertheless, the Letters Patent establishing South Australia as a British colony state:

> "**Provided Always** that nothing in those our Letters Patent contained affect or be construed to affect the rights of any Aboriginal Natives of the said Province to the actual occupation or enjoyment in their own Persons or in the Persons of their Descendants of any Lands now actually occupied or enjoyed by such Natives."[37]

In most of Australasia, these orders were largely ignored. Yet, the ethical problems raised by effectively stealing, albeit openly and legally,[38] land occupied by other people are still unresolved and continue to influence discussions of the sovereignty and Aboriginal title applicable to both Australia and New Zealand.

The imbalance between Great Britain's power to colonise and the ability of indigenous peoples to manage incursions by settlers was hardly addressed until 1836, when George Stevenson became Interim Protector of Aborigines in South Australia. Then, shortly after the abolition of slavery in the British Empire and 50 years after the First Fleet's arrival, there was a short-lived flurry[39] of similar "protectors" appointed in some Australasian colonies. This presumably occurred because the Colonial Office, at the time, was ruled by members of the Clapham Sect of evangelical Christians.[40] "Manifest Destiny"-type arguments were refined and presented to the Parliamentary Select Committee on Aboriginal Tribes (British Settlements)[41] and to the House of Lords Committee on New Zealand. On 14 May 1838 Dandeson Coates, Secretary of the Church Missionary Society, gave evidence before the House of Lords opposing the colonisation plans of the New Zealand Company. His doubts were shared by Lord Glenelg and Sir James Stephen with the result that the Colonial Office instructed Lieutenant Governor Hobson to appoint a Protector of Aborigines in New Zealand.[42]

Notwithstanding these christian interventions at least five reasons make it difficult to accept that British colonial policy was significantly inspired by humanitarian principles. First, the idea of humanitarianism as a principle of policy-making was always contested, it never became a set of universally-agreed precepts that could be clearly expressed in statute or policy instructions.[43] Second, Cook had already laid claim in the name of the Crown to territory in New South Wales and New Zealand despite having previously received the clearly-expressed opposition of humanitarians. His claims of British sovereignty were never repudiated by the British Government. Third, the British Government was aware that, for many years, it was incapable of enforcing humanitarian (or other) policies among the indigenous peoples of Australasia or even upon many of the non-indigenous people[44] settled among them. This was especially true of the areas beyond the Nineteen Counties[45] around Sydney Cove which were inhabited by squatters and their employees and parts of the interior of the North Island of New Zealand where Common Law was not universally enforced until the 20th Century.[46] Fourth, no matter how well-meaning and painstakingly designed, policies made in London often did not remain relevant to colonial conditions.[47] Often, colonial administrations were forced to amend or replace policies arriving from London by short-term expedients or delaying implementation.[48] Fifth, Protectors of Aborigines had few resources except the force of their own personality to influence policy-making or general behaviour. Their attempts to protect the interests of indigenous people, however well-intentioned, were overwhelmed by more powerful economic and political influences that were impelling the colonisation process.

2. Kith and Kin

Non-indigenous people who initially inhabited New South Wales and New Zealand[49] were overwhelmingly male and physically active. For the most part[50], they were from a long-established English underclass and was neither polite nor peaceful nor prosperous. Many were in Australia because of a brutal English legal system[51] which they usually encountered by committing petty (to modern sensibilities at least) theft of property.[52] There were only two attempts to transport convicts to New Zealand.[53]

Non-indigenous people[54] who arrived in Australasia shared many experiences and beliefs with the people they left behind. When young, vigorous people are separated from the families and societies which raised them, it is common for them to adopt behaviours which would scandalise middle class sensibilities "at home". For example, in New South Wales rum brewed in Bengal was both a comfort and currency in the early decades of colonisation. Its supply was monopolised by officers of the New South Wales Corps who mutinied against Governor Bligh in 1808 when he tried to restrain their activities which included racketeering, suborning the legal process and bribery.

In the first three decades of the 19th century non-indigenous society in New Zealand seems to have been another item on a long and notorious list of exports of unrelieved English debauchery to the rest of the world.[55] This unrestrained play of self-indulgent market forces is a model of what might have happened elsewhere in Australasia if convict settlement had not taken place under relatively strict military supervision. Colonisation in Australasia sometimes sat uncomfortably with the maintenance of control and good order in the British Empire. For example, some Waikato Māori, who were potential allies of Great Britain in World War I, were so alienated by confiscations of land, rapacious traders, dishonest and racist settlers and exploitation of indigenous women and children by non-indigenous people[56], that they refused to enlist for active service with the New Zealand Army.

Scandalous goings-on had two lasting effects. First, the "merriment and diversion"[57] provided were the foundation of commercial activity which took hold in New Zealand and New South Wales, even to the extent of introducing Māori, but to a much lesser degree Aboriginal Peoples, to commerce both as consumers and sometimes as suppliers. Commerce often originated illegally. For example, in New Zealand, it gave rise to a banking enterprise, albeit one that was short-lived and unregulated liquor sales (so-called sly-grogging). It remains impossible to adequately assess how important these commercial activities were in the lives of non-indigenous settlers, Aboriginal Peoples and Māori at that time. Anecdotal accounts of the treaty signing hui at Waitangi during 5 and 6 February 1840 indicate that many Māori grasped the mutual benefit of reciprocal trade. They also recognised its dependence on orderly relations between people. Many also found prosperity in trade.[58]

Second, the apparent social mayhem occurring in the colonies was seen by officials in London to be caused by British subjects.[59] The British Government accepted a degree of responsibility for the disruptive actions of its subjects and increasingly sought ways to bring a measure of order to the situation. For this reason, Sir James Stephen minuted on 15 March 1839:

> "1st. I assume as an established principle that the Colonization of New Zealand
> is, if not an expedient, at least an inevitable measure. It is in fact Colonized

already by British subjects of the worst possible character, who are doing the greatest possible amount of evil with the least possible amount of good, and who are living under no restraint of Law or Government."[60]

The British Government's responsibility for British subjects who chose to live in a territory outside Great Britain, without benefit of the rule of law and so without the King's Peace, was explicitly recognised by Lord Normanby, Secretary of State for War and the Colonies. In his instructions to Captain William Hobson RN dated 14 August 1839 he wrote:

> "… to rescue the Emigrants from the evils of a lawless state of Society it has been resolved to adopt the most effective measures for establishing amongst them a settled form of Civil Govt …"[61]

Neither Stephen nor Normanby submitted explicit reasons for the crown's[62] taking responsibility for its subjects who lived outside its territories and beyond the reach of a coherent legal system. It was almost as if ordinary colonists were like children whose selfish behaviour upset polite family gatherings and so deserved reproof.

The legal foundation for this duty was laid in 1608 by Sir Edward Coke.[63] He opined that a monarch's subjects owed a personal debt of gratitude to the sovereign for providing legal process which they should repay by being obedient. The crown had a duty to restrain subjects who are not grateful or whose behaviour could potentially undermine the crown's reputation and power and even interfere with its relations with other nations. It should do so by imposing[64] the King's Peace to ensure order and good conduct. The only sure way to promote order was to create colonies or protectorates to house and control the crown's subjects in foreign lands.

The extent of an empire growing in this way could not be limited by principles agreed beforehand or determined centrally because the creation of the next colony was always driven by the spread and enterprise of British subjects across the globe. In the British Empire, colonisation by the crown usually followed behind private initiative. In the late 1830s South Australia and New Zealand were just the latest examples of this phenomenon. British Governments did not always resort to colonisation when indigenous peoples were threatened by British adventurers. In those cases, where it declined to intervene to prevent depredations by British settlers, decisions made in London were often tainted by class and racism.

Kith and kin as a motive for colonisation was, on its own, neither sufficiently universal nor strong enough to impel British colonisation.[65] For example, in the Caribbean, British-born pirates set up bases[66] from which they disrupted lawful trade conducted by Spanish interests for many years before their activities grew to materially affect commerce based in London, on which the prosperity of the English nobility depended. Once that line was crossed the settlements were eventually colonised and the pirates admonished.[67]

The British Government accepted responsibility for ensuring order and good conduct in its Australasian colonies. But its practical application took various forms. Sometimes it verged on benign neglect. After 1790 the authorities in London or Sydney did not devote sufficient resources to establish and maintain order and control when random acts of settlement occurred in New Zealand. In New South Wales, from the late 1820s onwards, squatters invaded the back blocks beyond the Nineteen Counties with their flocks and faced negligible hindrance from the colonial government. By contrast, Acting Governor Grose and Governor Macquarie actively encouraged free settlers into New South Wales by granting them land along with costless labour in the form of convicts and indentured workers fed and clothed by the state. Or again, in much of the South Island of New Zealand after 1850, squatting was allowed on a first come, first served basis and only incurred an annual charge for a licence to occupy. Non-indigenous people, settlers, were encouraged by providing access to communal assets and activities at little or no cost.[68] In all these instances, the influence of kith and kin was not to initiate colonisation but rather to influence its character and who it benefitted.

3. Capital Relations

The economic and social progress of Australasian colonies depended on using land to grow useful produce. But the quality of land is highly variable even within small areas. Turning most landed estates in Australasia into profitable enterprises required consistent and significant capital investment over extended periods. Apart from land acquisition, the fertility of the soil was generally poor and, especially in the Australian Outback, often inconsistently and inadequately watered. A labour force had to be recruited, trained and equipped. Stock had to be obtained, secured by fencing and grazing improved. It was also necessary to provide the infrastructure required to carry wool and other products to British buyers and to receive payment in return.

In the early days of colonisation in New South Wales many of these requirements were supplied through the Commissariat Store. This store was a branch of the British Army and after 1813–1814 the UK Treasury. It was set up to feed and clothe the convicts and the regular soldiers. In New South Wales its functions expanded so that it also supplied convict labour, livestock, seeds and tools often on subsidised terms, which meant that they were paid for by the Treasury in London. In addition, some free settlers and New South Wales Corps officers invested their savings in shipments of merchandise which could be re-sold to settlers. Again, the main source of these funds was Great Britain.

It was only from around 1820, as the Bank of New South Wales became firmly established, that domestic financial institutions provided finance for land development. It seems likely that these domestic sources were always insufficient to meet the demand for investment funds. Colonisation of Australasia has probably always involved substantial capital expenditure which could not be raised in New Zealand or New South Wales.[69] In the long nineteenth century this meant that the extra capital investment required came predominantly from the London money and capital markets.

All parties to these capital flows had an abiding interest in ensuring that the price of assets, purchased with the aid of capital flows from overseas, would rise in the future. For lenders, a rise in price meant greater assurance that the money they advanced could, in all circumstances, be recovered by sale of those assets. Borrowers could also be assured that any investment they might make could be sold at a profit in the future provided the crucial inflows of capital continued. The monetary foundations of colonial society were based on debt. If increases in the capital value of the assets (i.e., capital gains)[70] could be assured, then more flows of capital could be expected to be made available in the future, especially if capital gains went untaxed. A money-go-round developed in both Australia and New Zealand which ensured that property prices kept rising. It was characterised by low or zero tax on capital gains, relatively simple procedures for borrowing for land purchase and ready access to new overseas loans. [71]

A colonial money-go-round of this type depends on the continuation of privately-funded international capital flows. On the one hand, it requires incurring international debts and, on the other, that debt service be constantly maintained.[72] If there be any doubt about the credit-worthiness of borrowers, borrowing from overseas cannot continue in which case the money-go-round ceases its motion. As a general principle, confidence of lenders in the long-term safety of their lending is materially improved by colonisation of the countries to which they lend. For example, if either the Australian colonies or New Zealand were to default on their obligations, lenders, especially those close to the English gentry[73], were able to recruit the British Government to obtain a remedy. Both Australia and New Zealand took great pains to ensure that their ability to borrow would not be doubted by London financiers. During the long 19th century, this included carefully aligning domestic politics so that they did not interfere with the international strategies followed by Great Britain even to the extent of allowing the British Government to exercise control over their own sovereignty. For example, it took the form of joining with the British military to subdue tribesmen in more distant colonies such as southern Africa[74], paying for battlecruisers that were ordered by the Navy Board[75], allowing the British Government to declare war on their behalf[76], adopting British commercial law and banking practice and, unquestioningly embracing free trade and fiscal austerity.[77]

Order and good conduct required to ensure that uninterrupted colonial exploitation by overseas capital continued, did not always extend to indigenous peoples. For some, this was because their aspirations and beliefs were inconsistent with the commodification of land[78] and the monetisation of economic and social life.[79] Others merely questioned why some kind of plural polity could not be established.[80] Yet others, who included a small minority of non-indigenous people, wanted to be left to live separately from the settler majority.[81] Settler governments were suspicious of all such sentiments which were regarded at least as recalcitrance and at worst as outright rebellion against the Crown. To control and manage the varieties of opposition colonial governments resorted to military conquest which, in the case of Aboriginal Tasmanians[82] and the scorched earth tactics employed by militia in Taranaki and Te Urewera in New Zealand descended into genocide.[83] The use of military might in this way shows that the ruling class in the Great Britain regarded the maintenance of colonial capital relations as of supreme importance in colonial policy.

4. Fatal Necessity and Military Threat

Most British military incursions in Australasia were on a local or regional scale. This was also true elsewhere in the British Empire, even in large territories like India. These local and regional wars were generally fought against locally-organised opponents. In contrast to the more recent "Great Game" conflicts in the Middle East or Afghanistan, the local challenges were not usually sponsored by one or other of the Great Powers. The British could muster a wide variety of lethal matériel, large bodies of trained soldiers, a Commissariat that could supply armies for as long as the conflict lasted[84] and, usually, adequate leadership. Most crucially, the unmatchable scope of the Royal Navy could be relied upon to reinforce these factors as required and for all other needs.[85]

During the long nineteenth century, therefore, Great Britain fought many geographically quite limited military engagements in the conduct of which it consistently displayed overwhelming advantages in technology, organisation and manpower.[86] For example, outside Australia and New Zealand indigenous peoples, armed with spears, were heavily defeated by British forces firing a relatively small number of Maxim guns.[87]

A country having placed itself at the centre of an empire makes an unconditional commitment to at least maintain the territorial integrity of its colonial property. This commitment is open-ended until such time it is formally abandoned. Lord Melbourne, the British Prime Minister during the late 1830s and early 1840s, talked of "the fatal necessity by which a nation that once begins to colonize is led step by step over the whole globe"[88]. The meaning of this striking statement is open to some conjecture. One of Melbourne's intentions was to convey the idea that a nation wishing to safeguard the integrity of its Empire was forced to maintain its armed forces at a level sufficient to forestall potential threats from other nations. Order and good conduct had to be maintained within its colonies lest any lapse in them offered an opportunity for intervention or mischief by another country. It may also be necessary to control, if not eliminate, unforeseen threats arising from across colonial borders by colonising the territories from which such threats might come.[89] By the late 1830s, the British Government perceived that first France[90] and later the USA[91], could possibly pose a military or more likely a diplomatic threat to its sovereignty over its Pacific colonies. It is far from clear how immediate such threats were. Yet, it was ever the way that extension of the borders of an empire can raise opposition from other nations even when it only takes the form of taxing or protecting its citizens living overseas. This opposition may take a variety of guises some of which must be actively addressed.[92] Others, like Baron de Thierry, self-styled King of New Zealand, were safely ignored or intrigued against[93] and others, like John Batman's claims over the site of what is now Melbourne, were eliminated by proclamation.[94] On occasion, military conflict may result from an assertion of independent sovereignty but only if the governments involved choose to seek military conquest such as during the New Zealand Land Wars. At other times, conflicts can be resolved by diplomatic negotiation or legal proceedings.

There is a further implication in Melbourne's statement; namely, once begun, colonisation takes on a life of its own. The effort and expense required to manage an extensive empire can prevent the central government from addressing other political priorities.

Roman Emperors tried, without permanent success, to limit the extent of their territorial claims by constructing physical barriers like Hadrian's Wall, the Antonine Wall and the *Limes Germanicus*. By contrast, the British adopted a policy of decolonisation (i.e., granting "independence" to compliant colonies) within the overall framework set by the British monarchy. But the process of decolonisation in the 20th century proved to be bloody and fraught with dangers to indigenous people, settlers and British-owned property; an outcome, although predictable, that was incapable of rational management. If that was what Melbourne had in mind, his perspicacity is to be applauded.

At the time, policy-makers recognised additional strategic advantages in colonising. For example, it was argued that it meant that Great Britain could control large areas of the globe without recourse to large armies of occupation through the ever-present threat of intervention by the Royal Navy. One illustration is the early and groundless belief in the idea that by colonising Australasia, Great Britain would obtain bases from which it could readily control the Far East.[95] Another was that in August 1839, when writing instructions to Captain Hobson, Lord Normanby, Secretary of State for War and the Colonies, summarised the strategic argument in favour of colonising New Zealand as follows:

> "We have not been insensible to the importance of New Zealand to the interests of Great Britain in Australia, nor unaware of the great natural resources by which the Country is distinguished, or that its geographical position must in seasons, either of peace of war, enable it, in the hands of Civilized men to exercise a paramount influence in that quarter of the globe. There is probably no part of the earth in which Colonization could be effected with a greater or surer prospect of national advantage."[96]

It was some decades before the full extent of the advantages to Great Britain of Australasian colonisation became clear. In the 20th century, the manpower, food and raw materials required to fight a series of international wars were supplied to a considerable extent from nations which were members of the British Empire.[97]

Australasia was largely colonised by British private interests which, like the Dutch, had become accustomed to searching the entire world for profitable investments. During much of the 19th century British capital flowed into North and South America, Europe (including Russia), the Far East as well as Australasia. This massive and un-precedented re-location of resources could only have occurred because the British Government provided suitable conditions. It did so by eliminating exchange risk by organising the gold exchange standard and by making land in its Australasian colonies and Canada as much like a landed estate in the "Home Counties"[98] as possible. The British upper class desired these conditions because they suited its commercial interests especially after the North American colonies were lost and slavery was abolished[99] in the British Empire. The English gentry used its dominance of the parliament to achieve these conditions, despite the First Reform Act 1832

> "The new parliament which met in 1833 contained 217 sons of peers or baronets; in 1865 the number was 180; the landed interest which was nearly 500 strong in 1833 had about 400 representatives in 1865."[100]

It is no coincidence that the start of colonisation of Australasia coincided with the widespread elimination of British investment opportunities elsewhere in the world, particularly in the American colonies. By 1780 Great Britain had lost control of North America apart from Canada and the British Empire, even in India, was facing competition from the Dutch and French[101] and the East India Company was weakened by competition from them. Finally, during the 1790s, investment opportunities for the British aristocracy in Europe were being increasingly circumscribed by the shadow of the coming war with France.

British investors began to seriously explore Australasia for profit. The accounts of Australia and New Zealand published by Cook and Banks stimulated considerable interest. If that were not enough, successive British Governments embarked upon policies to repress the working-class which were consistently sustained until the 1840s, well after the passage of the First Reform Act in 1832.[102] This repression was justified by officially-expressed fear of "Jacobinism"[103] but was, in truth, directed at reducing wage costs for employers in the face of increasing competition in international trade. Lower wages meant lower spending by British workers and ultimately lower profits for British producers and their investors. The relatively slow growth of British domestic markets as a result of sustained fiscal austerity[104] coupled with political repression provided an incentive for those who could accumulate capital to look overseas for ever-more profitable investment opportunities.

They searched Australasia, Canada, the Caribbean, China and Latin America. Within the next century they built a legacy of massive sheep stations, sugar and cotton plantations, vast wheatlands and cattle ranches, and subjugated China. The new[105] capital outflows that were stimulated paid for two broad forms of investment. Some people directly invested in the colonies. They or their agents carried accumulated wealth with them with which they bought or leased land, or set up their own businesses. Alternatively, the surpluses were deposited with London financiers from whom others borrowed to invest in these colonial activities. In these latter cases, debts were created which had to be serviced by regular payments. By this class of transaction, the financial interests of lenders in London and borrowers in the colonies were fused together for long periods.[106]

The result was a confluence between the views of financial sector interests and those of colonial and British Government politicians. These views often included opinions on economic, social and racial policy and were invariably informed by landed interests of non-indigenous people. Once interests as powerful as these are as fused together as they were in the British Empire there is no separating them except by massive and disruptive effort. In the case of Australia and New Zealand, it was in no-one's interest to make this happen.

Colonising Australasia

In important respects the pre-colonial societies settled in New Holland and New Zealand were similar. By 1790, both countries were inhabited by peoples who had no knowledge of how to make or work metal. Neither Māori nor Aboriginal Peoples had a written language. Both had been settled for many generations and had developed forms of communal living based upon collective occupation of territory by kin groups.[107] Both Aboriginal Peoples and Māori seem to have maintained relationships and communication with many other groups, some at considerable distance. However, neither used money. But despite the similarities between them New South Wales and New Zealand were colonised for different reasons. So, it must be historical factors originating in Great Britain which explain why the colonisations of New South Wales and New Zealand were so different.

5a. Why Colonise New South Wales?

The Grand Bargain began to collapse by the mid-1770s,[108] before Great Britain finally succeeded in losing the War of Independence. As a result, the Treaty of Paris was signed in 1783, which granted independence from Great Britain to the United States and proclaimed peace between Great Britain and France, Spain and the Netherlands. There was considerable political upheaval in Great Britain as petty personal vendettas between senior members of the British aristocracy made it impossible to form a stable government. Corruption in the corridors of power and incompetence in the military were laid bare and the subject of common abuse and ridicule. Hopes were destroyed. Plans were laid waste. Fears overwhelmed rational policy. British military authority was weakened only to find release in other parts of the globe.

But the greatest shock was that the sense of reality of the upper class, its boast of expertise in military command and in policy-making and its oft-repeated British expressions of good intent, were all exposed as largely vacuous.[109] Yet it was from this deep, almost moral, chaos[110] that the British Empire was reborn as a field of opportunity for transported felons and the younger sons of the English gentry.

It is said that in the 18th century, the number of criminal offences punishable by hanging multiplied from 50 in 1688 to over 220 in 1800.[111] But before the 19th century British gaols were not designed to permanently incarcerate felons as a punishment but only to hold prisoners pending sentence.[112] As the number of capital offences rose, the press of prisoners awaiting execution increased and could only be relieved by housing them in dismasted hulks[113] or shipping them to the colonies. But, instead of hanging those convicted of capital offences, the law permitted the Court to transport male felons convicted of capital crime, and to judge convicted women as "in want of clergy". As the 18th century passed, it became increasingly common for convicted felons to be transported[114] to colonies in the Americas as indentured servants[115] In the late 18th and early 19th centuries, political and economic repression became more common. Writs of *Habeas Corpus* were suspended from 1794 to 1795 and again from 1817 to 1818 and even in the 1830s workers such as the Tolpuddle Martyrs were transported for taking and administering illegal oaths. The loss of the American colonies also meant that no longer could prisoners be sent as indentured labourers to the plantations. If transportation was to be employed as a way of reducing the press of prisoners in England another site for an overseas penal colony had to be found.

Two years before the British Army's defeat at Yorktown, the House of Commons convened a committee to discuss transportation of offenders on 5 February 1779.[116]

Sir Charles Bunbury, in his Chairman's Report, stated that the Committee considered hulks secured at Gibraltar, premises on the Gambia and the Senegal rivers and New Holland as alternative destinations. Gibraltar was rejected because of the possibility of convicts absconding to nearby Spain; Senegal and The Gambia were dismissed on health grounds. New Holland was a long way from other Europeans, had a benign climate and was believed to have soils that could allow the colony to become self-sufficient relatively quickly. There is no indication in the available written records that the 1779 Committee discussed using New Zealand to establish a penal colony.[117] In 1784 An Act for the Effectual Transportation of Felons and other Offenders was debated and passed into law. Clark reports that:

> "In the short debate on the bill only one speaker, Mr Hussey[118], mentioned a place [in which to site transported convicts]: He said he meant New Zealand, lately discovered in the south seas."[119]

The uncertainties[120] created by the revolt of the American colonists reset the context for the moral, political and economic arguments of the day to the point of changing the way that people thought and acted together. Here was an opportunity for aspirants to official office to advance their cause for preferment. Concerned citizens[121] wrote to British government officials[122] suggesting a new home for Britain's North American subjects displaced by the revolt in North America and the need to find another destination for transported criminals.[123] An added advantage of any potential location was that it should not be owned by anyone. New South Wales and New Zealand appeared to satisfy both concerns.

Most influential among concerned citizens was James Matra who wrote "A Proposal for Establishing a Settlement in New South Wales"[124] dated 23 August 1783.[125] It rehearses the physical advantages of the country and its proximity to the resources of New Zealand as a suitable place of plantation of non-indigenous people which "may in time atone for the loss of our American colonies". He asserted that of a number of possible alternatives "… which know no sovereign"[126], "[n]one are [sic] more inviting than New South Wales". He proposed that an exploratory expedition be despatched to New South Wales consisting of two vessels. He argued that gardens should be established upon arrival, one vessel should be despatched to tell of the successful landing and the other should sail to "New Caledonia, Otaheite, and the neighbouring islands" to recruit families and women for the men left behind. He urged that successful colonisation of New South Wales would enable Great Britain to "powerfully annoy" Holland or Spain in the event of war. It seems that Matra obtained the ear of people of some influence such as Sir Joseph Banks, President of the Royal Society, Admiral Lord Howe, First Lord of the Admiralty and Lord Sydney, Home Secretary.

In 1785 the location of transported felons was placed before another parliamentary committee chaired by Lord Beauchamp.[127] The Beauchamp Committee considered three possible sites: Lemane on The Gambia, Das Voltas Bay in South-West Africa at the mouth of the Orange River and Botany Bay[128]. Lemane was rejected as unsustainable because its proponents envisaged transporting the prisoners in slave ships only to deliberately maroon them 400 miles up The Gambia without further support. Their fate would have been almost certain death from disease or attack by local tribesmen. The Committee, therefore, favoured Das Voltas Bay because it offered a counter-threat to the Dutch possession of Cape Town and relatively easy communication with London. But when surveyed by HMS *Nautilus* in September 1785[129] the site was reported as being "too dry and sterile to be settled"[130]. By default, this left Botany Bay although the Committee expressed concern about the cost of maintaining a penal colony so distant from England and was dubious about the claims that it would provide significant strategic advantages in any conflict with the Dutch in the Far East.[131] Nevertheless, so pressing was the domestic political problem of prison overcrowding that Botany Bay was accepted as the site of the new penal colony on the evidence of Joseph Banks and James Matra[132] and without benefit of further prior investigation.[133] This lack of preparation was possible because it was believed that New South Wales was home to no settled inhabitants.[134]

Hence, without considered debate on the matter, New South Wales came to be widely regarded as a part of the British Empire. Many European politicians, therefore, assumed that the disposal of the vast lands it encompassed was within the sole gift of the British Crown. This implied that the Crown could, without further ado, let alone legal and diplomatic ceremony, assume ownership of every part of the Australian continent. The Crown could retain any land it chose within the Crown demesne and make grants of estates to others of its choosing. The British Government did not find it necessary to seriously consider the present needs and future development of Aboriginal Peoples when granting pieces of land or planting its own subjects. Land in Australia was, therefore, regarded as identical with English Crown Lands and obliviousness[135] towards the Aboriginal inhabitants remained in place, with relatively minor deviations, over much of the next two centuries.[136]

The colony of New South Wales was initially financed by transfers of capital from London through the Commissariat, established to provide supplies to the British Army and which after 1813–1814 was a branch of the British Treasury. The colonial administration tried to solve the problem of feeding the prison population and its guardians by founding Government farms which were worked by convicts under convict overseers. Lack of equipment and expertise, not to mention want of incentive and physical vigour, meant that production remained below demands. From late 1788 to 1792 the colony in New South Wales endured "The Starvation Years"[137] during which Governor Phillip was forced to obtain emergency supplies from Cape Town and, unsuccessfully, seek more from Canton[138]. Ultimately, the problem of starvation was much reduced when military officers and free settlers started to work the land they were granted for profit, advantaged by the ready availability of convict labour victualled by the government. The Commissariat established a store at Sydney Cove to distribute rations to convicts and rank and file soldiers. Farm produce was sold to the Commissariat Store established at Sydney Cove, in exchange for store credits called store notes. These could be accumulated and exchanged for Treasury Bills drawn on the Treasury in London.

Plantation of Australia was not preceded by the usual English preparations for colonisation.[139] Land was ill-defined. Natives were not propitiated.[140] The territory was unexplored, let alone surveyed or mapped. Native society was assumed to be non-existent despite consistent evidence of repeated attempts by Aboriginal peoples to dissuade Europeans from making landfall. The determined refusal by non-indigenous people to accommodate the true state of the societies and cultures of Aboriginal peoples had a profound effect upon the way that colonisation of Australasia as a whole (i.e., including New Zealand) was undertaken. Most notably, it encouraged non-indigenous settlers to believe that they were entitled to own the land and that all other claims to it could be ignored. This entitlement took a variety of forms. For example, in the Australian colonies, the Crown assumed ownership of the land without compensation, let alone redressing the occupiers for their loss; in North America and New Zealand the British Crown did make a show of compensation in money or money's worth. The compensation offered, however, was invariably less than the upset price specified in Colonial Office instructions. Only in very recent times has discussion of redressing of, rather than compensation for, past injustices begun to form part of conversations between indigenous peoples and the descendants of settlers. Whatever form it took, the entitlement of non-indigenous people was frequently translated into day-to-day racism.[141]

In Australia, this presumption of ownership came to be justified by the doctrine of *terra nullius*. Although it gained increasing currency in legal circles throughout the 19th century it was not until 1889, at the earliest, that the term *terra nullius* was applied to Australia. *Terra nullius* means no-one's land.[142] The concept is originally derived from *res nullius* or no-one's law from which the Law of First Taker was derived. By the late 18th Century, lawyers accepted that land could only be owned by a person who both occupied and improved it. The Law of First Taker meant that since no-one owned or occupied or lived upon the land in Australia, no-one could own it. The Law of First Taker asserted that if there were no owners, then the land could not be sold or otherwise ceded by the people who roamed across it. Lawyers reasoned that it followed that lands devoid of people who could reasonably be regarded as land owners was available for the taking by any nation that wished to exercise sovereignty over it.[143] By "discovering" such a country and formally asserting sovereignty over it, a nation could choose how the land was to be defined, owned and used and by whom. Such reasoning provided the British Government with legal justification for asserting its sovereignty over the South Island of New Zealand in 1840 and over New South Wales in 1787 by dint of their "discovery" by Cook, respectively in 1769 and 1770.[144]

Such doctrines are implicit in the various commissions and instructions provided to Governor Phillip before he departed Spithead.[145] The First Commission was issued on 12 October 1786 and appointed Phillip "Governor of our territory called New South Wales" which extended from Cape York to South Cape and included all land to the west until 135 degrees west and all the islands adjacent in the Pacific Ocean between the latitudes 10 degrees 37 minutes south and 43 degrees 39 minutes south.[146] Phillip was given to believe that he was entitled to the obedience of all government personnel located in this vast and largely unknown area. Phillip's second commission was dated 2 April 1787. It appointed him Captain General of the Fleet and Governor-in-Chief of New South Wales and empowered him to remit sentences, to appoint justices, to punish, pardon and reprieve, to impose martial law and to grant land. Finally, on 25 April 1787, Phillip received his so-called 1st Instruction[147] which gave advice about managing convicts, soldiers and administrators and exploring, granting and cultivating the land.

He was specifically instructed to protect the lives and livelihoods of Aboriginal Peoples and to encourage friendly relations with them. His Instructions state:

> "You are to endeavour by every possible means to open an Intercourse with the Natives and to conciliate their affections, enjoining all Our Subjects to live in amity and kindness with them. And if any of Our Subjects shall wantonly destroy them, or give them any unnecessary Interruption in the exercise of their several occupations. It is our Will and Pleasure that you do cause such offenders to be brought to punishment according to the degree of the Offence. You will endeavour to procure an account of the Numbers inhabiting the Neighbourhood of the intended settlement and report your opinion to one of our Secretaries of State in what manner Our Intercourse with these people may be turned to the advantage of this country."[148]

There is no mention of the previous 60 000 years of occupation by Aboriginal peoples. Ferris asserts "*Terra nullius* was assumed"[149] but that assertion is questionable. The term *terra nullius* does not seem to have been used[150] in any of the documents issued to Phillip by the Crown or in the descriptions composed aboard HMS *Sirius,* HMS *Supply*[151] and the First Fleet[152] of the world which they entered on 26 January 1788. However, it is equally clear that the Crown expected that the "Natives" were neither to be "wantonly destroyed" nor that their "several occupations" to be subject to unnecessary interruption. Indeed, the Privy Council in London seems to have some form of co-habitation in mind as the First Fleet left Ryde Roads. This is not the same as implicitly assuming *Terra nullius* was a foundation of policy. It seems more likely that the extraordinarily wide military and executive powers with which the Crown anointed Governor Phillip[153], rather than the assumptions and beliefs that he brought from England, which justified his presumption that, in practice,[154] he was fully justified in applying The Law of First Taker to New South Wales.

5b. Why Colonise New Zealand?

New Zealand, by contrast, was sighted by many European, and probably many more Polynesian explorers.[155] Rumours of settlement[156] and chance visitations became less uncommon and in the last quarter of the 18th century, the South Pacific was progressively exploited by whalers, sealers, assorted beachcombers and sea captains recruiting crews or searching for slaves.[157] These venturers came to rely upon New Zealand (and New Holland) as sources of spars, firewood, water, fresh food and prostitution. The mixed bag of non-indigenous people (the vast majority of whom were men) who settled New Zealand was, in time, seasoned by missionaries, settlers, escapees from penal colonies, those with tickets of leave and military deserters. The immigrants brought expertise and experience. They even mustered some capital which they invested in trade goods, tools and implements and crudely assembled infrastructure. New Zealand offered access to products which were of immediate utility to the Royal Navy in its wars against the Dutch and the French. Eventually, informal trading and monetary links between New Holland and New Zealand crystallised into regular and formal, personal and mercantile arrangements. But establishment of effective political oversight over New Zealand took much longer.[158]

In the 1780s New Zealand, thanks to the painstaking work of Banks and Cook and their shipmates, was much better known in Great Britain than was New Holland. Yet, it was not until 1840 that the British Government colonised the country. There was a gap of 52 years between the arrival of the First Fleet at Botany Bay in January 1788 and Hobson's landing in the Bay of Islands in late January 1840.

The most obvious explanation for this delay is that between 1776 and 1840 the British Government was pre-occupied with:

- ❖ Fighting and financing wars against France and North American colonies;
- ❖ Incipient rebellion in Canada, China and India;
- ❖ Abolition of slavery and the uncertain future of the sugar estates of the English upper class; and
- ❖ The increasing disarray of the British East India Company.

The fiscal and legal administration of Great Britain dated from the time of Dowling's reforms in the 17th century. Yet the issues facing the Government called for considerable administrative expertise and effort from a civil service that was still structured along the lines of a household maintained by a landed magnate staffed by personal retainers. Much responsibility fell upon Cabinet Ministers to personally dictate policy and compose and oversee the instructions required to carry it out. Many highly competent and energetic men (they were always men), the most famous of whom were William Pitt and Lord Castlereagh, eventually buckled under the strain. It also required the mobilisation of an efficient Royal Navy without which no British foreign policy could have been carried out. Reform of technology, administrative procedures and strategy was, therefore, largely directed at improving the capabilities of the Royal Navy. By comparison, other parts of British government administration were left to muddle along with only vague design and resourced largely by personal initiative and energy.

The Government was further strained by political instability, King George III's increasingly serious illness, the Prince Regent's political ambitions, the social and industrial unrest as England, Scotland and Wales passed through the turmoil of the Industrial Revolution, the widespread enclosure of common land and agricultural depression weakened the traditional relationships which bound the common people to the land. There were also a series of mutinies in the Royal Navy anchored at the Nore and at Spithead in 1797 because of non-payment of wages[159]. When faced with social disturbance, the Government repeatedly resorted to highly repressive methods of social control administered by local Justices of the Peace. The lack of a coherent justice system meant that these methods tended to be patchy as to their liberality, competence and cruelty; inconsistencies which were a further cause of discontent. It is remarkable that during these years, incipient rebellion in the name of King Lud or Captain Swing centred upon the southern and eastern counties of England which were often the original homes of early free migrants to New South Wales and New Zealand.

There is also a remarkable difference between the official soul-searching[160] that preceded the plantation of New Zealand and the lack of considered debate over colonising New Holland. In the case of New Zealand, the British Government exercised unusual caution: visits had been made to Sydney and London by Māori chiefs; missionaries, including the "flogging parson" Bishop Marsden, had made extensive progresses through the country and were in regular touch with the Church Missionary Society in London; Special Commissioner Bigge reported to Lord Bathurst on the state of New Zealand in 1823[161]; a number of private organisations proposed plantations of non-indigenous people without success; James Busby, a British Resident was appointed in 1832 and thereafter sent voluminous correspondence to the Governors of New South Wales and the Colonial Office in London; an ensign was adopted for New Zealand vessels in 1834; the Declaration of Independence was signed in 1835; Captain William Hobson RN aboard HMS *Rattlesnake* was commissioned, in 1837, to visit New Zealand and make recommendations; and two Parliamentary Committees considered the matter in 1837 and 1838.

Plantation of non-indigenous people in South Australia and New Zealand was conceived in totally different circumstances from those which gave birth to Matra's proposals for New South Wales. By 1825 Great Britain had recovered some of the military (especially naval) superiority which was so carelessly cast aside in the Americas. Napoleon was defeated. Since the Battle of Trafalgar on 21 October 1805, Britannia really did rule the waves. Trade in slaves had been disrupted and slavery was about to be abolished in the British Empire albeit at considerable expense. A veneer of competence had been grafted onto the British political system. Increasingly, the British Empire was growing by means of treaties and was being drawn together not by trading relationships but by lending and borrowing. The Empire was no longer the area over which the King's Peace was to reign but increasingly represented the places around the globe in which British enterprise and capital could be profitably employed.

By the 1820s a newly minted theory of systematic colonisation was taking shape. Edward Gibbon Wakefield[162], while incarcerated for three years in Newgate prison for kidnapping a reputedly wealthy heiress, Ellen Turner, composed a detailed plan for "systematic colonisation" which he believed should be followed when the British government planted settlers in new colonies. These writings established Wakefield's reputation as an internationally recognised expert on colonisation.[163]

Wakefield's influence eventually extended throughout Australasia as well as Canada.[164] He argued that colonisation should aim at reducing "pauperism" in the home country by means of a "private speculation" that would be self-sustaining. To ensure that the venture did not require repeated calls upon the tax revenues of the home country, a balance between those who supplied capital and those who sold their labour must be installed. (Marx somewhat wryly described Wakefield's balancing act as trying to "manufacture wage workers in the colonies".[165]) A tax on land rents and the profits earned by the government from selling grants of land would furnish an emigration fund to pay for passages and temporary subsistence of poor emigrants. Wakefield believed that it was necessary to establish a "sufficient price" of colonial land. This price would not be so high as to make it impossible for labourers ever to purchase their own land but not so low as to make it unnecessary for them to work for those who contribute capital. This experience of wage work was intended to provide poor people with experience of the intelligent and prudent use of capital and so prepare them for productive land ownership. This balance between capital and labour implied by the doctrine of sufficient price does not seem to be significantly different from the *status quo* which obtained in England in the 1820s.

Wakefield summarised his ideas as an Appendix to "A Letter from Sydney" containing nine Articles.[166] Three of the most important are as follows:

> "ARTICLE I: That a payment in money of —— per acre be required for all future grants without exception.
>
> ARTICLE II: That all land now granted, and to be granted, throughout the colony be declared liable to a tax of —— per cent upon the actual rent.
>
> ARTICLE VIII: The grants be absolute in fee, without any conditions whatsoever, and obtainable by deputy."

They formed the kernel of the constitutions of the South Australia Land Company and the New Zealand Company, both of which were based on Wakefield's arguments. That reasoning was based on two presumptions. First, colonisation depended on the same precepts as any other enterprise which aimed to mobilise capital in order to earn a financial profit. Second, the suppliers of capital took precedence when it came to deciding on who should benefit and by how much. These two propositions were fused in the single argument that if only a valuable asset in land could be created and sustained, then posterity could be assured that the asset would be worked in a productive manner. This led directly to the interpretation of "sufficient price of land" to mean that anyone who bought land in a 'Wakefield Scheme' could be assured that its price would not be allowed to fall significantly in the future. This simple political principle was exported from the Wakefield colonies to all Australasian settlements and remained the cornerstone of their political economy at least until the end of World War I. It implied that anything which threatened to interfere with perpetually rising land prices came to be regarded as against the fundamental interests of the British Empire. In time these came to summarised in the notion of the Settler-Crown.

It is difficult to be certain how desperate were the living conditions in Great Britain and Ireland during the first three decades of the 19th century. Much has been written about this matter but little is based upon complete and rigorous analysis of the actual lives of people.[167] In part, this was because economic activity was largely rural. It was spread relatively thinly across the land so the true condition of people's state could only with great difficulty be assessed. Nevertheless, it appears that the living conditions for many people in England and Wales in the late 18th and early 19th centuries were desperate. Edward Gibbon Wakefield found a ready audience for his ideas among the many people dislocated from their rural upbringing by the Industrial Revolution and enclosure of the commons. He argued that Britain had too many people for the available work. His view was that colonies should not be run for profit or for prestige by the Home Country. Instead, he urged that they should be the means of liberating working people into self-reliance. For Wakefield, colonisation was less a matter of exercising the Royal Prerogative via the granting of Royal Charters and more akin to establishing a field in which English enterprise could be exercised. In this he was influential. After the French Wars, the British Government withdrew from the creation of large-scale colonies and left the field open for others to organise. The convict colony at Botany Bay was, therefore, one of the last of the old-style colonies founded under Royal Prerogative and patronage.

Warfare notwithstanding, financial problems were the most pressing and insoluble addressed by British governments between 1780 and 1840. From time immemorial English and British governments had financed their military and colonial adventures by borrowing from domestic and foreign lenders and by debasing the currency. When he became Chancellor of the Exchequer, Pitt's intention was to repay the entire National Debt (which stood at £231.8 million in 1783[168]). He introduced a Sinking Fund in 1786 so that on the eve of the outbreak of the French Wars in 1792 National Debt had been restricted to £241.6 million. But he soon relinquished his debt repayment ambition once wars against France and then the United States started. Both currency debasement and large-scale borrowing were employed to such an extent that much domestic politics in the 30 years following 1815 was devoted to unpicking the impacts of debasement by thorough-going currency reform and rebuilding the English financial system. The sea-change in financial policy resulted in the development of the gold exchange standard with the Bank of England at its centre. As the London money and capital markets grew in response to consistent official sponsorship, they became powerful instruments tying Britain's overseas possessions together into the British Empire.

Yet, over time, the inadequacies of the British Treasury became an ever more pressing constraint on government actions. The management of the Exchequer was virtually unchanged since the Dowling Reform of the 1660s.[169] This was the age of Exchequer Chests (the original tin boxes of "Tin Box Accounting" fame) each with multiple key-holders and maintained for separate purposes and managed without overall co-ordination between them. There was heavy reliance on revenues from indirect taxes, especially customs and excise duties. Lotteries were sporadically used to finance specific projects such as harbour works. All these revenue sources were very vulnerable to the rises and falls in the trade cycle and so inadequate to the task of maintaining the consistently heavy expenditures involved in foreign wars fought over a long period. New sources of revenue based on income or wealth were developed, including income tax, footman tax and window tax and in 1813 the Treasury was centralised and reformed.

The loss of the North American colonies also changed the British Government's approach to the possession of overseas territory. Loss of the War of American Independence broke the coherence of the system of protection of British trade provided by the Trade and Navigation Acts. It was no longer possible to secure trade between Great Britain and its colonies and between British colonies by tariffs and other trade restrictions. Pitt recognised this reality and attempted to reduce or abolish many customs and excise duties. Trade, especially with North America grew rapidly.

Ways of making and keeping a trading empire had to be found which did not just depend upon the British sovereign exercising ownership over significant areas of land. Increasingly, by treaty rather than conquest, Britain sought to secure relatively small colonies and other possessions in strategically important locations that could readily be maintained and defended by the Royal Navy. At the same time, profit from overseas ventures came less from trade than from interest on, and principal repayments of, debt raised in the revitalised London money and capital markets. Thus, hesitantly, almost by stealth, the seeds of a new kind of colonial empire were sown in London in the last two decades of the 18th century. It was destined to last largely intact at least until World War I. The British Empire, as it became known, was a subtle inter-twining of capital flows and Royal Navy influence that eventually framed many of the hopes and aspirations of perhaps half the population of the world for over a century. British colonisation of Australasia was begun at the outset of this process.

Two developments of political thinking lent vitality to official hesitancy over acquiring overseas territory. First, the influence of Jeremy Bentham[170] and his followers appears to have been considerable albeit far from obvious. It seems to have had the effect of fundamentally questioning whether governments should become involved in colonisation and, if so, when and in what form. The clarity of purpose which originally drove the development of Virginia for profit was lost and, by the late 18th century, decisions about colonisation became more nuanced. It was Bentham's decided view that colonies were costly to the coloniser and iniquitous to the colonised. He argued forcibly that they should all be emancipated.[171] These arguments gave rise to considerable discussion among British radicals during the 1820s and 1830s. On the one hand, many Philosophical Radicals were associated with the Wakefield schemes in South Australia and New Zealand with a view to earning profits from them. On the other, J S Mill favoured government involvement in colonisation on the grounds that only a government could make the long-term investments in infrastructure that were necessary for successful colonisation.

Second, the campaign against the slave trade and, later, slaver ownership arose from the practical application to everyday life of protestant beliefs in personal salvation. This thinking spilled over from the emancipation of slaves to a "manifest destiny" type belief that "advanced" nations should raise less civilised peoples into advancement. "Less advanced" peoples should, therefore, be protected not only in terms of their persons but also of their possessions. They were not to be exploited. British officials at the Colonial Office in London were much influenced by such doctrines that were promoted by the Clapham Sect.[172] One consequence was that policy-makers became very wary of causing harm to "innocent and inoffensive" peoples.

There was a crucial difference between British perceptions of Aboriginal Peoples living in New Holland and of Māori of New Zealand but this did not extend to changing the underlying profit motive for colonisation. By 1770 neither had been extensively observed although members of Cook's first expedition, especially the navigator

Tuapaia, managed to communicate with Māori, something they found impossible among Aboriginal Peoples.[173] To the English travellers Māori appeared organised and warlike but the Aboriginal Peoples of New Holland did not. No doubt it was reasoned that any Māori resistance to colonisation would be difficult to overcome but any defiance by Aboriginal Peoples would be short-lived. Hence when British Parliamentary Committees came to consider the location of a convict colony, the relative timidity of the Aboriginal Peoples made it appear that it would be unlikely that Great Britain would have to fight an expensive war in Australia before settlement could be established. The same could not be said of New Zealand. For a British Government operating under, what it believed to be, extreme pressure of time, New Zealand was not a viable option in 1788 even if it was in 1840.

When colonising North America, in the 17th and 18th centuries the English Government usually negotiated treaties with local peoples for access to land. It was also the course adopted when Great Britain came to include New Zealand in the British Empire in 1840. But this treaty-based course was not followed in New South Wales in the late 1770s, the South Island of New Zealand in 1840 and the rest of Australia before World War I. Yet, in the remainder of the long nineteenth century, the British Empire expanded throughout the known world largely by concluding hundreds of treaties of secession with all manner of peoples. Why were Australia and New Zealand treated differently?[174] In the face of domestic political pressures, England colonised Australia in 1788 and effectively repeated the action over the South Island of New Zealand in 1840[175] in the face of perceived threats from France and the USA.

Ultimately, the British Government was impelled by the political and commercial concerns of the ruling landed class to mobilise military power to add New Holland and New Zealand into its empire. It did so in order to fulfil barely articulated strategic designs. It was only in hindsight that it became clear that colonisation of Australasia was born, encouraged and facilitated by British financial interests. It was thought unnecessary for financial reasons to negotiate a treaty of cession with Aboriginal Peoples in New Holland, even if such a negotiation could have been undertaken. Butlin remarked:

> "In a settlement in which what was required after the initial stores were exhausted would be produced by convicts working under detailed direction, and in which the distribution of that output would be determined by the same authority, the need for money for internal purposes was not apparent. The colony was to be a special kind of prison and prisons do not require a monetary system."[176]

By contrast, financial interests knew that Māori were used to hard bargaining. By 1840, much of New Zealand was drawn into the British Empire that was fast becoming a financial entity. The change in approach between New Holland and New Zealand reflects the growing influence of finance in the rule of the British Empire. It was recognised by Colonial Office officials that a repetition in New Zealand of a New Holland-style annexation would quickly lead to military conflict which would undermine any prospect of land sales. Indeed, opposition from Aboriginal Peoples had already led to fighting over access to land and had led to a number of massacres. Consequently, Hobson was instructed to conclude a treaty of access with Māori which he did by two incompatible treaty texts, only one of which was, in practice, recognised in law.

Chapter Notes

1 *Laudabiliter* was a commendatory letter issued by Pope Adrian IV (the last English-born pope) in about 1155, which invited King Henry II to extend his sovereignty to Ireland. Adrian sought to bring the Roman Catholic community in Ireland directly under the influence of the Church in Rome. His aim was to undermine the local families that ran the Church in Ireland and to ensure that a levy of one penny per annum per household (Peter's Pence) was collected. The original text has been lost and its authorship, wording and structure is the subject of considerable dispute. Yet *Laudabiliter* was sufficient to ensure that other christian monarchs did not interfere in Irish affairs for many centuries.
2 The King's Peace was often expressed as the existence of "control and good conduct". The sovereign and afterwards the British Government determined the extent of control and what conduct counted as "good".
3 This was the Navigation Act System which started as a set or regulations in 1650 but between 1661 and 1849 took the form of a series of Trade and Navigation Acts. The System aimed to tie the economies of the colonies to that of first England and Great Britain. It also ensured that a prosperous merchant marine could readily supply skilled seamen to the Royal Navy. As a method of cohering the British Empire it was only partially successful because British trade faced severe competition from the Dutch and the French. Although it meant that Bristol and Liverpool were important slave ports and Glasgow was important for tobacco, increasingly the Empire was held together by the bonds formed by capital flows rather than traded merchandise.
4 Before the Wales Acts were enacted during the reign of King Henry VIII, English sovereigns were entitled Kings of England and, afterwards, of England and Wales. It was only in 1707 with the Act of Union that his successors became sovereigns of Great Britain and only in 1801 of the United Kingdom.
5 It is difficult to accept that these treaties resulted from negotiations between equals. The economic and military power in the relationship was overwhelmingly controlled by the British authorities. With the benefit of hindsight, it appears that during many of the "negotiations" indigenous peoples were forced to be impotent by-standers as the destiny of their lands was decided by British strangers who the natives were unlikely ever to encounter again.
6 Richard S Hill: *State Authority, Indigenous Autonomy: Crown-Māori Relations in New Zealand/Aotearoa 1900–1950*, Wellington, Victoria University Press, 2004, p. 11.
7 Robert Hughes: *The Fatal Shore: A History of the Transportation of Convicts to Australia, 1787–1868*, London, Vintage, 2003, pp. 414–424.,
8 Hugh Edward Edgerton: *A Short History of British Colonial Policy 1606–1909*, London, Methuen, 1941, distinguishes at least four types of British colonial process; namely, beginnings, trade ascendency, systematic colonization and responsible government, zenith and decline of *laisser-aller* principles and the period of Greater Britain. Unlike Edgerton, we use the term "colony" to indicate a territory the resident polity of which is institutionally subordinate to another, located elsewhere.
9 See George Louis Beer: *The Old Colonial System 1660–1754*, Vol I, New York, Macmillan, 1912, especially Chapter IV, pp.224–315.

10   This striking phrase was coined originally by Geoffrey Blainey in 1967 to emphasise the historical importance in the development of Australia of isolation resulting from the distances in time and space wrought by global travel in the 18th and 19th centuries

11   Colonial Department: "Rules and Regulations for the Information and Guidance of the Principal Officers in Her Majesty's Colonial Possessions", London, Clowes and Sons, 1837. This publication was revised at regular intervals during the 19th century. However, there appear to be no copies of the first edition of 1837 available in the public collections of New Zealand, despite the fact that official correspondence records that a copy was provided to Captain William Hobson RN in 1838 or 1839 before he departed on his journey to New Zealand.

12   For example, George Orwell in "Shooting an Elephant" recounts an event while he was serving as a police officer in Burma in which he feels impelled to shoot someone's elephant. He wrote: "Here I was the white man with his gun, standing in front of an unarmed native crowd—seemingly the lead actor of the piece; but in reality I was only an absurd puppet pushed to and fro by the will of those yellow faces behind. I perceived in this moment that when the white man turns tyrant it is his own freedom that he destroys. He becomes a sort of hollow, posing dummy, the conventionalized figure of a sahib." George Orwell: ebooks@Adelaide, University of Adelaide Library, n.d., n.p.

13   Lord Melbourne, UK First Lord of the Treasury, said in December 1837 "if we really are in that situation that we must do something, … it is only another proof of the fatal necessity by which a nation that once begins to colonize is led step by step over the whole globe." Quoted by Peter Adams: *Fatal Necessity, British Intervention in New Zealand 1830–1847*, Auckland, Auckland University Press/Oxford University Press, 1977, p. 5 (dedication page).

14   In practice, it required major changes in British foreign policy during the 1950s to finally quell the impetus for colonisation. Decisions to withdraw British forces "east of Suez" and allowing the "Winds of Change" to blow through Africa were important steps in this political process.

15   JR Seeley: *The Expansion of England: Two Courses of Lectures*, Boston, Little, Brown and Co, 1905. Sir John Robert Seeley (1834–1895) was Regius Professor of Modern History at Cambridge. The *Expansion of England* was originally published in 1883 and repeatedly translated and reprinted over the following 50 years.

16   Ibid, p. 156.

17   Ibid. p.69. In making this argument Seeley echoes the ideas of Edward Gibbon Wakefield.

18   Ibid p. 55.

19   For a similar argument see Arama Rata: "Intergenerational Financial Trauma", pp 21–29 in *Counterfutures,* Issue 14, 2023.

20   The phrase "Manifest Destiny" was first coined in an editorial composed by Jane Cazneau or John O'Sullivan in 1845. In its original form, it was a secular version of the belief that the United States of America was the home of the "chosen people" and meant that it was the duty and the right of the USA to spread republican democracy beyond its existing borders. This was to occur not by force of arms, but rather, as settlers entered new territories taking their democratic republican institutions with them. The doctrine has always been contested in American politics and was later adopted *mutatis mutandis* by Adolf Hitler for other purposes. See for example Albert K Weinberg: *Manifest Destiny: A Study of Nationalistic Expansionism in American History*, Chicago, Quadrangle Books, 1963.

21   Both Keith Sinclair: *A History of New Zealand, New Edition*, Auckland, Penguin, 1991, p. 69 and Michael King: *The Penguin History of New Zealand*, Auckland, Penguin, 2003, p.129 emphasise the influence of evangelical humanitarianism over New Zealand colonial policy. Similar claims do not seem to have been made about policy made for Australian colonies. It should also be recalled that, on occasion, religious intolerance spilt over into violence as in the massacres of Roman Catholics at Drogheda and Wexford in Southern Ireland in 1650–1651.

22   James Douglas, 14th Earl of Morton (1702–1768) was a natural philosopher interested in astronomy, medicine and agricultural improvement. He was elected Fellow of the Royal Society

in April 1733 and a founder and first President of the Philosophical Society of Edinburgh 1737. In 1738, he became Earl of Morton and was a representative peer for Scotland in the House of Lords. He was elected President of the Royal Society in 1764 and oversaw the operation of the Greenwich Observatory, measurement of the transit of Venus and measurement of a degree of latitude. He was a member of the Longitude Commission. He was not politically ambitious and devoted his time and much of his fortune to scientific enquiry.

23 James Cook (1728–1779) went to sea aboard Whitby colliers owned by the Walker brothers, usually plying between Newcastle and London and gained his mate's ticket. He also taught himself navigation and wrote scientific papers. At the outbreak of the Seven Years' War (War of Spanish Succession) in 1756 Cook volunteered for the Royal Navy. He was posted to North America as Master aboard HMS *Mercury* in which he surveyed the Saint Lawrence River at night during the Siege of Quebec. After 1768, Cook undertook three epic voyages into the Pacific Ocean. The First was as Lieutenant in command of HMS *Endeavour* (which meant that he was accorded the courtesy of being informally called Captain) from 1768 to 1771. It had a public purpose, sponsored by the Royal Society, to observe and measure the sun's Transit of Venus at Tahiti in June 1769 and a secret purpose to explore, chart and, if expedient take possession of, appropriate parts of New Zealand and New Holland. Despite striking the Great Barrier Reef, HMS *Endeavour* returned to England via the Torres Strait and Batavia (modern-day Jakarta). The records of this voyage published by Cook and Sir Joseph Banks caused a sensation and made both men famous. Cook's Second Voyage as Commander aboard HMS *Resolution* lasted between 1772 and 1775. His mission was to search for Terra Australis. Cook made two circumnavigations of the globe at unprecedentedly high latitudes which proved conclusively that the supposed southern continent did not exist. In 1775, Cook was promoted Post-Captain (meaning his name was "posted" as a Captain in the Royal Navy in *The London Gazette*) and in 1776 was ordered to search for passages to the north of Eurasia and North America aboard HMS *Resolution*. He failed to find either and was killed in Hawaii on 14 February 1779. During his voyages, Cook set high standards of meticulous exploration and recording of observations to the extent that some of his charts of New Zealand were still in use in the 20th century.

24 For a full text see http://nla.gov.au/nla.obj223065829/view.

25 Bruce Buchan: "Traffick of Empire: Trade, Treaty and *Terra Nullius* in Australia and North America", *History Compass,* Vol. 5/2, (2007), pp. 386–405. Buchan argued that at least since the mid-1700s, officials in London were aware of the idea that by inducing indigenous natives to "trade" and "traffick" they could, in time: "… create among the indigenous peoples a sense of personal interest that could be mobilised to maintain peace on the frontier and to oppose the incursion of other colonising powers." At p. 394, Buchan describes the beneficial impact of the appointment of Sir William Johnson to regulate trade in the American colonies.

26 It is unclear from the surviving texts of the period if it was the rules by which trade should be conducted or the idea of reciprocity between traders that should be imitated.

27 See Anne Salmond: *Two Worlds: First Meetings between Māori and Europeans 1642–1772*, Auckland, Viking, 1991.

28 John Barrow (ed): *Captain Cook's Voyages of Discovery*, London, Dent, 1954, p.72 "On Tuesday, May the 1st [1770], the south point of … [Botany] bay was named Sutherland Point …. This day Captain Cook, Messrs Banks, Solander, and a few other gentlemen, went on shore, and left more presents in the huts, such as looking-glasses, combs, etc., but the former presents had not been taken away."

29 Cook re-named New Holland as New South Wales on 21 August 1770. Ibid, p. 84.

30 James Cook to John Walker (his former employer in the Whitby coal trade), 13 September 1771. See McNab, op cit, 1908, Vol II, p. 80. Of Aboriginal Peoples Cook wrote: "It is said of our first parents that, after they had eaten the forbidden fruit, they saw themselves naked and were ashamed; these people are naked and are not ashamed. They live chiefly on fish, and wild fowl, and such articles as the land naturally produceth; for they do not cultivate one foot of it.

These people may be said to be in the pure state of nature, and may appear by some to be the most wretched on earth; but in reality they are far more happy than we Europeans, being wholly unacquainted, not only with the superfluities, but with many of the necessary conveniences so much sought after in Europe; they are happy in not knowing the use of them. They live in a tranquility which is not disturbed by the inequality of condition; the earth and sea, of their own accord, furnish them with all things necessary for life; they covet not magnificent houses, household stuff, etc; they sleep as sound in a small hovel, or even in the open air, as the King in his palace on a bed of down."

31 Frank Crowley: *A Documentary History of Australia*, (5 Vols), Melbourne, Nelson, 1980 Vol 1, p. 479 quotes T S Besnard, an Irish New South Wales squatter writing from his property in 1839 states "… our neighbours, the lawful owners of these splendid plains, who, by the way, are of very quiet demeanour…" evidently thought that the Aboriginal peoples owned the land of Australia.

32 The term Pākehā is the Māori word for non-Māori inhabitants of New Zealand. Originally, I intended to use the term "pākehā" to mean all non-indigenous residents of Australasia. But it was argued by a number of people that such a use would not be understood in Australia and ran the risk of using Te Reo wrongly. For these reasons I use instead the term "non-indigenous persons".

33 See William Blackstone: *Commentaries on the Laws of England*, 4 vols, Oxford, Clarendon Press, 1765–1769.

34 See *Blackstone's Commentaries on the Laws of England*, Book the First, Chapter the Seventh: Of the King's Prerogative. http://avalon .law.yale.edu/18 th century/blackstone_bkTch7.asp. Accessed 1 April 2021.

35 These tales were often told by seafarers suffering from scurvy and other dietary (not to mention personal and social) deprivations as a result of long voyages often in search of fresh food and potable water. Such people were ill-equipped to report dispassionately on what they saw from the decks of their vessels as they coasted by.

36 See Crowley, op cit, 1980, Vol. 1, pp. 58–60, p. 135, pp. 262–264 and pp.318–319.

37 Transcription of Letters patent establishing the Province of South Australia, 19 February 1836. Accessed at legislation.sa.gov.au/lists-and-index-to-sa-legislation/letters-patent.

38 On 21 August 1770, according to Barrow, op cit, 1954, p. 84 "Previous to their leaving the island, Captain Cook displayed the English colours, and took possession of all the eastern coast of the country, by the name of New South Wales, for his sovereign the King of England.

39 This initiative was followed by the appointment George Langhorne as Missionary in modern-day Victoria in 1837, Captain Gayner as Protector in Western Australia in 1839 and George Clarke as Protector in New Zealand in 1841. Similar appointments were made in the Northern Territory in 1864, in New South Wales in 1880, Queensland in 1897 and Tasmania in 1912

40 Lord Glenelg, Secretary of State for War and the Colonies 1835–1839 and Sir James Stephen, Permanent Under-Secretary of State at the Colonial Office were members of the Clapham Sect.

41 See *Report of the Parliamentary Select Committee on Aboriginal Tribes (British Settlements)*, (Reprinted with Comments by the "Aborigines Protection Society"), London, William Ball and Hatchard and Son, 1837. A copy of this report was sent to Governor Gipps on 31 January 1838.

42 W David McIntyre and WJ Gardner (eds) *Speeches and Documents on New Zealand History*, Wellington, Oxford University Press, 1979, p. 13 states that Normanby's instructions to Hobson provide that all contracts with Māori for cession of land "should be made by yourself, through the intervention of an Officer expressly appointed to watch over the interests of the Aborigines as their Protector." This placed George Clarke, the person appointed as Protector of Aborigines in New Zealand, in the impossible position of having to serve two directly conflicting policy aims.

43 For example, British commercial interests, such as the New Zealand or the South Australia companies followed their own self-interests in trading with, and investing in, Australia and New Zealand irrespective of the actions and beliefs of governments, humanitarians, and clerics.

44 Australasian colonies outside the established settlements were so lacking in effective law

enforcement that it appears that bribery of officials, fraud, perjury under oath and payment for suitable evidence were widespread throughout the 19th century. For example, the writ of the Common Law does not seem to have been established throughout the North Island of New Zealand until after World War I.

45 The Nineteen Counties were defined by Governor Ralph Darling, first in 1826 and extended in 1829, as the limits of the Colony of New South Wales. They were Gloucester, Durham, Northumberland, Cumberland, Camden, St Vincent, Hunter, Cook, Westmoreland, King, Murray, Argyle, Roxburgh, Bathurst, Brisbane, Philip, Wellington and Bligh.

46 It is remarkable that Matthew Moorhouse, the first non-interim Protector of Aborigines in South Australia from 1839 until he retired in 1856, led a group of volunteers who committed the Rufus River massacre of 30 to 40 Aboriginal people in 1841.

47 Despatches from Auckland or Sydney could take 100 days to reach London and another 100 days for any reply to be conveyed in return. Thus, it took at least nine months before matters of some complexity could be addressed in the Australasian colonies.

48 The classic example is Governor FitzRoy's financial innovations by which he successfully sought to ward off public bankruptcy of the Colonial Government of New Zealand during 1844 and 1845.

49 Most pre-colonial arrivals seem to have washed up on New Zealand shores through shipwreck, as fugitives from "justice" and onerous working conditions or as missionaries. Some, like sealers, were even deliberately marooned by their (often Sydney-based) employers. Others staffed semi-permanent whaling stations and timber camps. Missionaries were relatively early settlers in both New South Wales and New Zealand but very few others freely chose to settle and work on the lands.

50 There is far from complete agreement about the numbers of people transported. For example, Hughes, op cit, 2003, pp. 159–160 states that of the 150 000 transportees recorded by the Home Office between one half and two thirds were repeat offenders, 80% were thieves, most were city dwellers, most were propertyless, 75% were single and their average age was 26. But according to Blainey, op cit, 2014, p. 67 by the time the last transported convicts arrived in Western Australia in January 1868 a total of 163 000 had been transported since the arrival of the First Fleet.

51 During the period 1688 to 1800 the number of crimes punishable by death rose from 50 to 220. Most were defined in defence of property. Systematic transportation was introduced by the Piracy Act (often called the Transportation Act) 1717 and suspended by the Criminal Law Act 1776 after the American colonies were closed to the victims of the British justice system. The last shipload of transported felons sent to the American colonies docked on 16th April 1776 at Jamestown, Virginia. Transportation seems to have been often employed as an alternative to the death penalty by courts unwilling to commit convicts to hang for what were seen as relatively minor transgressions. Transportation was resumed in 1788 and lasted until 1867.

52 Grand Larceny was a capital and, hence, a transportable offence. For such an accusation to be sustained the object of theft was supposed to be valued at a minimum of one shilling. Hence, transportation could be avoided if the valuation of the property involved could be reduced below this amount. It is sometimes unremarked that transportation of capital felons was widely accepted during the 18th Century. For example, Egerton, op cit 1941, p. 226 states: "The system was very popular with the English Government, who instead of being obliged to maintain the convicts could obtain five pounds for them from contractors, who in turn disposed of them on Colonial markets at about ten pounds a head; with the colonists who were assigned efficient labour at a cheap rate; and with prisoners who were able to work their way to independence."

53 These were the so-called Parkhurst Boys. Between 1842 and 1852 about 1500 boys between the ages of 12 and 18 were transported from the reformatory attached the Parkhurst Prison on the Isle of Wight. Most were sent to Western Australia, Victoria, Tasmania and Norfolk Island. 92 came to New Zealand aboard the *St George* in November 1842 and another 31 were brought by

the *Mandarin* in November 1843 (having already deposited 51 in Tasmania a month before). Thereafter, New Zealand and South Australia successfully petitioned the Colonial Office against further transportation. By contrast, Western Australia successfully urged that it continue. The boys were pardoned on arrival provided i) they were apprenticed [i.e. indentured] to a local employer and ii) agreed not to return to England during the term of their sentence. Considerable research appears to have been undertaken into the Western Australian apprentices but none could be discovered on those sent to New Zealand.

54   Non-indigenous people in New Zealand are generally known by the Māori word pākehā.
55   Sinclair, op cit, 1991, p. 46 decorously states that: "By 1838, there were about two thousand Europeans living in New from Zealand. Five or six hundred of them had settled round the Bay of Islands, where Kororareka had become a busy little town. A good many visitors or residents have left us portraits of this early settlement, few of them very flattering."
56   Such opposition might only emerge after several generations. See Michael King: *Te Puea: A Biography*, Auckland, Hodder and Stoughton, 1978, especially Chapter Four, pp. 79–97.
57   Adam Smith: *An Inquiry into the Nature and Causes of the Wealth of Nations*, CJ Bullock ed, New York, PF Collier & Son, 1909, p. 137. Smith stated: "People in the same trade seldom meet together, even for merriment and diversion, but the conversation ends in a conspiracy against the public, or in some contrivance to raise prices."
58   William Pember Reeves: *The Long White Cloud: Ao Tea Roa*, London, Allen and Unwin, 1956, p. 128 states: "The crews of these [whaling ships] found among the rum-shops and Māori houris of Korororaka a veritable South Sea Island paradise. The Māori chiefs of the neighbourhood shared their orgies, pandered to their vices, and grew rich thereby." Reeves does not mention that there was also a ready trade in re-victualing and re-fitting visiting ships. The chiefs also charged harbour dues.
59   This belief may have been encouraged by missionaries in New South Wales and their influential supporters in London and by the despatches of the British Resident in New Zealand, James Busby.
60   McIntyre and Gardner eds, op cit, 1979, p. 8.
61   Ibid, p. 12.
62   The term "Crown" is a slippery fish legal concept. Its meaning appears to alter to suit the purposes of its user. For example, it can be said to refer to the maximum power than can be collectively mobilised by the state or community. Alternatively, it is sometimes used to signify the person of the sovereign when exercising the Royal Prerogative. Finally, some colonists in the 19th century appear to have regarded the term "Crown" as referring to the person of the monarch to whom they (and presumably by implication all British subjects) owe fealty.
63   Steve Sheppard: *The Selected Writings of Sir Edwards Coke, Volume I*, Indianapolis, Liberty Press, 2009.
64   It should always be recalled that during the 18th and early 19th centuries communications between London and distant colonies could occupy years so that direct contact of colonial affairs by Colonial Office officials is a figment of a post-electric telegraph imagination.
65   For example, in parts of Africa it was not until 1870 that this step was taken and then only in competition with other European powers during The Scramble for Africa.
66   It should be recalled that many so-called pirates were supported by merchants who supplied them with ships and equipment in return for a share of the profits.
67   It should be recalled that many so-called pirates operated under Letters of Marque which made their activities sanctioned by the English monarch or some other sovereign authority in return for a share of the booty.
68   Initially, organised state assistance was reserved for non-indigenous settlers only; it was not available to Aboriginal Peoples or to Māori. This racially-based policy was consistent with the view that natural-born subjects of English monarchs enjoyed a personal relationship with the Crown; a belief that stretched rationality to breaking point. Such doctrine implied that, in

practice, Māori and Aboriginal Peoples were given access to a more restricted set of rights than were natural-born British subjects. In the case of Māori this was in direct repudiation of the promise granted in Article 3 of the Treaty of Waitangi, 1840. Claudia Orange: *The Treaty of Waitangi*, Wellington, Allen and Unwin/Port Nicholson Press, 1987, p. 42 reports the Article in question as: "The Queen extended her protection to the Māori people and granted them 'all the Rights and Privileges of British subjects'...."

69 Sources of reliable data on overseas borrowing through public issue of bonds and other debts by borrowers located in Australia and New Zealand do not exist for the period before 1865. During the 19th century after that date, it is only possible to find data for exports of capital from London but no data on imports of capital from any other destination. Even after 1865 there is little information, except anecdotes, about other kinds of capital flows such as direct overseas investment or personal remittances. Yet the nature of the country, on which most economic activity was based and from which demands for capital arose, did not suddenly change after 1865. See Leland Hamilton Jenks: *The Migration of British Capital to 1875*, London, Jonathan Cape, 1938 and Irving Stone: *The Global Export of Capital from Great Britain 1865–1914: A Statistical Survey*, Basingstoke, Macmillan, 1999.

70 Capital gains are made when the sale price of an asset, like a house, is higher than the price paid to buy ownership of it. If a tax is imposed on such capital gains, then the attractiveness of all assets is reduced because the prospective gains from buying and then selling it are reduced.

71 Michael Turnbull argued that such a money-go-round is part and parcel of Wakefield's Systematic Colonisation. Michael Turnbull: *The New Zealand Bubble: The Wakefield Theory in Practice*, Wellington, Price Milburn, 1959. Presumably, the argument could also be applied *mutatis mutandis* to South Australia.

72 Debt service means timely payment of interest on, and capital repayments of, outstanding debt. New Zealand is one of the very few countries which has never defaulted on its sovereign debt obligations.

73 Presumably this is the foundation of the practice of London financial institutions in recruiting members of the upper class, including royalty, as business representatives.

74 Both New Zealand and the Australian colonies supplied volunteers and horses to fight in the First Boer War in South Africa.

75 Both were *Indefatigable* class battlecruisers which were relatively obsolete (less heavily armed, slower and carried less armoured protection) compared to the more up-to-date British *Lion* class and German *von Moltke* class designs. They mounted 12 x 12 inch and 16 x 4 inch guns and 2 x 18 inch torpedo tubes. HMS *New Zealand* was paid for by the New Zealand Government, commissioned in 1912 and gifted to the UK. She had a complement of 800. She operated with the Royal Navy Grand Fleet as part of the First Battlecruiser Squadron and saw action at Heligoland Bight and Jutland. She was sold for scrap in 1922. HMAS *Australia* was commissioned into the Royal Australian Navy in 1913. She had a complement of 820, half of whom were serving with the Royal Navy. She saw action in the Pacific and Far East and was scuttled in 1924.

76 In Australia and New Zealand the respective Governors General declared war on Germany in 1914. The same occurred in Australia in 1939. However, it was the New Zealand Prime Minister who declared war in that year.

77 British policy was not labelled or lauded as "Austerity" during the 19th century. Nevertheless, British Governments consistently sought to commit as few of their own resources as possible to the prosecution of their policies. In following this course, they used many of the policy techniques that came to be known as "Austerity" during the 21st century.

78 Commodification of land is the term applied to the legal and social changes required to make land a thing, like a landed estate, which can satisfy the wants of humans viewed as individuals. In both Australia and New Zealand it involved demolishing or ignoring the cosmologies, social structures and beliefs which gave life to communal ownership and occupation of land and use

of natural resources and replacing them with those associated with the institutions of individual ownership.

79 This is said to be the foundation of the Māori King in New Zealand. No similar initiative seems to be evident in Australia. Nevertheless, pastoral use of the hunting ranges over which Indigenous Aboriginal peoples roamed was met with shows of armed resistance and the deaths of sheep, cattle or stockriders.

80 For example, Wiremu Tamihana Tarapipipi Te Wahoroa. It was not until the 20th century that similar arguments were voiced in Australia.

81 The Parihaka settlement founded by Te Whiti and Tohu in Taranaki is but one such example.

82 Hughes, op cit, 2003, p. 120 calls the elimination of Tasmanian Aborigines "… the only true genocide in English colonial history." This may be an exaggeration in view of the exploits of the English Parliamentary Army in Southern Ireland and the British Army in India.

83 Scorched earth tactics were employed against Tuhoe people at Ruatahuna in May 1869 and around Lake Waikaremoana in June 1870 which attempted to "wipe out the economic bases of Tuhoe's survival". See Judith Binney: *Redemption Songs: A life of To Kooti Arikirangi Te Turiki*, Auckland, Auckland University Press/Bridget Williams Books, 1995, p. 165 and p. 227.

84 Local rebellions have a limited life because the participants have to break off hostilities in order to plant the next season's crops or hunt for food, and have no source of supply except the land in dispute. They often fail for this reason.

85 The Royal Navy was of particular strategic value because it could be used to control the scale of conflicts. The Royal Navy gave Great Britain the options to unify local conflicts into larger wars or to separate conflicts from each other. In these ways, the Royal Navy was, in practice, an effective instrument for determining the geographical extent of those countries in the Empire that afforded access to the sea.

86 The Crimean War 1853–1856 exposed a number of fundamental weaknesses in British military capabilities which threatened to undermine the entire adventure. As a result, over the following decades, British Army logistics and medical provision were re-structured and reformed, more effective weapons were introduced, formal infantry officer training became more common and promotion on merit started to occur. These changes increased the competitive military advantage with which the British Government faced the indigenous peoples of the Empire in the second half of the 19th century.

87 The effects of this superiority were startling. In the New Zealand Land Wars Lieutenant-General Cameron repeatedly used armoured steam boats to avoid and encircle Māori forces. On 25 October 1893 700 police with Maxim guns were attacked by 6000 Matabele tribesmen armed with spears and rifles near the Shangai River in Southern Rhodesia (Zimbabwe). 1600 tribesmen were killed and the British suffered four casualties. On 1 November 1893, further south, at the Battle of Bambesi, a British contingent armed with five Maxim guns and a Hotchkiss cannon firing shrapnel were surprised by many thousands of Matabele of whom 2500 were killed.

88 Quoted by Adams, op cit, 1977, p. 5 and p. 101. Unfortunately, Melbourne's exact meaning is unclear. It is possible that he was expressing dislike of being forced into a decision to colonise by circumstances that he could not control or, merely, that it was advisable to set prior limits beyond which any contemplated colonisation should not be allowed to expand.

89 One of the reasons provided by Lord Normanby, the Secretary of State for War and Colonies, to Captain Hobson RN on 14 August 1839 was that New Zealand was important "to the interests of Great Britain in Australia". See McIntyre and Gardner, op cit, 1979, pp. 10–11.

90 On 15 March 1839, Sir James Stephen, Permanent Under-Secretary of State for Colonies asked "Should we acquire the Sovereignty of all the Islands [of New Zealand] and brave the discussion which must follow with the United States and with France with all the arduous responsibility of protecting the Inhabitants of so extensive a Dominion?" See Ibid, p. 9.

91 In 1845, Lieutenant Wilkes, Commander of the United States Exploring Expedition reported that some of the "scientific gentlemen" engaged in the expedition arrived in the Bay of

Islands from Sydney in time to witness the hui leading to the first signings of the Treaty of Waitangi. By 30 March 1840, three vessels of the United States Navy, USS *Flying Fish,* USS *Porpoise* and USS *Vinciennes,* lay at anchor off Kororareka (nowadays called Russel) in the Bay of Islands. See Charles Wilkes: *Narrative of the United States Exploring Expedition Vol II*, Pennsylvania, Wiley and Putnam, 1845, p. 375. Accessed at http://www.enzb.auckland.ac.nz/document/?wid=1247&action=null 16 April 2022. The accuracy of Wilkes's account, the real threat to British sovereignty posed by the US and the perception of the presence of the United States Navy in Sydney, New Zealand and London are some of the questions raised by these events worthy of further investigation.

92 In the first half of 1840, the Nanto-Boredelaise Company (La Compaigne de Bordeaux et Nantes pour la colonisation de Ille du Sud de la Nouvelle-Zelande Et Ses Museum) under the sponsorship of Louis Phillipe, King of France, attempted to colonise the South Island of New Zealand. The King appointed Captain Lavaud of *L'Aube*, a naval corvette, Commissaire du Roi, to prepare for and oversee the French and German settlement of Bank's Peninsular. Lavaud left France on 19 February 1840 and arrived in the Bay of Islands on 10 June 1840 unaware that Hobson had already (on 21 May 1840) proclaimed British sovereignty over the South Island by reason of Cook's discovery in 1769. When Hobson understood French plans, he ordered HMS *Britomart* to Akaroa to show the British flag. Upon investigation, Lavaud concluded that the legal basis of the proposed French colony was highly dubious deeds of sale and purchase concluded by a whaler Langlois which, among other things, promised French citizenship and French protection to Māori. Instead of asserting French sovereignty, Lavaud carefully avoided provoking armed conflict between Great Britain and France and concentrated on ensuring that settlement proceeded peacefully and cooperated with British magistrates. His actions earned him the Légion d'Honneur on his return to France on 1843. See Peter Tremeum: *Kai Tahu Land Sales to Captain Langlois and the Nanto Bordelaise Company on Bank's Peninsular*, Wai 27, doc T3, May 1989, pp. 38–39.

93 This was how Charles, Baron de Theirry was treated before and after he arrived in New Zealand on 4 November 1837 to set up an independent kingdom on 40 000 acres of land he thought he had purchased in 1823 while a student at Cambridge University. James Busby, the British Resident in New Zealand, spent considerable effort to mobilise opposition to de Theirry's enterprise among northern Māori. See Robyn Hyde: *Check to Your King*, Auckland, Golden Press, 1936.

94 On 2 September 1835, Governor Bourke proclaimed that Batman and his companions were trespassing because they did not possess licences to occupy. See CMH Clark: *Select Documents in Australian History 1788–1850*, Sydney, Angus &Robertson, 1955, pp. 93–93.

95 McNab, op cit, Vol I,1908, pp.45–49 called Sir George Young's Plan.

96 McIntyre and Gardner, op cit, 1979, pp. 10–11.

97 For example, the largest manpower contributions (in millions mobilised) to the Entente forces in World War I by selected countries of the British Empire were as follows:

COUNTRY	NUMBER MOBILISED	KILLED
UK	4,006,000	702,410
INDIA	1,440,437	53,486
CANADA	619,636	59,680
AUSTRALIA	416,000	58,961
SOUTH AFRICA	231,500	12,452
NEPAL	200,000	N.A.
NEW ZEALAND	117,175	18,060

N.A. Not available. Source: http://nzhistory.govt.nz?war/british_empire_facts_and_stats. The various sources disagree for a summary see https://en.wikipedia.org/wiki/World_War_I_casualties.

98 The Home Counties are here defined as the counties that existed before 1965 that were

circumadjacent to London, England. They comprise Essex, Hertfordshire, Kent, Middlesex, and Surrey. In modern times, these areas, together with Greater London, have become among the most prosperous in the UK and their inhabitants have become a by-word for self-satisfaction and conservative political attitudes.

99 Great Britain and the United States outlawed international trade in slaves in 1807. In 1808 they set up the West Africa Squadron which operated until 1860 as a joint naval operation to ensure that their anti-slave trade laws were respected. Slavery was made illegal throughout the British Empire by the Slavery Abolition Act 1833 which came into effect on 1 August 1834 (except in Ceylon (Sri Lanka) and St Helena). However, existing adult slaves did not finally receive their freedom until 1840. Owners of slaves were paid £20 million (estimated to be around 5% of British GDP) for the loss of their property. The British Government borrowed this sum from Rothschilds and the debt was not finally extinguished until 2015 when remaining undated gilts originally issued to ex slave owners were withdrawn and replaced with ordinary gilts with a fixed maturity. About half of the compensation was received by Caribbean plantation owners and the remainder by absentee landowners in Great Britain.

100 See E L Woodward: *The Age of Reform, 1815–1870*, Oxford, Clarendon Press, 1938, , p.87.

101 One side effect of the demise of the Trade and Navigation Acts was the elimination of the large surpluses which the landed aristocracy of Southern England accumulated by finance of smuggling. This wealth found its way into new enterprises which collectively became known as the Industrial Revolution and into the British colonies.

102 The first Reform Act 1832, although labelled "Great" by many of its proponents, was not remarkable for its radical impact. It added only around 270 000 to an electorate of 435 000 in England and Wales. See Woodward, op cit, 1938, pp. 84ff.

103 Jacobins were members of a republican movement which originated in Brittany in the late 1780s. They were responsible for the overthrow of the French monarchy and the Reign of Terror and were the forerunners of many left-wing political movements in the 19th century. The term "Jacobinism" was widely and loosely employed in Great Britain during the late 18th and early 19th centuries as an epithet designed to associate a person or political idea, often without benefit of factual evidence, with support for violent, radical and republican thoughts, policies and actions. We might regard any hint of Jacobinism as the antithesis of the "good conduct" that the King's Peace sought to establish.

104 For long periods in the long 19th century the British economy also displayed signs of an overvalued exchange rate in the form of low inflation, low productivity growth, low levels of domestic investment and loss of overseas markets by British exporters.

105 Unfortunately, we cannot know with certainty whether or not this pattern was new because it was not until after the middle of the 19th century that sufficiently reliable estimates of capital flows out of London money and capital markets became available.

106 The fusing of interests was reinforced as colonial businesses took on the structures of Joint Stock Companies. Shareholders (or members) of such companies had an interest in receiving a continual flow of dividends while colonial managers also benefitted from generating profits.

107 There is some archaeological evidence that Māori travellers visited Dark Point in New South Wales before there was contact between Aboriginal Peoples and europeans. Andrew Crowe: *Pathway of the Birds: The voyaging achievements of Māori and their Polynesian ancestors*, Auckland, Bateman, 2018, p. 209.

108 The last shipload of felons transported from Great Britain arrived in Jamestown, Virginia in April 1776. Yet many believe that the British loss of the Battle of Yorktown, Virginia in September and October 1781 signalled to the British Government led by Lord North that war against the American rebels and their French, Spanish and Dutch allies could no longer be prosecuted with any hope of success.

109 A similar level of vacuity of such claims was discovered on the Western Front by working class soldiers fighting for France, Germany and Great Britain during and after World War I. Incipient

revolt was the result. By contrast, very similar experiences among Dominion forces seems to have been forged into a sense of nationhood in Australia, Canada and New Zealand.

110   Chaos may be an over-statement. It certainly risks over-estimating the importance of the United States in world history. The gentry lost confidence in their own political expertise to the extent that, in 1783, they thrust the High Tory, William Pitt, the Younger (1759–1806) and the son of Pitt the Elder, Lord Chatham, into the role of First Lord of the Treasury (since 1878, when coined by Disraeli, called Prime Minister) at the age of 24, a position he retained for nearly 19 of the next 23 years. He did so with the active assistance of King George III in bribing supporters and opponents and by carefully concealing his personal beliefs and policy intentions. He acted concurrently as Chancellor of the Exchequer. His main policy was to economise on Government spending and find new methods of taxation in order to reduce the National Debt. It is believed that Pitt was asexual and was known to be fatally addicted to port. He died, worn out in office. The influence of the Younger Pitt in the form of "Austerity" and cheap government extended at least until World War I.

111   See Leon Radzinowicz: *A History of English Criminal Law and it's Administration* Volume I, Movement for Reform, London, Steven and Son, 1948. The Appendix gives a list of 18th Century capital offences set out under 21 different headings. For example, the Black Act 1723 is said to have introduced more than 350 criminal offences punishable by execution. Many appear to have involved wearing blackface and killing game of the estates of the local aristocracy.

112   A modern example is Fulton County Jail in the State of Georgia USA. This facility was designed to hold people pending trial. Once sentenced, the accused were supposed to be sent to a State prison to serve their sentence.

113   Many of the hulks lay in creeks around south east England, often close to the ports from which they previously sailed on active service. Apart from the impacts on local communities of pollution and want of hygiene it is also conceivable, for example, that the presence of a sizeable prison population incarcerated on hulks in Langstone Harbour might have undermined discipline aboard Royal Navy vessels berthed in Portsmouth. It is not known whether and to what extent the existence of these prison hulks influenced the conduct of ships of the Royal Navy based nearby nor how such considerations may have provoked urgency in the search for alternative sites to house transported felons.

114   By the final quarter of the 18th century, England had enjoyed a long history of disposing of its undesirables by banishing them to some place that was either inhospitable or inaccessible and preferably both. It was a tendency which potentially touched all walks of life. The ruling class employed arbitrary incarceration of ruling sovereigns and their families without benefit of warrant or trial in a variety of strongholds at least since the time of King Edward II; seamen often marooned shipmates, like Alexander Selkirk (Defoe's model for Robinson Crusoe), who proved intolerable; and whole villages would deliberately ignore the existence of members of the community who committed acts such as incest.

115   Transportation was conducted under a contract system by which the master of the vessel involved was paid a fixed price for each prisoner delivered to the New World and, in addition, could keep the proceeds of their sale to their new employers. The incentives in such a system encouraged ships' captains to transport skilled artisans and to keep them in good shape during the voyage because such labour attracted a premium when sold as indentured workers on arrival.

116   Journals of the House of Commons, Volume 37, p.125.

117   Alan Moorehead: *The Fatal Impact: An Account of the Invasion of the South Pacific 1767–1840*, New York, Harper & Row, 1966, p. 134 states: "As early as 1779 the matter was considered by a committee of the House of Commons. New Zealand was rejected on the grounds that the Māoris there were too ferocious…". Unfortunately, he does not provide evidence to support of this statement.

118   This appears to have been William Hussey MP (c.1724 to 26 January 1813). He was a wealthy Salisbury clothier with a thorough understanding of financial matters. He was a prominent civic

leader and became Mayor of Salisbury in 1779. He was MP for St Germans from June 1765, for Hindon from 1768 and for Salisbury from 1774 until his death. He inherited a fortune from his father which was enhanced by two lucrative marriages. He commanded considerable respect in the House of Commons but never served in government.

119   Clark, op cit, 1988, Vol I, p.65.
120   The period 1775 to 1785 saw a ferment of social and political ideas. One has only to recall that during this period Immanuel Kant published *Critique of Pure Reason* (1781), Thomas Paine published *Common Sense* (1776) and *The American Crisis* (1776–1783), and Adam Smith published *An Inquiry into the Nature and Causes of the Wealth of Nations* (1776).
121   They included James de Lancey, Admiral Sir George Young and James Matra.
122   Including Lord Howe, First Lord of the Admiralty, Lord Sydney, Home Secretary, and Evan Nepean, Under-Secretary of the Home Department which was then responsible for colonial affairs.
123   Presumably transporting felons to the Caribbean, for example, would have reduced the price that could be obtained in the slave markets and so undermined the profitability of the Atlantic slave trade.
124   McNab, op cit, Vol I, 1908, pp. 36ff.
125   James Mario Matra (1846–1806) was born in New York. He joined the Royal Navy as a Captain's Servant in 1761 and sailed under Lieutenant James Cook as Midshipman aboard HMS *Endeavour* between 1768 and 1771. He was a lowly paid diplomat in Tenerife and Constantinople during much of the 1770s. In May 1785 he testified before the House of Commons Committee investigating the resumption of transportation. In 1786 he was appointed British Consul in Tangier and died in office. See Alan Frost: "James Mario (Maria) Matra (1746–1806)", *Australian Dictionary of Biography*, Australian National University, https://adb,anu.edu.au/biography/matra-james-mario-maria-13084/text23669, accessed 27 February 2022.
126   Presumably, Matra had New Zealand in mind at this point. See McNab, op cit, 1908, Vol I, p.36.
127   See Andrew Tink: "The Role of Parliamentary Committee Witnesses in the Foundation of Australia", *Australasian Parliamentary Review*, Spring 2005, Vol 20(2), pp 33–38.
128   It is perhaps surprising that sites in New Zealand were not seriously considered by the Beauchamp Committee. Indeed McNab, op cit, 1908, Vol I, pp. 58–66 includes an anonymous, undated account in which the relative advantages of New Caledonia, New Holland, New Zealand and Norfolk Island as sites for penal settlements are canvassed. Of these alternatives, only New Zealand has never housed transported adult convicts. McNab appears to believe that it was drafted by Matra or Sir George Young and to have been written between 1783 and 1786. However, I have been unable to find references to a discussion of that proposal which canvassed the reasons why New Zealand was not actively considered as a possible site for a penal colony.
129   HMS *Nautilus* commanded, in 1786, by Commander Thomas Thompson, was an unrated Echo Class ship-rigged sloop of war. She was built at West Itchenor in 1784 and wrecked at Flamborough Head on 3 February 1799. She was armed with sixteen 6-pounders and six 12-pounder cannonades. She carried a complement of 125. Thompson died on The Gambia at the end of 1786 and his report was presented to the Committee by his chosen successor Lieutenant Tigge.
130   Hughes, op cit, 1987, p. 64.
131   For a more detailed account see ibid, pp. 56–67.
132   Both had been aboard HMS *Endeavour* when Cook explored the eastern seaboard of New South Wales in 1770.
133   Hughes, op cit, 1987, p. 1 Hughes notes that "In 1770 Captain James Cook had made landfall on the unexplored east coast of this utterly enigmatic continent, stopped for a short while at a place called Botany Bay and gone north again. Since then, no ship had called; not a word, not an observation, for seventeen years, each one of which was exactly like the thousands that had

preceded it, locked in its historical immensity of blue heat, bush, sandstone and the measured booming of glassy Pacific rollers." If Hughes is anywhere near accurate, the authorities in London must have been singularly desperate to settle on Australia as a solution to their political problems. They must also have been acutely insensitive to the deprivations that their chosen policy was bound to inflict on the convicts and their keepers. It is remarkable, therefore, that the reasons for their desperation have gone largely unrecorded.

134 It is now (2023) estimated that, "before the coming of European civilization", the continent of Australia was home to perhaps 1 million indigenous inhabitants. However, there is very substantial disagreement about this estimate. Geoffrey Blainey, op cit, 2014 p. 16 states: "My inclination, on present evidence, is to conclude that in most centuries the Aborigines were fewer than 500,000…." See also CMH Clark: *A History of Australia,* Vol 1: From the Earliest Times to the Age of Macquarie, Melbourne, Melbourne University Press, 1988. At p.4 he wrote: "On … the mainland of Australia the estimates … have always differed; some put the figure as high as one million four hundred thousand, while others put is at approximately three hundred thousand. Estimates of the number of Tasmanian Aboriginals … also differed greatly, some missionaries suggesting two hundred thousand while secular observers put the figure as low as between four thousand and seven thousand". Whatever The accuracy of these estimates it is plain that the continent of Australia was very sparsely populated when the First Fleet arrived.

135 Until well into the 20th century, Aboriginal inhabitants exercised few of the rights of ordinary Australian citizens. For example, they could not take oaths, could not vote in General Elections and could not be granted passports. Only in New South Wales and South Australia were they permitted to own real estate. As a result, a number of apocryphal tales are told about this period. For example, it is said that Aboriginal Australians were generally regarded as "beasts of the field" and so went untaxed and the reason why Albert Namantjira was granted citizenship was so that his £7,000 annual income from the sale of paintings would be subject to income tax.

136 Only very recently has it become common for historians to regard fighting between Aboriginal peoples and non-indigenous settlers in Australia as a war. In part, this is because there has been long-standing intellectual resistance to the idea that Great Britain was engaging with other nations for control and ownership of the land of Australia. See for example John Connor: *Country by country: Australian frontier wars, 1795–1928*, Chapter 17, pp. 388–407, in John Crawford and Ian McGibbon eds: *Tutu Te Puehu: New Perspectives on the New Zealand Wars*, Wellington, Steele Roberts, 2018

137 See Hughes, op cit, 2003, Chapter 4, pp. 84–128 provides a detailed account of this period. From the date of the arrival of the First Fleet no vessel arrived in Sydney until the *Lady Juliana* landed on 3 June 1790 with another 222 female convicts "and some flour" (pp. 104–105).

138 It was during this last attempt that HMS *Sirius* was wrecked off the coast of Norfolk Island in March 1790.

139 Governor Arthur Phillip was left by the Admiralty to assemble all the requisites for the establishment of a self-contained convict colony. His success in doing so was such that only two glaring oversights came to light in the years ahead; he purchased insufficient women's clothing and was not afforded a list of the sentences of which the prisoners in his care had been convicted. See Jenni Ferris: "Governor Phillip's First Commission", https://www.governor,nsw.gov.au/assets/Uploads/Governor-Phillips-Commissions.pdf, p.5.

140 The Australian continent was settled in a number of waves over at least 60 000 years by the ancestors of Aboriginal peoples who came by sea or passed over the land bridges with Asia that were eliminated about 6000 BCE by a long, slow rise in sea-level, which started about 16,000 BCE. In the centuries before the First Fleet arrived, the Australian Continent was visited, intermittently, by explorers from Europe, China and, certainly adjacent territories. However, after the land bridges with Asia disappeared, no-one from outside appears to have settled the country, except temporarily and, then, dictated by availability of seasonal food. Few explored even limited areas of Australia with the care that Cook devoted to his charting the entire coast

of New Zealand, New Holland and the west coast of North America. See Geoffrey Blainey: *A Shorter History of Australia*, Sydney, Vintage, 2014, Chapter 2, pp. 17–24.

141 For examples see Robert E Bartholomew: "No Māori Allowed: New Zealand's Forgotten History of Racial Segregation, How a Generation of Māori Children Perished in the Fields of Pukekohe", Auckland, Robert E Batholomew, 2020.

142 It is important to emphasise that "no-one" in this context means "no-one before the coming of the Pākehā". It is as if time before the arrival of the English does not exist for the purposes of adjudicating the Common Law. The idea of an ordinary person or the "man on the Clapham Omnibus" was coined by Lord Bowen J in the 1880s and used by Lord Greer J in 1903. So was the absence of ownership of land in Australia in the late 18th century, because "ordinary men" had yet to be conceived and "the Clapham Omnibus" that was their chosen mode of transport had not been invented?

143 Since the time of Queen Elizabeth I, it was ruled that "discovery" of a country was only valid if it accompanies (or is at least closely followed by) occupation by the nation claiming sovereignty over it. It is unclear why this condition seems to have been ignored in the case of New South Wales (presumably a lapse of seventeen years between discovery and occupation was officially considered to be sufficiently short to qualify as occupation). Nevertheless, Elizabeth's rule was at the forefront of official thinking about New Zealand some 50 years later, until Hobson chose to ignore it in May 1840.

144 Sir James Stephen was unsure whether a claim to sovereignty over the South Island would prove substantial. This was because the original discovery was not followed by settlement within a relatively short time.

145 For a summary of texts see Ferris, op cit, n.d.

146 Phillip was appointed Governor of Australia east of the present site of Alice Springs and, depending on the meaning of the term "adjacent", of southern New Guinea, the southern Solomon Islands, New Caledonia, the New Hebrides, Norfolk Island, Fiji and New Zealand north of the Banks' Peninsular.

147 Also known as his "Amended Commission".

148 "Governor Phillips's Instructions 25 April 1787 (UK)", pp. 6–7 accessed at foundingdocs.gov.au/transcripts/new2-doc-1787.pdf

149 Ferris, op cit, n.d., p. 3.

150 Bruce Buchan: "Traffick of Empire: Trade, Treaty and *Terra Nullis* in Australia and North America 1750–1800", *History Compass*, Vol 5, Issue 2, (2007), pp. 386–405, at p. 387 states: "To be sure it [the record] does show that a doctrine of *terra nullius* was not applied to Australia prior to 1889, but it also shows that other, more deeply entrenched European concepts, ideas and assumptions were applied in the colonial dispossession of Indigenous Australians." This dual use of the term "*terra nullius*": the legal doctrine *versus* the summary description of political and social reality remains a source of considerable confusion.

151 HMS *Sirius* ex HMS *Berwick* ex *Berwick* was built as a merchantman at Rotherhithe in 1780 and engaged in the Baltic trade. She was damaged by fire and bought by the Royal Navy in 1781. She was rebuilt, refitted and coppered at Deptford. She carried four 6-pounder guns and six 18-pounder cannonades as a 6th rate. She was renamed *Sirius* during preparations for the voyage to Australia on 12 October 1786 and served as Phillip's flagship for the First Fleet until Cape Town. There he transferred to the armed tender HMS *Supply*, the fastest vessel in his command, with the intention of providing for the arrival of the rest of the fleet. HMS *Sirius* departed Ryde on 13 May 1787. She was wrecked at Norfolk Island on 19 March 1790.

152 The remainder of the First Fleet consisted of six transports carrying convicts, marines and other personnel *Alexander, Charlotte, Friendship, Lady Penrhyn, Prince of Wales* and *Scarborough* and three store vessels laden with food and other supplies *Golden Grove, Fishburn* and *Borrowdale*.

153 Of Phillip's powers Watkin Tench, Captain of Marines, commented "Nor have Government been more backward in arming Mr Phillip with plenitude of power, than extent of dominion.".

See Watkin Tench: *A Narrative of the Expedition to Botany Bay*, London, Debrett, 1789, Chapter 10 accessed at gutenberg.net.au/ebooks/e00083.html Chapter 10.

154 Hughes, op cit, 1986, p. 12 remarks "They [i.e. Aborigines] neither sowed nor reaped, they appear to have wrought no changes on the face of the country. They were seen as culturally static primitives lightly wandering in an ecologically static landscape, which seemed to eliminate any claims they might have had to prior ownership." The accuracy of this summary is debatable given that the indigenous peoples appear to have used fire to drive prey into carefully planned and co-ordinated ambushes.

155 Andrew Crowe: *Pathway of the Birds: The voyaging achievements of Māori and their Polynesian ancestors*, Auckland, Bateman, 2020. At p. 209 he reports the discovery of a basalt Polynesian adze found in 1928 at Dark Point in New South Wales. He conjectures that Polynesians may have visited Australia before the arrival of non-indigenous settlers.

156 An unsubstantiated rumour recounted by Primavère Lesson, Surgeon on *La Coquille,* stated that "a Scottish gentleman" accompanied by "sixty peasants" embarked in 1782 "to establish himself on the shores of the River Thames or in Mercury Bay" in New Zealand. However, all trace of this attempt at colonisation is now lost to history. See Andrew Sharp (ed), Diana Quarmby (trans): "Duperry's Visit to New Zealand in 1824", Wellington, Alexander Turnbull Library, 1971, pp 106–107 and footnote 175 where Sharp argues that Lesson's anecdote is a garbled version of other events involving Rev Thomas Fyshe Palmer and the vessel *Plumier* in 1801. See also Rüdiger Mack: "The Mystery of the Scottish Gentleman Emigrant from 1782", *Journal of Pacific History*, Vol 32, No 2 (Dec 1997), pp 243–249.

157 These were the notorious "Blackbirders" who sailed the Pacific Ocean in search of indigenous peoples they could enslave and sell in South East Asia.

158 An early attempt was by Philip Gidley King, Governor of New South Wales. He issued a Government and General Order on 26 May 1805 extending his protection to Otahetians, Sandwich Islanders and New Zealanders who "are protected in their properties, claims for wages, and the same redress as any of His Majesty's subject." See McNab (ed), op cit, 1908, Vol I, pp. 258. Most historians argue that King's initiative was largely ineffective.

159 Presumably this was an economy measure arising from Pitt's stranglehold on public expenditure. It is noteworthy that Hobson, Shortland and FitzRoy all served for many years in the Royal Navy soon after the mutinies and all resorted to late or non-payment of their public servants between 1840 and 1845. See Michael Littlewood: "Robert Fitzroy and the Insolvency of the New Zealand Government, 1843–1845", 16 June 2021 downloaded as PDF from: papers.ssrn.com/sol3/papers.cfm?abstract_id=3867025.

160 The change in the nature of the debate about colonisation of the Antipodes might be chimerical. It is possible that the appearance to modern eyes of latter-day soul-searching is nothing more than a product of selective culling of official correspondence in conformity with political attitudes to colonisation which have become more humanitarian. In any case, many public displays of hand-wringing accompanied massive redistributions of land into the hands of non-indigenous persons occurred in both New Holland and New Zealand.

161 Bigge's report on conditions in New Zealand was based on a variety of verbal evidence including testimony from officers of HMS *Dromedary*. He was an important source of accounts of disorderly conduct by crew of visiting vessels and of attempts at placing escaped convicts among Māori. He recommended that the jurisdiction of the Governor of New South Wales be clarified to include New Zealand, that the Governor be given the duty to appoint magistrates and constables and that occasional visits be made by a ship of the Royal Navy. Commissioner John Thomas Bigge to Earl Bathurst, 27 February 1823. See McNab, op cit, 1908, Vol I, pp. 587–596.

162 Edward Gibbon Wakefield was an incorrigible and venal manipulator of other people. After failing to settle at the East India Company and Gray's Inn, he obtained minor roles as a diplomatic messenger in the aftermath of Waterloo. In 1816 Wakefield eloped to Edinburgh with his first wife, 16 years-old Eliza Prattle who died in 1821. Wakefield embarked upon

lengthy, costly and ultimately fruitless litigation to question the will of Eliza's father that was the source of his late wife's (and potentially his) fortune. In 1826 he lighted upon a 15 years-old schoolgirl, Ellen Turner, daughter of a very rich silk manufacturer. He kidnapped the girl and married her at Gretna Green. He was sentenced to three years' imprisonment in 1827 and incarcerated in Newgate Gaol where he wrote works attacking capital punishment and about colonisation including *A Letter from Sydney* (1829). After release in May 1830, he assisted in setting up the colony of South Australia. He continued to propagandise for his idea of systematic colonization, gave voluminous evidence to House of Commons Select Committees on Disposal of Land in British Colonies and on New Zealand, helped form the New Zealand Company which combined with the New Zealand Association and was an influential adviser to Lord Durham during his Commission in Canada. He served as a Director of the New Zealand Company from 1840 until 1849. Early in 1844 he became heavily involved in trying to save the New Zealand Company from liquidation. He suffered a stroke but recovered sufficiently to become involved in select committee hearings into the company's affairs. Further illnesses followed but Wakefield assisted John Godley to found the Canterbury Association. He published *A View of the Art of Colonization* in 1849 and helped draft the 1852 Constitution Act. He embarked for New Zealand aboard the *Minerva* on 12 October 1852 and landed at Lyttleton on 2 February 1853 and at Wellington on 7 March 1853. He was elected to the Wellington Provincial Council and the first General Assembly in 1855. His duplicity and attempts at manipulation meant that he was trusted by no-one. In December 1854 Wakefield contracted rheumatic fever and retired from public life until he died on 16 May 1862.

163 See M F Lloyd-Pritchard (ed): *The Collected Works of Edward Gibbon Wakefield*, Glasgow, Collins, 1968 especially pp. 93–185, "A Letter from Sydney, The Principal Town of Australasia", which was published anonymously in 1829.
164 Bernard Attwood: *The Economic History of Australia: An Introduction*. Accessed at https://eh.net/encyclopedia/the-economic-history-from-1788-an-introduction/p.3/.
165 See Karl Marx: *Capital* Vols I and II, trans. Eden and Cedar Paul, London, Dent, 1933, p. 849.
166 See Lloyd-Pritchard, op cit, 1968, pp. 178–185.
167 See for example J L Hammond and Barbara Hammond: *The Village Labourer 1760–1832: A Study of the Government of England before the Reform Bill*, Abingdon, Alan Sutton Publishing, 1995 and E P Thomson: *The Making of the English Working Class*, Harmondsworth, Penguin Books, 1970.
168 B R Mitchell and Phyllis Deane: *Abstract of British Historical Statistics*, Cambridge, Cambridge University Press, 1962, Table Public Finance 5, pp 401–403, Nominal Amount of the Unredeemed Capital of the Public Debt of the United Kingdom at the end of each financial year 1691–1939.
169 Sir George Downing (1623–1684) was employed by Charles II to reform the Treasury. He introduced the system of votes which linked Parliament's agreement to expenditure with specific items of spending. He was appointed Secretary to the newly-instituted Commissioners of the Treasury. In this capacity he introduced a number of accounting innovations.
170 Jeremy Bentham (1748–1832) was a philosopher and social reformer who is the founder of utilitarianism. As such he was the fount of many ideas that were once considered radical but which have become commonplace over the past two centuries. He rejected the doctrines of natural law and natural rights which he called "nonsense on stilts". He advocated individual and economic freedoms and denied the existence of "society". He called for separation of church and state, freedom of expression, equal rights for women, the right to divorce, decriminalising homosexuality and abolition of slavery, capital and corporal punishment. He was opposed to colonisation. He influenced many English philosophers including J S Mill. On his death his body was desiccated is now housed at University College, London.
171 Jeremy Bentham: "Emancipate Your Colonies! Addressed to the National Convention of France Anno 1793. Shewing the Uselessness and Mischievousness of Distant Dependencies on a

European State" in John Bowring ed: *The Works of Jeremy Bentham Volume 4*, 1838, pp. 407–418 downloaded from http://If-oll.s3.amazonnows.com/titles/1925/0872.04_Bk.pdf.

172 Sir James Stephen, long-time Permanent Secretary at the Colonial Office and Lord Glenelg, Secretary of State for War and the Colonies from 1835 to 1839 were both believed to subscribe to Clapham Sect sentiments. The term "Clapham Sect" was not coined by Stephen until 1844 and referred to a group originally centring on William Wilberforce and Henry Thornton. Members did not subscribe to a set doctrine but were christians who drew no distinction between social action and evangelism. They held disparate ideas but were against slavery, supported extension of the franchise and shared close personal friendships and family relationships. Most were conforming members of the Church of England and lived close to each other in the, then, upper class suburb of Clapham.

173 Much later, in the 1830s, Captain William Hobson, First Governor of New Zealand and James Busby, British Resident in New Zealand, both argued in some detail that British settlement should take the form of "factories" of limited extent.

174 This question is not original. For example, Banner, op cit, 2005, p. 2 asks "British land policy in Australia was different from land policy in otherwise similar colonies before and after. Why?" However, Banner neglects to mention that British sovereignty over the South Island of New Zealand was asserted by virtue of "discovery" by Cook.

175 It should be recalled that Governor George Grey insisted that "waste" lands on the South Island of New Zealand should be purchased from Māori. "Waste" to the Governor and his seniors meant land which was not being used for residences, burial grounds or cultivation. It did not mean that the land in question was of no value to Māori. For example, "purchase" of the Wairau and lands to the south (roughly 3 million acres) was the condition demanded of Ngati Toa by Governor Grey for the release, in January 1848, of Te Rauparaha who was kidnapped on 23 July 1846 and held without warrant or trial. Even further south, so faulty were the transactions conducted by Kemp, Mantell and others that it took more than a century and several official enquiries before any recompense (let alone redress) was offered to the affected tribes, most notably Ngai Tahu.

176 S J Butlin: *Foundations of the Australian Monetary System 1788–1851*, Sydney, Sydney University Press, 1968, p. 12.

CHAPTER 2

PLANTING NON-INDIGENOUS PEOPLE, ENTERPRISE AND SOCIETY

Plantation of non-indigenous people in New South Wales was the direct result of Great Britain's failure to effectively govern its New England colonies. This stemmed from a failure of British aristocracy to see beyond its immediate need to repress ordinary citizens. To the British ruling class its New England colonies provided a repository for transported felons and a source of profit. So, the loss of the American War of Independence meant that an alternative home for these unfortunates was required and profitable opportunities must be sought elsewhere. Botany Bay was that alternative home which began to be settled in 1788, 52 years before New Zealand was colonised in 1840. Other sources of profit only emerged later.

It was during the half century following the arrival of the First Fleet that the nature of the British Empire began to change. New South Wales was begun as a prison but later was made to turn a profit. From its inception, New Zealand was colonised by non-indigenous people for individual gain based on investment capital raised from Great Britain. By 1840, capital from London was made available to all Australasian colonies.

Plantation of non-indigenous people in Australasia began in earnest on Saturday, 26th January 1788 when the First Fleet entered Port Jackson (Sydney Harbour). On the following day the Union Jack was planted in the presence of Governor Philip and his most senior officials and the land was formally claimed for Great Britain. Most observers of these events watched from the vessels of the First Fleet lying at anchor. Clearing the site at Sydney Cove for a settlement and erecting tents and huts then began.[1]

It was not until the 6th February 1788, that the women convicts were brought ashore. In a procedure lasting from five o'clock in the morning until six o'clock in the afternoon the women prisoners were subjected to a "strict search" for stolen goods which was widely evaded and were then ferried ashore in longboats. A total of 732 convicts and 245 marines[2] disembarked the First Fleet at Sydney Cove. Arthur Bowes Smyth, Surgeon aboard *Lady Penrhyn,* reported that:

> "The men convicts got to them very soon after they landed, and it is beyond my abilities to give a just description of the scene of debauchery and riot that ensued during the night."[3]

On the following day there was a parade, enlivened by martial music, at which Governor Philip's commission was read, followed by a formal luncheon for the officers and senior officials. On the previous evening, the lower classes, had already conducted their own celebration despite being assailed by violent thunder squalls and temperatures of over 70 degrees Fahrenheit.

In this way, colonisation of Australasia started with the delivery of selected representatives of the more unruly and militaristic elements of late 18th Century English society into New Holland, which was, for non-indigenous people, a completely alien environment. This small, transported, wholly non-indigenous population put down the roots of colonies in Australia and New Zealand and was an important reason why the two countries prospered or languished to the extent that they did.

The society that initially coalesced at Sydney Cove was very simple. Non-indigenous convicts were forced to colonise New South Wales and Royal Marines were compelled to guard them while being overseen by senior officers and colonial administrators. The daily necessities of all groups were supplied by the Commissariat[4] which was a branch of the British Army and was the source of hand tools, seeds, clothing and food rations and the pay of rank-and-file soldiers.[5] A store was established in Sydney Cove operated by the Commissariat from which personal supplies could be drawn according to pre-determined schedules irrespective of appetite and need. Governor Philip insisted that all residents received the same set allowances. Blainey[6] recounts that a convict called Black Caesar ate his whole weekly ration in a day. Women were allowed only two-thirds of the men's ration no matter what sustenance they each required. The Commissariat also acted as an agent for the employment of convicts by private landowners, who included missionaries.

The Colonial Office envisaged that the convict society would become self-sustaining[7] within two years and provisioned the First Fleet accordingly. Governor Philip tried to establish Government farms to grow the produce that would feed the people under his care. But the soils around Sydney Cove were sandy and unproductive and the farms were worked largely by the calloused hands of gangs of convicts overseen by "trusty" convict overseers. Lack of agricultural equipment and draft animals, not to mention want of agricultural expertise, incentive and physical vigour meant that farm production remained consistently below demands for it. From late 1788 to 1792, the colony of New South Wales endured "The Starvation Years"[8] during which Governor Philip was forced to obtain emergency supplies from Cape Town and unsuccessfully seek further victuals from Canton.[9] Rations were drastically reduced, starvation became commonplace and scurvy even appeared among the convict population.

From the date of the arrival of the First Fleet on 26 January 1788 no vessel arrived in Sydney until the *Lady Juliana* landed on 3 June 1790 with another 222 female convicts "and some flour".[10] In fact the British Government had contracted the firm of Campden, Calvert and King to organise two further fleets to convey the core of the newly-recruited

New South Wales Corps, more supplies and more convicts to Sydney. But the Second[11] and Third[12] Fleets were not as disciplined as the First under Philip. Many passengers of the Third Fleet were recruited directly from prison hulks and were often ill on embarkation. There were also cases of mis-treatment by crew members.

The spectre of starvation did not finally evaporate until some members of the New South Wales Corps and very few free settlers arrived to work the land for profit. Corps members were advantaged in variety of ways. They were entitled to more rations than other residents, they could obtain goods at the Commissariat Store at advantageous prices, they could select the most productive land and they were advantaged by the ready availability of subsidised convict labour and some animal-drawn farming equipment. Over time, members of the Corps managed to take over many of the holdings originally granted to Emancipated convicts. With the opening of the Hawkesbury Valley in 1794, more fertile land was settled.

For some years, Governor Philip[13] has been requesting the Colonial Office to recruit competent farmers to become free settlers.[14] But, by 1800 only 23 free settlers had come to Sydney.[15] Under instructions to Governor Phillip dated 25 April 1787 convicts and free settlers of "good conduct and disposition to industry" were entitled to a grant of land. Further instructions dated 20 August 1789 permitted additional grants for non-commissioned marine officers and privates. Commissioned officers were allowed grants from 1792 onwards. In addition, land could be occupied under Crown licence, which did not involve alienation of the land to the occupier and was normally for a period of 12 months.

It is now necessary to summarise the process by which land ownership emerged as part of the development of "free settlement" in the early colonial history of New South Wales. A more detailed account can be found in Chapter 4 "Marketable Land in Australasia".

At first, land was distributed directly by the hand of the Governor or Acting Governor, a method predicated on the assumption that all Australia was already composed of crown lands.[16] The first free settlers who landed in January 1793 comprised five men, two women and six children. Only one, Thomas Rose, was an experienced farmer and was married with four children (three boys and a girl). Each man received 30 acres, each woman 20 acres and each accompanying child 10 acres. It seems that girls did not count because Thomas Rose was granted a total of 80 acres on 28 May 1793. Arthur McMartin has conjectured that, for reasons of security, Acting Governor Grose directed Rose and the other free settlers[17] to settle on unproductive "hungry" land to the west of Sydney so-called because it proved to require plentiful manuring.[18] At the outset of colonisation land was tilled by hand either by hoe or by spade. Fertility of the soil was enhanced by spreading and hoeing in wood ash and by turning in the sod.[19] At about the same time Grose granted highly productive land near Parramatta to Lieutenant James Macarthur[20]. It betrays a singular inability by Grose to understand what was intended to be achieved by courting free emigration by expert farmers and his overwhelming desire to propitiate the officers he commanded. Grose freely granted land to officers of the New South Wales Corps and endowed each with 10 convicts supported by the colonial government for every 100 acres granted. Leading figures of the Corps were enabled to establish prosperous estates based on what Hughes describes as Government-sponsored slave labour which came to be known as the Assignment System.[21]

In the Australian colonies, the governments facilitated a primary market for waste land.[22] Estates in land, but not the land itself, were made available to everyone who was not a convict. In New South Wales before 1832, this involved applicants being given *gratis* a crown grant upon application to the Governor.[23] These grants were normally in *fee simple* so that they did not involve the grantees in obligations to the crown. In some cases, licences to occupy required that proprietors promise to progressively improve the land. The land involved was first surveyed at significant expense by the colonial government. Once a crown grant was made, the landed estate could be enjoyed as the grantee saw fit although sometimes there were conditions for cultivation, fencing or residence. Crown grants could also be alienated as the holder wished.

In order to clarify my text, it is convenient to distinguish between three types of land market. First, there was the Pre-Primary Market. This was only applied in New Zealand and consisted of the colonial government purchasing land from Māori. Second, there was the Primary Market for land in which the colonial government disposed of land to settlers. Disposal might be by sale or lease but always involved some form of crown grant. Hence, the supply of land onto the Primary Land Market was determined by the Governor's willingness to make crown grants. Third, there was a Secondary Market on which land was bought and sold among settlers and sometimes indigenous peoples.

After 1832, when Ripon's Rules (see Appendix 1 below) were introduced, the Primary Market in Australia was conducted through public auctions. Purchasers bid for the freehold specified by crown grant, or a leasehold over a fixed period with or without right of renewal or an annual licence to occupy. In the Australian colonies boundaries were usually surveyed by the Government. By contrast, in New Zealand, although the Government rejected the idea that Māori owned the land, the costs of boundary surveys were paid by them because they were regarded as "sellers". The Government charged the original Māori occupiers for this service.[24] For many years, out in the back blocks of the Australian colonies and in the South Island of New Zealand, most runs operated by squatters remained ill-defined and, in practice, largely unpoliced.

Estates in land specified by crown grant, lease or license to occupy could be traded on a secondary market. Secondary markets in Land were organised by private investors who made and maintained institutions for the exchange of landed estates. Surveyors, lawyers, real estate agents, auctioneers and providers of finance all combined locally to make transactions possible. From time-to-time, especially in the last quarter of the 19th Century, governments sought to encourage small-scale landowning by purchasing and sub-dividing large runs then on-selling the smaller holdings on deferred terms. Other government support for transactions in landed estates extended to guarantees of title under the Torrens System of land registration which became widespread after 1860. For the most part, governments did not intervene[25] in transactions involving land arranged on the secondary market in Australia and New Zealand.[26] The operations of private monopolists were of much greater influence than governments over land market outcomes.

The central aim of all this activity was to sell land for a price higher than that at which it was bought. This required a market in land. So, the process of making markets was crucial in creating landed estates which could be bought and sold. But making such markets changed the character of the thing being bought and sold. Land became a landed estate. The land of Australasia was no longer a tangible entity from which people and the natural world grew and to which they returned after death. In the colonised world, land became real estate defined solely in legal documents that made no mention of the land's history or its physical, social and cultural attributes. Estates were legal claims. Land became a commodity, each "piece" defined by cadastre[27] in relation to other "pieces" of real estate.[28] The massive advantage that estates have over the land which underlies them is that estates are readily re-defined, relatively easily bought and sold and capable of transfer from person to person, company to company or government to government across the world. Estates also allow English-trained lawyers to maintain that the land underlying landed estates always remains in the ownership of the Crown. We shall learn that all these attributes are much sought after in lawyerly circles.

The grants were administered by commissioners who were supposed to make sure that the conditions which were attached to them (e.g., ownership of adequate capital, support of sufficient stock or requirements for cultivation) were adhered to. The activities of the commissioners could be intrusive and detract from the real purpose of making the grants which was to spread cultivation as quickly as possible. Nevertheless, this was broadly the system by which much of the South Island of New Zealand was settled by squatters.

In New South Wales, under Grose, the system of personal distribution of crown grants was riven with favouritism. For example, in May 1793 he directed Thomas Rose onto unproductive land. Yet, in the previous February, he not only granted John Macarthur fertile land further to the west in Parramatta but also made him paymaster for the New South Wales Corps and Inspector of Public Works. These appointments meant that Macarthur took personal charge of much of the finances of New South Wales. Unlike the pay of their subordinates, the officers of the New South Wales Corps were paid in London. This gave the officers access to sources of capital not available to others. It meant, for example, that Macarthur as Corps Paymaster could use his position organise a ring to monopolise the purchase of rum. With other Corps officers, Macarthur also used his position to dominate colonial affairs by racketeering, monopolising the sale of spirits and food and controlling access to convict labour. It also enabled Macarthur to access large areas of grazing land.

Eventually the influence exercised by the Corps officers became entrenched and a political interest called the Exclusives became a feature of New South Wales politics. Inevitably, these activities gave Macarthur extra-legal power which he used to suborn litigation for his own and his associates' benefit. Such power courted opposition from successive governors. He was sent by Governor King to England for trial by Court Martial for shooting his Colonel in 1801 and escaped. He managed to invoke the patronage of Lord Camden, Secretary of State for War and the Colonies who made him a crown grant of 10,000 acres of his choosing. He was also permitted to purchase nine merino rams and one merino ewe from the royal flock at Kew and the sheep formed the basis of his wife's[29] masterly flock improvements which lasted until her death in 1850. He returned in 1805 and, by 1806, the Macarthur family owned a flock 5,000 strong.[30]

Having been part of the military junta which deposed Governor Bligh, Macarthur left for England again in 1809 and did not return until 1817. During that time, he intrigued intensively with his high tory associates against Governor Macquarie,[31] perhaps the most visionary and energetic Governor ever appointed to Australasia. Macquarie acted on the belief that the future of the colony was to be found among the activities and energies of Exclusives,[32] Free Settlers and Emancipists[33] who would choose to make the country the basis for their future lives. In 1817 Macquarie granted a charter for the Bank of New South Wales.[34] He also improved communications, opened the country surrounding Sydney to free selection and designed and oversaw the construction of many public buildings. One unintended consequence of Macquarie's belief was that for many decades after the introduction of representative government the politics of New South Wales was dominated by a running battle between Exclusives and Emancipists.

But Lord Bathurst, who in later life called himself an ultra tory and who became Secretary of State for War and the Colonies in 1812, would have none of such "open society" nonsense. He saw no reason why New South Wales should ever be anything but a penal colony and prisons have no need for money or democracy let alone banks and deliberative assemblies. In 1819 Bathurst appointed John Thomas Bigge as Special Commissioner to determine how far New South Wales could be "made adequate to the Object of its original Institution". This meant that, contrary to Governor Macquarie's ideas, Bathurst was intent on eliminating free settlement and re-establishing the penal colony of New South Wales on more enduring foundations. Bigge arrived on 26 September 1819 to conduct his investigations which he completed in February 1821. It appears that he only took evidence from the largest landowners, like Macarthur, and he was highly critical of Macquarie.

There is no need to rehearse the details of Bigge's three lengthy reports except in one respect. The recording of crown grants during the period before 1819, appears to have been inconsistent and unreliable. When Bigge arrived in Sydney, it was officially estimated that grants totalling 324,251 acres had been made in New South Wales and a further 57,423 acres provided in Van Diemen's Land.[35] Complaints about delays in conducting surveys remained. Incentives in the system encouraged accumulation of large estates. People who were granted an acreage which was not economically viable or who were unable to fulfil their obligations for cultivation often sold their provided grants to richer or larger landowners like John Macarthur and William Wentworth, both of whom accumulated large estates. Often land transfers subsequent to the initial crown grant went unrecorded. It was also suggested that crown grants had been made on the grounds of manufactured evidence of capital owned or improvements made.

Commissioner Bigge reported that the records did not provide a reliable link between the identity of grantees, the amount of land held, the stock lent by the Government and the stores supplied by the Commissariat. (Presumably, the estimates of crown grants issued were also in doubt.) As a result, he could not vouch for the accuracy of land returns made by the colonial administration.[36] Bigge reported on the six-step procedure for making crown grants which appears to have remained relatively unchanged from the time of Acting Governor Grose until the end of Governor Macquarie's rule in 1819–1820[37] as follows:

1. Applications for crown grant could be made in Sydney on an appointed day in the year (although exceptions were made for settlers bearing instructions from the Colonial Secretary or for convicts whose sentence had expired);
2. A list of grantees and the acreage of the grants allotted[38] to each is prepared by the Governor and sent to the Surveyor-General;
3. The Surveyor-General or his deputy publish the list in the *New South Wales Gazette* and, after the time for objections expires, measures off the allotted land;
4. The Surveyor-General sends the measurements and description of the boundaries of the land to the Governor;
5. The Governor transmits them to the Colonial Secretary's office where a grant is made out, sealed and registered; and
6. The grantee pays the fees and receives the grant.

The area of land allotted and any indulgences such as the use of convict labour, loans of government herds or access to stores are at the discretion of the Governor. The acreage of each grant issued after 1810 was highly variable and, unlike those made in Governor Philip's time, no limit was placed upon the maximum size of an individual grant. Once a crown grant had been obtained the title to the land could be sold, given or bequeathed by the new owner at will.

Considerable speculative activity on the secondary land market began to emerge after 1810, especially in town and some suburban sections close to Sydney. The colonial government appears to have made no attempt to manage the primary or secondary markets for land in New South Wales. Responsibility for making, describing and recording crown grants was shared between the Colonial Secretary, the Surveyor-General and the Commissioners for Crown Lands. The only centralised record of crown grants was a chronological list by grantee registered by the Colonial Secretary. This system of personal administration by the Governor persisted until the early 1820s, by which time the system of crown grants was hard pressed and thought to be close to collapse. Rapid increases in free settlers, encouraged by Macquarie's vision, could not be adequately serviced by the personal allocation of land by the Governor.

Macquarie's successor, Thomas Brisbane, tried to improve land administration. He removed some delays in settlement by issuing tickets-of-occupation which permitted immediate occupancy without initial survey and security against the charge of trespass without alienating the land. He appointed more surveyors to reduce backlogs. He also tried to ensure that grantees had an interest in using the land productively. He insisted on promising land only to those with the inclination and ability to make productive use of it and ruled that settlers should maintain one convict labourer at their own expense for every 100 acres they were granted. Between May and December 1825, Brisbane went so far as to supply more than 500,000 acres of crown lands to the primary land market at 5s per acre.

In 1825 the population of New South Wales has been estimated as 38,313 having been 13,116 in 1815 and was destined to become 71,304 in 1835.[39] Despite this rapid population growth, little appears to be known about the early history of residential housing in New South Wales[40] although the early 1830s saw restrictions on size and drainage of, and access to, housing lots brought into effect. For example, in The Rocks, wealthy traders built grand mansions along the ridge overlooking Sydney Cove while down the slope were dark, insanitary shanties housing the working class who lived close to their work in the houses of the rich. Later, similar patterns of ramshackle working-class housing close to major industrial development took root in Balmain, New South Wales, and Fitzroy, Victoria. Presumably, these properties were let rather than sold to their occupants. However, there is also mention of "pay off as rent".[41]

It is reported that there was speculation in urban sections in Sydney during the late 1820s and early 1830s and in Auckland during the early 1840s.[42] In New South Wales, the estates that formed the basis of homes of the gentry were based on sizeable crown grants made by a succession of Governors. These estates were sub-divided and re-subdivided into residential sections on which individual homes could be built. This was organised by the land owners, auctioneers or real estate companies. It is not known how the transactions involved were financed although settler's letters occasionally mention involvement of banks and traders in these transactions. In Auckland, after 1840, town sections were purchased at crown auction (reputedly by Sydney speculators) and subsequently subdivided into smaller lots and offered for sale. It was not before the turn of the twentieth century that ordinary non-indigenous workers could aspire to a detached house on a quarter acre section.

Auctioning Crown Land

Frederick Robinson, 1st Viscount Goderich[43] was made Secretary of State for War and the Colonies for the second time in November 1830. On 9 January 1831, he wrote to Governor General Ralph Darling, Governor of New South Wales, setting out how sales of crown land were henceforth to be conducted. His instructions remained largely intact in Australia and New Zealand until World War I.[44] Disposal of crown lands in New South Wales from its foundation involved making grants to eligible settlers on condition that they cultivate the land. But, by the late 1820s, Goderich concluded that the system had failed.[45] Goderich did not agree with Wakefield's ideas on colonisation then all the rage. It is true that they were based on the free flow of capital, trade and people around the world which accorded with Goderich's broad philosophical inclinations. But Goderich made no attempt to ensure that the British government, when choosing emigrants, regulated the supply of labourers to "be as nearly as possible proportional to the demand for labour"[46] or that "no excess of males be conveyed to the colony free of cost".[47] He was of the view that financial burdens provided an incentive for making improvements which was absent when free grants of land were made. Free grants led to possession by people who were either "unable or unwilling" to make improvements. In 1831 he broke decisively with British colonial tradition and determined that all disposals of crown waste lands in the colonies by free grant would cease.[48] Henceforth, all land disposals in British colonies would be by means of public auction.[49]

Ripon's Rules represent a major change to the Grand Bargain under which the British Empire was originally formed. No longer did access to crown lands depend upon the "grace and favour" of the sovereign and the disposal of crown lands ceased to depend upon the exercise of the sovereign's pleasure. Ripon's Rules meant that crown waste lands would henceforth be obtained by anyone who could pay the price they fetched at public auction. They, therefore, mark the end of the use of royal charters to unlock colonial territories as part of the Grand Bargain.

This change represents yet another example of the belief, commonly expressed in the long nineteenth century, that free trade in open markets leads to coherent settlement of differences and peaceful co-existence which all parties have an interest in preserving. This thinking underlay Morton's Hints, Classical Economics and the free trade treaties that Cobden negotiated with France in the 1860s. In accord with this policy, detailed regulations were promulgated for New South Wales on 1 August 1831 to govern the conduct of public auctions of crown waste lands.[50]

Ripon's Rules (see Appendix 1 for a full text) stipulated that no land within 100 feet of the coast would be made available. The colonial government reserved the right to construct roads and extract building materials and to mine coal and precious metals[51]. All free persons could purchase any quantity of land. Land was to be surveyed before sale and normally to be made available in lots of 640 acres (1 square mile). There was to be three months' prior notice of sale of land by the government at public auction. If application were made to purchase land, then one month's notice of public auction was required. To make a bid a 10% deposit must be paid and, if successful, the balance must be tendered within one calendar month. Non-payment would mean that the deposit will be lost and the land will be re-auctioned.

The 1831 regulations were incorporated word-for-word into the 1837 edition of the Rules and Regulations which summarised the "Terms upon which the Crown Lands will be disposed of in New South Wales and Van Diemen's Land".[52] Colonial officers were told that:

> "No land is disposed of … otherwise than by public sale, and it has been deemed expedient to prepare, for the information of settlers, the following summary of the rules which it has thought fit to lay down for regulating the sales of land in those Colonies."[53]

The Colonial Office envisaged a largely domestic system of land disposal. The various applications were to be made to local officials in New South Wales and Van Diemen's Land. Auctions were to be held locally. It appears that overseas advertisement of sales or the results of bidding did not occur. Presumably, the Colonial Office entertained a model of settlement which involved settlers taking their capital with them to Australasia and, on arrival, deciding upon the most appropriate use of their funds and time. Nevertheless, agents were not precluded. But unlike more modern provisions, there was no active encouragement of overseas investment except by granting remission, to some serving military and naval officers, of some of the purchase price.[54]

The disposal of crown lands was to be under the direct control of the Governor of each colony. This course was chosen to avoid the peculation and cheating which attended some of the land grants made in the North American colonies prior to independence. An open market for crown lands was relied upon to eliminate the worst excesses of monopoly, fraud and graft by virtue of the "sunshine of information" that was allowed to flood the process. But, it is extremely debateable whether this alone was ever going to be sufficient to prevent underhand trades in a large and disparate colony like New South Wales with few bidders and a press, which had yet to develop judgement that was independent of vested interests. Hence, it is likely that early bidders in the process probably made substantial gains at the expense of the British Government.[55]

In 1843, these regulations were further elaborated.[56] *Inter alia* they required that:

"1. All lands will be disposed of by sale alone, and must have once at least been exposed to public auction.
2. The lowest upset price[57] will be not less than 1l. [£1] per acre; but the Government will have power to raise the same by proclamation, though not again to reduce it.
3. The lands will be distinguished into three different classes, viz, Town lots, Suburban lots, and Country lots…
5. Town and suburban lots will in no case be dispersed of except by public auction, but country lots which have already been put up for auction and not sold, may be disposed of afterwards by private contract at the upset price.
6. No lands will be sold by private contract except for ready money[58]. When sold by public auction, one-tenth, at least of the whole purchase-money must be paid down, and the remainder within one calendar month, or the deposit will be forfeited.
7. Lands will be put up for sale in lots, not exceeding one square mile in extent."

The Governor was also given discretion to raise (but not lower) the lowest upset price that would be accepted at auction for town and suburban lots and not more than one tenth of country lots offered for sale. He was also given discretion to "dispose by private contract, at a price not less than the lowest upset price for the district of blocks comprising 20,000 acres or more". Thus, the Governor replaced the Sovereign and became directly involved in the management of sales of Crown waste lands to settlers.

The 1843 Rules and Regulations followed closely the procedures that had been developed by the New Zealand Company for the sale of land in its settlements. Like the New Zealand Company, it became possible for UK investors to make deposits towards the purchase of land in New Zealand[59] through the Bank of England and to receive an entitlement to name, within six months, a "proportionate number of emigrants for a free passage". This form of assisted passage represented a new element of policy because the emigrants were to be intending wage workers "chosen from the class of mechanics and handicraftsmen, agricultural labourers, or domestic servants"[60]. With this provision the Colonial Office appears to have adopted some aspects, at least, of Wakefield's idea of extending British society into the rest of the world by populating colonies with a cross-section of the population of Great Britain.[61]

Squatting

The terms "squatting" and "squatter" carry different cultural connotations in the UK, the USA and in Australasia. In the UK and the USA calling someone a squatter implies that they are occupying or using real estate in an unauthorised way. It is often applied to disadvantaged people who, without being able to squat, would be homeless. From 1862, this activity in the USA was regulated under various Homestead Acts which helped settle 160 million acres west of the Mississippi River. In Australasia, by contrast, squatters are people who own or at least control very extensive estates often originally acquired by means that were outside existing land laws. They are often collectively termed the "squatocracy" in order to convey their privileged and political influential position in society.

In the current context, squatting is the occupation and use of land without owning a freehold or leasehold title to it and is a method of acquiring land which is not covered by Ripon's Rules. The lands beyond the Nineteen Counties in New South Wales and outside the town, suburban and country sections on the South Island of New Zealand were regarded as crown land but was never allocated through open public auctions. Indeed, this land was never offered on the Primary Land Market. Rather, a squatter could occupy territory by driving flocks or herds onto grazing lands and by acquiring a licence to occupy from the colonial government. The activities of squatters were often only cursorily policed. It represents a type of land proprietorship which is rarely found in closely settled societies. It was the main way that the hinterlands of New South Wales, Victoria, Queensland and South Australia and the South Island of New Zealand were occupied by a small minority of non-indigenous settlers. Squatting on crown lands was reported from the outset of planting non-indigenous people in New South Wales[62] but it was not before 5 September 1826 that Governor Darling attempted to control it.

Darling created an area in the vicinity of Sydney called the limits of location. This was extended on 14 October 1829 to become the outer boundary of the Nineteen Counties. By his order settlers were only able to take up land within these boundaries. The order was widely ignored and unauthorised occupation of crown lands both within and without the set boundaries continued. On this land extensive sheep rearing became established and by the 1830s wool had become the largest export from New South Wales.[63] By 1840, an area 200 miles wide running from Moreton Bay (present-day Brisbane) through Port Phillip (i.e., Melbourne) to Adelaide[64] was occupied by "maybe less than one thousand"[65] pastoralists who were without legal tenure to the land that they occupied and were widely referred to as "squatters".

In order to regulate the situation, on 28 August 1833, the New South Wales Legislative Council passed an Act for protecting the Crown Lands of this Colony from Encroachment Intrusion and Trespass. Under this measure Commissioners of Crown Lands in the Colony of New South Wales were appointed by the Governor. They were charged with preventing "intrusion, encroachment and trespass" of crown lands, to which end they were permitted to set up "beacons or landmarks" to signify the existence of crown lands. Unsurprisingly, this measure did not prevent widespread squatting which rising wool prices had transformed into a highly profitable occupation. On 29 July 1836, "an Act to restrain unauthorized occupation of Crown Lands in New South

Wales" was passed. From 1st January 1837, it became an offence to occupy or improve crown lands located beyond the boundaries of the Nineteen Counties circumadjacent[66] to Sydney without first having obtained a valid licence-to-occupy or a licence to "depasture"[67] animals. Those found guilty faced fines up to £50 for a third or subsequent offence and free settlers found counterfeiting licenses could be transported for up to seven years or imprisoned for up to four years. Convicts committing the same offence faced seven years transportation or four years in irons performing public works such as road making. It was under the authority of this Act that Governor Bourke proclaimed the Batman Treaty, which laid claim to modern-day Melbourne and Geelong, illegal because it involved trespass on crown lands.

From 1830 onwards, squatters continued to expand their activities despite not enjoying legal title to the lands they occupied. They were able to do this because of the lack of effective enforcement of the existing law. Not only were the Commissioners of Crown Lands under-resourced in the areas outside the Nineteen Counties but also wool growing by squatters was highly lucrative and so bribery of officials became just another cost of "doing business". Crown lands on which squatting took place were often traditional hunting grounds of Aboriginal peoples. Beasts depasturing the land were fair game and were frequently speared. Employees of squatters looking after the flocks were also killed. Lord Glenelg, a noted humanitarian, who became Secretary of State for War and the Colonies in 1835 sought to extend protections to Aboriginal peoples in the form of reserves, policing the crown lands, appointing protectors, providing schooling and religious instruction, and guaranteeing traditional rights.[68] However, no new resources were forthcoming to provide for any of these new policies. Governor Gipps believed that:

> "The lands [i.e., Crown Lands] are the unquestionable property of the Crown and they are held in trust by the government for the benefit of the people of the whole British Empire. The Crown has not simply the right of a landlord over them, but exercises that right over them under the obligations of a trustee."[69]

But he was never able to muster the resources and political support required to bring his vision into a practical reality.

By contrast, some squatters and their employees were intent on driving away or killing the bands of Aboriginal people who traversed what the settlers claimed was "their land".[70] At the same time, other squatters actively protected Aboriginal peoples. In the absence of protection from the government, the killings continued. The massacre of aborigines at Myall Creek in 1838 was a direct result of inadequate policing in the areas beyond the Nineteen Counties. It was, according to Gipps, "of frequent occurrence" but rarely investigated by the local constabulary. In the case of the Myall Creek massacre, Gipps quickly charged the perpetrators, seven of whom were hanged after two trials. This antagonised squatters so that they became implacably politically opposed to Gipps. Some squatters organised into a Black Band to pay for the defence of those charged with the Myall Creek killings and to intimidate potential witnesses. The Black Band became the extra-legal enforcers of discipline among, and the organ of subsequent direct action by, squatters.

The early 1840s was a time of falling wool prices but many sheep had been purchased with funds borrowed from banks at rates of 10% to 15% p.a. Many squatters were forced to sell their flocks for boiling down for tallow and banks experienced liquidity difficulties when loans could not be serviced. Some squatters also exploited the isolation of their employees by paying their annual pay in the form of "orders" which were often impossible and always expensive to spend. They commonly charged excessive prices for rations deducted from wages and charged shepherds and stockmen well above market prices for losses of livestock.[71] Finally, in 1844, most of the 24 newly elected seats in the Legislative Council were won by squatters and their adherents. That election result destroyed any faint possibility that Glenelg's humanitarian ideas would survive. So, they expired quietly and unremembered.

The scene in New South Wales was set for full-blown political confrontation between Governor Gipps and the squatters which dominated local politics until Gipps returned to England on 11 July 1846. On 2 April 1844, Gipps issued a regulation that from July 1845 squatters would be subject to the following conditions:

❖ Each squatter must pay £10 p.a. for each separate station over which they had propriety;
❖ Stations could be no larger than 20 square miles (12,800 acres); and
❖ No licence could be obtained to cover a station capable of depasturing 500 head of cattle or 4,000 head of sheep.

The Pastoral Association aroused furious opposition. For the first time, individual squatters that occupied several runs more than seven miles apart would be forced to purchase a separate annual license to occupy for each property. For example, Wentworth complained that his annual bill for licenses would rise from £10 to £150. In an apparent attempt to quieten the tumult, the rest of Gipps's proposals for a progressive freeholding of squatted land appeared in the *Sydney Morning Herald* on 13 May 1844 having been leaked by Mr Icely under Gipps's authority.[72] It was reported that Gipps was proposing that after five years' occupation a squatter could purchase the freehold of 320 acres of his run at £1 per acre. Then, provided the squatter continues to pay the £10 p.a. grazing licence he has security over his run for a further eight years after which the freehold of a further 320 acres could be purchased. This pattern of progressive freeholding could continue in eight-year instalments for as long as the squatter wished.

Some influential squatters believed, quite erroneously, that they already enjoyed the land they occupied as if they held it in fee simple.[73] Hence, the grazing licence was widely regarded as a tax, illegally imposed. The Colonial Office rejected this line of argument in short order. The squatters persisted in demanding tenure for 21 years coupled with a pre-emptive right of purchase even though the Colonial Office understood that such a combination of rights would:

> "… give him [the squatter] also the power, in fact, of effectively defeating all competition in the purchase of land, by the means it would afford him [sic] of selecting and appropriating whatever spots he might think most for his interest to possess."[74]

Undismayed, the squatters took their objections and demands to the Parliament in London. Eventually, Orders-in-Council were issued in March 1847 which awarded squatters occupying runs on crown lands, leases of 14 years in length with a right of pre-emptive purchase. Thus, an influential and privileged political interest that represented highly conservative beliefs was established and secured in a prominent place at least until World War I.

Nevertheless, as early as the late 1850s demands began to be made to release crown land for settlement. The argument surrounding the issue became known as the "Land Question". Large areas of all colonies were leased to squatters who grew wool for export mainly to Great Britain. Increasing numbers of immigrants had been enticed to Australia by the prospect of obtaining land but on arrival found it beyond their means or even unavailable. One result was that in Melbourne a convention was held from 15 July to 6 August 1857 to set out the foundations of a Land Bill which was intended to be widely accepted. In the event, the draft bill was never legislated but the exercise did make the disposal of land a matter of enduring Australian class politics.[75] For example, the Melbourne Convention passed a resolution which laid out the right of every adult to select land subject to seven conditions. The conditions included substantial occupation (i.e. no absent proprietors), payment of 10% of the purchase price on occupation, water and water frontages, land on gold fields and land near settlement to be exempt from selection and the price not to exceed £1 per acre.[76] It appears that none of the new colonial legislatures took the advice of the Melbourne Convention when drafting subsequent land laws. Nevertheless, its activities are a measure of the concern about unlocking the land from the hands of squatters which was to last for at least the next 50 years.

By 1861 the first of the 14-year leases issued under the 1847 Regulations were falling due for renewal. On 18 October 1861 the New South Wales Parliament passed the Crown Lands Alienation Act and the Crown Lands Occupation Act. Together these Acts became known as the Robertson Acts.[77] The first set out the rules by which crown lands could be alienated and the second codified the rules of occupation. For the purposes of the Acts, crown lands were lands vested in the crown which have not been dedicated to a public purpose or which have not been granted or promised to be granted in fee simple by the Governor on the advice of the Executive Council.[78] The main political purpose of the Acts was to allow all-comers to purchase or settle the type of land that heretofore had been mostly occupied by squatters. Most of the land in question was un-surveyed at the time of the passage of the Acts. Three other colonies (Tasmania, Victoria and Queensland) adopted the New South Wales model by introducing similar legislation at much the same time.[79] By contrast, the events in New Zealand after the passage of the Constitution Act 1852 were largely dictated by the activities of Provincial Governments each of which passed its own legislation.

Unlike the cases of the New Zealand Provinces, there is little new information to be garnered from a detailed examination of the various Acts governing alienation of crown lands which were passed in the Australian colonies. Hence, we shall confine our narrative to the experience of New South Wales. The principle of permitting free selection prior to survey was an important feature of the Robertson Acts. It was adopted in Tasmania in 1858, in Victoria in 1862 and Queensland in 1860. Crown lands were opened for selection and could be purchased at auction. Individual settlers were able to secure only one run in any given round of alienations of crown lands. A uniform upset price of £1 per acre was established, of which a quarter, or 5 shillings per acre, was payable on purchase and the remainder had to be paid over three years. Land so purchased could be freely resold after a year. Leases of crown lands were granted for a uniform 14 years at a rent of £10 p.a. Settlers were recompensed for any improvements that they made, which included the costs of boundary surveys. The system was administered by locally-based Land Commissioners. Selections could be registered through agents in the main centres of population.

The Robertson Acts did not reduce the economic and political dominance of the squatocracy. As with all systems of land administration, there was considerable gaming by existing squatters and lease holders. Local administration distant from the centre of political power provided opportunities for peculation and dishonesty by local officials. Ignorance of the nature and extent of land open for selection provided opportunities for existing squatters to monopolise water sources or fertile land to the disadvantage of their neighbours. Sometimes squatters employed "dummies" to secure their chosen selections and undertake to on-sell the land to their sponsors after a year; a process known as "peacocking". The Robertson Acts did not open settlement to all-comers because further legislative change was required for that to occur. Nevertheless, the land policies adopted under the Robertson-style Land Acts did lead to a significant reduction in un-occupied lands. By 1907, only just over half of all lands in Australia were unoccupied.

New Zealand Land

The foundations of landed estates in New Zealand are different from those underpinning Australian land. From the outset of British colonisation of New Zealand, Colonial Office officials assumed that Māori must be accommodated into what passed for British imperial designs in London. No blueprint for the transfer of power was drawn up apart from the instruction that Hobson "… treat with the Aborigines of New Zealand…"[80]. The transfer was placed in the hands of Captain William Hobson RN who was an experienced naval commander used to quieting conflicts and acting sensitively to the possible diplomatic consequences of his actions. But the Colonial Office declined to provide Hobson with more than general written instructions. In particular, he was not supplied with a draft treaty to present to Māori on behalf of the British Government. Nevertheless, care was taken to ensure that Hobson sailed to New Zealand via Sydney where he spent three weeks as the guest of George Gipps, Governor General of New South Wales.

Gipps was Hobson's immediate superior in the British colonial hierarchy and had developed decided ideas about the nature of the crown estate that he oversaw. In January 1840, while Hobson was in Sydney the sale of land in New Zealand was the subject of public controversy which Gipps defused by forbidding a private auction of South Island land. At about the same time, Gipps also attempted to conclude a treaty with ten Māori chiefs over the disposal of their land. The text of this unsigned treaty has survived[81] and Gipps expanded upon the ideas it contains in speeches delivered subsequently before the New South Wales Legislative Council.[82] Like the Treaty of Waitangi the unsigned treaty proposes agreement to three propositions; namely, the grant of sovereignty over New Zealand to Great Britain, the British Government to have a monopoly over the purchase of New Zealand land from Māori and Māori to become British subjects. The similarities with Hobson's draft of the Treaty of Waitangi are so close that I presume that Gipps conveyed these ideas to Hobson during January 1840.

After landing in New Zealand in late January 1840 Hobson seems to have spent much effort in drafting the instrument now known as the Treaty of Waitangi. It is composed of three articles:

> Article 1 accords Great Britain the right to govern New Zealand;
>
> Article 2 permits the British Government to bring land held by Māori into the crown estate by means of sale and purchase; and
>
> Article 3 conveys to Māori all the rights and responsibilities of British subjects.

Of these, Articles 1 and 3 did not require the British Government to immediately engage with Māori in order to provide the benefits promised in the Treaty. Only Article 2 involve the British Government in some form of active policy that immediately involved Māori and which took the form of a market upon which Māori land was to be bought and sold. The British colonisation of New Zealand began, therefore, with founding a land market created and managed by British interests.

Definition of Ownership of Land in New Zealand

Between 1838 and 1846, British views changed about the meaning of land, the nature of title to land and the question of who owned the land. In 1838 Colonial Office officials were incapable of deciding upon the ownership of land in New Zealand. Existing law provided an inadequate guide to the matter. On 14 August 1839, Lord Normanby, Secretary of State for War and the Colonies wrote to Lieutenant Governor Hobson about the proposed annexation of New Zealand as[83]:

> "… a measure essentially unjust and but too certainly fraught with calamity to a numerous and inoffensive people, whose title to the soil and to the Sovereignty of New Zealand is indisputable, and has been solemnly recognised by the British Govt."

Whoever holds the combination of title to the soil and sovereignty of New Zealand can determine what form title shall take, who can own it and what can be done with it. Thus, in August 1839, Colonial Office officials appeared to have judged that Māori were just as much owners of New Zealand as the crown was of the land of Great Britain and Australia. This implied that Great Britain could only replace Māori as owners of the land if Māori were to grant or sell it or if the British crown took the land by conquest.[84] It followed that the system of land disposal employed in New South Wales, Tasmania and South Australia could not be used in New Zealand.

In the event, the form of land ownership in New Zealand was unilaterally imposed by the British Government. By the Letters Patent dated 16 November 1840, a distinct Colony of New Zealand was established.[85] A Legislative Council and Executive Council was set up and the Common Law as enacted in Great Britain was applied to New Zealand. The Governor was given the power to transfer crown waste lands to private persons and corporate bodies. This implied that until the land of New Zealand was owned by the crown, transfers of title to estates in it could not be legally valid and were unenforceable under the Common Law. The New Zealand colonial government had first to obtain ownership of the land before landed estates could be created and then distributed to settlers. While casting about for an owner of the land, the Colonial Office accepted that Māori were proprietors of the land so it was recognised that before the crown could issue crown grants to settlers it first had to obtain uncontested control over the land of New Zealand. Thus, between 1840 and 1846 the colonial Government set up a Pre-Primary Market in New Zealand land.[86] In doing so, the Colonial Office built a façade of transactions with Māori, by which it could portray them as "sales" made "voluntarily" as if they had taken place in any town or village in South East England.

The initial step was to assert the crown's right of pre-emption. Article the Second of the Treaty of Waitangi states[87]:

> "… the Chiefs of the United Tribes and the individual Chiefs yield to Her Majesty the exclusive right of Preemption of such lands as the proprietors thereof may be disposed to alienate at such prices as may be agreed upon between the respective Proprietors and persons appointed by Her Majesty to treat with them in that behalf."[88]

Successive Colonial Governors interpreted this provision to mean that their administration had been given the sole right to buy the land of New Zealand from Māori. In other words, the Treaty of Waitangi anointed the colonial government with the power of a monopoly buyer (i.e., a monopsony). By this reasoning, it meant that no-one other than the crown could obtain unencumbered ownership of New Zealand land or unencumbered title to estates in New Zealand land. If a person desired to own a landed estate in New Zealand, then she was forced to approach the colonial government to obtain it.[89]

The Pre-Primary land market involved the definition of the extent of owned land compared with wastes. In his instructions to Captain Hobson RN dated 14 August 1839, Lord Normanby declared that Ministers of the Crown have been restrained from assuming sovereignty over New Zealand for some time. He famously stated that Ministers:

> "… have deferred to the advice of the Committee appointed by the House of Commons in the year 1836, to inquire into the state of the Aborigines residing in the vicinity of our Colonial Settlements; and have concurred with that Committee in thinking that the increase of national wealth and power promised by the acquisition of New Zealand, would be a most inadequate compensation for the injury which must be inflicted on this Kingdom itself, by embarking in a measure essentially unjust, and all too certainly fraught with calamity to a numerous and inoffensive people, whose title to the soil and to the

Sovereignty of New Zealand is indisputable, and has been solemnly recognised by the British Govt [sic]. We retain these opinions in unimpaired force; and though circumstances entirely beyond our control have at length compelled us to alter our course,[90] I do not scruple to avow that we depart from it with extreme reluctance...."[91]

In 1839, just before Hobson set sail for the Antipodes, the British Government believed, without explicit qualification, that Māori society held title to the entire soil of New Zealand.[92] Thus, in direct contrast with New South Wales and Tasmania, at the time of drafting Hobson's instructions, the British Government held the opinion that title to the entire land surface of New Zealand (together with, presumably, parts of the surrounding seabed and the associated airspace) was already owned by some Māori tribe or another. There was, therefore, no part of the country to which anyone else could claim a proprietary right. The term 'title' could (and can) be read in several ways. For example, it might merely mean having the right to use or determine the use of land. Alternatively, it could mean that a certain tribe was holding a particular piece of land by force of arms, or that several different rights (of varying significance) are held by several tribes over land over which a powerful tribe has some form of veto control. It might even mean that a particular tribe is able to dispose of the land under its jurisdiction by means of gift or sale. It seems likely that the Colonial Office had the last meaning in mind when drafting Normanby's Instructions to Hobson.

Although the legal framework into which the new colony of New Zealand was fitted was largely imported from the Colony of New South Wales, the Colonial Office recognised that the situation in New Zealand was radically different from that which obtained in Australia. The Colonial Office accepted that New Zealand was inhabited by a "numerous and inoffensive people" and, unlike New South Wales, could not be regarded as an uninhabited land. It is true that the South Island was "discovered" and claimed for Britain by Cook in 1769. But although the claim was made, it was never followed by occupation; but more important perhaps, neither was the claim ever repudiated. In the 1830s, the British Government had no intention of relying upon the doctrine of "discovery" to assert sovereignty over New Zealand.[93] Despite Cook's claims and by complete contrast with Australia, the British Government regarded it as essential to involve local inhabitants in its proposed colonisation. Attwood states:

> "The Colonial Office's key players maintained that acknowledging the sovereignty of the natives and their title to land, and in turn acquiring the natives' consent to relinquishing them both, made the possession of foreign lands more honourable for the British nation and more just in the eyes of God—and more peaceful to boot."[94]

The method of involvement chosen by the Colonial Office was to arrange some form of market for land.[95] Yet it did so without having first firmly settled upon a meaning of the term "land" in a New Zealand context.

At the close of the 1830s, the Colonial Office accepted that Māori had title to both "occupied" or "settled" and "unoccupied" or "unsettled" lands, i.e., all the territory in New

Zealand. Indeed, Hobson was explicitly instructed to conclude "fair and equal contracts" with Māori for cession of "Waste Lands"[96] to the crown. But the meaning of the term "waste lands" is not clear and was used inconsistently. To successive British Governments, waste lands were lands for which the crown had no immediate or prospective use and so were surplus to its present and future requirements. But like any civilisation dependent on shifting agriculture, Māori provided for future needs by controlling and conserving land which was not in current use. The land occupied by a given tribe comprised the land in current cultivation, the land over which food and other materials was gathered, the land resting after cultivation, land required to house anticipated population growth as well as areas of cultural importance such as the final resting place of the dead. Colonial New Zealand governments consistently refused to recognise this meaning, presumably on the ground that Māori were regarded as a dying race. Alternatively, "waste lands" might mean not currently in use (i.e., land not at present occupied or settled) or it might mean land deliberately not used productively according to european custom (e.g., grouse moors or monuments like battlefields). Another meaning is that "waste lands" are lands which have not been altered by the hand of man, like a hunting territory or a location of valuable minerals. In all such cases, the definition of waste depends upon the intentions and plans of its proprietors. But Aboriginal peoples and Māori were never consulted about such matters.

In 1839, therefore, the British Government accepted that Māori had the ability to cede title[97] to land, including unoccupied land. As a logical consequence, if it were found that Māori land had been obtained unfairly, then the title to the land falsely taken should revert to its original owners, not the crown. Both Busby and Hobson speaking at the hui at Waitangi in February 1840 made this very point.[98] But during 1840 the official view on land ownership started to be radically altered. The change seems to have coincided with the appointment of Lord John Russell as Secretary of State for War and the Colonies. The Letters Patent dated 16 November 1840 *inter alia* grant to the Governor of New Zealand full power and authority in the name of Her Majesty to "make and execute":

> "… Grants of waste land, to us belonging within the same, to private persons, for their own use and benefit, or to any persons, bodies politic or corporate, in trust for the public uses of our subjects their resident, or any of them.
>
> PROVIDED ALWAYS, that nothing in these our Letters Patent contained shall affect or be construed to affect the rights of any Aboriginal natives of the said Colony of New Zealand, to the actual occupation or enjoyment in their own persons, or in the persons of their descendants, of any Lands in the said Colony now actually occupied or enjoyed by such natives."[99]

Already, we can detect a change in the fundamental precepts about land which underlay British policy. The Letters Patent distinguish "Grants of waste land" to private persons from lands "actually occupied or enjoyed" by natives. It is implicit, therefore, that waste land is counted among the land which is neither occupied nor enjoyed as defined by Colonial Office officials. So, for example, if land has been acquired illegally or unjustly from Māori but remains unoccupied or not enjoyed it must be waste. Moreover, if it is waste, it must be part of the crown estate presumably on the grounds that such "waste" is held in trust by the crown for the benefit of all members of the British Empire. If that land is not of immediate use to the crown, it can be endowed with a crown grant and sold through auction. This directly contradicts Hobson's assurance to Māori at the Waitangi hui that land falling into such a category would revert to its original owners.

Furthermore, the Land Commissioners[100] who were to investigate land claims of land purchased before 14 January 1840 were only permitted to allot a maximum of 2,560[101] acres[102] to a given claim. This implies that any surplus above this acreage was never owned by Māori and now could not be owned by the settler involved. Since it was legally owned by no-one, legal logic concluded that legal ownership of it reverted to the crown.[103]

But the Government's ideas on land ownership continued to develop. In late 1841, the New Zealand Company concluded an agreement with Lord John Russell.[104] The agreement was in three parts:

1. The Crown will grant to the Company "under the public seal of the Colony" as many acres of New Zealand as shall be equal to four times the number of pounds sterling as have been spent in an approved manner. This land was not to exceed 160,000 acres and was to be "at or in the neighbourhood of" Port Nicholson or New Plymouth. This land was to be selected in continuous blocks the external boundaries of which were to be surveyed by the Government. Further claims by the Company would be disclaimed. Native reserves were to be safeguarded.
2. The Company would receive a charter of incorporation for 40 years allowing it to buy, sell, settle and cultivate land in New Zealand. It would also be able to advance funds to aid development of agricultural production but was expressly prohibited from "engaging in banking or any other commercial undertakings".
3. The Crown would sell 50,000 acres to the Company at a discounted price. The Government retained the option of requiring that the assistance of emigration to New Zealand should be supervised by the Commissioners of Colonial Lands and Emigration.

The Native title over the acreage gained by the Company was regarded as duly extinguished. Hence, it only remained for crown grants to be issued for it to be held in freehold title. By this means, the Company became virtually an agent of the crown in the settlement of New Zealand in the southern districts of the North Island and in Nelson.

By 1846, this view had developed even further so as to become an extreme version of the Lockean view. In that year, Earl Grey[105], by then Secretary of State for War and the Colonies, indicated to Governor Grey that, in his view[106]:

> "The Queen, as entitled in right of her Crown to any waste lands in the Colony, is free to make whatever rules Her Majesty may see fit on the subject. The accompanying Charter authorizes the Governor to alienate such lands."[107]

He fundamentally disagrees with the view that Māori held title to the entire land of New Zealand. He holds that such a view mistakes "… the ground on which the right of property in land is founded"[108]. In addition, he states that:

> "I must find it a vain and unfounded scruple which would have acknowledged their right of property in land which remain unsubdued to the uses of man. But if the savage inhabitants of New Zealand had themselves no right of property in land which they did not occupy, it is obvious that they could not convey to others what they did not themselves possess, and that claims to vast tracts of waste land, founded on pretended sales from them are altogether untenable."[109]

Earl Grey also removed "enjoyment" as a possible qualification for possession. Active subjection of the land occupation remained the sole criterion for land ownership.

Earl Grey's views directly contradict the promise made on behalf of Hobson at the hui held at Waitangi in February 1840. There, Busby, speaking on behalf of Hobson, stated that:

> "[He] … had often told them that land not duly acquired would not be confirmed to the purchaser, but would be returned to the Natives, to whom it of right belonged; that this the Governor would be prepared to do."[110]

In the event, returning land purchased in an irregular manner was rarely returned to the Māori that sold it. Instead, Commissioners were required to limit Māori sales to 2,540 acres (4 square miles) and to add any land remaining to the crown estate.

Earl Grey had every opportunity to understand the implications of his opinions because they were expressed very soon after the 1845 General Inclosure Act came before the British Parliament. That Act aimed to ease the process of enclosing what remained of the commons in England and Wales by establishing Enclosure Commissioners who were enabled to bring forward enclosure schemes without the need for the passage of individual private acts of Parliament.

Locke's Doctrine of Land Ownership

Debates on the General Inclosure Bill (which became law in 1845) extended over much of the early 1840s and involved discussion of the philosophical foundations of private ownership of land.[111] These principles were most fully[112] enunciated by John Locke and were widely shared and discussed within Parliament, many of the members of which owned land that was part of the estimated six million acres that had been enclosed by the English Parliament since 1750. Locke's doctrine on land ownership was the philosophical and moral justification for the existence of private property and was at odds with many Māori sensibilities.

In Locke's view, personal ownership of property was grounded in the Law of Nature. He stated:

> "Before the Appropriation of Land, he who gathered as much of the wild Fruit, killed, caught, or tamed, as many of the Beasts as he could; he that so employed his Pains about any of these spontaneous Products of Nature, as any way to alter

them, from the state which Nature put them in, *by* placing any of his *Labour* on them, did thereby *acquire a Propriety in them*; But if they perished in his Possession, without their due use; if the Fruits rotted, or the Venison putrefied, before he could spend it, he offended against the common Law of Nature, and was liable to be punished; he invaded his Neighbour's share, for he had *no Right, farther than his Use* called for any of them, and they might serve to afford him Conveniences of Life.

38. The same *measures* governed the *Possession of Land* too: Whatsoever he tilled and reaped, laid up and made use of, before it spoiled, that was his peculiar Right; whatsoever he enclosed and could feed, and make use of, the Cattle and Product was also his."[113]

Locke's doctrine provided the justification for the privatisation of common land for the benefit by private land owners. It also provided a reason to colonise the ranges of so-called primitive tribes, like Australian Aboriginal peoples and Māori, because it meant that those demesnes only extended to dwellings, burial grounds, cultivations and such reserves required for undertaking shifting agriculture. Acceptance of Lockean precepts, therefore, would lead to a narrowing of the interpretation of the guarantee contained in Article Two of the Treaty of Waitangi, even before it had been properly tried in practice.[114] From such reasoning it followed that any land remaining within a given ceded territory was crown land. Clearly, by 1846, the British Government expected Governor Grey to fully and faithfully carry out Lockean doctrine on land ownership.[115]

This expectation rested upon a philosophical understanding of a particular meaning of "labour". Locke was only concerned with individual ownership by persons already "civilised". Hence, in New Zealand, "labour" meant the improving (i.e., changing) the state of Nature by individual effort for individual benefit. Effort organised and performed communally, activities which safeguard future productivity by conservation or abstinence and skills passed orally, do not count as Lockean "labour". Thus, they do not provide evidence of a property right let alone a right to land ownership. Yet, these are some of the defining features of the economic organisation of Māoridom prior to, and in the first two decades of, colonisation.[116]

Crown Pre-emption

The 1837 edition of the Rules and Regulations presumes that the crown estate is already secured in each territory. It does not, therefore, discuss the means by which the crown acquires the lands of Aboriginal peoples. (However, it is possible to infer that it implies a crown monopoly over the purchase and initial sale to settlers of Aboriginal land.) Normanby stated in his instructions to Hobson: "… that henceforward no lands shall be Ceded either gratuitously or otherwise, except to the Crown of Great Britain"[117] Moreover, in the so-called Unsigned New Zealand Treaty emerges in Sydney in early 1840 that we read:

"And the said Native Chiefs do hereby on behalf of themselves and tribes engage, not to sell or otherwise alienate any lands occupied by or belonging to them, to any person whatsoever except to Her said Majesty upon such consideration as may be hereafter fixed and upon the express understanding that the said Chiefs and Tribes shall retain for their own exclusive use and benefit such part of their said lands as may be requisite for their comfortable maintenance and residence."[118]

This represents an explicit, draft agreement (which was never signed) by 10 Māori chiefs to sell land in New Zealand only to the crown. Its general effect would be an agreement by Māori to grant to the crown a monopsony (i.e., a sole monopoly over the ability to purchase) over Māori land.

While retaining a broad similarity with the Unsigned Treaty, the wording of the Treaty differs in three notable respects from that employed by Normanby and Gipps:

"Article the Second

Her Majesty the Queen of England confirms and guarantees to the Chiefs and Tribes of New Zealand and to the respective families and individuals thereof the full exclusive and undisturbed possession of their Lands and Estates Forests Fisheries and other properties which they may collectively and individually possess so long as it is their wish and desire to retain the same in their possession; but the Chiefs of the United Tribes and the individual Chiefs yield to Her Majesty the exclusive right of Preemption over such lands as the proprietors thereof may be disposed to alienate at such prices as may be agreed upon between the respective Proprietors and persons appointed by Her Majesty to treat with them in that behalf."

First, faithful to Normanby's instructions, the land transactions between Māori and the crown envisaged by both the Treaty and te Tiriti are not confined to the monopsony power of the crown. According to the Unsigned Treaty, however, the crown's monopsony can only be exercised if Māori "retain for their own exclusive use and benefit such lands as may be requisite for their own comfortable maintenance and residence". It follows that if this condition were to be violated any exercise of the crown's monopsony power would be morally and legally invalid. However, in neither the Treaty nor te Tiriti does such a safeguard exist. Rather, in both documents the initiation of the sale process is left entirely to the wishes revealed by Māori to the crown. Hence, on this basis, the Treaty and te Tiriti envisaged a somewhat more permanently open pre-primary market for Māori land than did the Unsigned Treaty.

Second, Hobson was instructed to negotiate a crown right to monopolise acquisition of Māori land by gift or purchase. The crown's monopsony is summarised in the Treaty as "the exclusive right of Preemption".[119] *The Oxford English Dictionary* defines 'pre-emption' as "purchase by one person or corporation before an opportunity is offered to others; also the right to make such purchase". This wording is capable of a variety of interpretations ranging from the mandatory exercise of monopoly purchasing, through a sole right to purchase which may or may not be exercised at the sole discretion of the crown,[120] to a right of first refusal constrained by time. On the face of it, the Treaty merely gives the crown an exclusive right to buy Māori land before it is more widely offered for sale. It does not appear to automatically confer a perpetual monopsony on the purchase of Māori land neither does it compel the crown to exercise that monopsonistic power whenever Māori wish to sell. By complete contrast, in te Tiriti there is no mention of such a right. Like the Treaty, but unlike Gipps's unsigned treaty, it is merely agreed to sell land to the Queen at a price to be agreed with her agent.[121]

Third, the Unsigned Treaty does not specify how a price for land in New Zealand is to be arrived at. It merely talks about "... such consideration which may be hereafter fixed ...".[122] This could mean that the New South Wales Governor or his agents would dictate the price to be paid. By contrast, both the Treaty and te Tiriti state that the price to be paid for land sold by Māori would be agreed by Māori sellers and the crown's buying agents. In both the Treaty and te Tiriti a negotiation over the price of land is envisaged whereas in the Unsigned Treaty the matter is left undecided if not implicit.

It would not be surprising, therefore, if many rangatira were confused about the nature and extent of the land purchasing powers that were assumed by the Colonial Government. Many, but not all, chiefs appear to have broadly understood the nature of crown monopsony. However, other chiefs believed that no more than a right of first refusal by the crown had been agreed in the Treaty. Yet others, appear to have believed only that land would be sold to the highest bidder; a belief that perpetuated well into the 1880s.[123]

With the elevation of Governor Grey pre-emption was invariably interpreted by the British Government and by the colonial administration as a crown monopsony over Māori land. This right was unequivocally upheld all the while the colonial administration could command sufficient resources to make land purchases on a scale desired by Māori and non-indigenous settlers alike. Before he departed from England to take up the position of Governor of New Zealand, FitzRoy asked Stanley, the Secretary of State for War and the Colonies, about the possibility of waiving pre-emption "in certain cases under defined restrictions".[124] Stanley's concerns were almost entirely financial and unrelated to the ethics of the crown exercising the power of monopsony.

In 1846 debate was ended when the meaning of the term "Pre-emption" was redefined by Governor Grey.[125] Grey made it illegal for " ... any person ... to purchase any estate in land from any person of the Native race ..." or to use or occupy "... any land not comprised within a grant from the Crown". Crown pre-emption meant the crown's claiming the sole right to acquire Māori land plus the sole right to issue titles to landed estates specified in crown grants.[126] In future, all legally valid transfers of land from Māori proprietors to another person had to pass through the hands of the crown. In effect this version of pre-emption was using a market mechanism to act as the substitute for the doctrine of *terra nullius* in New Zealand. It was, for example, no longer legally possible for Māori to lease out land of which they were proprietors. Finally, in Governor Grey's Proclamation XIX, "any person" included anyone either Māori or non-indigenous person. In so doing, it moved many informal uses of Māori land beyond legal protection of the crown.

The New Zealand Government exercised the crown's right of pre-emption between 1840 and 1862[127] and effectively from 1873 until after World War I. There, the Pre-primary Market took the form of payments to Māori by the crown or the New Zealand Company in its various guises. Although these transactions were officially called "sales", they are more accurately described as payments paid by the state monopsonist (i.e. the state acting as a monopoly buyer) to Māori for quieting, for the time being at least, claims to the occupation of land. Experience showed that much of the land involved in these transactions was inadequately defined, often the recompense paid was inadequate and not infrequently was wrongly and unfairly distributed.

Redress for hurts committed between non-indigenous people, Māori and Aboriginal peoples by their various representatives and agents has yet to become subject for serious discussion in Australasia. Instead, questions about how to address past wrongs have been exclusively framed in terms of compensation for harms that can be proved, beyond a reasonable doubt, to have occurred. The issues of what can and should be done to redress current and future residents for the harms caused by our ancestors have yet to be accurately posed, let alone addressed.

The success or otherwise of Wakefield's plans depended upon the extent to which a relatively open market for land could be transplanted into the society that eventually coalesced in New Zealand. Only such a market could nurture and sustain the following arguments which recur throughout the nineteenth century. First, economic assimilation of Māori, by participating in a land market, would ultimately mean the spread of (capitalist) civilisation and material well-being among "Natives". Second, existing settlers may crystalise profits from rising land values through the medium of market sales thereby encouraging new investment in land in the future.[128] Third, relatively open access to land meant that the colonial government could sustain the argument that ownership of land in New Zealand brought with it unrivalled opportunities for settler advancement. None of these reasons was thought to be consistent with land continuing in communal ownership.[129]

Yet all these events could not have taken place if it had not been possible to settle debts. When a landed estate is auctioned buyers incur a debt to sellers. If that debt is not settled according to the terms and conditions of sale, then the transaction is at least partially negated. Indeed, in auction sales organised by the crown, the buyer loses his deposit and the land is re-auctioned. This means that a market in landed estates lives alongside a method of settling debts. Pre-colonial land deals in New Zealand often involved payment by both trade goods and currency. But sales of crown grants to landed estates usually specified tender of currency (i.e., cash on the fall of the hammer) if purchases were to be concluded. The Primary Land Market in Australasia could not function without access to some form of money. But money did not exist in pre-colonial times. Colonisation of Australasia involved not just acquisition of landed estates but also the assembly of ways of paying for them.

Chapter Notes

1. Hughes, op cit, 2003, p.88. Large trees were felled, their roots dug up and cultivation all begun without the aid of draft animals or ploughs.
2. In addition, 306 ships' crew, 22 children of convicts, 54 wives and children of marines and 14 officers and passengers are also known to have landed. There is considerable disagreement about the muster roll carried by the First Fleet. Some have suggested that the muster of crew members is a gross under-estimate and that the true compliment of the first British settlement was closer to 1,700 than the 1,373 officially recorded.
3. Arthur Bowes Smyth: "Journal" http://firstfleet.uow.edu.au/s_women.html and https://commons.wikimedia.org/wiki/Category:Arthur_Bowes_Smyth. The account of general debauchery and riot may be open to doubt because it seems that Smyth remained aboard the *Lady Penrhyn*. Not that it is of any lasting historical significance, but some historians now believe that Hughes over-stated the levels of moral turpitude exhibited in the aftermath of disembarkation of the women convicts at Sydney Cove.
4. The Commissariat was transferred to the UK Treasury in 1813–1814 so that from that date the government of New South Wales was paid for as if it were a branch of the British Government.
5. The pay of officers and administrators were paid in London because that was where their employees were located (i.e. in Whitehall or at Horseguards). Pay could only be obtained from London by negotiating bills of exchange to be drawn in Sydney; an expensive and time-consuming process.
6. Blainey, op cit, 2014, p. 30.
7. The parallel with New Zealand is striking. The Colonial Office seems to have been exceptionally susceptible to nostrums involving self-sustainable finance. It continued to act as if profit from sales of land "purchased" cheaply from Māori and sold at higher prices to non-indigenous settlers would provide a reliable source of income for the New Zealand colonial government. The events from 1840 to 1845 show how misguided its policies were.
8. For an account of this period see Hughes, op cit, 2003, Chapter 4, pp 84–128.
9. It was during this failed attempt that HMS *Sirius* was wrecked off the coast of Norfolk Island in March 1790.
10. Hughes, op cit, 2003, pp. 104–105.
11. The Second Fleet comprised *Lady Julianna*, HMS *Guardian*, *Justiian*, *Surprize*, *Neptune* and *Scarborough*. It departed between 29 July 1789 and 19 January 1790 and arrived between 3 June 1790 and 28 June 1790. HMS *Guardian* sank off Cape of Good Hope.
12. The Third Fleet comprised *Mary Ann*, HMS *Gorgon*, *Matilda*, *Atlantic*, *Salamander*, *William and Ann*, *Active*, *Queen* (which departed from Cork), *Albermarle*, *Britannia* and *Admiral Barrington*. It departed between 16 February 1791 and 19 April 1791 and arrived between 9 July 1791 and 16 October 1791.
13. Philip suffered from kidney stones and was forced by ill-health to relinquish his post in July 1792 and returned to England. He left Major Grose, Commanding Officer of the New South Wales Corps, in charge of colonial administration as Acting Governor.
14. Unlike the situation in New Zealand, the colonial administration did not have to first obtain ownership of the land of Australia before it was dispensed to settlers. In January 1793 Acting Governor Grose was confronted by the first free settlers to arrive in New South Wales.
15. Hughes, op cit, 1987, p. 106.
16. This proposition assumed that the British crown owned the land of New South Wales. Ferris's assertion that this assumption was based on the assertion of *Terra nullius* by the authorities in London has already been questioned. Rather, the preceding argument suggests that it arose directly from the very wide powers to dispose of land by which Governor Phillip was anointed, which were granted but never justified by the crown.

17 Walter Brody, Frederick Meredith, Edward Powell and Thomas Webb also arrived with the Rose family on the *Bellona*.
18 Arthur McMartin: "Rose, Thomas (1754?-1833)" *Australian Directory of Biography*, National Centre of Biography. Australian National University. https://adb.anu.edu.au/biography/rose-thomas-2604/text3583. McMartin reports that Rose regarded his decision to take up his original grant was a major mistake.
19 This was a method widely used in vegetable gardens and allotments in rural England. Provided the sod was completely turned upside down so that any green matter was smothered it was highly effective in improving the fertility and, in time, the ease of working the soil.
20 This was just the beginning of John and Elizabeth Macarthur's holdings. Crowley, op cit, 1980, Vol 1, pp. 136–138. Despite Captain John Macarthur's self-promotion while in London to face court martial, his lengthy absences from New South Wales probably means that his wife was principally responsible for the very successful merino breeding programme undertaken on the Macarthur estates.
21 Hughes, op cit, 1987, p. 109.
22 Officials defined "waste land" as those parts of the Crown's demesne which was not required for public purposes.
23 In the British colonies in America this method of creating estates in land had been rife with favouritism and graft. Governors had become accustomed to using land grants as a way of influencing the political life of the colonies they ruled. Ripon's Rules and the 1837 edition of the rules and regulations issued by the Colonial Department specifically ruled out this method of distributing titles to landed estates.
24 Surveying a piece of colonial land in the 19th Century took place without the assistance of geodetic triangulation. It usually took the form of a chain and compass survey of a boundary path cut through any obstructing vegetation.
25 An exception was Governor Gipps who despatched his Colonial Secretary to the auction rooms of Hebblewhite and Vickers in Sydney on 6 January 1840 to put a stop to what was advertised as "The First Public Sale of Land in New Zealand" to take place in New South Wales. See Edward Sweetman: *The Unsigned New Zealand Treaty*, Melbourne, The Arrow Printery, 1939, pp. 55–56.
26 It might be argued that in the so-called Wakefield Colonies of South Australia and New Zealand there were attempts by the New Zealand Company to ensure that sales of landed estates on the secondary land markets took place at escalating prices. For example, the New Zealand Company tried to encourage speculation in New Zealand landed estates by organising lotteries for land orders in London. Crowley, op cit, 1980, Vol 2, p. 62 also refers to 80 acre land orders in South Australia. But, detailed evidence of such practices is difficult to find. In part, because they were highly circumscribed by the parlous state of New Zealand Company finances after 1843.
27 A cadastre is a public register which documents the ownership and location of a piece of land.
28 This property explains the importance of surveyors and surveying in colonial life during the long nineteenth century.
29 Elizabeth Macarthur (1766–1850) was the daughter of a Devonshire farmer. She married John Macarthur in 1788 with whom she gave birth to eight children. She was separated from her husband for many years while he was in England courting influence in his vendetta against a succession of Governors. In 1817, by the time he returned, Mrs Macarthur had increased the Macarthur estate to 60,000 acres. They became further estranged as he slid into mental illness which led to his being declared a lunatic and deprived of his seat on the Legislative Council in 1832. Elizabeth managed the extensive Macarthur estates upon which she dramatically improved the breed of Australian merinos by judicious and repeated cross breeding with Spanish rams so that the fineness of their wool became unparalleled and wool yields rose. She did this by means of the meticulous accuracy of her record keeping until her death. She is insufficiently recognised as an astute observer of public affairs and as a leading pioneer of the Australian wool growing industry.

30   Blainey, op cit, 2013, p.39. It is likely that these flocks were bred by his wife, Elizabeth, during Macarther's absence overseas.
31   Lieutenant-Colonel Lachlan Macquarie (1762–1824) was Captain-General and Governor-in-Chief of New South Wales between 1810 and 1821. He developed policies initiated by Governor King to open New South Wales to free settlers and emancipists. He was responsible for significant public works such as Sydney Hospital and the road across the Blue Mountains to Bathurst. He had experienced the ills which lack of an organised monetary system bestowed on society while serving in India and Sri Lanka. He became convinced of the virtue of a domestically-based bank and eventually succeeded in fostering the Bank of New South Wales in 1817. His bitter denunciation of "petty banking" or the issue of personal promissory notes may have been coloured by his support for a local bank.
32   Military officers, senior administrators and free settlers without the "stain" of being transported convicts. They formed the Exclusives who were the self-styled colonial gentry who concentrated on accumulating large estates and flocks. They formed an exclusive group of families which spurned contact with the rest of the population.
33   Emancipists were former convicts which had served their sentence and had had their rights as British subjects restored to them or were accorded absolute or conditional pardons. The last were often termed Ticket of Leave Men. They included very able men such as Simeon Lord who became a leading figure in the commercial life of Sydney.
34   Currently branded Westpac.
35   These amounts include endowments made by the crown for glebe to benefit individual parishes, for the support of female orphans, for the benefit of schoolmasters at Parramatta, Richmond, Wilberforce, Castlereagh and Pitt Town and for commons at Richmond and Windsor.
36   Bigge was very critical of Macquarie and so he may have exaggerated these deficiencies. Bigge's Reports on his Commission of Inquiry was published by the British Parliament in three reports: "First Report: Report of the Commissioner of Inquiry into the state of the colony of New South Wales", 19 June 1822; "Second Report: The Judicial Establishments of NSW and Van Diemen's Land", 21 February 1823; "Third Report: Report of the Commissioner of Inquiry on the state of agriculture and trade in the colony of New South Wales", 13 March 1823.
37   John Thomas Bigge: "Report of the Commissioner of Inquiry on the State of Agriculture and Trade in the Colony of New South Wales" accessed at unw.gutenberg.net.au/ebooks13/1300241h.html#ch-02. See especially section entitled "Regulations respecting Grants of Land and Allotments in Towns". This was the third of three reports that Bigge submitted to Bathurst.
38   From 1817, prospective settlers were allowed to make applications on first arrival which reduced the costs of separate travel to Sydney to make application and to wait upon the administrative process.
39   Australian Bureau of Statistics: *Historical Population Statistics*, Canberra, Commonwealth of Australia, 2019 Table 1.1. These estimates are of persons actually resident in the country but do not include indigenous peoples before 1961 and residents of the Jervis Bay Territory before 1915 and after 1993.
40   For some information see Wendy Thorp: *Inner West Council suburb history*, Leichhardt Municipality Heritage Study, Inner West Council, 1990.
41   Lennie Lower: *Here's Luck*, Sydney, Eden Paperbacks, 1989. Whether or not self-help associations like friendly societies were also a source of housing finance in some cases is a matter that requires further investigation.
42   Many such reports appear to be the result of complaints by under-bidders in the public auctions for land. For example, see S.M.D Martin: "New Zealand: In a Series of Letters", London, nd. Facisim Edition, Kiwi Publishers, Christchurch, pp 125-128.
43   FJ Robinson (1782–1869) was an able and pragmatic tory who gave long service as MP and Cabinet Minister (including Prime Minister). He became 1st Viscount in 1827 and the Earl

of Ripon in 1832. He was twice Secretary of States for War and the Colonies. He was deeply affected by his wife's mental illness and is rumoured to have burst into tears during an interview with King George IV who offered him a handkerchief.

44   These became known in Australia as Goderich's Regulations or Ripon's Rules. They were repeated word-for-word in the 1837 Rules and Regulations. See Colonial Department, op cit, 1837.

45   Advertisements for the first sales of Auckland town lots sold on 9 April 1841 stated that the sales were to be held under "Government Regulations dated 1 August 1831". The reason for this minor curiosity is that, at the time of the sale, New South Wales legislation still applied to New Zealand. The Ordinance by which New Zealand adopted New South Wales legislation was not promulgated until 3 June 1841.

46   Lloyd-Pritchard, op cit, 1968, p. 180.

47   Ibid, p. 180.

48   His decision was conveyed to Lieutenant-Governor Darling of New South Wales in a despatch dated 9 January 1831. In that despatch he announced his intention of drafting regulations for the conduct of land sales. These regulations followed on 20 January 1831. Accessed from www.enzb.auckland.ac.nz/document/?wid=8731&page=0&pageaction=null.

49   During this period there was much discussion in British official circles about how to make the administration of Government more efficient and effective. It is possible that this change of policy was one of the results of these deliberations. See for example Graham Bowrey, Freda Hui and Ciarstan Smark: "An 1831 discussion on New Public Management", *Accounting History*, Vol 22, No 3, February 2017, pp 370–386.

50   *The Sydney Gazette and New South Wales Advertiser,* Tuesday, 2 August 1831, accessed from https://trove.nla.gov.au/newspaper/article/2201850/499158.

51   This reservation appears to date from the times of Elizabeth I. For example, in 1568, all deposits of gold and silver were nationalised by the English Crown.

52   When the Rules and Regulations were first drafted New Zealand was not yet a British possession. In 1840, however, it became part of New South Wales, hence, the following applied from the outset of Crown Colony Government.

53   Rules and Regulations, op cit, 1837, p. 62. On 15 September 1842, Lord Stanley, Secretary of State for War and the Colonies, wrote to Governor Gipps that the British Government had maintained the principle that "… the Waste Lands of the Crown shall never be alienated except by Sale." See Crowley, op cit, 1980, Vol 1., p 33–34 on colonial opposition to this.

54   Rules and Regulations, op cit, 1837, p. 55–59. The level of remission depended on officers' length of service and their seniority. Governors were permitted to allocate land to qualifying military and naval officers (which included those retired after serving the British East India Company) outside the normal schedule of land auctions, thus contravening the requirement for public sale of lands. It was also made possible for officers to be granted land "to the amount of the remission to which they are entitled". All officers seeking remission had to wait two years before they could receive a Crown Grant.

55   It is extremely difficult to make an accurate assessment of the truth of this statement. The potential losses can, in theory, be calculated by the difference between total welfare of the colonial population plus the welfare resulting from revenues of land sales and the welfare that could result from making grants of land freely available. In practice, this would involve making estimates of the welfare that could be generated in circumstances different from those which actually obtained, a task which is surrounded with much uncertainty.

56   Colonial Office: "Rules and Regulations for Her Majesty's Colonial Service", London, Clowes and Sone, 1843, Chapter XIII, Sale of Waste Lands in the Colonies, Sec II, The Australian Colonies and the Falklands, pp 116–119.

57   "Upset price" means the lowest price the Government would accept for the land at auction.

58   "Ready money" means cash or its close equivalent. This effectively means that colonial governments could not provide such as deferred payments to purchasers of Crown land.

59 Colonial Office, op cit, 1843, Section 9. Deposits were payable in £100 units to the credit of the Agent-general of the Crown Colonies. The Agent-general would issue a certificate which could be exchanged for a certificate issued by the Colonial Land and Emigration Commissioners that will entitle the holder to obtain credit for that sum in any purchase.

60 Ibid. Section 10 makes assisted passages available on the following conditions: For every £100 deposited 4 adults may be nominated for a free passage (2 children between one and fourteen = 1 adult); Each assisted emigrant must be approved by the Colonial Land and Emigration Commissioners and must accord with their rules about the selection of labourers; Purchasers of land and their families could not qualify for free passage.

61 Lloyd Pritchard, op cit, 1968, p. 165. This implies that the Colonial Office did not oppose "Manifest Destiny" of British colonisation.

62 Squatters also exercised proprietorship over large areas of the South Island provinces in New Zealand.

63 Attwood, op cit, 2008, p. 4.

64 Ibid, p. 3.

65 Blainey, op cit, 2013, pp. 73–74.

66 Circumadjacent is a term employed in leases to indicate the area of land immediately adjacent to, and surrounding, a given location.

67 Depasturing means feeding animals on the pasture growing upon an area of land.

68 See Henry Reynolds and Jamie Dalziel: "Aborigines and Pastoral Leases—Imperial and Colonial Policy 1826–1855", *University of New South Wales Law Journal,* Vol 19(2), 1996, pp 317–317 and 327–328.

69 From a letter from Gipps to Lord Stanley dated 18 April 1843. See Samuel Clyde McCulloch: "Gipps, Sir George (1791–1847)", *Australian Dictionary of Biography*, Australian National University, https://adb.anu.edu.au/gipps-sir-george-2098/text2645.

70 It was reputed that measures adopted to quieten Aboriginal peoples included poisoned food and branding as well as shooting. See Crowley, op cit, 1980, Vol 2, pp. 79–81.

71 See Crowley, op cit, 1980, Vol 2, pp. 45–46, pp. 51–53 and pp. 63–64.

72 Despatch from Sir George Gipps to Lord Stanley (Non. 107), dated 17 May 1844 printed in *NSW Government Gazette,* Saturday 28 June 1845, pp. 671–672.

73 Ibid, p. 678.

74 Ibid, p. 679.

75 See Crowley, op cit, 1980, pp. 354–357.

76 Ibid p. 355 provides a full list of the conditions proposed by the Convention.

77 The architect of the legislation was the Prime Minister of New South Wales Sir James Robertson (1816–1891). Robertson entered the New South Wales Parliament in 1858 and was Prime Minister of New South Wales on five occasions before he resigned through ill-health in February 1886. He was a firm advocate of land reform to enable poorer people to settle on the land. His proposals were bitterly opposed by the Pastoral Association and the Robertson Acts only passed the New South Wales Legislative Council because 21 new seats were created to swamp the squatter vote.

78 Here is yet another definition of "waste lands". This definition widens the earlier notions of "waste lands" because it includes land that the Governor intends to grant in fee simple at some future (but unspecified) time.

79 New South Wales: Crown Lands Alienation Act, Crown Lands Occupation Act, 1861 (Robertson Acts); Tasmania: Waste Lands Act, 1858; Victoria: Land Act, 1860 (Duffy's Act); Queensland: four Lands Acts, 1860; South Australia: Crown Lands Act, 1872. For more details see "Land Tenure and Settlement", pp. 263–354 in *Year Book Australia* No 2 1909, Canberra, Australian Bureau of Statistics, 1909.

80 McIntyre and Gardner, op cit, 1979, p. 12.

81 See Sweetman, op.cit, 1939.

82 On 14 January 1840, before Hobson departed for New Zealand, Gipps issued a proclamation making purchases of land in New Zealand null and void.
83 McIntyre and Gardner, op cit, 1979, p. 11.
84 It appears that at no stage in their deliberations prior to 1839 did Colonial Office officials consider the possibility of a British expedition to New Zealand to secure military conquest of the whole country.
85 See McIntyre and Gardner, op cit, 1979, p. 54.
86 It should be noted that this did not bring a system of individual ownership into existence. That monumental change had to await the Native Lands Act of 1862 which is discussed at some length below.
87 The following wording is taken from the English version of the Treaty of Waitangi. In the Māori version called Tiriti o Waitangi, which most Māori signed in 1840, the idea of Crown pre-emption is not mentioned and Tiriti merely states "… the Chiefs all will give to the Queen the sale and purchase of those parts…" of land they are willing to sell. See IH Kawharu (editor): *Waitangi: Maori and Pakeha Perspectives of the Treaty of Waitangi*, Auckland, Oxford University Press, 1989, Appendix, p. 320.
88 Orange, op cit, 1987, p. 258.
89 The meaning of "pre-emption" was disputed for many years. In part this was because the version of the Treaty of Waitangi that was signed by most Māori and called Tititi o Waitangi does not mention the idea of pre-emption. Instead, for many decades many senior Māori thought that the colonial government had obtained only the first right of refusal over any land that might be offered for sale.
90 Presumably, the commercial activities of the New Zealand Company and its fore-runners were the "circumstances" which forced the Colonial Office to make the policy decision that colonisation of New Zealand was inevitable.
91 McIntyre and Gardner. op cit, 1979, p. 11.
92 To be more precise, "soil" in 1839 also included subterranean levels, the airspace above and to varying degrees, the adjoining seabed and water courses. At various subsequent dates, the Crown reserved to itself ownership of "mines of precious metals' and naturally occurring gold, silver, uranium and petroleum (1840, 1948, 1847, 1945 and 1937 respectively). The Crown is also the predominant owner of the seabed out to the 12-mile territorial limit. The airspace above the land is not apparently owned by anyone although its use is heavily regulated by the crown, thus making difficult its profitable exploitation. Specific exceptions to this general position include Lake Waikaremoana and the Whanganui River.
93 On 21 May 1840, "discovery" by Cook was the reason given by Hobson for asserting British sovereignty over the South Island of New Zealand. It was also the justification for the issue of Letters Patent on 16 November 1840 entitled "Charter for erecting the Colony of New Zealand and for creating and establishing a Legislative Council and an Executive Council". See McIntyre and Gardner, op cit, 1979, pp 54–57.
94 Attwood, op cit, 2020, p. 170.
95 It might also be argued that the Colonial Office sought to establish the authority of the Crown by seeking the widespread adoption of the English Common Law a latter-day variant of the idea of the King's Peace. The resources devoted to the construction of a legal system appear to have lagged behind Hobson's attempts to buy land so, it seems that it was believed that the spread of Common Law would follow acceptance of market relationships. In the two-horse race to bring civilisation, therefore, the land market (albeit considerably hobbled) came first and Common Law was a distant second.
96 The instruction to employ fair and equal contracts in the transfer of waste land from Māori to the crown is contradicted by the crown's assertion of a monopoly right of land purchase from Māori (i.e., the right of preemption). If only the crown can buy land then sellers of land are placed at a disadvantage because they cannot take advantage of competition between alternative buyers to drive up the sale price.

97　Attwood, op cit, 2020, p.6 states "… that sovereignty and rights of property in land were made or not made—*historically,* in that they came into being only as the result of deeply historical processes…." If Attwood is correct, then "ceding title" could perhaps be construed as any historical process which involved some measure of agreement between at least two parties and which resulted in the extinguishment of "Native Title". If so, the discussion of this matter over the years has been unnecessarily confused by legal arguments which were not considered to be of practical importance in the early 19th century except in the United States as a result of Marshall CJ's judgements on the matter of native title.

98　W. Colenso: "The Authentic and Genuine History of the Signing of the Treaty of Waitangi', Facsimile Edition, Christchurch, Kiwi Publishers, 1890/1996, p. 17 and p. 19. Hobson was reported at p. 19 as saying "… that all lands unjustly held would be returned; and that all claims to lands, however purchased, after the date of the Proclamation would not be held to be lawful." The very fact that he made such a statement reinforces the belief that the precepts underlying Normanby's instructions set out above were valid at this time. This despite any conversations to the contrary Hobson may have had with Gipps in Sydney during late 1839 and early 1840.

99　McIntyre and Gardner eds, op cit, 1979, pp 56–57.

100　Two commissioners, EL Godfrey and M Richmond, were originally appointed by Governor Gipps of New South Wales on 7 July 1840 but their report on certain Northern claims was not confirmed by Hobson until August 1842 shortly before he died.

101　The maximum extent of each claim was apparently arrived at without benefit of consultation with Māori or existing non-indigenous land owners.

102　This limitation was part of an 1831 New South Wales Ordinance. (2,560 acres equal 4 square miles.) It was repealed in February 1842 and replaced by a scale of 4 acres for every £1 expended which was derived from the compensation paid to the New Zealand Company as part of the agreement concluded with Lord John Russell in 1840.

103　E Wilson Wilson: *Land Problems of the New Zealand Settlers of the 'Forties' Thesis presented for Honours in History in Degree of Master of Arts, 1933*, Dunedin, AH and AW Reed, nd, p 75. Claims were reduced to the maximum permitted without allowing settlers to choose which part of the holding they would relinquish.

104　Alexander Mackay: "A Compendium of Official Documents Relative to Native Affairs in the South Island, Volume One", Enclosure in No 28—Agreement. Accessed at nzetc.victoria.ac.nz/tm/scholarly/tei-Mac01Comp-t1-g1-t5-g1-t2-g1-t28-g1-t2.html#name-131542-mention.

105　Adams, op cit, 1987, p. 188 describes Earl Grey as "… the most ideologically committed of all the heads of the Colonial Office to a narrow interpretation of the land guarantee…."

106　This is contained in a despatch which contained the 1846 Constitution Act, a new Charter and instruction for the gradual implementation of representative government dated 23 December 1846.

107　McIntyre and Gardner eds, op cit, 1979, p. 59.

108　Ibid, p. 60.

109　Ibid, p. 60.

110　Colenso, op cit, 1890/1996, p. 17

111　For example, Lord Palmerston in supporting the Inclosure Bill on 4th July 1845 in the House of Commons argued that "… the common land of the country does not belong to the community at large, but to a certain number of individuals resident in the neighbourhood." See https://api.parliament.uk/historic-hansard/commons/1845/jul/04/commonsenclosure-bill#S3V0082PO_18450704_HOC_26. Palmerston recognised that he could not agree that the commons were owned by the crown in trust for everyone for to do so would mean that it was possible to agree to communal ownership in general, contrary to Lockean ideas.

112　Locke may not be the originator of this doctrine. John Winthrop, the Reverend John White and the Reverend Francis Higginson appear to have assembled "Reasons for Plantation of New England" in about 1628 which was found in John Winthrop's papers after his death.

They argued: "That which lies common, and has never been replenished or subdued, is free to any that possess and improve it, for God hath given to the sons of men a double right to the earth—there is a natural right and a civil right. The first right was natural when men held the earth in common, every man sowing and feeding where he pleased. Then as men and their cattle increased, they appropriated certain parcels of ground by enclosing and peculiar cultivation, and this in time got them a civil right." Locke's parents were both puritans and it seems possible that Locke, who was born in 1634, was exposed to such arguments at home in his youth. See winthropsociety.com/doc_reasons.php edited by Marcia Elaine Stewart.

113   Locke, op cit, 2005, pp 294–295, emphases in original.
114   Adams, op cit, 1977, p. 188.
115   Such were the philosophical roots of the enduring non-indigenous myth of the rugged pioneer hacking a civilised nation from recalcitrant and trackless bush and the founding precepts of neo-liberal political economy. Such deep-seated conjunctions of belief may explain why the privatisation of New Zealand society has been so readily accepted and so little critically interrogated since 1984.
116   It is also remarkable that such a view of property almost completely ignored the possibility of corporate ownership and the collective (i.e social, economic and political) power that it might entail. This issue was not raised in New Zealand until the 1870s when John Ballance rose to political prominence and the works of Henry George on the taxation of land became widely read. The obvious contradiction between ownership by an individual and ownership by a collectivity like a company was eventually resolved by the legal artifice of granting the attributes of a "natural person" to companies.
117   McIntyre and Gardner, op cit, 1979, p. 13.
118   Sweetman, op cit, 1939, p. 64.
119   It is a matter of some interest to enquire about the source of this usage in the Treaty. Adams, op cit, 1977, pp. 139–140 suggests that pre-emption in the sense of a crown monopsony over Māori land was discussed by Labouchere on 12 or 13 March 1839 and argues that it had been integral to the Colonial Office's policy towards New Zealand for some time before that. Orange, op cit, 1987, p. 37 suggests the wording appears in notes provided to Hobson by James Freeman.
120   This is the sense employed by Adams, ibid and Orange, ibid.
121   The relevant wording in te Tiriti is as follows:
"The Queen agrees to protect the chiefs, the subtribes and all the people of New Zealand in the unqualified exercise of their chieftainship over their lands, villages and all their treasures. But on the other hand the Chiefs of the Confederation and the other Chiefs will sell land to the Queen at a price agreed to by the person owing it and by the person buying it (the latter being) appointed by the Queen as her purchasing agent."
122   Sweetman, op cit, 1939, p. 64.
123   On 28 August 1885, John Ballance recalled, during the course of debate on Want of Confidence, that he asked a Māori rangatira, Wahanui, appearing before the Native Affairs Committee of Parliament: "Will you explain what you understand by the pre-emptive right?" Wahanui replied: "I understand it is this: I shall sell my land to the highest bidder—to the man who shall give me the most money." John Ballance MHR, Parliamentary Debates 1885, Volume 53, p.354.
124   See Rose Daamen: "The Crown's Right of Pre-emption and Fitzroy's Waiver Purchases", Rangahaua Whanui Theme D, Wellington, Waitangi Tribunal, August 1998, p. 57.
125   Proclamation No XIX, 16 November 1846.
126   Crown grants were normally couched in terms of fee simple which meant that their owners did not owe payments in service to the crown. Such grants could be readily re-sold or leased on the secondary land market.
127   Between 7 February 1840 and 5 August 1914, the crown asserted the legal right of pre-emption over purchases of Māori land between the following dates: 7 February 1840 until 26 March 1844 when waived; waivers nullified 15 June 1846; pre-emption redefined 16 November 1846

and abandoned on 15 September 1862. Between 15 September 1862 and 5 August 1914 the Government often borrowed heavily to obtain title to Māori land so making it very difficult for private buyers to compete. In this it was aided by compulsory purchase powers introduced in the Native Land Purchase and Acquisition Act 1893.

128   Butler, op cit, 1964 and Turnbull, op cit, 1959.
129   Maurice Ormsby has pointed out that, on the contrary, they always have been consistent with leasehold title.

CHAPTER 3

MONETISATION OF AUSTRALASIA

British colonisation was based on the exploitation of land for monetary gain. Uses of colonial land expanded alongside the scale and scope of monetary transactions. This Chapter sets out the starting point for the evolution of colonial money in Australasia. In New South Wales and New Zealand, the monetary systems were based on English-style banking practices. Ordinary banking involved the creation and negotiation of short-term bills, the issue of notes and the taking of deposits. During much of the nineteenth century British monetary authorities believed that banking profits depended largely on the private issue of bank notes and that this activity could be controlled by manipulating bank gold reserves. For this reason, the system became widely known as the Gold Standard System. But frequent crises during the Long 19th Century showed that the operation of this system was neither smooth nor automatic.

Foundations
The history of the use of currency in each society is not just a matter of a succession of money commodities, such as coins and banknotes. Of more lasting importance are the social institutions by which money commodities operate and change and through which they become widely accepted by a wide variety of people. For example, Easton speculates that:

> "Pre-contact Māori had already been involved in barter-like transactions, which prepared them for those with the anonymous European. Even when money became involved, it was a 'fully backed' currency, in which the currency equalled (roughly) its market value in metals. In contrast with today's transactions with notes or cheques, the exchange involved two items of similar 'intrinsic' value."[1]

Easton seems to argue that use of a specific currency in, for example, pre-colonial New Zealand land transactions was really a kind of barter in which the coins were valued according to their content of precious metals such as silver or gold. (In other cultures, units of currency may be exchanged according to their use values for example as fishing weights or ornaments.) Presumably Easton adopts this argument because no evidence of sustained monetary institutions in pre-colonial New Zealand has so far been discovered.

There also appears to be no evidence that Māori (or Aboriginal Peoples) did value pre-colonial coinage according to the market value of the metals it contained.

Money commodities, or objects widely accepted as media of exchange such as cattle, shells, coins and bank notes, should be distinguished from the social structures which ensure that money commodities functions as potential users expect. These structures may take several forms and can be commercial, communal or personal or some combination of the three. Their precise configuration depends largely upon the risks and opportunities encountered when buying and selling, lending, and borrowing or saving and investing. From very early times[2] these social structures have brought peoples together from across the globe.[3] For all these reasons, money is always "on the wing". Hence, when attempting to elucidate how money worked in different social contexts it is a mistake to concentrate on the money commodities found to have been used in a single society at a particular time and to apply any findings to another time or to other economic or social circumstances.

Similar conjectures to those made by Easton about Māori do not appear to have been made about Australian Aboriginal peoples. Before non-indigenous people planted themselves in New Holland and New Zealand there is no evidence[4] of the use of currency (however fully backed by "precious" metals) and no indication that personalities or social structures played a part in forming monetary institutions. In the absence of this type of evidence the mere existence of trade in the form of barter of one good or obligation for another cannot be accepted as evidence for the use of currency or money in pre-colonial times.

Instead, I assume that, before British colonisation, indigenous cultures in New South Wales or New Zealand introduced neither monetary commodities nor monetary institutions. Money commodities and the institutions that made them work which emerged after colonisation began were physically imported, ready-made, from beyond the seas by British colonisers, British missionaries and the beachcomber society which peopled the colonies alongside their indigenous neighbours. Even after plantation of non-indigenous people begun in earnest the British Government made no attempt to provide a monetary system for the colonies of Australasia. In the case of New South Wales this is perhaps understandable. S J Butlin remarks:

> "The colony was to be a special kind of prison and prisons do not require a monetary system."[5]

But 52 years later, New Zealand, which was hardly touched by the taint of transportation and convict settlers and the colonisation of which was supposed to be financed predominantly from sales of land, was neglected in precisely the same way by the Colonial Office. The main reason why the Colonial Office compounded this error of omission is presumably that it believed that the institutions which make for a reliable monetary system would spontaneously emerge as trade developed.[6]

This official neglect means that the foundations of Australasian monetary institutions was probably based on a wide variety of expectations developed and experiences undertaken overseas. This might account for the lack of a coherent foundation for Australasian monetary institutions and the variety of monetary operations might be interpreted as a grounding for institutional competition. But, as we shall find, Australasian monetary institutions centred on cartelised banking. Neither Australia nor New Zealand provided welcoming homes for many of the institutional innovations which took shape in London during the long19th century.[7]

Commissariat

In one respect New South Wales stood alone. The British Government determined that plantation of non-indigenous people in New South Wales would follow the example of British colonisation of the North American colonies and the Caribbean islands by using workers that were employed under compulsion. But, in the case of Australia, the workforce was composed of one-third of Great Britain's incarcerated population that was transported to that destination between 1788 and 1868, together with their spouses and offspring. These people were indentured for periods of 7 or 14 years after which they could apply for a Ticket of Leave which would permit them to leave the penal colony. In humanity, therefore, the Colonial Office was duty-bound to make arrangements for the material succour of the prisoners and their keepers not to mention those administering them. It discharged these obligations through a branch of the British Army called the Commissariat. The structure and management of the Commissariat during the 18th century was opaque and seems to be often peculiar to individual regiments.[8] At the time New South Wales was planted, the Commissary or Commissariat was a name given to a set of relatively haphazard processes which brought food, drink, fodder, tools and implements, clothing and footwear and distributed them to prescribed recipients. In 1788 and for some time after, all victuals and other necessities had to be imported into, and distributed within, Australia by the Commissariat. To this end, a Commissariat store was established in Sydney to dispense supplies to colonial officers, the military and their prisoners. The Commissariat was also, initially, the paymaster for rank-and-file marines.[9] Salaries of senior military personnel and government officers were payable in London and had to be drawn upon by bill of exchange.[10] Butlin also remarks that Governor Phillip met even small, unforeseen expenditures by means of bills drawn on the Treasury in London.[11] The Commissariat also oversaw the allocation of convicts to Government farms, and later to free settlers, and the leasing of Government-owned live stock. From 1798, the small number free settlers among the general public (by 1800 only 23 free settlers had arrived in New South Wales) were permitted to make purchases at the Commissariat Store. Agriculture in New South Wales developed from a foundation of government farms manned by convict labour and stocked with government-owned horses, sheep and cattle. Starting 1793 under Acting Governor Grose, successive Governors made crown grants of land to commissioned officers, emancipists and free settlers which were fully supported by convict labour and permission to lease Government-owned livestock.

Along with visiting vessels, the Commissariat Store provided a market for the produce of the newly developed land. It accepted produce such as grain and cattle and paid for it by Store Receipts. Butlin states:

> "It is not clear how early this system developed. Not until the colony was producing some of its own supplies could it have commenced—1790 or 1791 at the earliest. By 1795, however, it was fully established …"[12]

These receipts were periodically purchased (i.e., withdrawn from domestic circulation) by the Commissariat which exchanged them for bills drawn on the Treasury in London. Butlin[13] records the observations of Elizabeth Macarthur about how the Commissariat system worked. On 1 September 1795, she wrote to Miss Kingdon as follows:

> "In payment for [in the case under discussion, grain] the Commissary issues a receipt, approved of by the Government, and those receipts pass current here as coin and are taken by masters of ships and adventurers who come to these parts with merchandise for sale. When any number of these have been accumulated in the hands of individuals they are returned to the Commissary, who gives a bill on the Treasury in England for them.… Pigs are bought upon the same system, as would also sheep and cattle if their numbers would admit of their being killed."

Commissariat Store Receipts were, therefore, a source of UK and international currency, which was not restricted in its convertibility into gold by the 1797 Bank Restriction Act.[14] Treasury Bills were particularly highly valued by army officers who wished to use bills of exchange on the Treasury to engage in trade with visiting ships' captains.[15] Because Store Receipts were readily convertible into Treasury Bills they came to be regarded as effectively guaranteed by the British Government and circulated in New South Wales as a kind of note issue, until the early 1820s.

It is clear that even though the British Government neglected to provide New South Wales with any monetary arrangements let alone a monetary system, the Commissariat Store provided access to internationally acceptable currency from the early days of food and fodder production in the colony. Through its offices it was possible for pastoralists like Lieutenant and Mrs Macarthur to acquire internationally negotiable currency by selling their produce to the Commissariat Store.[16] The links between the colonial monetary system and the London Money and Capital Markets probably date, therefore, from the inception of planting of non-indigenous people at Sydney Cove.

But the system of drawing bills on the Treasury in London was inefficient for other kinds of payment such as bills for casual workers or unforeseen repairs. It meant that workers for the colonial government of New South Wales, paid by means of a Treasury Bill signed by the Governor did not receive the remuneration that had been agreed in Sydney. While the workers could be sure of ultimately receiving pounds, shillings, and pence for their labours, negotiating bills through an agent in London was costly and took many months. This could only have placed considerable strain on the workers' finances. Governor Phillip asked that he be supplied with dollars to meet these everyday expenses and in February 1792 3,870 ounces of Spanish silver dollars were shipped to Sydney.[17] They do not appear to have stayed within New South Wales any longer than the 7,500 silver dollars purchased by Governor King for similar purposes in 1803. The drain of widely acceptable international coinage was a direct consequence of the virtual absence of earnings from exports and the continued dependence of the penal colony on imports for daily needs.

Form its inception in 1788 until probably the 1820s the colony of New South Wales was beholden to the UK Treasury as payment for employment in Sydney. So long as the Treasury maintained the link between Store Receipts and Treasury Bills, the economy of New South Wales was not impeded. But if ever a more austere budgetary regime were to hold sway in London, then it is probable that limitations would have been placed on the ability of colonists to acquire Treasury bills through the Commissariat in Sydney. In any case, any increase in the Treasury Bill rate in London would increase the cost of receiving Treasury Bills as payment for employment in Sydney. Most important is the fact that, even after the Bank of New South Wales started business in 1817, the growth of colonial liquidity and lending was not the result of decisions made in Sydney but of those made by Treasury officials in London.[18]

One result was that supplies of domestic currency were not consistent with the state of the colonial economy. Initially, at least, the colony of New South Wales relied totally upon imports of food and other comestibles, clothing and tools. In the absence of export revenues, imports could only be purchased either by means of bills of exchange drawn on the British Treasury or by currency imported either by free settlers, marines or members of the New South Wales Corps (who guarded the prisoners) or by vessels seeking re-fitting. These last three sources were probably of minor importance in the early years of the colony. So, whenever imports occurred, currency was sent overseas to pay for them. This meant that there was less currency available for circulation within New South Wales with the result that domestic trade was restricted. A very similar sequence of events was reported in the early years of the settlement of New Zealand.[19]

By 1799 Governor King was convinced that coinage was of considerable importance as a means of exchange and he arranged for £1,200 of copper coins, to be shipped to Sydney.[20] He also set out detailed schedules of the sterling equivalent of a wide variety of non-British coins. Governor King issued a General Order on 19 November 1800 which listed the local value in Sydney of a variety of foreign coins in terms of pounds, shillings and pence as follows:[21]

	£	s	d
A guinea	1	2	0
A half-Johanna	2	0	0
A gold mohur	1	17	6
A Spanish dollar		5	0
A Johanna	4	0	0
A ducat		9	6
A pagoda		8	0

	£	s	d
A rupee		2	6
A Dutch guilder		2	0
An English shilling		1	8
A copper coin of 1 oz			2
A copper coin of 1/2oz			1
A copper coin of ¼oz			½

It seems safe to conclude that Governor King was well aware that a very wide variety of coins was circulating in New South Wales in the early years of the 19th century. But, in the absence of adequate statistical returns we can form no reliable estimates of how large the stock of such money was, the uses to which the currencies were put or how widely these uses were spread through society.

It is likely that a similar serendipitous mixture of the world's coinages was also available in New Zealand at about this time because it seems that Sydney and New Zealand attracted a similar assembly of missionaries, whalers, sealers and casual traders. But direct evidence of the use of coinage in New Zealand at this time is sparse. Payments for land in New Zealand in the late 18th and early 19th century included a wide range of so-called "trade goods" and currency. Nevertheless, Richard Cruise[22], writing in 1824 stated:

> "The females were exhibited in fewer numbers, and their relatives manifested an avidity for lucre, in proposing conditions on which they would permit them to visit the ship."[23]

Firth also mentions examples of currency being used as ornament.[24] It appears that Māori rangatira imposed berthing charges (a form of "invisible" export) from the vessels that touched their shores in search of cargoes of timber or flax. We do not know if any payments owing were settled in coin or some other currency such as rum, gunpowder or firearms.

The Sydney-based Commissariat Store managed money and money-like tokens for about 40 years. So far as is known, nothing comparable existed in New Zealand at the same time.[25] Rather, if money commodities were used in pre-colonial New Zealand, it seems likely that originated largely in Sydney[26] or the Far East.

Coinage

Neither New South Wales nor New Zealand was blessed by the Colonial Office with the means to legally regulate the production and issue of domestic currency. Yet, both societies developed monetary expedients of their own. These are much better known in the case of Australia largely because Governor Macquarie reported on them at great length although his predecessors had occasion to mention them. As for New Zealand, a number of travellers' tales date from the first three decades of the 19th century but they contain very few observations of monetary transactions. No doubt this is because, before 1845, unlike New South Wales, New Zealand had no Commissariat to act as a primitive central banker.

In both Australia and New Zealand, it was some time before institutions which fostered the wide acceptance of money came into being. Initially, if trade and exchange were conducted at all[27] it was by means of barter. For example, in early New Zealand, on the one side, incomers offered relatively standard commodities such as muskets and barrels of gunpowder, iron nails, barrels of rum, sacks of flour and sugar, iron or steel axe heads or blankets in a variety of colours in response to offers from Māori of sexual partners and victuals (like pigs, fish or fresh water), industrial products (such as timber and flax), or services like occupation of land.[28] The pioneering anthropologist

Raymond Firth boldly stated that Māori did not use money before non-indigenous people plantation began.[29] There appears to be no reason to doubt the general accuracy of this assertion.

Nevertheless, over time, the terms of trade changed. For example, Māori required longer nails that could be ground "at the millstone" to serve as wood chisels or boring instruments.[30] For some time afterwards the same was true of New South Wales. There, barter was common with wheat and rum important trade commodities to the extent that in 1813 the road between Sydney and Liverpool cost Governor Macquarie "400 gallons of rum".[31] In the period before organised colonisation, missionaries concluded elaborate deeds of sale and purchase with Māori for extensive estates in northern New Zealand[32] the consideration for which included a wide range of trade goods and specified currency.[33]

In the absence of monetary institutions in New Zealand, it is only possible to offer conjectures about the use of currency specified in pre-colonial sale and purchase agreements. It is possible that the currency involved was ultimately to be used in Sydney or in exchanges with captains of visiting vessels or to be displayed a mark of wealth, power, and intelligence (i.e., mana). Whatever the intentions that lay behind the details of the sale and purchase agreements it is evident that mere tendering of coin is not evidence of the use of money unless it is accompanied by some evidence of the existence and use of monetary institutions. Until such evidence emerges we can only agree with Firth that pre-colonial New Zealand was probably without money or monetary system.

Promissory Notes

When coinage is not available, people who are familiar with the use of money commodities and who are aware of the convenience of reliable monetary institutions, often tender promises-to-pay in settlement of debts. Such promises-to-pay are called promissory notes and are a written promise (i.e. like an IOU) to pay a stated amount in a specified place, at or by a specified date.[34] In law, these notes need not be printed and may be inscribed on anything, including livestock, or paper of any quality.[35] Many historians have established that, in New South Wales, promissory notes were issued by a wide variety of companies and people to pay for goods and services . But the use of such notes in New Zealand has been less commonly described; indeed, their very existence is often only known from passing references in private correspondence.

In Sydney, during the first five decades of colonisation, private promissory notes circulated as if they were domestic currency. Indeed, they came to be known as "Currency." "Currency" circulated at less than its face value unlike the combination of Commissariat Store Receipts, Treasury Bills and foreign currencies which collectively came to be known as "Sterling"[36] because it traded at close to its face value. Despite the convenience enjoyed by everyone engaged in domestic trade in having access to media of exchange, the value of these privately produced promissory notes suffered because they could easily be forged, they had an uncertain life because they were often written on poor quality paper and in ink that quickly faded and there was no guarantee that their issuers commanded the wherewithal let alone the intention to fulfil the "promise to pay" that the notes conveyed. It was not until about 1810 that printed promissory notes became commonplace. The acceptance of promissory notes varied widely between localities, which reflected the fact that some issuers were regarded as trustworthy and others were not. In Sydney, although not it seems in New Zealand, the issue of promissory notes was known as "petty banking".

But "petty banking" is a first important step towards the development of money which is adaptable to commercial circumstances. Its creation is based on a promise to pay someone a consideration (the more modern term is a personal cheque). It is, therefore, an acknowledgement of a debt between parties to a transaction. For this reason, it is often called debt-based money. The ultimate value of a given promissory note bears no relation to its cost of production which can be as little as the time, pen, ink and paper involved in its drafting. Rather, a receiver of such a note will value it according to the trust which can be placed in the promise of payment it conveys. For the government of a well-regarded country like the UK the worth of a promissory note issued by the UK Treasury is invariably taken at its face value (i.e., its value inscribed on its face). So, it is said that a "pound is a pound."

The economic importance of promissory notes is that they can be adapted to accomplish many kinds of transactions undertaken in many circumstances. Such instruments are composed by purchasers and can be tailored to reflect the terms and conditions of the transaction being undertaken. They can also be created when and if the purchaser chooses. This flexibility of use is the monetary concomitant of the commodification of land.

The fact that promissory notes can be created out of nothing means that a bank, for example, can create readily-accepted money.[37] It does this by allowing its customers to issue promissory notes (i.e. write personal cheques) to a greater value than the deposits it holds on their behalf (i.e., permit the account in question to be overdrawn). Normally, these notes are paid into other banks as deposits and so enhance the ability of all banks, including the one that permitted the original overdraft, to allow greater overdrafts. The only restraints on this process are the need for banks to hold sufficient liquidity to supply day-to-day demands of customers for cash and to meet the costs of cheque clearing.[38]

Governors King, Bligh, and Macquarie attempted to regulate the circulation of the products of "petty banking" with only partial success.[39] In 1800 Governor King believed that if a sufficient supply of coinage could be ensured, then the use of privately-issued promissory notes would decline. He believed this would result in an increase in the acceptability of locally-created means of exchange.[40] He tried to ensure that only forms printed by the Government-owned press would be allowed to circulate but his orders were widely ignored. Governor Bligh issued a General Order on 3 January 1807 proclaiming that promissory notes should be settled in "Military and Colonial Notes". Again, the Order was widely disregarded. Finally, in June 1810, Governor Macquarie proscribed written promissory notes for £5 and under and notes payable in "currency". He subsequently required that the notes be printed and should be payable in sterling, which should be used for the payment of all duties and fees to public departments. In October 1813, Macquarie banned all convicts, even those with a ticket of leave, from issuing promissory notes and free persons would be subject to a fine of £20 for each note they negotiated. Yet, despite this lengthy, albeit desultory, campaign against promiscuously-issued promissory notes they continued to circulate in New South Wales for many years. Indeed, their demise had to await the formation of note-issuing, deposit-taking banks serving New South Wales and Tasmania and the development of wool exports in the late 1820s and early 1830s.

The monetary history of New Zealand is much less developed than that of the Australian colonies notwithstanding several outstanding pioneering efforts.[41] During the 1840s and 1850s, promissory notes issued by prominent traders and entrepreneurs, circulated in commercial centres such as, Auckland, Dunedin, Nelson and Wellington and possibly more widely. Presumably, they were also issued before this[42] and even perhaps afterwards despite the active development of nation-wide banking in the 1860s and 1870s. Unlike New South Wales, which was favoured from the outset of colonisation, by the operation of the Commissariat, New Zealand had no secure source of coinage, apart from that accumulated in payment for exports, until the arrival of Imperial troops in 1845, also paid for through the Commissariat. Hence, whenever the total value of exports fell below the total value of imports there was a fall in the stock of currency held in domestic hands. The resulting shortage of coin encouraged the invention of substitute media of exchange for domestic trade. The invention sometimes took the form of promissory notes.[43]

In the British Empire, this sequence of events arose because the main method of colonisation adopted in the 19th century was by forming and maintaining markets. For example, in 1830, the Society for the Diffusion of Useful Knowledge wrote:

> "If we range through the great Polynesian ocean to exchange our own articles of manufacture for those commodities which its islands produce in such abundance, we are bound to give instruction for the mind as well as our clothes and implements."[44]

There were many possible reasons for adopting this approach. Buying and selling were simple to understand by Europeans, who were used to trading. More complex social interactions were simplified and interpreted in terms of exchanging or trading. European participants regarded buying and selling as a litmus test of good faith and civilisation. Successful trading could only take place in relatively settled social conditions and in the presence of mutual benefit.

No market functions unless some acceptable way of settling debts is agreed upon (often tacitly or by custom) between buyers and sellers. When markets are very localised and the participants within them relatively well-known to each other a debt might readily be settled by no more than a simple verbal promise to pay.[45] When that promise is written by a person, a company or an institution widely known to be trustworthy, it might itself also be traded for other goods and services because it is more likely to be accepted by sellers. Thus, issuers of promissory notes of good reputation[46] might come to expect to make an income from creating and issuing them during commerce.[47]

Banking

During his military service, which included holding the positions of Paymaster of the King's troops in the Bombay Presidency, Deputy Governor of Colombo after the defeat of the Dutch and Colonel in charge of the London District, Governor Macquarie became well acquainted with the strategic military advantages of a stable and efficient monetary system.[48] He became convinced of the importance of a working bank for colonial development while passing through Cape Town on his way to take up the Governorship of New South Wales aboard HMS *Dromedary*. Accordingly, he requested permission to grant a charter to a bank to be based in Sydney. This proposal was rejected by Lord Bathurst, Secretary of State for War, and the Colonies presumably because, if enacted, it would have been contrary to the sentiments of the Bullion Committee 1810[49] the views of which appear to have been widely accepted by the House of Commons.

Official thinking about currency matters was dominated by the Report of the Select Committee on High Price of Bullion which was issued on 8 June 1810. The findings of the Committee were based upon the argument that the profitability of privately-owned banks (which included the Bank of England) largely depended upon their ability to print and issue bank notes at minimal cost. This Committee, whose members included David Ricardo and Henry Thornton, concluded that banks had over-issued paper (i.e., notes and bills) while convertibility into gold had been suspended since 1797. It recommended a staged return to full gold convertibility to be managed by the Bank of England "so as to provide a sufficient check and control in the issues of paper from the Bank of England." The Committee advised that once convertibility at the Bank of England was achieved, it would be some time before banks in other parts of the United Kingdom "could be compelled to pay in specie". These views represented a "bullionist" analysis of banking which held that the main thrust of banking policy should be aimed at control of issue of banknotes by private companies. No doubt Bathurst shared these views which, together with the legalities involved, dictated his attitude to Macquarie's granting of banking charters.

Over time, and despite this rebuff, Macquarie became more firmly convinced that the future of New South Wales lay in settlement by free settlers and emancipists, a necessary condition of which was a dependable monetary system. He, therefore, set out on the long, circuitous march towards disobeying the Colonial Office and Lord Bathurst. His journey was delayed in 1812 by the British Government sending £10,000 in Spanish dollars which Macquarie ordered to be manufactured into "holey dollars" valued at 5s and "dumps" valued at 1s 8d and issued through the Commissariat store.[50] This importation was insufficient to meet the growing needs of the colonial economy. In addition, in 1812–13, the Commissariat was fully incorporated as a sub-department of the UK Treasury. Deputy Commissary-General Allan was appointed to run the Commissariat in Sydney. Allan misled Macquarie into believing that he was authorised to issue notes to replace Store Receipts. In time, the deception was discovered along with the unsuccessful speculations that Allan was conducting using the notes he created. Allan was recalled and replaced by Drennan in 1819 whose administration of the Commissariat turned out to be just as flawed as that of the man he succeeded.

**INTERNATIONAL MONETARY INSTITUTIONS
1821 ONWARDS**

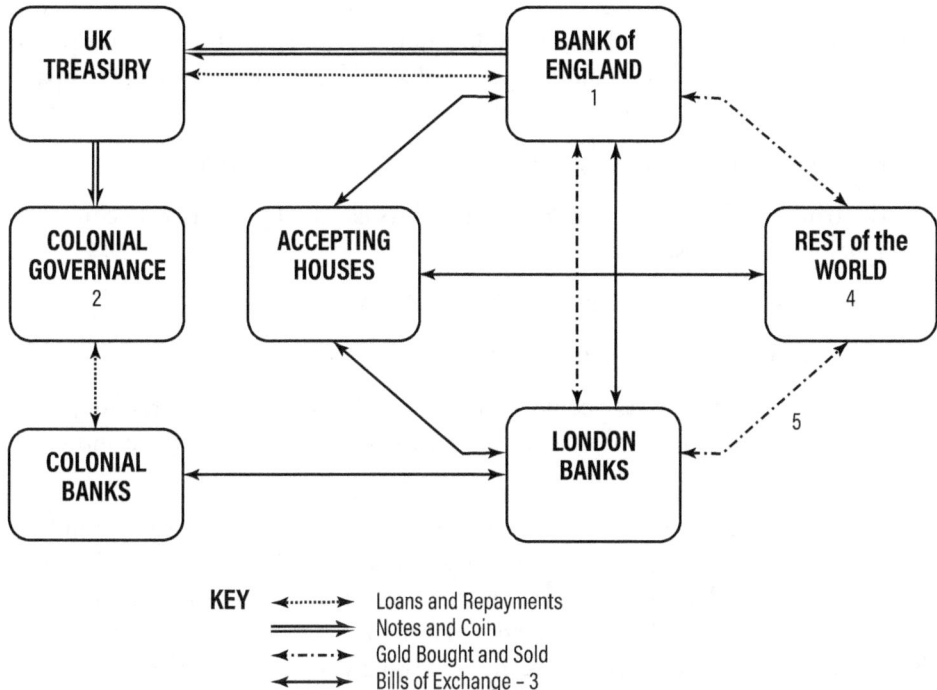

KEY
- Loans and Repayments
- Notes and Coin
- Gold Bought and Sold
- Bills of Exchange - 3

NOTES
1. Gold was purchased and sold at £3-17s-101/2d per troy ounce 95% fine by the Bank of England from 1821 on.
2. Includes merchant venturer companies.
3. Balances emerging between financial institutions were invariably cleared by transfers of gold coin or bullion.
4. Rest of the World includes central banks, treasuries of non-English countries and companies with international reach. Many such private companies became members of the Accepting Houses Association.
5. Gold in sufficient quantities was discovered in 1747 in Russia, in 1840 in California, in 1852 in New South Wales and Victoria, in 1861 in New Zealand and in the 1890s in South Africa.

Thus, it was not until 20 November 1816 that Macquarie could assemble sufficient support from the mercantile class of Sydney to ensure that a joint stock bank could be launched. That day, 14 leading citizens[51] met in Judge-Advocate Wylde's chambers to discuss the progressive decline in the value of "currency". Two days' later a further meeting, under the chairmanship of Lieutenant Governor Molle, approved the desirability of a sterling medium of exchange and resolved to form a public colonial bank.[52] Wylde advised Macquarie that it was true that there was no mention in his Governor's Commission of his being able to grant charters to companies. But Wylde also reasoned that because Macquarie was able to grant charters for boroughs there appeared to be no legal impediment to his providing the bank with a charter granting limited liability to its subscribers.[53] On 12 February 1817, the directors of the Bank asked Macquarie to grant them a charter for seven years along the proposed lines. A charter, signed by Macquarie, was delivered on 22 March 1817 backdated to 12 February. It granted "… by charter under the colonial seal … all the rights, immunities, privileges and title of a corporation and of a joint stock company, indemnifying all subscribers against risk and liability beyond the amount of their respective shares." [54] Among The rules of the Bank of New South Wales[55] were the following:

> The purposes of the company were to discount, loan and deposit;
>
> The Bank would be run by a President and six elected Directors who could appoint a Chief Cashier and Secretary;
>
> Notes could be issued in denominations of 2/6, 5/-, 10/-, £1 and £5;
>
> No paper with more than 3 months to run is to be discounted; and
>
> Loans secured by mortgage could be made provided loans were not for longer than 12 months, were no larger than £500 and bore interest at no more than 10%.

The charter and operating rules are very conservative and accurately reflect the thinking of the Bullion Committee. Nevertheless, they contain the principle of limited liability and the right to lend on the security of first mortgage. These significant innovations were not allowed in any British bank before Macquarie agreed to them. Nevertheless, in the course of the next century, both became increasingly accepted (or at least not openly discussed) and without them it is difficult to imagine how the settlement of landed estates in New South Wales would have been possible.

Macquarie reported these developments to Bathurst in a despatch dated 29 March 1817. The Bank of New South Wales opened for business at 10am on 8 April 1817 but it was almost another year, in March 1818, before Macquarie's despatch reached Bathurst and the British Government learned what had happened. Bathurst referred Macquarie's despatch to the crown law officers on 6 August 1818 who opined in October:

> "… we are of opinion the Governor was not legally empowered either by his commission or instructions to grant such a charter and that it is therefore null and void"[56]

Bathurst wrote to Macquarie on 29 October 1818 conveying the legal opinion and instructing him to inform the Bank subscribers that they were in the same position as a member of any other partnership formed for trade purposes. This meant that subscribers to the Bank of New South Wales must accept unlimited liability for the bank's losses. But Macquarie and the directors of the Bank reasoned that if this opinion were to become widely known in Sydney it could undermine the confidence with which the Bank was viewed. It risked precipitating a run on the Bank and a halting of ordinary payments in the colony.

Macquarie did not respond in detail for almost two years, until 1 September 1820, by which time the Bank has been operating for more than three years. He argued that the

Bank had succeeded in its main purpose and that monetary relations in New South Wales had been regularised. Contrary to Bathurst's instructions, he proposed to do nothing and to allow the Bank to continue to operate under its present charter for fear that confidence in the Bank would be lost[57] and lead to widespread bankruptcies. Bathurst did not pursue the matter. Neither Bathurst nor Macquarie made mention of the permission to lend on the security of first mortgage which meant it became part of Australian banking practice. Thus, the Bank of New South Wales was born of determined sponsorship by the Colonial Government but its early years were conceived in a bed of legal sophistry in Sydney and fertilised by administrative indolence and inattention in London. Yet the fact remains that this initiation of banking in New South Wales is the origin of the nexus of transactions, the "golden cords", by which the colony was drawn into the international banking system centred on London. Repeated around the globe, the same process safeguarded the integrity of the British Empire for more than a century.

During the 18th and early 19th centuries the "business of banking" consisted largely of issuing banknotes, buying and selling trade bills and bills of exchange and taking deposits. Compared with modern financial institutions, lending other people's money was not a major activity. After the passage of the Country Bankers Act in 1826 any bank which was founded more than 65 miles outside London could issue its own notes. Within the 65-mile circle note issue was a monopoly of the Bank of England. In practice, it meant that a number of banks were formed in major provincial trading centres like Bristol, Exeter, Norwich and Liverpool. They maintained a note issue through their branches but operated a so-called headquarters branch in London which did not issue notes. Its main task was to engage in trading in bills on the London Discount Market. Provided a bank held sufficient cash to meet the day-to-day demands for cash of its customers and other banks, when they presented notes for payment, there is nothing to prevent its note issue business from continuing. By contrast, official attention was directed elsewhere and a view developed that note issue by banks should be carefully controlled which had its clearest expression in the Report of the Bullion Committee in 1810.[58]

Dealing in bills was a method of raising short-term credit for the conduct of domestic and foreign trade. These bills were promises to pay a specified sum of money, at a specified place, at a specified time in the future. They worked like delayed promissory notes.[59] Once accepted [60]by a reliable institution, bills ensured that producers or their customers could be sure of obtaining short term loans (at a price called the rate of discount) which would ensure that trade could take place even if liquidity was tight. Such bills could be repeatedly re-discounted during their lifetime with other financial intermediaries, like discount houses, as the need for liquidity arose. Most of the large discount houses or acceptance houses were located in the City of London and enjoyed close business relationships with the Bank of England which was itself a discount house. (Appendix Three contains a detailed description of the bills mechanism.)

In outline, the mechanism worked as follows. When a manufacturer had to pay a supplier in the future, the supplier would issue a bill drawn on the manufacturer. This bill was for a sum to be paid to the supplier at a future date, say 90 days or three months hence. On maturity of the bill, the manufacturer pays the supplier and the bill is cancelled. In the meantime, the supplier, if in need of credit, could sell (or discount) the bill at a bank for an amount below its face value and the bank would collect the full value from the manufacturer when the bill fell due. This bill finance mechanism was the main method of financing trade during the Industrial Revolution. It remained the main way that Australasian exports and imports were financed until 30 years after World War II. This system of finance was remarkably flexible. For example, if a borrower required further accommodation an existing bill could be redeemed on maturity by issuing another short-term bill. Long-term lending secured by a mortgage on real estate was not a matter for deposit-taking banks; it was the preserve of solicitors and wealthy individuals who were often themselves landowners.

For much of the early 1820s, the financial sector of New South Wales can be characterised as a confused collection of private enterprises exhibiting no specialities. Many issued notes, many made loans, many took deposits and all seem to have discounted commercial paper while also acting as merchants and general traders. Many traders and merchants accepted "all kinds of colonial produce at market prices".[61] Until the Bank of Van Diemen's Land and the Bank of Australia opened for business in 1823 and 1826 respectively, the Bank of New South Wales was the only banking company.

These confused financial arrangements were further complicated between 1822 and 1825 when Governor Brisbane presided over an attempt to introduce a "dollar standard"[62]. Brisbane envisaged the use of dollars in cash payments as the colonial accounting standard. But the outcome was confusion because silver dollars traded at a variable discount against sterling despite attempts by the colonial government to stabilise its value.

The monetisation of New Zealand took a broadly similar course to that followed earlier by New South Wales and later by Australia. Some of the most salient similarities can be summarised as follows. First, in both territories, the monetary system centred upon privately owned deposit-taking banks which were heavily supported by the two colonial governments and which fostered close working relationships with the London Money and Credit Markets.[63] So close were these international links that it might be possible to argue that banks within Australia and New Zealand were more closely bound together by their dealings with the London Money and Capital Markets than they were with each other in the colonies.

Second, much later, the extension of banking was encouraged by the development of wool exports[64] and the discovery and exploitation of gold deposits. Thus, both Victoria, from 1851, and New Zealand, from 1861, were able to create their own supplies of international currency simply by extracting and refining gold within their respective territories. This gold could be obtained by banks in exchange for bank notes which they created at minimal cost.

Third, the Commissariat played an important role in the public finance of both New South Wales and Tasmania from the outset of the colonies and in New Zealand for over 20 years after 1845. For considerable periods it was an important source of foreign currency throughout the Australasian colonies.[65]

Both Australia and New Zealand developed as settler societies the prosperity of which was founded upon ready access to land. But landed estates did not include any minerals, coal, oil or gas that were found on it. Lending on the security of land or on the products of land have always been an important part of the operations of Australasian banking systems.

But they were not identical. For many decades in Australia, most pastoral land was leased or occupied under license. Proprietors paid a relatively small annual fee to squat and had an incentive to make the maximum operating profit from occupying the land. Borrowing, if undertaken, was not for land purchase but for improvements in the form of stock, buildings, grasses and fencing and for the development of infrastructure such as roads, railways and drought resistance.[66] Lending was often secured by liens on future production or stock. This latter practice was also made legally possible in New Zealand in 1858.

But the histories of Australia and New Zealand also differed. Most New Zealand landed estates were sold by the crown and were granted in fee simple.[67] Proprietors purchased a freehold estate before it could be occupied. Financial companies operating in New Zealand faced demands for loans for land purchase and acquisition of leases. Virtually the only security available to back these loans was the future value of the land and the value of the produce it yielded. Occupiers had a vested interest in owning the land they occupied in the prospect of making a capital gain on sale. That gain was more, the greater the extent of public provision of infrastructure and the greater the acreage of land owned in fee simple.

By contrast, in England, traditionally, banking business largely consisted of sales and purchases of short-term financial instruments (like bills) and was not at all involved in lending against the security of real property.[68] Colonial Office officials cleaved to British banking lore which in the 18th and 19th centuries held that lending on the security of land was far too risky to be financed by buying and selling short-term liabilities such as bills of exchange or accepting sight deposits.[69] Indeed, the Bank Charter Act 1844, various legal judgements and a series of colonial banking regulations (see Appendix 7) forbade banks from lending on landed security. Banks in Australia and New Zealand eventually developed as deposit-taking mortgage banks, the note-issuing and discount business of which was of decreasing importance.[70] Hence, despite differences between the Australian and New Zealand monetary systems prior to World War I, in the long-run, this difference in the pattern of land tenure between Australia and New Zealand had little impact on the form of monetisation that took shape. Bank-based monetisation of both Australian and New Zealand society was determined by the same private companies, often owned largely by British interests, and actively (albeit covertly) supported by successive settler governments.[71]

Monetary Adaptation
The Australasian monetary system has evolved quite differently from the English system which was its original progenitor. For time immemorial, banks could only be legally formed in Great Britain and its possessions by means of either a Royal Charter or by

private Act of Parliament. Banks were partnerships with unlimited liability. The sole exception was the Bank of New South Wales which Macquarie had illegally chartered in 1817.

In 1826, the UK Parliament passed the Country Bankers Act. This allowed a joint stock company (with more than six partners) to set up as a bank that issued banknotes provided it was located more than 65 miles from London. Nevertheless, shareholders had to continue to accept the risk of unlimited liability. In addition, the Bank of England was permitted to open branches outside London. Several new banks were incorporated in important British trading[72] centres. These new banks had access to the discount market via local branches of the Bank of England. For many years, this pattern was also followed in Australia and New Zealand. Several Australasian banks were incorporated under the 1826 Act including the Bank of Australasia, the Union Bank of Australia and (much later) the National Bank of New Zealand. The new legislation did not materially alter the nature of banking in the colonies. Indeed, the Union Bank of Australia which opened in New Zealand in 1840 remained predominantly an "exchange bank" until the 1860s.[73] This meant that it earned a small profit from discounting bills but made most of its surplus from the issue of notes to its customers.

The rapid development of wool-growing in New South Wales, Victoria and South Australia during the 1830s and 1840s was associated with bankers, traders and stock and station agents. For many years, prosperity was distributed liberally until a trade cycle downturn in the early 1840s led to the closure or merger of many banks formed in the preceding decade. It also forced some traders to leave banking altogether. Not until the discovery of gold in Victoria in 1851 did recovery set in. But when it did, the boom lasted until the 1890s. Three developments conspired to fundamentally change the colonial model of banking permitted under the 1826 Country Banking Act.

First, in the 1850s and early 1860s gold was discovered in commercially viable quantities in both Australia and New Zealand. For example, in Victoria after 1851 and New Zealand from 1861, a number of banks opened for business and began purchasing domestically extracted gold with their own notes and depository receipts. This meant that international currency could be obtained locally at relatively low cost by local banks.[74]

Second, when lending to wool-growers Australian banks often sought to place "a trustworthy merchant" between them and the pastoralist borrower.[75] The idea was to ensure that the bank's lending remained at short-term while the merchant could offer longer term finance if it chose. This policy was developed to such an extent that, in time, the Bank of New Zealand placed several layers of merchant financiers between it and ultimate borrowers. But Sinclair and Mandle have argued that many so-called merchants were also involved in land ownership and the profitability of their businesses often depended on produce from land. In many cases, there was a conjunction of risks which the acquisition of an intermediary merchant could do little to mitigate because of the close links between farming and business.[76]

Third, in the late 1860s, the Privy Council[77] ruled that chartered banks were allowed to take possession of landed property if a borrower, having offered a mortgage over land to secure a loan, were to default on the conditions of the loan. It seems that, in law, this was a breach of the conditions of supply under the Sale of Goods Act, notwithstanding existing banking law and regulation. In other words, a bank could assume title to land only if that title had been acquired in the course of its banking business.[78] This ruling meant that banks were in practice permitted to lend against the security of land.

At the same time and before World War I, the financial systems of both the Australian colonies and New Zealand were tightly tied to the London Money and Capital Markets. This meant that they operated within the framework of currency management, called the Sterling Exchange Standard, overseen by the Banking Department of the Bank of England. Transactions between banks were denominated in Sterling (i.e., English pounds, shillings, and pence). The Resumption of Cash Payments Act 1819 (Peel's Act) set the price of a troy ounce of gold 95% fine[79] as equivalent to £3-17s-$10^1/_2$d in coin. This price was guaranteed by the Bank of England and was available to all-comers. Every bank transaction expressed in sterling was as "good as gold". But gold was only infrequently used to settle banking debts because banks maintained banking relationships with each other. If a bank owed money to another bank it was normally granted short-term accommodation so that it could settle the debt. Only in abnormal circumstances,[80] therefore, were inter-bank debts settled by gold flows between institutions. Thus, such gold flows were an important sign that the bank owing the debt was "in trouble" which meant that the bank concerned could no longer rely upon credit from other banks.

When a bank issues a bill on behalf of a customer it makes a contingent advance to that customer, who may wish to borrow against it in the future. The more bills a bank issues the greater the volume of credit it potentially creates. The more credit it creates, the greater the volume of payments to other banks it will have to meet in the future. If all banks expand their business through credit creation at much the same rate, then no single bank incurs a substantial net debt with the rest of the banking system. Banks can continue this lending policy because they will expect that any temporary deficiency they incur with the rest of the system will be matched by a surplus in the future. By contrast, if a bank finds that its receipts from bills collected are consistently less than its payments on bills owing then it will have to adjust its business operations by reducing the number of bills it issues.

During the Long 19th Century, Australia and New Zealand probably had highly seasonal patterns of exports and, to a lesser extent, imports. At some times of the year Australasian banks were in deficit to the system in London and other times in surplus. Regular patterns of deficit and surplus were largely anticipated and met by means of borrowing from other banks or holding liquid reserves. These reserves were commonly called London Funds. If they came under downward pressure, then, as rule of thumb, Australasian banks restricted advances and discounts to colonial customers. But this was not an automatic mechanism; individual colonial banks remained free to notice or ignore the signals provided by the London Money and Capital Markets.

Although individual colonial banks were free to take notice or ignore the signals emanating from the London Money and Capital Markets, the bank in question will undertake a combination of the following adjustments:

- borrow gold or sterling from other banks,

- sell bills for gold or sterling on the London markets,
- borrow gold or other currency from overseas, or
- reduce the flow of bills it will have to meet by reducing credit granted to customers.

These adjustments display features of the classical gold standard system. For example, the rise in borrowing from other banks raises interest rates charged between banks, increased gold imports by banks in London when purchased by the Bank of England Banking Department on behalf of the Bank of England Issue Department allows an increase in sterling money supply to take place and a reduction in bill dealing means that colonial credit is curtailed. All are examples of the way that colonial banks interacted with the London Money and Capital Markets in the normal course of banking business. None of these links is automatic and the gold standard system was not mechanical.

**INTERNATIONAL MONETARY INSTITUTIONS
1826 ONWARDS**

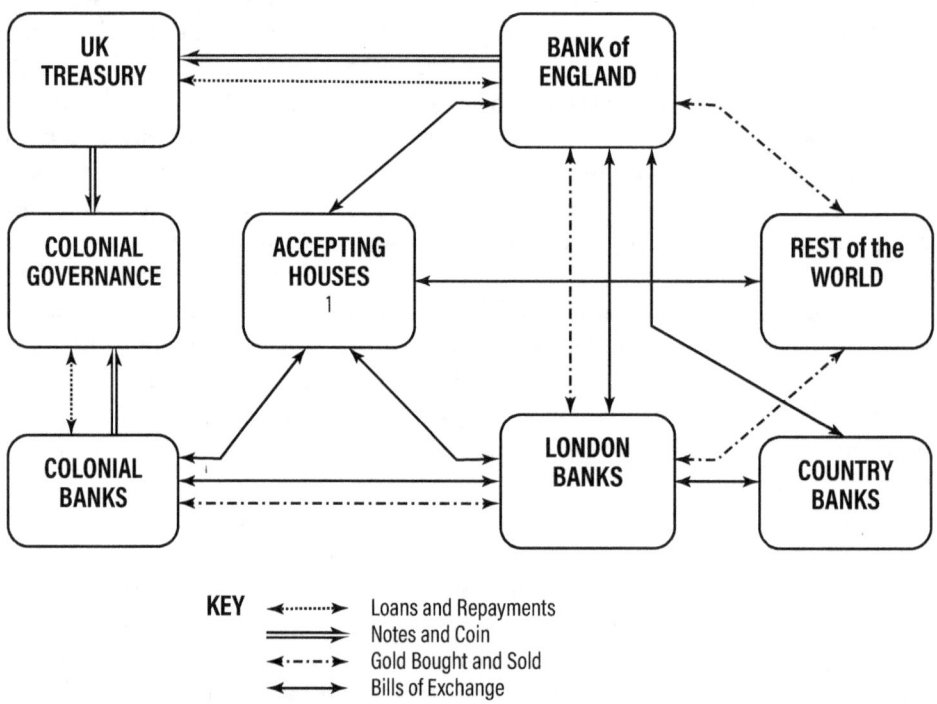

Notes
1. Overend Gurnsey & Co commanded over 50% of Accepting House transactions by 1826. The company acted as effectively lender of last resort in the 1826 crisis, a role the Bank of England declined to fill.

More important it incorporated no centralising tendency.[81] Adjustments were directed to the individual needs of each bank. Consequently, they were only conducted as vigorously and for as long as a given bank faced difficulties. There was no procedure by which the adjustments of individual banks were collected to safeguard the international financial system, except perhaps through bill market transactions. But these were likely to involve restriction or extension of credit by regionally based banks rather than gold movements. There was no "steady state" or "equilibrium" towards which the system gravitated unbidden as a result of the above adjustments. Rather, the gold standard at this time (1826–1845) seems to have been quieted and enjoyed a period in which it was subject to few perturbations.

Rather, control of adjustment to changed circumstances always remained with the affected bank or banks. The innovations embraced by banks operating in Australia and New Zealand could only become part of generally accepted banking practice so long as the so-called disciplines of the gold standard system (sometimes called the rules of the game) were not circumvented or ignored to a material degree. These disciplines were invariably self-imposed by the banks themselves under the growing influence of influential members of the London Discount Market[82] headed by the Bank of England. But individual actions taken in isolation by individual banks to adjust to outside circumstance were insufficient to prevent regular recurrence of international financial crises during the 19th and early 20th centuries (see Appendix 4). Only during the Baring Crisis in 1890 did the Bank of England, oversee international financial arrangements as part of a consortium of central and private banks which harvested to significant advantages in its future dealings with the Government of Argentina. The rules of the game were concocted without regard to the interactions that existed between banks. They prescribed actions by a bank to prevent failure but these actions often risked undermining other banks in a beggar-thy-neighbour fashion.[83]

Colonial banking appears to have been highly collusive with written inter-bank agreements negotiated on deposit rates and rates of discount.[84] Agreements between banks in the Australian colonies and New Zealand became more comprehensive and restrictive, at least until the 1890s. During the second half of the 19th century, customers of banks only rarely enjoyed the advantages of price competition.[85] Competition, when it existed, took the form of multiplication of bank branches and minor variations in characteristics of deposit and lending products. Collusion made the colonial banking industry appear more predictable than could be justified by the actual risks it was taking. This appearance of stability was particularly attractive to London accepting houses. Each bank could assume that its competitors would react to changes in the wider world as it would. Many innovations, such as stock mortgages or product liens, were shared by collective agreement or by legislation. Most important of all, each bank manager could implicitly rely upon the word of his (always a he) counterpart in another bank. For all these reasons banks in Australia and New Zealand duplicated many of the functions performed by banks in many other parts of the British Empire.

The colonial monetary systems also contained institutions which were not replicated elsewhere. It is these which reflect the peculiar risks which businesses and personal customers faced in the two countries. Most notable among them in Australasia were stock and station agents. In the 19th century these institutions served many of the financial and other needs of farmers including brokering stock and land acquisitions, supplying equipment, seeds and chemicals, storing, brokering and acting as agents for exports like wool and grain and supplying short-term and long-term credit.[86] Trading banks enjoyed close links with these organisations through inter-locking directorships and large credit facilities. Prior to 1890, stock and station agents were among the largest companies in Australia and New Zealand. Ultimately, the fundamental weakness of this method of managing system risks was exposed by a sustained fall in export prices and land values. The close links between the management of banks and associated stock and station agents meant that the risks being taken by the different organisations were very closely related and were never spread between organisations that were truly financially independent. Worse, the risks that banks were being led to undertake were being taken by a notionally independent organisation over which banks had no day-to-day control. Substantial risks were hidden from the bank's own management systems and banks did not control the ultimate use of the money that had been borrowed by the institutions with which they were associated.

Chapter Notes

1. Brian Easton: *In Narrow Seas: The Economic History of Aotearoa New Zealand*, Wellington, Victoria University Press, 2020, p. 62.
2. See for example Benjamin Bromberg: "The Origin of Banking: Religious Finance in Babylonia", *The Journal of Economic History*, Vol 2, No 1, (May 1942), pp. 77–88 and R D Baker: "The Implausibility of the Barter Narrative & Credit Money in Ancient Babylon", *The Developing Economist*, 2014, Vol 1, No 1, pp 3–31.
3. See for example Joseph Manning: *The Open Sea: The Economic Life of the Ancient Mediterranean World from the Iron Age to the Rise of Rome*, Princeton University Press, 2018.
4. Evidence of the everyday use of currency might take the form of caches of monetary commodities such as coins either deliberately or accidentally accumulated or of accounts or tallies kept in terms of a unit of account. So far as is known, no such evidence has yet come to light in pre-colonial Australasia.
5. S J Butlin: *Foundations of the Australian Monetary System 1788–1851*, Sydney, Sydney University Press, p. 12.
6. This view is contradicted in the Kauwaeranga Judgement delivered by Fenton CJ in the Native Land Court on 3 December 1870. Fenton states that "…Lord John Russell …[wrote]… to John Thompson Esq, who had asked for a charter of incorporation of a proposed New Zealand Agricultural, Commercial, and Banking Company." Russell declined the request on the ground that British sovereignty over New Zealand "… is expressly disavowed…". See pp.237–8 in Alex Frame: "Kauwaeranga Judgement Law in the Pacific", *Victoria University of Law Review*, Vol 18, 1984, pp. 227–45.
7. For example, colonial banking remained focussed on trading in bills of exchange and gold, advancing on landed security and taking deposits. The development of a colonial capital market and dealing in futures and options did not take place before World War I.
8. The original soldiery sent to New South Wales in 1787–1788 was composed of Marines. In 1789 a new body was recruited in Great Britain and named the New South Wales Corps. It has not been possible to discover whether or not the Commissariat that provided succour for the Marines was the same as, or different from, the one that served the New South Wales Corps.
9. It is not known when the operation of this function was changed. But it is known that Lieutenant John Macarthur was appointed Paymaster of the New South Wales Corps by Acting Governor Grose after Governor Phillip left for England on 11 December 1792 to be (successfully) treated for kidney stones.
10. As in New Zealand in the 1840s, because they were paid in London their salaries were subjected to income tax, withheld at source. See Littlewood, op cit, 2016.
11. S J Butlin, op cit, 1968, pp. 15–16.
12. Ibid, p. 31.
13. Ibid, pp. 31–2. From the clarity of her account, it is obvious that Mrs Macarthur was well-acquainted with the system of Store Receipts and was, even as early in 1795, concerned to increase the size of the flocks of the Macarthur family.
14. The Bank Restriction Act 1797 removed the requirement of the Bank of England to redeem banknotes in gold. The suspension of gold convertibility lasted from 27 February 1797 and was extended annually until 1 May 1821. The receipts issued by the Commissary store in Sydney were exempt from the 1797 Act.
15. In their ability to accumulate Store Receipts, and so international currency in the form of bills of exchange on the Treasury, coupled with the use of martial threat, officers of the New South Wales Corps could exercise market power over the purchase and subsequent sale of imported commodities like rum. This source of market power led directly to the so-called Rum Rebellion during which Governor Bligh was incarcerated by mutinous elements of the New South Wales

16   Corps whose activities he tried to moderate.

16   Lieutenant Macarthur held a commission bestowed in Great Britain and so was paid in London. He would have been forced to access his officer's pay by bill of exchange on the Treasury. Given the priority that they accorded accumulation of sheep numbers, it seems unlikely that the Macarthurs would have sold substantial numbers of carcases to the Commissariat Store.

17   Butlin, op cit, 1968, pp.16–17 suggests that there were a large number of clipped or cut silver dollars among them. It is possible that they were accumulated as a result of Great Britain supplying the forces defending Holland against the French armies in early 1792. Presumably, these silver dollars were shipped to New South Wales in late 1792 because of the emerging dependence of Sydney on supplies of silver currency from a silver currency area like Asia or, possibly, because the British Government wished its own coins to be conserved at a time when war against France was declared to be imminent.

18   Butlin, op cit, 1968, p. 103 reports that both Mr and Mrs Macarthur expressed the same opinion several times between 1814 and 1822.

19   C A Sharp (editor): *The Dillon Letters: The Letters of the Hon. Constantine Dillon 1842–1853*, Wellington, AH & AW Reed, 1954, p. 19 where Dillon writes to his mother: "I left England without a letter of credit and the consequence is that I can get no money but at a great loss, as of course the risk is great."

20   Butlin, op cit 1968, p. 36. The pennies were despatched immediately and the other coins arrived a year later. The total shipment comprised £550 of pennies, £350 of halfpennies and £300 of farthings. King brought the coins into circulation by requiring that purchases from the Commissariat Store be paid for by tendering these coins.

21   Ibid, p. 40. Sovereigns are not included in King's list because the circulation of gold sovereigns ceased after about 1603 and they were not struck again in England until 1817 as part of the Great Recoinage. Note also that the value of a guinea was often greater than the official price of £1–1s-0d.

22   Richard A Cruise: *Journal of a Ten Months' Residence in New Zealand*, 2nd Edition, London, Longman, Hurst, Rees, Orme, Brown and Green, 1824, Reprinted by Capper Press, Christchurch, 1974, p.166.

23   The ship was HMS *Dromedary* which started life as a merchant vessel *Kaikusroo* built in Bombay for the East India Company and launched in 1799. She was purchased for the Royal Navy in 1805 and commissioned as HMS *Howe* a 40-gun frigate. In 1806 she was converted to a 24-gun storeship and renamed *Dromedary*. In 1809, she carried Governor Lachlan Macquarie to New South Wales. In 1819, she was refitted as a convict ship and transported convicts to Tasmania. For the return voyage she was re-fitted as a timber transport and visited New Zealand in 1820 for kauri spars. On the return voyage to England, she carried Commissioner Bigge to England along with his criticisms of the tenure of Governor Macquarie. In 1826, she sailed for Bermuda where she was used a prison hulk and kitchen for workers building the new dockyard. She was broken up in 1864.

24   Raymond Firth: *Economics of the New Zealand Māori*, Wellington, Government Printer, 1972, p. 443. However, this observation appears to have been derived from Maning, op cit, 1922, p. 2. Maning was destined to become a Judge in the Native Land Court in which capacity he displayed scant regard for Māori customs. Firth also notes in footnote 7, p. 443 that Maning said that D'Urville reported that pigs weighing about 40 kilos were sold by Māori in Otago Harbour for between 16 and 18 shillings. D'Urville visited the South Island of New Zealand in 1828 and 1840.

25   The Commissariat started to operate in New Zealand in 1845 and was not wound up until 1867. Its spending is thought to have had a positive impact on the growth of the Auckland and Wellington economies during this time; other parts of New Zealand do not appear to have been so favoured. This conclusion is largely based on anecdote and the matter deserves intensive investigation.

26 The same monetary institutions which create currency can be employed to destroy it. This might occur if a government wished to reduce the supply of coins by melting them down into ingots which remain in its vaults uncirculated.

27 Cook's journals and logs record that Indigenous Aboriginals in New South Wales did not understand the concept of trade and could not be induced to engage in it. This was different from his experience in other Pacific Island communities such as Tahiti and New Zealand where indigenous peoples were observed to be acquisitive and enthusiastic traders.

28 In New Zealand, as contacts multiplied, demands for trade goods changed. Muskets and powder were demanded as payment more frequently especially during the period of the so-called Musket Wars in the 1820s and 1830s. See for example RD Crosby: *The Musket Wars: a History of Inter-Iwi Conflict 1806–45*, Auckland, Reed, 2001.

29 Firth: op cit, 1972, p. 443 when writing about the period 1810 to 1830 states: "Goods changed hands by process of barter, since for decades, there was no money economy in New Zealand, nor any medium of exchange".

30 Anne Salmond: *Two worlds: first meetings between Māori and Europeans 1642–1772*, Auckland, Viking, 1993, pp. 374–376 quoting Crozet's account of Marion's voyage in the Pacific she states that Māori offering fish in exchange for nails: "… later on … demanded nails four or five inches in length. Their object in asking for these nails was to make small wood chisels with them. As soon as they had obtained, they took it to one of the sailors and by signs engaged him to sharpen it at the millstone…."

31 R F Holder: *Bank of New South Wales: A History, Volume I: 1817–1893*, Sydney, Angus and Robertson, 1970, p. 5. No doubt other expenditures were also involved.

32 On some occasions, these sales between missionaries and Māori were concluded with the intention of safeguarding the ownership by Māori of the land. The belief motivating such deals seems to have been that missionaries could be trusted by Māori to hold onto the title they obtained in the face of pressures to sell whereas certain important members of hapu could not.

33 For example, the so-called Fairburn Purchase was concluded between Māori and missionaries of the Church Missionary Society (CMS) in January 1836 and was later estimated to amount to 75,000 acres of South Auckland. The consideration was paid in five instalments the first of which consisted of 90 blankets, 24 axes, 24 adzes, 26 hoes, 14 spades, 80 dollars, 900 pounds of tobacco, 24 combs, 12 plane irons. The other four instalments were said by Fairburn to be worth in total £902. See D Moore, B Rigby and M Russell: "Old Land Claims", Rangahaua Whanui National Theme A, Wellington, Waitangi Tribunal, First Release July 1997, (Chapter 3: The Fairburn Purchase, pp 79–97), p. 82. http://www.waitangitribunal.govt.nz/assets/Documents/Publications/wt-theme-a-old-land-claims.pdf accessed 30 March 2021. This transaction was intended to prevent Māori land from being sold to non-indigenous land sharks.

34 Sometimes the notes included a fixed date in the future, or they stated that they would be settled on demand or sometimes they contained both promises. For example, notes of John Jones issued in Dunedin in the 1850s were payable on sight in Dunedin or on two days after sight in Waikouiti.

35 Latterly trading banks have succeeded in reducing the ways in which promissory notes can be legally recognised and negotiated. For example, banks in New Zealand now refuse to process all personal cheques, however validly drawn. The reason given was that all payments by cheque were processed by a single company which was a sub-contractor to the New Zealand banks and which found continuing the business uncongenial.

36 Butlin, op cit, 1968, p. 67 states that Governor King referred to the Spanish dollar as a "sterling coin". This was because it traded in Sydney at close to its face value.

37 This ability is not limited to banks. Anyone or any institution can offer the same service. Whether or not it is used depends on how trustworthy the person or institution is thought to be by members of the community.

38 In 2021, all New Zealand banks ceased the use of cheques as a means of payment. The reason

was that the sole supplier of cheque-clearing services, Payments NZ Ltd, a company jointly owned by the trading banks, announced that it was no longer worth its while to continue to supply the service.

39 The practice of issuing promissory notes appears to have been widespread among Sydney traders such as Simon Lord, senior officials like the early Governors and even some convicts.

40 Governor King does not seem to have considered the waste of social resources involved in supporting a medium of exchange the value of which is uncertain. Ultimately, this is the reason for a government to ensure that at least one trustworthy medium of exchange is in circulation as in the case of the Earl Grey's insistence on opening the Colonial Bank of Issue in New Zealand in the 1840s.

41 The most important contributions have been: Harry Dodgsun Bedford: "The history and practice of banking in New Zealand", unpublished DLitt thesis, University of Otago, 1916; S J Butlin: *Australia and New Zealand Bank*, London, Longmans, Green & Co, 1961; Raymond Firth, op cit, 1972; and the *History of New Zealand Money Project*, Victoria University Wellington, jointly chaired by D K Sheppard and Jan Whitwell. All these pioneers are deceased and much lamented.

42 It seems possible that an analysis of the accounts of early traders, missionaries and storekeepers might yield information about the circulation of promissory notes or credit notes in pre-colonial New Zealand. Unfortunately, so far as is known no such analysis has yet been undertaken.

43 It is also possible to explore Fitzroy's financial innovations from this point of view see Ken Matthews: "The legal history of money in New Zealand", Reserve Bank of New Zealand *Bulletin*, Vol. 66, No. 1, pp. 40–49. See also Michael Littlewood: "Robert FitzRoy and the Insolvency of the New Zealand Government, 1843–1845" accessed at https://papwrs.ssm.com/sol3/papers.cfm?abstract_id=3867025.

44 *Society for the Diffusion of Useful Knowledge: "The New Zealanders"*, Library of Entertaining Knowledge, London, Charles Knight, 1830, p. 424.

45 It should be recalled that a bank cheque is neither more nor less than a form of promissory note. For example, when personal and company cheques are uttered by bank customers to customers of other banks they go through a "clearing" process. When clearing takes place between local banks local reputation is of considerable importance in ensuring acceptance of such promissory notes or cheques at face value.

46 A promissory note issued by a trader of relatively high reputation could be expected to realise a higher proportion of its face value than a note issued by someone of lower repute. This proportion is called the rate of discount when the actual value of the note is lower than its face value. Thus, the proportionate difference between the actual value of a note in market transactions and its par face value (i.e. the discount rate) is a measure of the reputation of its original issuer. The smaller the difference, the higher the reputation.

47 Butlin, op cit, 1968, pp. 92–94 lists a number of such petty bankers in Sydney and Van Diemen's Land. They include Hogan and Allen; Gordon; Murray; Bird; Wentworth and Walker. It has not yet proved possible to compile a comparable list for New Zealand.

48 For a fuller account see Holder, op cit, 1970, p. 6.

49 See Great Britain, Parliamentary Papers, House of Commons, 1810, 349, Vol 3, pp 1–252.

50 "Holey dollars" were manufactured by punching out the centre of a Spanish silver dollar coin. "Dumps" were the blank punched out circle of metal.

51 Holder, op cit, 1970, p. 11 states that the meeting was attended by Wylde, D'Arcy Wentworth, Alexander Riley, Simeon Lord, Robert Campbell snr., Charles Hook, J R O'Connor, William Browne, Thomas Macvitie, Richard Brooks, James Birnie, Richard Jones, Robert Jenkins and J T Campbell secretary to Governor Macquarie. These "magistrates, principal merchants, and gentlemen of Sydney formed the majority of those agreeing to the outline Constitution of the Bank of New South Wales that was published on 30 November 1816. Many were also significant issuers of promissory notes which the proposed bank was supposed to make redundant. The

active role played by Macquarie's administration in promoting and founding the Bank of New South Wales is particularly noteworthy.

52   Ibid, p. 12. Holder notes that the record of this meeting is the first entry in the minute book of the Bank of New South Wales.

53   In the early 19th century, all banking companies (defined as companies engaged in the business of banking) were legally partnerships with unlimited liability. This meant that their members accepted that they were personally responsible for any losses the business may incur. When losses were large, as in the case of the City of Glasgow Bank in 1858, many members of the company could be forced into bankruptcy. Such unlimited liability was, at the time, considered to be an important guarantee of the moral probity with which the banking business would be managed.

54   Holder: op cit, 1970, p. 17.

55   Ibid, p. 16.

56   Ibid, p. 51.

57   The risk of a loss of confidence in the management of the Bank of New South Wales was real. In 1820 the Chief Cashier, Francis Williams, was asked to resign for making unauthorised loans amounting to £2,000. By January 1821, a full accounting of Wiliams's activities revealed a shortage of £12,000 in notes. Apparently, Williams was in the habit of issuing notes as a favour to friends and had given credit for payments which were never made. Despite the fact that he had gained nothing from his actions he was charged with embezzlement. See ibid, pp. 29–30.

58   See Report of the Select Committee on High Price of Bullion, GBPP, 1810, 349, Vol 3, pp. 1–252.

59   They were often issued by banks on behalf of the customers. In doing so, bills were transformed into bank instruments which meant that a holder of a bank bill had a claim against a bank of known reputation rather than on the parties to the underlying trade the credibility of which might be difficult to establish.

60   Accepting a bill involved stamping or signing the bill for which a fee was charged. If the bill was not paid on presentation, the holder of the bill could have recourse to the accepting house for payment.

61   Butlin, op cit, 1968, p141. This was the practice of merchants like John Blaxland, John Dickson, S Lord, P Carrigan and Daniel Cooper.

62   The reasons for doing this are obscure. The policy appears to have been advocated by Major Gouldburn, Colonial Secretary and Deputy Commissary-General Wemyss and rooted in their long-standing antipathy Macquarie's enforcement of "sterling" and a general dislike of the Bank of New South Wales. See ibid, pp. 144–146.

63   For a broadly-based discussion of these links see Herman M Schwartz: *In the Dominions of Debt: Historical Perspectives on Dependent Development*, Ithaca, Cornell University Press, 1989.

64   In Australia, after 1830 and in New Zealand after 1850.

65   This is not to mention the significant impact it had upon the development of particular regions within the colonies. For example, it is doubtful whether Hobart and Sydney could have grown as they did in the absence of the activities of the Commissariat. In addition, it seems clear that, in New Zealand, both Auckland and Wellington benefitted considerably from war finance whereas Nelson remained relatively untouched by it.

66   The economic structures of Australia and New Zealand, especially in the long 19th century, have a significant feature in common; namely, they must accept (or take) prices secured on commodities sold on international markets to pay for imported capital goods the suppliers of which are able to exercise a degree of market power which allows them to be price makers.

67   In New Zealand, as a whole, the proportion of total landed estates in fee simple was undoubtedly larger than the proportion held under other forms of tenure. However, the extent of landholding in the South Island and Hawkes Bay was such that the total acreage under leasehold was larger than the acreage of freehold.

68   For further details see George J Goschen: *The Theory of Foreign Exchanges*, London, Effingham Wilson, 1898 and Paul Einzig: *A Dynamic Theory of Forward Exchange*, London, Macmillan, 1967.

69 Bedford, op cit, 1916, pp. 7–13 reproduces a circular despatched on 30 May 1846 entitled "Regulations and Conditions for the Observance of which Provision should be made in the Charter or Legislative Enactment relating to the Incorporation of Banking Companies in the Colonies". It precisely reflects this policy approach and includes the provision that the "Debts and Engagements of the Company on Promissory Notes, or otherwise, not to exceed at any time thrice the paid-up Capital with the additional amount of such Deposits as may be made with Company's Establishment by individuals in Specie or Government Paper." An earlier version called the Treasury Regulations for Colonial Banks was issued in 1840 copies of which were not transmitted to New Zealand because it was still being administered from New South Wales.

70 This did expose colonial banks to significant credit risks when either export prices or the price of land fall. In that case, borrowers had access to lower incomes with which to service outstanding debt and the securities against which that debt was secured are of lower value. Thus, both the Australian and New Zealand monetary systems were forced to endure periods of significant losses, bank collapses, bankruptcies and great business and political uncertainty.

71 In 1894–1896 the Bank of New Zealand Ltd. was effectively nationalised by the New Zealand Government to prevent its closure and in 1911 the Federal Government of Australia founded the Commonwealth Bank of Australia.

72 Many of the techniques of banking that were refined in Australasia before World War I were originally developed to facilitate the capture, transportation and ownership of slaves, the ownership and development of plantations and the sale of the products forthcoming from them. By the late 18th century banks located in UK ports associated with the slave trade, like Bristol, Glasgow and Liverpool, were at the centre of important financial networks (composed of so-called country banks) which were beginning to find a wide variety of outlets for their expertise and resources in the British Empire. P J Cain and A G Hopkins: *British Imperialism 1688–2015*, Third Edition, London, Routledge, 2016, note at p. 83 that "An alliance between land and money was firmly in place well before the economic and political consequences of industrialisation compelled attention."

73 Butlin, op cit, 1961, p.155 records that in the case of the Union Bank of Australia in New Zealand during the early 1840s "business was necessarily mostly exchange, with some holding of deposits and modest note issue".

74 Chief among them in New Zealand was the Bank of New Zealand founded by a cabal of Auckland speculators in land and other assets who had intimate connections with leading figures in Provincial and National governments. It was closely associated with Thomas Russell, Minister of War, John Williamson, Superintendent of Auckland, Frederick Whittaker, and Edward Stafford both sometime Prime Ministers of New Zealand.

75 Keith Sinclair and WF Mandle: *Open Account: A History of the Bank of New South Wales in New Zealand*. Wellington, Whitcombe & Tombs, 1961, p. 34. David Larnach, Managing Director and Chairman of the Bank of New South Wales 1853–96, wrote in 1865 that he "… prepared to agree that advances to squatters were 'perfectly legitimate' if 'confined to not over 5s per head upon sheep, and so long as you have a substantial Merchant between you and the Squatter' ….

76 Sinclair and Mandle, op cit, 1961, p. 44.

77 The records of the Judicial Committee of the Privy Council at this time appear to be incomplete and it is not possible to give a precise reference for this judgement. However, it is recorded that in 1870 a case between John Cherry and two others and the National Bank of Australia ruled that the assumption of landed title by the bank was judged to be legal because it took place as a result of the borrower defaulting on the conditions agreed in the original transaction contrary to the Sale of Goods Act and so happened in the normal course of banking operations. See humanities-.research.exeter.ac.uk/privycouncilpapers/public/trial/view/id/1088?order=searchRank&direction=ASC. Accessed 15 March 2021.

78 The words "acquired in the course of its banking business" proved more than sufficiently capable of flexible interpretation to permit banks operating in the Australian colonies and in New

Zealand to become, by 1890, very substantial lenders against landed securities.

79 The fineness of gold specified by different monetary authorities varied. In the United States Gold Standard Act 1900, it was 90% pure and in Russia it was 99%. The Royal Mint regularly sampled the gold content of the gold coinage it issued called the Report of the Pix. The mints at Melbourne and Sydney consistent recorded gold content in excess of 95%.

80 There never was a precise definition of circumstances that were considered "abnormal". It was often equated with "unexpected" and so was coloured by personal and professional judgement about the honesty and professionalism with which the bank concerned was run.

81 This feature means that it is debateable to label the Gold Standard System as a system at all.

82 The role of acceptance houses is unclear at this time. Later in the century and particularly before World War I the London Accepting Houses Committee became very influential albeit highly secretive.

83 Many of the so-called disciplines of the Gold Standard system only emerged to public view during periods of financial instability when rescues were organised among banks. But it should always be recalled that many of the arrangements were negotiated in extreme secrecy and it is possible that the "rules" that were allowed to appear in public may have been nothing more than an acceptable story for public consumption.

84 See Sinclair and Mandle, op cit, 1961, pp. 235–236, Appendix 2, The Banking Agreement of 1868 in which deposit and lending rates are agreed between the main banks. Its title suggests that negotiation of this agreement was at least an annual event.

85 Neo-classical economic theory asserts that open price competition between firms like banks leads to supply of the maximum flow of product at the lowest possible price for all customers. However, this conclusion may not hold true in the presence of risks and uncertainties, the management of which is assisted by the existence of banks.

86 There are tales, no doubt apocryphal, that managers of the local branch of a pastoralist's stock and station agency were given a standing order that when the cheque for the season's wool-clip arrived he was to despatch a new dress to the farmer's wife.

CHAPTER 4

MARKETABLE LAND IN AUSTRALASIA

Colonial development in Australia and New Zealand rested upon the ability to translate land into money and turn money into land. Only then did it become possible for someone to buy land cheap and sell it dear. During colonisation the meanings of both land and money changed. The meaning of land was defined so that it became as much like money as possible while money was re-invented so that it could stand for a given piece of land. This Chapter describes how this was achieved in Australia and New Zealand.

The Meaning of Land
Few historians have enquired about the meaning of the term "land" that was in common usage in England and Australasia at the end of the 18th century.[1] "What was meant by land?" is an important question because answers to it throw light upon what the various parties to British colonisation (non-indigenous settlers, Aboriginal peoples, Māori, prospective emigrants and the British Government including its colonial administrations) each perceived as the nature and extent of customary and legal titles and the various personal and collective rights that emanated from them. This is quite apart from the many customary meanings that the term "land" and its variants like "country", "soil", "earth" and "demesne" have accumulated over the years.[2] It is perhaps the main inheritance of the Norman Conquest to modern-day Britain, that land has come to be defined, almost exclusively, as a lawyerly entity of crown-granted landed estate within the Common Law. The result was that in the British Empire the legal meaning of land became paramount and other more customary and colloquial usages were largely overridden, ignored or forgotten by the post-Norman Conquest legal system and other, less formal, social processes.

It took more than three generations to establish and enforce the Common Law throughout the Australasian colonies. It is by no means certain that all parties to the colonisation of Australia and New Zealand shared even a broad conception of the meaning of "land" during the long 19th century. For much of that time, the apparently neutral action of merely calling something "land" often provoked misunderstandings and disagreements that deeply influenced colonial social relationships.

In the Common Law according to Blackstone:

> "Land hath also, in its legal signification[3], an indefinite extent, upwards as well as downwards. … So that the word "land" includes not only the face of the earth, but every thing under it, or over it. And therefore if a man grants all his lands, he grants thereby all his mines of metal and other fossils, his woods, his waters and his houses, as well as his fields and meadows."[4]

By this legal principle, anyone in legitimate possession of land can determine the use of the land surface specified in the title deed also the air above it and the ground beneath to the centre of the earth. Blackstone makes it plain that this does not mean that a person's ownership is absolute or allodial[5] because:

> "… it being a received, and now undeniable, principle in the law, that all the lands in England are holden mediately or immediately of the king. … A subject therefore hath only the usufruct, and not the absolute property of the soil."[6]

This doctrine implies two important conditions. First, the crown absolutely owns the land over which it is sovereign and grants title to an estate in it through the exercise of the Royal Prerogative. This landed estate can be bought and sold. But it means that should the land become owned by no-one then title to it immediately reverts to the crown estate. Since the Glorious Revolution in 1688, the Royal Prerogative has been exercised, in practice, by the government of Great Britain. The power it embodies is not supposed to be arbitrary which means that the government should not place limits on the ownership of landed estates without offering fair compensation.

Second, the granting of title to an estate in land means that the terms of the original grant can be altered by a subsequent exercise of the Royal Prerogative through changes to the "law of the land." An early example is the Case of Mines of 1568 which established that all mines of gold and silver in England belonged to the crown[7] in the person of the sovereign. This right was transferred to the crown in the form of government representing the people by the Bill of Rights 1689 during the Glorious Revolution when the Divine Right of Kings was abolished or, perhaps more precisely, subsumed by the Parliament of the representatives of the people.

Starting in the twentieth century, in both Australia and New Zealand, the crown in the form of the government has, by legislation, reserved to itself the ownership of a wide range of minerals deposited beneath the surface of the earth and rights to access the air above.[8] In addition, over the last two centuries the crown has progressively reserved rights to access for many network services such as roads, wharfs, water and sewerage reticulation, telecommunications[9] and gas and electricity supply systems thereby, in effect, retrospectively changing the terms of the original crown grants under which the land in question is held. Blackstone opined that, under the Common Law, such legislation is lawful[10] provided it is not arbitrary and is performed with caution.[11] This process has occurred at different times and to different extents in different colonies with the result that even the legal meaning of "land" has taken a different meaning in various parts of Australasia from that it takes in England and Wales.

Land in New South Wales

The Common Law meaning of land in New South Wales is like that articulated by Blackstone. The title to land is derived originally from a crown grant made under Royal Prerogative nowadays exercised, in practice, by a representative democracy. In theory, the grant extends beyond the land surface it defines upwards to the heavens and downwards to the centre of the earth. But over time, this extent has been limited and landowners no longer own a wide variety of minerals and other resources which Blackstone's definition includes. For example, Section 7 of the Crown Lands Act 1884 passed by the New South Wales Parliament states:

> "All grants of land issued under the authority of this Act shall contain a reservation of all minerals in such land and shall contain such other reservations and exceptions as may by the Governor be deemed expedient in the public interest."

Section 7 also provides that owners of title to land containing minerals may be permitted to remove those minerals only on payment of a royalty and subject to prescribed conditions.

It is almost impossible to express Aboriginal people's meaning of land that they occupied into the language of the Common Law.[12] At the time of the First Fleet and before, Non-indigenous people had no understanding of the ways of life of indigenous Aboriginal peoples.[13] The many different languages, the absence of permanent settlement and sustained agriculture, the lack of shared experience, the fleeting periods of contact all meant that non-indigenous people learned little about the variety of ways that Aboriginal peoples related to the land they inhabited. Much of our current knowledge about this matter represents a reconstruction of the past created for our own times and purposes. It now seems that Aboriginal peoples roamed over a clearly designated territory that was "owned" by no person or institution (in the sense of holding a sole unchallenged right to control usage and to alienate) and upon which succeeding generations subsisted without apparent alteration to their environment. But it is also possible that this interpretation may be mythical.

A more careful[14] description was published in 1845 by Edward Eyre, the explorer and colonial administrator,[15] who took considerable pains to understand the customs of Aboriginal peoples during the late 1830s and early 1840s. In his discussion of Aboriginal property in land[16] he states:

> "It has generally been imagined, but with great injustice, as well as incorrectness, that the natives have no idea of property in land, or proprietary rights connected with it. ... As far as my own observation has extended, I have found that particular districts, having a radius of ten to twenty miles, or in other cases varying according to local circumstances, are considered generally as being the property and hunting grounds of the tribes who frequent them. These districts are again parcelled out among the individual members of the tribe. Every male has some portion of land, of which he can always point out the exact boundaries. These properties are subdivided by a father among his sons during his own lifetime, and descend in almost hereditary succession. A man can dispose

of or barter his land to others; but a female never inherits, nor has primogeniture among the sons any peculiar rights or advantages. Tribes can only come into each other's districts by permission or invitation, in which case, strangers or visitors are always well treated."

It is not possible to judge at this distance in time the accuracy of Eyre's account or how relevant it was for New South Wales in the late 1780s. Eyre was not an expert anthropologist and was writing about his experiences in the late 1830s, more than 40 years after the arrival of the First Fleet. Moreover, it is possible that his account was coloured by a desire to impress George Grey who was soon to be made Governor General of New Zealand. Nevertheless, the Colonial Office soon appointed Eyre to New Zealand as Lieutenant Governor of New Munster which suggests that his views were accorded a measure of respect[17] at the time.

In his review of the founding of the colony of New South Wales, Professor Attwood argues that anthropological observations, like those of Eyre, did not impinge on the way colonisation was set in train. Indeed, it appears that the leaders of the First Fleet made no attempts to negotiate access to land with the Aboriginal peoples but also the Colonial Office made no subsequent attempt to ensure that the omission was rectified. He provides three reasons for this[18]:

1. "Despite quite frequent communication between Governor Phillip and his officers and the tribesmen at no stage did it result in a change in British preconceptions about the primitive character of Aboriginal society
2. There was no need for Phillip to negotiate about access to land because the colony was initially well-resourced in this regard. It was also believed that Aboriginal peoples could contribute nothing other than seafood which the British could harvest themselves. In any case, Phillip realised that the superiority of British arms and the decimation by British-borne disease would ensure British access to any amount of land should that course of action become necessary.
3. The conditions which led to a kind of negotiation of sovereignty in New Zealand were absent in New South Wales before 1800. Entry by Britain was abrupt and there was no time to build an understanding of language, customs and social organisation. Moreover, unlike New Zealand in the 1830s, there was minimal competition with other would-be colonising powers such as France (the immediate presence of de la Pérouse notwithstanding), Holland, Russia and the United States that conceivably might have forced Phillip into negotiation."

None of these reasons is particularly persuasive, especially during the years following the initial period of colonial establishment. First, Phillip took considerable pains to learn the local dialects and entertained Aboriginal people for considerable lengths of time. It is true that this did not appear to enable a significant increase in understanding. To find reasons why this was so we will probably have to enquire into the limitations in the experience, education and training of Phillip and his officers and those overseeing their actions. Second, the initial period of relatively plentiful stores was succeeded by two or three years of increasing starvation which would normally have increased pressure to develop alternative home-grown food supplies and access to cultivable land. That this does not appear to have occurred in the case of New South Wales may be because the colony lacked the wherewithal (e.g., capital goods plus agricultural expertise and effective planning) to make this a practical policy option and so was forced to continue to rely upon unreliable imports of stores in order to forestall widespread malnutrition. Third, it seems likely that the absence of rapidly increasing demand for land from settlers meant that the colonial administration did not recognise the need to secure suitable land from Aboriginal peoples before the 1820s. So, in summary, it seems that the British Government colonised New South Wales for no better reason than it could do so without risking becoming embroiled in costly hostilities with Aboriginal peoples or other colonial powers and because it meant that the government could transfer a pressing domestic political problem to the colonies far out of plain English sight.

If this assessment is an accurate representation of official British thinking, it is also evidence for a total absence of planning or design for the future Australasian colonies. It shows that a well-established, long-term policy agenda was not in place before the First Fleet sailed nor for some decades afterwards. It also implies that the legal and political heritage established by the British Government was the result of choices made under short-term pressures as circumstances changed. Moorehead suggests that the relationship of the Aboriginal inhabitants of New Holland to their environment was of an unconscious intimacy that was different from that enjoyed by Māori:

> "They had the art of living for the day, they knew how to laugh and enjoy themselves, and if they had no ambition at least they possessed the Greek quality of Φιλοτιμώ—the knowing of one's place in the world."[19]

But caution is necessary. It is quite impossible to make any kind of judgement about the level of intimacy with their environment enjoyed by Aboriginal peoples compared with that enjoyed by Māori. Unless new evidence emerges, no answer to this question can possibly be based on fact.

No such sensibility was shared by most of the convicts and their guards. There is no place in the Aboriginal or Māori worlds for Common Law ownership of estates in land by individual persons. But there may be armed resistance when the sound of marines' or colonists' muskets drives away the birds that would otherwise be trapped or netted for food. Inevitably, attempts at cultivation by convicts and their keepers encroached upon the Aboriginal peoples' hunting grounds and with Aboriginal people for the same fisheries.[20] But for Aboriginal peoples and Māori living communally, such competition for things is not merely a matter of a dispute between alternative owners; between individual, self-interested dogs quarrelling over a bone. It runs far deeper than that. Competitive individualism was and still is, an active denial[21] of the legitimacy of the community upon which was founded the very existence of the societies formed by Aboriginal peoples and Māori.

Moorehead describes Aboriginal society collapsing into extinction[22] over the next 40 years along with its tribal laws. European diseases such as smallpox, whooping cough and measles played their part as did sterility as a result of Venereal Disease and wholesale killing of Aboriginal people by settlers. Of Aboriginal peoples he says:

> "They thought that their tribal hunting grounds were their own, and when they found this was not so, that they owned nothing, that they had virtually no rights of any kind, that they were aliens in their own country, they were bewildered and resentful; and when all their protests failed, they succumbed into listless serfdom."[23]

The lost unique, intimate relationship between Aboriginal peoples and the country they inhabited has been more recently described. For example, Ambelin Kwaymullvia wrote in 2005:

> "For Aboriginal peoples, country is much more than a place. Rock, tree, river, hill, animal, human—all were formed of the same substance by the Ancestors who continue to live in land, water, sky. Country is filled with relations speaking language and following Law, no matter whether the shape of that relation is human, rock, crow, wattle. Country is loved, needed, and cared for, and country loves, needs, and cares for her peoples in turn. Country is family, culture, identity. Country is self."[24]

The contrast between this description of Country and the Common Law description of land is stark.

These multi-dimensional descriptions of land show how the Common Law concepts of landed estates and their tenure are but a shadow of the ideas upon which notions about communally-held land were founded. By isolating certain legally defined properties from the more holistic, traditional notions of land, the legal system allows some degree of commensurability between pieces of land to take place but omits the very characteristics which make a piece of land valued by its proprietors. If ever an attempt were made to translate the concept of land understood by Aboriginal peoples into the Common Law it is obvious that it would face considerable conceptual and linguistic problems. Those problems would require much advice from Aboriginal peoples, Māori, anthropologists and lawyers skilled in framing widely-accepted legal documents. No such attempt was tried in New South Wales. As we shall see the attempt made to do this in New Zealand was never attended by the requisite skills or knowledge to make it work.

But these difficulties were unimportant compared to those which sprang from the Pandora's Box of land tenancy as it was opened by the colonisation of New South Wales. Whether or not the land surface of the continent of Australia was or was not owned by its indigenous Aboriginal occupies in the late 18th century is still a matter of heated dispute.[25] For our present purposes, however, the outcome of that debate matters little. The crucial fact is that it was firmly believed in official circles in London that the British Government had followed up Cook's "discovery" with "possession"[26] in the form of the convict colonies at Sydney Harbour and, later, Norfolk Island and Tasmania. In 1788, Britain alone had chosen the burden of exercising sovereignty over New South Wales, and no person owned any part of it. Hence, the British Government in the guise of the

Crown could unilaterally make indisputable grants of its land surface[27] without needing to consult its Aboriginal occupiers on the matter. The British arrived in 1788, planted a colony with convicts and did so without entering into a conversation about the future guardianship of the land.

Crown grants could be very simple in this newly-settled world because they did not need to take account of many pre-existing conditions and circumstances. Ownership, in the British sense, did not exist in New South Wales when non-indigenous people were planted. As a consequence, there was no need to construct deeds to landed estates which traced the chain of previous ownership back to an original grant by the sovereign as was the case in English law. Or, if there was, the chain of past owners was very short and simple to describe. It was possible in everyday practice to define a piece of New South Wales solely by its cadastral boundaries abstracted from its physical features, historical associations and place in the community. Starting from such an abstract grant it is a relatively short step to achievement of registration of title to land.[28]

The extent to which this simplification, obtained by selecting a single feature of land, assisted in developing the finance of trade in land cannot be underestimated. An indisputable abstract title divorced from history, other sections of land, and details of ownership and usage has many of the features of a bill of exchange the value of which does not depend on the physical characteristics of the underlying trade, or even the reputation of the parties to it, but rather solely upon the trust with which its acceptor is viewed. A landed estate is land shorn of the very properties which make it valuable to a community. The absence of the complexities of history, social relationships, physical features, and cultural associations makes land defined in this way easy to trade. The management of land within a wide portfolio of securities is also facilitated because different types of landed security can be compared consistently by the financial yield each produces. Once such landed estates are classified according to the risks they embody, lending against the security of land is greatly facilitated.[29]

Crown Wastes

The term "waste" has taken a variety of meanings over the years. To the British Government in the 1830s it meant nothing more than the land for which the crown had no purpose that could be decerned by the government of the day. Such land was deemed surplus to the needs of the crown and could be sold or given to other owners. Governor Gipps still believed that the crown held its landed estate as a trustee for the benefit of all the people of the British Empire. But increasingly demands for colonial land as a source of profit became more insistent and it appeared that the crown's landed estates were preventing people from bettering their lives by settling in the colonies.

In 1842 the British Government linked the proceeds of land sales with the work of the Colonisation and Emigration Commissioners to protect indigenous people and to encourage settler immigrants. It passed legislation to ensure that the only disposals of crown waste lands throughout Australasia would be by means of grants in fee simple purchased at public auction. On 22 June 1842, the British House of Lords passed The Waste Lands Act[30] into law. This was "An Act for regulating the sale of waste land belonging to the Crown in the Australian colonies". This system was authored by the Colonial Office in London and allowed no exceptions:

> "1. ... within the Australian colonies the waste lands of the Crown shall be disposed of in the manner and according to the regulations hereinafter prescribed and not otherwise."

Nevertheless, colonial Governors were allowed to exempt land from sale so that it could be reserved for the use and benefit of Aboriginal inhabitants. The Colonisation and Emigration Commissioners had the duty, dating from their formation on 10 January 1840, to:

> "... guard [indigenous people] against personal outrage and violence; to protect them in the undisturbed enjoyment of their proprietary right to the soil, wherever such right may be found to exist; to make it an invariable and cardinal condition in all bargains and treaties made with the natives for the cession of lands possessed by them, in occupation or enjoyment...."[31]

In the Australian context, Reynolds and Dalziel also remark that:

> "... revenue generated by land sales was to be used to fund emigration and after the enactment of The Sale of Waste Lands Act 1842, fifteen percent of the Land Fund was to be expended for the benefit, civilisation and protection of the Aborigines."[32]

The exemption of the lands of Aboriginal peoples is listed together with a long list of other uses. These included military defence, public worship, schools, cemeteries, quays and landing places and land required to fulfil promises to Military and Naval Settlers.

All land put up for auction was to be first surveyed at the expense of the colonial authorities. Lots could not exceed one square mile. Lots were designated as Town Lots covering all the land within a designated town, Suburban Lots located within five miles of a designated town and Country Lots consisting of the remainder. A minimum upset price was set at £1 per acre although the Governor could raise this. A deposit of 10% of the purchase price was due on the fall of the hammer with the remainder due in one calendar month.

The Act also instructed the Colonisation and Emigration Commissioners[33] to devote "... one equal Half Part at least of..." the gross proceeds of the sales of waste lands to the payment of passages of selected emigrants who could not afford the fare to the colonies. This introduced the principle of assisted passages for poor immigrants.

Finally, the legislation gave Governors the ability to negotiate sales of blocks of more than 20,000 acres by private treaty. These blocks did not have to be surveyed although they had to be recognisable by landmarks which would be surveyed. The boundaries of the blocks were to form parallelograms in which no side shall be more than twice the length of any other side.

In order to make a profit from raising sheep, pastoralists could not usually afford to buy the extensive acreage necessary. Leasing of the land was their only option (aside from leaving farming altogether). But the 1842 Act did not allow crown lands to be leased to pastoralists for longer than one year, which for colonies in Australia, especially New South Wales, was a major omission. Indeed, it forced Gipps to employ the device of issuing annual licences of occupation (as distinct from longer-term leases) for pasturing of stock in order to circumvent the problem.

Although New Zealand was included in the list of Australian colonies it seems unlikely that the 1842 Crown Waste Lands Act had any effect upon the country. The reason is that the colonial government in New Zealand had first to purchase any land it offered for sale to settlers. But by the time the 1842 Act became law it seems probable that that the colonial administration in New Zealand was bankrupt. Hence, it simply did not have the resources to make the 1842 Act a reality. The failure of land auctions to provide a sound footing for the Colony of New Zealand meant that it was necessary to replace at least some of the provisions of the 1842 Act as they applied to New Zealand. The 1842 Act was repealed by the Waste Lands Act 1846[34] which also removed New Zealand from its scope.

Crown Land in New South Wales

From the outset of non-indigenous settlement, the British Government assumed that the entire land surface of Australia was already the property of the crown because it agreed to exercise sovereignty over the entire continent without exception. Indeed, it presumed that since Cook claimed British sovereignty over New South Wales at Cape Weymouth on 21 August 1770 Great Britain owned the surface of Australia, everything above it and everything below it to the centre of the earth. Hence, the British Government set about distributing the land as if the entire continent of Australia consisted of crown land.

In recent years, a vivid illustration of how this occurred has been reported as part of the Griffiths Case heard before the Supreme Court of the Northern Territory. This litigation concerns a successful claim for compensation from the Government of Australia by the Ngaliwurru and Nugali peoples who are members of the Makalamayl, Wujaiyi, Yanturi, Waitawul and Maiyalaniwang estate groups. It was found that these people had rights over land located at the confluence of the Victoria River and Timber Creek in the Northern Territory which were constrained or nullified by various government actions. The background to the case provides a clear and legally verified account of how the land in question became commodified.

In 1855 Augustus Gregory was employed by the West Australian Government in marking out roads and stock routes and exploring for grazing lands. He was appointed to lead an expedition comprising 18 men to explore the north of Australia. He sailed from Moreton Bay in August 1855 and reached the Victoria River in the following month. Gregory established a base camp at the confluence with Timber Creek and explored the surrounding country. The report he presented on his return indicated that the Timber Creek area had extensive areas of grazing.

But it was some time before non-indigenous people arrived in Timber Creek. Some pastoral leases[35] were granted in the Victoria River district in the late 1800s but it was some time afterwards that the various holdings were stocked with cattle. Even later still Timber Creek became a centre for the supply of cattle stations in the surrounding district. Increasingly, Aboriginal peoples were excluded from their traditional lands by the owners of cattle stations. The result was:

> "During these early years of settlement, relations between the local indigenous groups and the European settlers ranged from open warfare, and massacres, to what was at times friendly cooperation."[36]

It was not until the early 1900s that Aboriginal peoples were recruited to work on the cattle stations. Between 1920 and 1960 a rhythm of work was established in which the at the beginning of the wet season the stock camps closed and the Aboriginal workers "returned to the bush" only to return for the next season. Wages were often paid in kind in substandard goods and at rates below those received by non-indigenous workers. Aboriginal women were employed as poorly remunerated domestic servants and often the subject of physical and sexual abuse. Housing was primitive and often without potable water and sanitation. Unsurprisingly, dissatisfaction let to strikes at Pilbarra in 1946 and at Wave Hill in 1966. The latter dispute lasted 7 years and resulted in some land grants to Aboriginal peoples.

It is with considerable trepidation that I try to draw lessons from this short sequence of events. Nevertheless, it is remarkable that these events did not take place very quickly. The various stages by which settlement was established such as discovery, occupation by settlers, stocking, fencing and irrigation and slaughter of cattle for market were separated by considerable gaps in time. Each stage involved changes in land tenure and the development of new financial methods to pay for the required investment. Eventually the rights of run-holders conflicted with the way of life of Aboriginal peoples so seriously that only the Commonwealth Government could untangle the differences to permit commerce to continue.

Discontinuous development of this type consigns many commercial activities to mayhem or illegality for periods of time. This is because, for example, as cattle are introduced, Aboriginal peoples attacked them as if they are game with the result that runholders attacked the indigenous people. Only when means of co-existence, like work as stockmen or domestic servants are innovated will this stage of development end and another begin. It may be that the norms of everyday life in a country that is owned by nobody but many have use of it may become characterised by rough justice dispensed within communities closed to the outside world.

Land in New Zealand

In New Zealand the ownership of land, although not the nature of the land itself, has been the subject of active controversy from the day that settlement in the country was first mooted. A wide range of opinion about the compatibility of the concept of ownership common among non-indigenous people with Māori culture still exists. Different legal structures have tried to mimic features of tribal proprietorship[37] within the framework of personal ownership.[38] This involves attempting to describe communal proprietorship of land in terms Common Law title. For the most part, these attempts have failed and have left a bequest of new problems for those who inherit them.

The form of tenure to the title of a landed estate in New Zealand, has been overwhelmingly one of *fee simple* despite the deep inconsistencies between Māori communal values and the principles of individual property rights in Common Law. Yet, despite these obvious, fundamental and long-standing differences, no attempt has ever been made in New Zealand to find systematic ways of reconciling them except in isolated cases. The exceptions include entities like the Thermal Region of Rotorua,[39] Lake Waikaremoana[40] or the Whanganui River.[41] In those cases, the entity in question is deemed to be "owned" by itself or by no individual person. In effect, legislation has decreed, on a case-by-case basis, that certain entities are deemed to be subject to ownership arrangements peculiar to themselves. Such exceptions mean that the "land" in question is perpetually removed from any legal processes which involve its alienation. They do not, therefore, involve changing the meaning of the term "land" albeit in the above cases they cease to be "land" in its fullest sense. The land involved in all the exceptions remains cadastrally-defined pieces of landed estates just as it is recognised by the Common Law.

Limitations to the rights attached to "land" similar to those to be found in Australia have also been introduced into New Zealand Common Law from time-to-time. They have generally involved taking away rights which owners of land would expect to otherwise enjoy. Nowadays, they include use of air rights without Government permission and ownership of deposits of uranium, oil and gas and precious metals. But again, the land underlying this type of legislation is the land recognised in Common Law.

Remarkably, Māori culture has barely touched the idea of New Zealand land. We can gain some idea of how little when we contemplate the following account of what tribal land meant to Māori everyday existence:

> "… the pre-European Māori had come to understand the relationship of one resource to another and of each to the environment as a whole.
>
> The forests provided much of the raw material for their economic activities. It provided timber for a wide range of purposes, bark for roofing, raupo for thatching, toetoe for lining, aka creepers for eel pots and lashings, harakeke or native flax for clothing, cordage and nets.
>
> The forest also provided food. Edible berries were collected from kahikatea, rimu, matai and miro trees. Hinau yielded an edible pulp. The Māori also cultivated vegetable food.
>
> Mineral resources were utilised to manufacture tools. Basalt, different varieties of greywacke and other rocks provided stone for adze blades, pounders and sinkers. Obsidian flakes were fashioned into knife-like implements. Greenstone supplied material for adzes and chisels. Sandstone was used for grinding.
>
> Animal products were used in a wide variety of ways. Whalebone was used for combs, ornaments, pins, fish-hook barbs and weapons. Dog skins and bird feathers were utilised for cloaks.

The rat, dog, many species of birds and virtually all accessible species of fish and shell fish were drawn upon for fresh food."[42]

Durie CJ[43] has stated:

"The land was a whole entity. Soil, rocks, sand, water and air were part of a territory but different parts were distinguished for the purposes of use by individual members."[44]

While the land was held communally certain individuals had "the right to extract, subtract or sever different resources at prescribe places based on historic use".[45] So the meaning of land to different members of the community differed according to history and circumstances. But that meaning always remained within the gift of the community and so could be reversed or augmented.

Such a rich list of resources could potentially be accessed by a variety of hapu,[46] sometimes from other tribes, at different times or on different occasions. Pan-hapu and pan-tribal relationships were thus created. But to sustain them required an investment in the sort of constancy and care that all but the most dysfunctional families enjoy from, and bestow upon, their members. In another context, this has been explained in the case of Māori as:

"… the very notion of ascertaining 'ownership' involves an outright rejection of the paradigms of tikanga Māori whereby people were of the land and did not 'own' it."[47]

Presumably, this is also the idea that is also being conveyed when Aboriginal peoples were described by explorers as "nomadic" or as "hunters and gatherers".

Because resources varied from place-to-place in New Zealand, Māori created no single form of relationship with the land they occupied or method of land management.[48] It is difficult to find evidence that the settler-dominated Parliament (once it was finally established in 1855) attempted to accommodate the complexity of the concepts of land commonly-held within Māoridom.[49] Rather, it is common to find references to Māori "communism" or "beastly communism" when the question is discussed. It is also true that, beginning with the ascent of Governor Grey in 1846, New Zealand settler politics set about ensuring the assimilation of Māori on terms largely of Grey's own making. It is therefore unremarkable how little legislation was affected by Māori culture in the first 25 years of New Zealand's membership of the British Empire.

The Legal Framework: New Zealand

The concept of "owning" land in the sense of controlling its use and alienation, without risk of challenge, was imported into New Zealand in the minds of non-indigenous people and their English-trained lawyers. Most non-indigenous people originated in England and relatively few came from Scotland where a different system of property law prevailed. When those same immigrants came to explain Māori land tenure they usually adopted a conceptual framework and a vocabulary which had become engrained over many centuries of legal practice in England.[50] Before 1840, by complete contrast, determination of the rights and wrongs of the proprietorship of land in New Zealand was, in practice, largely in Māori hands.[51] There is, therefore, no reason to believe that, in 1840, at the time of te Tiriti and the Treaty[52], it was possible to readily translate concepts such as "own", "sell", "alienate", "dispose", or "purchase" from Māori to non-indigenous settler culture and vice versa.[53] For at least a generation, Māori and non-indigenous residents often talked past each other when land or landed interests were under discussion. Indeed, it might be possible to sustain the argument that only with the emergence of John Ormsby, Wi Pere and Wi Parata after the end of the New Zealand Land Wars, that Māori understanding of non-indigenous meanings of land began to develop. Despite the radical views of John Ballance and Sir George Grey, who were both enthusiastic advocates of land nationalisation, understanding of what land meant to Māori achieved less progress.[54] Moreover, Māori practice in land dealings changed as sales took place. Indeed, the very act of engaging in sale and purchase of land and other things with non-indigenous people changed the way Māori did things and, over time, how they thought about land. Hence, nowadays, it is often impossible to reliably disentangle so-called traditional Māori practices from accounts by non-indigenous people of presumed Māori behaviours.[55]

Before 1840, non-indigenous people gained access to extensive estates especially in Northland. Although the transactions involved were often couched in terms which mimicked the appearance, even if they did not represent the substance, of the Law of Contract,[56] two features mean that they were not contracts legally binding in Common Law.[57]

First, there seems to have been widespread misunderstanding about the nature of many of the agreements. Some non-indigenous people believed that the land in question had been purchased outright in the European sense that an individual person obtained the right to control its use and to alienate the property to another. They believed that all other claims to the land had been quieted and unquestioned control over its future use and ownership had been passed to them as purchasers. Hence, subsequent to concluding the transaction, such non-indigenous purchasers assumed that they exercised full control over the use and disposal of land without regard to the claims of others or of its previous "owners".

Non-indigenous ownership of this kind was in direct contrast to Māori beliefs that only some forms of occupancy and use were allowed to non-indigenous purchasers and then only in the expectation of receiving a variety of forms of on-going service in return.[58] As a consequence, there was often much dispute about the terms and conditions of the transactions and the adequacy of any consideration involved. To some extent, these arguments were suppressed by the growing practice of negotiating and settling purchases in the presence of all interested parties.[59] But the steady stream of petitions and complaints concerning land transctions that has continued ever since is testament to the fact that suppression is not the same as quieting claims, let alone conclusively (or finally) settling them or redressing wrongs.

Second, the Common Law probably did not extend throughout New Zealand until shortly before World War I. Until the Common Law extended throughout the country, no legal jurisdiction existed in New Zealand that could legally adjudicate upon criminal acts or civil disputes. In 1840 the establishment of the English Common Law system was regarded by many Māori as the main potential advantage of agreeing to te Tiriti. But it would not be for at least another generation until this advantage became available to most of them in most of the country. It is true that when the Native Land Court was set up in 1865, under Chief Justice Fenton,[60] it could be said that some form of consistent adjudication of disputes about Māori land ownership became available throughout New Zealand.[61] But, in setting up a special Court in which claim and counter claim about landed estates was adjudicated, much was lost because the Court employed a standard,[62] formulaic[63] process of investigation and sometimes took little notice of the intricacies of Māori culture.[64] In any case, the Native Land Court was an inadequate substitute for the fall majesty of the Common Law which was overwhelmingly available only to Māori leaders.

Meanwhile, the ownership of Māori land was publicly discussed largely in terms of the problems faced by non-indigenous settlers in trying to acquire title to landed estates. Settlers, brought up in the shadow of the enclosures of common land, had come to realise that communally-held rights could not be depended upon. In the British Isles, communally guaranteed rights of access to land and land-based resources were undoubtedly valuable and often meant the difference between survival and death from starvation in the "hungry months" of the year[65]. But such commons could easily be destroyed by powerful magnates and landlords who then enclosed them for their own purposes and profit.[66] This provides an abiding negative memory and sound reason why settlers tended to seek title to land in *fee simple*. By contrast, Māori regarded land as the source of life and a fount of resources the use of each might involve a manifold of rights of use. Moreover, settlers and their trappings might be regarded as an additional resource the rights of access to which could be claimed. Thus, if we take the perspective of the purchase of a fixed block of land, many different rights might have to be quieted depending on the number and nature of the resources involved if anything like the level of control traditionally implied by a *fee simple* title is to be established. This might take some years if the use rights can only be exercised at greater than annual, or at unpredictable, intervals.

The establishment in New Zealand of *fee simple* title to land was encouraged by the Colonial Government and, more particularly, its agent, the New Zealand Company[67]. The latter emphasised the availability of fertile land and the fact that crops could be grown throughout the year. In one leap would-be settlers could avoid the twin scourge of landlordism and the hungry months. But this could only be true if *fee simple* title could be established in place of Māori communal ownership. Hence, the very basis of the colonisation that was embarked upon in New Zealand actively invited deep conflicts between cultures. It is clear that such conflict was anticipated by Colonial Office officials who provided permission for Governors Hobson, FitzRoy and Grey to provide for exceptions for Māori within the operation of Common Law.[68] Some even opined more generally that a standard Common Law approach to legality should be softened so that different systems of the law would apply in different countries.[69] This did not occur to any meaningful extent and land laws in New Zealand were based upon an insecure foundation of unresolved, unacknowledged and deep-seated conflict between cultures, which subsequent political developments were ill-prepared to solve.

By 1840 the British Empire was becoming a field over which British capitalists roamed in search of profit and the constant aim of the Colonial Office was to facilitate settlement by non-indigenous people. This meant that land had to be made available in a form that settlers wanted, which meant it had to have the following characteristics:

- Land defined by its cadastral boundaries fixed by survey lines rather than defined by geographical limits to socially-determined rights or cultural memories[70];
- Title to land must be represented by a very long, unconditional lease from the Crown, e.g. *fee simple*, and held by individuals so that, for example, there is no commons and no customary access or use;
- Title means that all alternative claims on the land or rights over it must have been quieted[71] so that control over the use and alienation of land must be in the hands of the title holder; and
- The value of titles to land must be allowed to rise over time to provide capital gains to purchasers and to attract the next generation of settlers.

These features were introduced virtually from the foundation of the Colony[72] and remain at the heart of the notion of land in New Zealand to this day.

Until early 1840,[73] the land surface of New Zealand was presumed by Colonial Office officials to be owned by its Māori proprietors[74] and, unlike Australia, could not be legally occupied unless purchased.[75] From the outset, the Colonial Office, envisaged that the government of New Zealand would be financed from the profits earned from the sale of land to settlers. That was as true for the British Government as it was for the New Zealand Company. But before settlers could be sold land, the colonial administration had to purchase land from Māori so that it could be endowed with a crown-granted title and on-sold.[76]

In New Zealand the British Government had a two-fold aim when it introduced a pre-primary and primary market for land to New Zealand. First, it sought to ensure that all land in New Zealand would eventually be derived from some form of title ultimately derived from the crown. Second, it judged that market processes, however approximately followed, were sufficiently fair and reasonable to justify the belief that traditional Māori rights of use and occupation had been fully and fairly extinguished. The confluence of these policy aims is clearly shown in the working of two commissions[77] set up to investigate pre-colonial land purchases and to recommend crown grants for legally valid land claims.

The first was inaugurated in September 1840 by New South Wales legislation.[78] Three Commissioners (Francis Fisher, Colonel Edward Godfrey and Captain Matthew Richmond)[79] were appointed by Gipps to enquire into the validity of land purchases in New Zealand prior to colonisation. Its work began in January 1841 and did not end until September 1844.[80] The second was appointed by Lord John Russell and comprised William Spain, who, on Hobson's instructions, investigated land purchases by the New Zealand Company. Spain's enquiries lasted from May 1842 until September 1844.

There appears to be no record of the criteria that were applied by either commission in making judgements about the validity of land claims. The matter appears to have been left to the discretion of the commissioners. But they commanded little inkling of what the elimination of customary tenure would be in New Zealand. This is shown by the choice of legal commissions rather than open-ended consultation to investigate and settle the concerns of Māori and non-indigenous people about land ownership. It was widely believed by the political classes in England that "true" title to land was created solely by permanent occupation and cultivation and that land tenure that did not satisfy all three criteria of permanence, occupancy and cultivation did not truly constitute ownership by anyone.[81] Thus, all land adjudged not validly purchased did not revert to its original owners but rather became the crown's property. Both commissions, in keeping with this highly individualistic notion of ownership, born of intensive land use in long-settled societies, supposed that a valid transfer of title would have taken place when all relevant parties knew what was being transferred, knew what consideration had been paid and agreed to make the transfer and accept the payment.[82] In effect, the commissioners tried to find evidence of the existence of some species of individually negotiated contract. Presumably, the commissioners assumed that such contracts were the natural outcome of a market for land in New Zealand.[83] But, in retrospect, it is now plain that such an assumption is unwarranted. Contracts can be onerously obtained, may have unforeseen adverse consequences and may be deliberately constructed to deny some parties of their legitimate rights. Such possibilities seem not to have been entertained by the commissioners.

When no evidence of a contract could be found the claim was disallowed and the land concerned became part of the crown estate contrary to Hobson's explicit promise at the hui at Waitangi. Thus, not just land claims by non-indigenous people were at risk in the hearings before the commissions. Unless Māori could also legally prove that they permanently occupied and cultivated the land in question then their proprietorship might also be terminated and the land in question added to the crown estate. In this way, the first two land commissions set a precedent which left Māori out of the policy discussions about land questions and used narrow English legalism to secure Māori land for non-indigenous settlers. But with the appointment of Lord John Russell as Secretary of State in late 1839, land ownership became increasingly discussed in terms of occupation and use or "subjugation" of the land. So it was that in 1846 Earl Grey instructed Governor Grey that Māori ownership of land extended only to those pieces which were occupied and cultivated. All remaining land was owned by nobody and so was crown estate.

In the event, Governor Grey did not faithfully obey Earl Grey's arguments.[84] Faced with a population that was overwhelmingly Māori, many of whom had grown doubtful about the guarantees contained in the Treaty of Waitangi, he could not implement the radical changes to the ownership of land envisaged by the British Government. Instead, he temporised.[85] First, he cloaked his actions within a stream of elaborately misleadingly[86] optimistic reports about how rapidly Māori adopted the Common Law and were assimilating into New Zealand every-day life. Second, behind this over-optimistic public screen he cultivated personal relationships with certain powerful chiefs through appointments, presents, loans, pensions and visits and used the generous grant-in-aid afforded New Zealand by the British Government to undertake a formidably ambitious programme of land purchase sufficient to satisfy the likely future demands of prospective non-indigenous settlers. Hence, he was able to simultaneously avoid censure from his masters in London[87] and from settlers. By such means he could leave the difficult issue of what was meant by landed property in New Zealand to be resolved by someone else and to another time when non-indigenous settlers formed the majority of the population.[88]

Thus, it was not until after the first settler government was formed under the New Zealand Constitution Act 1852 that the full-bloom of the Lockean view of land ownership was translated into the narrow legalism[89] that passed for legal process in New Zealand during the second half of the 19th century[90]. For that, three steps were taken: First, it was necessary to instil individual title in land[91] in *fee simple* among Māori; Second, to install a stand-alone Land Court to investigate land ownership, the judgements of which could not be challenged by the Supreme Court because the Native Land was designated a Supreme Court and so constituted its own Court of Appeal; and Third, to preside over or condone a range of legal, but nevertheless unethical practices[92] which were remarkably successful in helping land speculators, local businessmen, existing and new settlers and financiers to prise Māori land away from communal tribal ownership.[93]

It also transformed the meaning of land because certificates of title issued by the Land Courts referred to areas of land or pieces defined by fixed and impermeable boundaries, without any reference to their history, traditional usages and cultural significance for local people. This meant that Māori land could become what settlers wanted; a commodity to buy and sell solely at face, or exchange, value. It nevertheless also served as a constant reminder to Māori of their culture which had been deliberately left out of the deliberations of the Land Court.[94]

Sales of Crown Waste Lands

On 3 September 1840, E Deas Thomson (New South Wales Colonial Secretary) wrote to Hobson telling him that he had approved of a number of concessions for Government officers serving in New Zealand.[95] The reason given was that, in a world before the invention of public transport, government officials required to live somewhere close to their place of employment.[96] So, it was considered necessary to reserve from the public auction allotments suitable for their accommodation. For example, those earning at least £200 per annum and whose duties required residence in the town could claim immediate possession of one town allotment of no more than a quarter of an acre in return for a deposit of £5. The remainder of the purchase price would be payable when an average price for the block or section is established on the basis of the sale prices of one third of the allotments in that situation.[97] Other, less valuable, concessions, were available to those earning between £100 and £200 per annum or not considered as having to live in town to perform their duties.

These concessions provoked anger especially among those closely associated with the activities of the New Zealand Company in Wellington despite their having been authorised in New South Wales and some months before Hobson became legally responsible for the auction of crown waste land in New Zealand. Nevertheless, despite the legality of the procedure, accusations of sharp practice have continued to be made down the years.[98] For example, Stone[99] reports that both Mathew and Cooper asked Hobson for permission to select lots in the new capital before the public sale of crown land. According to Stone: "The governor agreed to concede this privilege to all officials, provided that, after the first auction of town lands, they paid the average price realised for similar lots at the sale." This description represents nothing more than an imprecise summary of the instructions that Hobson received from Gipps's Colonial Secretary.

Bassett[100] is also highly critical of Hobson's closest associates. He claims that the officials had an unfair advantage because they had prior knowledge of the sites to be auctioned and the upset prices that were set by the Government. It is true that publicity of the sale was limited[101] by the haphazard publication schedule and very limited public circulation of the first "Government Gazette" and the lack of an Auckland newspaper before the *New Zealand Herald and Auckland Gazette* commenced operations in July 1841. It is also true that Shortland (the then Colonial Secretary), Mathew (Surveyor-General) and Cooper (Colonial Treasurer) each made substantial purchases at the auction in addition to taking advantage of the allotments reserved to them. Whether these circumstances were sufficient to unfairly manipulate market outcomes remains debatable in the absence of other evidence. Bassett neglects to point out that upset prices had been set by Ripon's Rules for nearly a decade and the demand for town lots from Sydney speculators was such that the land on offer was a matter of common knowledge. He also ignores the fact that some officials under the terms of Gipps's circular could, in effect, access credit granted by the Government that was not available to other purchasers. This is likely to have been a far more potent source of market disturbance than anything mentioned by Stone or Bassett. Nevertheless, it is on such flimsy evidence that accusations of corruption and peculation on the part of Hobson's entourage have been sustained for over a century and a half.

After the sales, it was complained that the officials of the Colonial Government took advantage of these concessions to manipulate the subsequent public auctions for personal gain.[102] Contemporary Auckland and Wellington opinion and a procession of subsequent historians have labelled these concessions as the cause of "land jobbery". Three officials, in particular, are suspected of profiting personally from organising the land sales; namely, Shortland, Mathew and Cooper. By contrast, Hobson has been judged "squeaky clean".[103]

On 9 December 1840, Lord John Russell wrote to Hobson about the sale of the crown demesne.[104] He instructed that Hobson should first clearly separate the crown demesne from the lands of private persons and those retained by Māori. Once done, the sales should proceed according to "fixed principles":

1. All Crown lands should be surveyed as soon and as accurately as possible.
2. From these land reserves should be set aside for public use.
3. No public land "is ever disposed of gratuitously."
4. Surveyed districts are to be disposed of by public sale at a uniform price.

5. "Every possible method is to be adopted for expenses of the Land Department, including surveys, and other works as may be indispensable to give an exchangeable value to the land."
6. No more than 50% of the net sale proceeds will be deducted for public services or benefit of Māori.
7. Such a deduction of 50% will only be made when there is a deficiency of other sources of funding for such services.
8. At least 50% of net proceeds should be spent on assisting emigration.
9. Emigration will be effected by, or under the supervision of, the Colonial Land and Emigration Commissioners.

These principles were already well-established in New South Wales. In particular, the crown demesne could not be sold without first being surveyed. The first surveys were conducted at the expense of the crown. In the following years in New Zealand, the costs of survey, which were substantial, were transferred from the crown to the Māori proprietors.

The New South Wales Government Gazette, Issue 23, Tuesday 22 March 1841, re-published a notice of sales of town allotments in Auckland dated 25 February 1841 signed by Willoughby Shortland, Colonial Secretary. It is difficult to judge how widely the news of this sale was propagated given that, at the time, New Zealand had no Government Gazette of its own and no daily newspapers. The conditions of sale had been refined since Goderich's time and the latest version was set out in September 1840. Gipps instructed that they be read out at the commencement of every land auction.[105] He also ruled that that the notes of existing Sydney banks would be accepted in payment for land in New Zealand and that the balance remaining after payment of the deposit could be remitted either in Sydney or Auckland.[106] On 19 and 20 April 1841, the first sale of town allotments was held. This was followed by a sale of suburban sections on 1 September 1841. These suburban lots put up for sale, together with the Government's upset price of each, were listed in the *New Zealand Herald and Auckland Gazette* of 10 July 1841.

In the first two auction sales held in 1841, on 19 and 20 April and on 1 September, the crown encountered strong demand for allotments. It seems that bidding was infected with speculative fervour that was not repeated for some years. Between 19 April 1841 and 19 November 1851 the crown conducted 51 separate public land auctions.[107] (This excludes transfers to the New Zealand Company, which occurred in January and February 1844, under the terms of the 1841 agreement concluded with Lord John Russell.) Between February 1842 and June 1844, 979 allotments were offered for sale but purchaser bids were not forthcoming on 749 of these.[108] This period coincides with a severe recession in New South Wales and New Zealand. Butlin stated of New South Wales that:

"Sales of Crown land were £324,072 in 1840, only £92,174 in 1841 and a mere £9,174 in 1844."[109]

Comparable data do not exist for New Zealand. Nevertheless, there is evidence to suggest that a pattern similar that found in Australia occurred in New Zealand. First, land sales in New Zealand went through a similar slough judging by successful sales of crown land. Second, it was in this period that land sales by the New Zealand Company fell to low levels. By May 1843, it had become clear that the Company's debts could not be serviced and its bills were being dishonoured in London. In mid-1844, the Company suspended its operations.[110] Third, this period coincides with retrenchment by the Union Bank of Australia of its New Zealand operations.

For a colony such as New Zealand with no effective method of tax collection, this lack of land sales dramatically reduced the revenues of the Colonial Government so that its usual costs could no longer be met from revenue. This fact seems to have paralysed government administration which continued to offer land for sale as surveys were completed but without great financial success. With Hobson's death on 10 September 1842, Shortland as Colonial Secretary was left in charge of the government of New Zealand. He dealt with the chronic weakness of government revenues just as if he were left in charge of a Man-o'-War[111] on foreign station. He issued, as Hobson did before him[112], bills drawn on the UK Treasury that the UK Government honoured. But such actions were merely a stopgap. By the time Governor Fitzroy arrived in New Zealand around Christmas Day[113] 1843,[114] the finances of the New Zealand government were not only decrepit[115] but also misleadingly reported.

Despite land sales being at the heart of its plans the UK Government neglected to provide sufficient funds for land purchase yet burdened the New Zealand state with a large, expensive and obligatory Civil List.[116] The results were that settlement was held in check and the colonial administration had recourse to financial arrangements for which it did not have time to arrange prior approval from the Colonial Office. They included issuing more bills drawn on the UK Treasury to meet current expenditure[117] and issuing debentures in small denominations as legal tender. It would appear that lack of finance for the colonial administration was a perennial problem. This was not assisted by the haphazard and inconsistent way that the colonial government's accounts were drawn up between 1840 and 1842.[118] Shortland appears to have investigated the possibility of waiving the crown's right of pre-emption while he was Acting Governor following Hobson's death.[119] However, it was left to Governor FitzRoy to introduce a number of innovations which included waiving crown pre-emption to try to bring a semblance of order to colonial finances.

Pre-Emption Partially Waived

Before he departed from England, FitzRoy asked Lord Stanley, then Secretary of State for War and the Colonies about the possibility of waiving pre-emption "under certain defined circumstances"[120]. Stanley's concerns were almost entirely financial. He advised FtzRoy that:

> "In the event of its being advisable to waive pre-emption, [he] was to keep two objects in view. Europeans were to be prevented from acquiring land from Māori at a cheaper rate than they would have encountered if they had acquired land from the Government[121]. And if such purchases were made a contribution should be paid by the purchaser to the emigration fund, perhaps concurrently

with payment to the Māori owners. A portion of this payment, equivalent to at least the amount required under the Imperial Act [of 1842], could then be devoted to emigration."[122]

Governor Robert FitzRoy arrived in New Zealand, around Christmas Day 1843. Shortly afterwards he discovered that he had been seriously misled about the state of the New Zealand public finances.[123] The New Zealand economy, along with that of New South Wales, was in depression. The government finances almost entirely depleted.[124] The colony was £24,000 in debt, many public servants had not been paid for some time, some government revenues owed to the government had not been received and the colonial government's credit with the local branch of the Union Bank of Australia was all but exhausted.[125] Revenue from land sales had virtually ceased. The crown was effectively incapable of exercising its right of pre-emption. FitzRoy is quoted as stating to the Legislative Council on 23 May 1844:

> "... that when he left England the Government there had an impression that New Zealand could pay its own expenses, even at the rate of 50,000l per annum...."[126]

Governor FitzRoy announced to a gathering of Māori chiefs on 26 March 1844 that he would entertain applications to waive the crown's right of pre-emption. Māori chiefs were told that they could deal directly with purchasers for the sale of "a few hundred acres"[127] provided they paid a duty to the crown of 10/ – per acre and provided permission from the government was obtained beforehand. Such sales would be investigated to ensure that they were prudent and would not lead to problems for tribes in the future. Successful purchasers were issued with a certificate which could then be used to apply for a confirmatory grant from the crown one year after the date of purchase. On 10 October 1845 a second proclamation reduced the duty on sale to one penny per acre.[128] The immediate result was a temporary rise in land sales.[129]

It seems likely that the Colonial Office was just as misled as FitzRoy about the state of New Zealand finances. The Colonial Office expressly forbade the issue of debentures to cover any deficit in the government budget or to reduce the colonial establishment paid for by the Civil List. Shortage of Colonial Government funds prevented significant land purchases by the crown, and many Māori had expressed dissatisfaction to FitzRoy about their inability to sell land. FitzRoy was acting within a series of interlocking cleft sticks. He wrote to Lord Stanley on 15 April 1844, as follows:

> "I cannot break up the Government establishment without your Lordship's express authority; I cannot reduce the salaries of officers whom your Lordship has authorised to receive them; I can neither raise nor draw bills,—and until the Legislative Council has met and passed an ordinance, I cannot raise supplies by taxation."[130]

FitzRoy energetically cast about for solutions to the multiple political and financial dilemmas[131] that he faced. First, like his immediate predecessors, FitzRoy issued debentures drawn on the UK Treasury to which the Legislative Council gave the status of legal tender[132] within New Zealand.[133] Second, he tried to institute a policy of free trade with its associated loss of customs revenue. He proposed that this shortfall should be met by direct taxation on land and houses; a form of wealth tax. Such was the opposition from settler interests that he was forced to abandon his plans for taxation of capital in favour of new and higher customs duties which were re-established in April 1845.[134] Third, he suggested to gatherings of Māori chiefs that he might find a way round the straitjacket of the Waste Lands Act by adopting the stratagem of Governor Gipps who gave permission for occupation of land under short leases. Fourth, on 27 February 1844, he waived the right of pre-emption in favour of the New Zealand Company[135] over 150,000 acres for the proposed Scottish settlement in New Munster, up to 150,000 acres in or near Wairarapa and not more than 250,000 acres elsewhere in the North Island. Fifth, Fitzroy proclaimed that, subject to a long list of conditions, he was prepared to waive the crown's right of pre-emption over some parts of Auckland. But, despite all these measures, in the absence of proceeds from renewed land sales the public finances of the colony were destined to remain in a state of collapse.

Auctions of New Zealand land held by the crown during 1843 and 1844 were largely ignored by prospective bidders. In an attempt to revive transactions in land, Fitzroy announced, on 26 March 1844, that, upon application to the Governor, where considered appropriate, the crown could forego its right of pre-emption and would allow suitable prospective European purchasers to deal directly with Māori sellers. Conditions were attached to the transactions which meant that there was nothing like free trade in Māori land. They included reserving one acre in ten for the purposes of supporting the building and use of schools or hospitals or general Government purposes, payment of a fee of 4/– per acre on application for a waiver, making a crown grant after at least 12 months had elapsed since the payment of this fee for which 6/– per acre would be charged and survey of the allotment at the cost of the purchaser.[136] However, after initial sales of 600 or so acres, sales again languished and Fitzroy reduced the duty payable to 1d per acre on 10 October 1844. This resulted in the sale of around 100,000 acres in quick order.[137]

It is unsurprising, but nevertheless remarkable that even *in extremis* Fitzroy chose not to alter the legal characteristics of New Zealand land that had begun to evolve.[138] Applications for a waiver of crown pre-emption over a specified area of land had to be made in writing to the Governor who would then either issue a consent or refuse.[139] In making his decision the Governor was to take the following factors into account:

- The nature of the locality;
- The state of neighbouring and resident Māori;
- The abundance or deficiency of land;
- The disposition of the Māori concerned towards the Europeans and the Government; and
- The views of the Protector of Aborigines.

No waivers were to be given for sites of pa, urupa or land about them. No waivers would be given in the area between Tamaki Road and the sea to the north. All surveys of land under waiver must be performed at the purchaser's expense.[140] One-tenth of land purchased under waiver must be conveyed to the crown for public (especially Māori) purposes. A fee of 10/ – per acre is payable for the nine-tenths of the land over which consent for a waiver is granted, to be devoted to the general purposes of government. Deeds of transfer must be deposited with the Surveyor-General as soon as practicable. At least 12 months must elapse between the granting of consent and the issue of a crown grant for which a fee of 4/ – per acre is payable. On 10 October 1844 a further proclamation reduced the payment due to the government for a waiver from 10/ – to 1d. It is estimated that 148 claims (47 under the March Proclamation and 101 under the October) were preferred under the two proclamations entailing somewhat less than 100,000 acres were sold under the two FitzRoy proclamations.[141] Some land involved in the Orakei Claim, situated in or near Remuera, was sold under FitzRoy's second proclamation.[142] For the most part, the natures and location of these claims and the identities of the beneficiaries of the abandonment of pre-emption await detailed investigation. Dr Maurice Ormsby correctly points out that the question of who benefitted from the suspension of pre-emption and to what extent remain to be systematically explored.

Incipient insurrection among northern tribes and concerted defamations in London by settler interests meant that Fitzroy was recalled in late 1845. Like much of the Colonial Office's dealings with FitzRoy the management of his replacement was so ham-fisted as to be deliberately malign.[143] FitzRoy was relieved of his commission as Governor in a dispatch from London dated 30 April 1845 that was received in New Zealand on 1 October 1845.[144] The decision was announced to the House of Commons on 5 April 1845 and had become common knowledge in New Zealand by mid-September.

The Meaning of Land Ownership

The discussion of Māori land ownership is couched in largely non-indigenous concepts using terms such as "titles", "claims" and "rights". The earliest official investigation of the matter appears to be that of the Board of Enquiry into Native Affairs which reported in July 1856. It stated:

> "NATIVE TITLE TO LAND AS TRIBES …
>
> 4. It appears that the title or claim to land by Tribes, arose from occupation, dating sometimes from remote periods, and from more recent conquests, followed by occupation either by themselves personally or by remnants of the conquered people.
> 5. That this title existed no longer than could be defended from other tribes
> 6. That the boundaries were in some cases clearly defined and admitted by adjoining tribes, but that in many others they were quite the reverse, and were causes of constant quarrels.
> 7. That narrow belts of land as being claimed by two tribes, could not have been occupied by either without causing a call to arms. That there is no part of the country which is not claimed by some party or another."[145]

This represents a fair summary of the information, that was current among officials of the colonial government, about the ownership of Māori land during the 1850s and 1860s.

It is noteworthy because it is written from the perspective of senior chiefs who would be most concerned with matters of high policy for their tribe or iwi, such as warfare or land sale. It is also silent about what ownership of Māori land means for the occupiers. Since then, surprisingly little written about land in New Zealand has been concerned with the nature of land ownership among Māori. If we are to take most non-indigenous commentators at face value there is virtually no variation in the forms of communal Māori ownership and the rules that determined how they operated.[146] Yet even under a regime of predominantly individual ownership it is possible to conceive of, and, in some cases, identify a wide variety of methods of communal ownership. It seems likely that a similar variety of arrangements also existed in Māoridom before and after 1840. But, at that time, few observers thought it worthwhile to report upon them. So, we have no accurate points of comparison between then and now.

Thus, we must start at a different place and journey in a different direction from that taken by English law, if we are to throw any light at all on Māori communal land ownership systems. Carwyn James has argued:

> "The legal and political legitimacy of constitutional arrangements within the Māori world must be understood as an assessment of mana, not only in the context of other fundamental values, but also in the range of sources of mana and the accountability and authority inherent in the different sources of mana. Mana is the central concept of Māori leadership, and at its core is the idea of spiritually sanctioned authority. An individual's mana comes from the gods, one's ancestors, and one's own actions. It has therefore been described as a power, influence and authority that is both ascribed and achieved.
>
> The land itself is a source of mana. To be more precise, it is the development of a relationship with the land that accrues mana. Ownership per se is not the key criterion, rather it is the occupation and use of the land over generations that would establish mana. This relationship with the land must be based on substantive action and cannot be purely exploitative."[147]

If then we push open the door labelled mana we might find some answers to the questions we raise. However, first we must note that James's view is apparently directly contradicted by Fenton who stated:

> "There is no such thing as *mana* of land. *Mana* is personal. A chief may—or might have had, I should say, for the day is past—sufficient *mana* to greatly influence his power of managing or directing the disposal or withholding from sale of land, but this power is derived from his position of *pater populi,* [the father of], enabling him to protect what he thinks to be the interests of his tribe. He may have no interest in a piece of land, yet able to retain it from sale. I have never recognised or believed in the existence of such an intangible thing as *mana,* as unrecognisable as the consequential damages were by the Alabama Commission.[148] None of the old Judges recognised such a thing as land *mana* as conferring a title to land recognisable by the Courts."[149]

We should recall that Fenton was the "old Judge" who designed, drafted much of the legislation for, and set the procedures and protocols of, the Native Land Court, over which he presided as Chief Justice for nearly 20 years. There are elements of prospective self-fulfilment and retrospective self-justification in such statements. It is hardly surprising, therefore, to learn that the Native Land Court did not regard mana of land as evidence of title. But, as an economist who has survived for more than 70 years without benefit of formal legal training, I find it surprising to learn that Fenton, who apparently had no difficulty in accepting the lawyer's creation myth embodied in the "Crown", found the idea of mana to be "intangible".

By contrast, Edward Shortland, who observed and recorded Māori culture over many years, was of the view that mana of the land arose from the original proprietorship assumed upon possession of previously unoccupied land. He said that mana in its ordinary use signifies power but when applied to land it "corresponds somewhat to the power of a trustee".[150] Thus, *rangatira* could apportion land among their relatives and other members of a tribe according to well-established rules, which were considered fair and reasonable. Once made, these allocations gave good title to beneficiaries and their descendants. The mana over such appropriated land was with the head of the family in rightful possession. This description is consistent with the view that the central political institution in Māoridom during the 18th and 19th centuries was not iwi (or tribe, nation) but, in reality, were hapu (or sub-tribe, clan).[151]

Indeed, crown colony administration, successive settler governments and the Native Land Court found it convenient to deal with a version of Māori authority simplified into a few distinct tribes and leading chiefs. For example, Ballara, describing the Manawatu-Rangitikei purchase in 1849 states that:

> "… McLean arrived to buy the land, insisting that Ngati Apa reunite themselves to sell and receive the purchase price. He informed them that he would not acknowledge any interior boundary in their sale within the limits of their claims in the mountain ranges… McLean also imposed a pyramidal model of the tribe on Ngati Apa by refusing to accept that individuals could belong to more than one hapu…"[152]

This suggests that, in McLean's eyes at least, it was important to ensure that land payments were distributed on a hapu-by-hapu basis.[153] Each member of a hapu was apparently duly recorded as receiving his or her share so that it was not possible for someone to receive more than one share even if they could establish claims through more than one hapu.

Ballara also argues that where a paramount chief who supported land sales could not be found, it was common to 'manufacture' one. The example she gives is that of Te Hapuku who was encouraged and supported by McLean to ease land sales throughout Hawkes Bay.[154] Thus, modern conceptions of the tribe or iwi as a paramount political and social organisation among Māori may be an artefact arising from interaction with non-indigenous institutions such as the Native Land Purchase Commission, the Native Land Court and the Waitangi Tribunal. By contrast, Ballara asserts:

> "... it must not be forgotten that many patterns of local Māori behaviour, including the paramount importance of hapu in economic and social organisation, persisted relatively unchanged from at least the 18th to at least the mid-20th century."155

The crucial role played by hapu is endorsed by Firth. He argues that:

> "Data as to the precise definition of rights as between the *hapu* and the tribe are difficult to obtain, due partly to the lack of clear distinction between the two social units. The actual position seems to have depended very much on the status of the *hapu* concerned, some being important enough to rank practically as independent tribes, others of lesser size being much more closely affiliated with the parent body."156

It is to be expected, therefore, that the management of land within Māoridom is much more akin to the management of an inherited family concern than of an asset with exchange value. Much land is under the proprietorship of particular families whose title is unquestioned from generation-to-generation. Errors and encroachments would be confronted and managed as they occur. The produce of the land would be the property of its proprietors. But, proprietorship never extended to an ability to alienate the land to someone outside the tribe without openly seeking and obtaining agreement from all concerned. Even then, it would be possible for very powerful chiefs to veto the alienation.

This is precisely the situation in which Governor Gore-Browne found himself when negotiating the purchase Teira's land in Waitara in the face of stated opposition from Wiremu Kingi Rangitake. It mattered not one jot that Wiremu Kingi had no personal claim on the land because, as a senior chief, he was acting in his role of trustee over what he believed to be the long-term interests of his people. It is also very likely that Teira was mobilising Gore-Browne's interest in purchase as a way of indirectly challenging the chiefly authority of Wiremu Kingi.

This method of owning land has usually been termed "collective" or "communal". Not infrequently it has been equated with communism and, particularly in the 1850s and 1860s, often qualified by the term "beastly". However, so far as is known no studies have been undertaken into the precise forms of ownership and control of land that were actually exercised by hapu. Yet, it is known that a number of possible alternative collective structures can be envisaged each of which is consistent with the general idea of communal control of property. They include, but are not necessarily confined to:

- Cooperatives in which each member shares in the ownership and benefits of the land;
- Corporations by which land is owned by an entity that is owned by a community;
- Trusts that hold and manage land on behalf, and for the benefit, of beneficiaries who may yet to be born;
- Partnerships formed by an agreement between independent parties to pursue a particular business or social goal;
- Condominium Associations formed by all those who have the right to use the

land but none of whom own it; and
- ❖ Land that is itself regarded as a natural person and so legally able to own itself, e.g. the Whanganui River.

The Waitangi Tribunal noted in its Muriwhenua Fishing Report (Wai 22)[157] that the rights[158] of hapu took a number of forms. For example, it noted that:

> "The location of traditional fishing areas is known by Māori today and was much commented on by early European visitors… Best… observed: Thus, in former times the Ngai Turanga hapu of the Urewera had rights to the waters of the Turanga river between Otara and Okehu… they had the fishing privileges of the stream. Beattie… noted that in Southland the natives assembled every October and November to catch lamprey. The best stations on the river were well-known, and only certain hapu had the right of working them. Nicholas… commented on the existence of sharply defined fishing rights at Kawakawa in Northland, the limits being marked out by stakes driven into the water. He observed several rows of these stakes belonging to different hapu, each having their prescribed boundaries…"

Each of these communal forms of ownership is governed by its own set of rules. Under Common Law, such rules would have to be generally specified in considerable detail in writing. They can become the subject of litigation based around the rights of individuals that have been specified. Such rights to land might be split between different people, places and times and may be part of complex hierarchies in which a given right will supersede another right if the circumstances dictate. By contrast, in families, like hapu, these matters are not normally formally litigated. Usually, they are raised, discussed, sometimes at very great length, and decided upon. During each step of this process unwritten rules and protocols will guide family members and others entitled to participate to behave appropriately.

When McLean, Chief Commissioner for the Purchase of Native Lands, appeared before the Waikato Committee in 1860 at the bar of House of Representatives the following interchange was recorded:

> "Will you describe the meaning of tribal right in regard to the transfer of land?—It varies so much in different parts of the country, I should wish to know what particular part of the country you refer to, as the custom which prevails in one place does not in another."[159]

Later he was pressed further on the same subject:

> "When a *hapu* alienates, who represents it, and is the consent of all its members necessary?—In some tribes the different *hapus* must be consulted, in others the chiefs; much depends upon the personal character of the latter. I did not say that *hapus* or subdivisions of tribes had not a right of transfer of property. The various *hapus* or families which compose a tribe most frequently have the right of disposal, but not always; the custom varies."[160]

McLean summed up the situation by saying that Māori "have no fixed rule". He most assuredly did not say that Māori do not follow any rules; he was at pains to emphasise the great variation in practices that existed at the time of his speaking.

Despite the diversity of local customs, it is, nevertheless, possible to deduce some general governance principles. If no effective rules exist to regulate communal activities, then group possession of property places every member of the group in a position of responsibility or liability for the actions of every other member. This is the case irrespective of the individual legal positions of the members. If it is believed that society is best advanced by individual enterprise and ownership seeking its own destiny, then having to devote resources to deal with such collective liabilities and responsibilities will be regarded as detracting from the achievement of society's full material potential. But communal responsibility may also be the result of close interdependence between the owners which may occur for reasons other than ownership of property held in common. For example, we might think of interdependencies resulting from downstream pollution, pollination by bees and moths sharing airspace or access to shared resources like stocks of fish. Other sorts of interdependence conceived in shared experience or born of genealogy, for example, might prove to unify society thus reducing potentially wasteful conflicts. By the same token, the structure of the rules and regulations of the owning community may serve to mitigate the adverse consequences of such interdependence. Unfortunately, there appears to have been little investigation, apart from that of Ballara, of the ways in which Māori communal ownership of land and other resources was regulated in practice during the 19th century.

By contrast, for followers of Locke, land could only be owned by people who had changed it some way. Changes were limited to cultivation which, in the Māori world, could shift over considerable areas during a succession of growing seasons; construction of residences; and establishment, of burial places. Those politicians of a Lockean persuasion might argue that much of New Zealand in 1846 consisted of land which was not immediately used by Māori in these ways. Benthamites could look askance at large areas left apparently untouched for long periods. Hence, followers of John Locke and Jeremy Bentham could agree with Earl Grey's view that ownership of land by Māori was distinguished by cultivation and occupation and that what remained was "waste", the ownership of which the crown could assume.

It should be recalled that this course of action was seriously proposed by the Secretary of State, Early Grey, in 1846 without compensating those who claimed proprietorship of the land and who formed the vast majority of New Zealand residents at the time. Nevertheless, even before settlers formed a majority of the population, the same arguments, augmented with moralistic overtones, could be heard in support of a wide range of actions aimed at gaining access to Māori land. For example, Walter Brodie was bold enough to assert:

> "It was, I repeat, we who made New Zealand what it was in 1840; we, by personal sufferings and exertions, laid the foundation of an empire; we civilized and Christianized the savage; we broke up and cultivated the soil; we introduced cattle, trade, and the arts of civilized life. This land, once a land of

terror, had become by our means the safe abode of men of all nations. We by purchasing their lands, which were perfectly valueless to the native, gave them the value which they now possess; and without us, the Governor would never have been invested with the rule of the Antipodes."[161]

Despite Brodie's rhetorical flourish and obvious prejudice, experience proved Earl Grey wrong. Virtually all of the South Island and most of the North Island of New Zealand had been purchased by the crown from Māori. It is true that in the subsequent century many adjustments to the purchases were agreed or imposed. These often took the form of compensatory payments of money, land or other assets. But, that most of New Zealand was destined to be purchased[162] rather than conquered, means that, in practice, the experience of settlement showed the wisdom of the belief, current in the 1830s, that Māori were indeed the original owners of all the land of New Zealand. Consequently, there was no "waste" anywhere. Thus, including such waste lands in the crown estate would have the effect of cutting the tribes affected off from possible future economic development based around use of that land. In some cases, this has meant that sales and purchases of land made long ago by ancestors of present-day Māori and for which inadequate compensation was paid nowadays may attract a payment to compensate for the deficient prices originally paid.[163] On the face of it, it is nowadays accepted that the land was originally alienated in exchange for a consideration, i.e. sold, by Māori. It follows that it is now accepted that Māori held an ownership interest in the land in question. It will be recalled that it was Marshall CJ's view that Aboriginal proprietors had no ownership interest in the land they occupied. As a consequence, they held nothing that could be sold (or given) to another. It is not known whether or not the historical process outlined above has led to a questioning of Marshall CJ's doctrines of Aboriginal title. At the very least they must be considered seriously open to question even if they cannot be judged dangerously misleading.

Yet this interpretation neglects to mention that before Great Britain took possession of New Holland and New Zealand two distinct types of customary practice which governed the use and ownership of land; one Aboriginal and the other Māori. It is now impossible to be certain, but I presume that these practices evolved over many centuries and were widely known and widely accepted and followed. With colonisation, the convicts, settlers, missionaries, officials and their fellow travellers brought with them the law of property relation encapsulated in the Common Law of England. Now, suddenly, Australia and New Zealand each had two types of rules governing how land was to be used and distributed; neither of which could be translated into the others. British colonial governments also set about imposing the Common Law on their newly seized territories in place of Aboriginal and Māori traditions. In so doing, anyone with some knowledge of the Common Law was advantaged over the most powerful, erudite and persuasive of indigenous people. Moreover, in this unpremeditated action a problem was posed to succeeding generations which has never yet been solved; namely, do traditional practices have a place in ruling colonial society and, if so, how can that result be achieved?

Chapter Notes

1. In New Zealand the list is largely confined to Richard Boast, Sir Eddie Durie and Ann Parsonen.
2. Classical economists regarded "land" as all the gifts of nature embodied in a section of the surface of the earth. Such a view regards land solely as a factor of production measured in terms of the quantity of a well-defined good. When regarded as part of s state of nature a given piece of land stretches upwards into space and downwards to the centre of the earth. I have already remarked that restrictions on the ownership and use of real estate mean that "land" in this unlimited sense does not form part of the story of the colonisation of Australia and New Zealand.
3. There are many other ways of defining "land". They include the social nexus that surrounds its occupation or use, the economic or use value of land, the personal emancipation that land ownership can bring and metaphysical or historical properties of particular territories. Some of the differences we describe above are related to parties using different conceptions of land when in conversation with each other.
4. William Blackstone: *Commentaries on the Laws of England*, 1st edition, Oxford, Clarendon Press, 1765–1769, Book the Second, Chapter the Second, p. 18. Consulted at Avalon.law.yale.edu/subject_menus/blackstone.asp. Accessed 30 May 2021.
5. In Mauritius, Quebec, South Africa, Sri Lanka, some European countries and many parts of the USA ownership of land is absolute or allodial. Allodial ownerships means that the beneficial owner owns the land in question and does not hold an estate in the land that has been granted by the Crown. It has been proposed that New Zealand should adopt allodial land ownership without apparent interest from lawyers, politicians or the general public. See Law Commission: "Tenure and Estates in Land", Preliminary Paper No 20, Wellington, June 1992.
6. Blackstone, op cit, 1765–1769, Book the Second, Chapter the Seventh, p. 105.
7. The term "Crown" is a lawyerly myth and is any entity which manifests the mythical conception of the maximum extent of public power that a given polity (which is notionally governed by a monarchy) can muster. At a given time, the crown of a given place need not necessarily be identical to the crown in the same place at another time. Moreover, the crown is an ideal type of considerable slipperiness which, in practice, requires much careful handling before it can be meaningfully discerned by others.
8. Australian Law Reform Commission: "Traditional Rights and Freedoms—Encroachment by Commonwealth Laws", Final Report, ALRC Report 129, Sydney, The Australian Law Reform Commission, December 2015, Chapter 18, pp. 459–493; Richard Boast and Neil C Quigley: *Regulatory Reform and Property Rights in New Zealand*, Chapter 5, in Susy Frankel ed. *Learning from the Past, Adapting for the Future: Regulatory Reform in New Zealand*, Wellington, LexisNexis, December 2011.
9. This began in the 1790s with the installation of semaphore and later electronic telegraph systems to connect the Admiralty in London with the main anchorages of the Royal Navy such as the Downs and Spithead.
10. It is tempting to comment that the Bill of Rights 1689 passed the shadow of the crown's prerogative to the people's representatives while ensuring that its substance remained firmly within the grasp of the ruling class.
11. Australian Law Reform Commission, op cit, 2015, p. 461.
12. The main reason why this should be so is that the Common Law is based upon natural persons who are responsible for their own actions. Describing collective realities in the language of individual persons leaves out many of the collective beliefs, hopes, aspirations and disciplines which are entailed in living collectively. By contrast, communities which have collective responsibilities for the actions performed by their members seek to ensure that the actions of individual members do not undermine the benefits that the community creates and shares. In practice, the difference between the two may be more a matter of theory than reality.

13 Governor Phillip made significant efforts to learn the local dialect and even had Aboriginal people kidnapped so that he could interrogate them. However, so intense was the struggle for survival during the early years of the of the Sydney settlement that little progress was made in exploring the wider cultural and physical environment in which the survivors of the First Fleet found themselves.
14 I emphasise that a careful description is not necessarily a generally truthful one.
15 Edward John Eyre was born on 5 August 1815 at Whipsnade, Bedfordshire and died on 30 November 1901 at Whitchurch, Devon. He was educated at Sedburgh grammar school and emigrated to Sydney without attending university. Between December 1837 and July 1838 he was the first to drive sheep and cattle from New South Wales to Adelaide. Between 1839 and 1841 he made three explorations into the centre of Australia and walked across the Nullarbor Plain to Albany in Western Australia. He returned to England in 1845 and published a narrative of his travels (see below). Served as Lieutenant Governor of New Munster in New Zealand 1848–1853, Lieutenant Governor of Saint Vincent 1854–1861 and Governor of Jamaica 1862–1865. For many years he was embroiled in disputes over his handling of revolts in Jamaica but was ultimately officially vindicated.
16 Edward John Eyre: "Manners and Customs of the Aborigines of Australia", Chapter IV published in *Journals of Expeditions into Central Australia and Overland from Adelaide to King George's Sound 1840–1841*, Volume II, London, T & W Boone, 1845. Consulted at Gutenberg. net.au/ebooks/e00048.html#manners. Accessed 11 June 2021.
17 Respect for Eyre's abilities did not extend as far as his immediate superior, Governor George Grey.
18 See Attwood, op cit, 2020, pp. 36–38.
19 Moorehead, op cit, 1966, p. 133.
20 Ibid, p. 141–143.
21 The denial is multi-dimensional and deep-rooted. Buying and selling communally owned assets for personal gain, articulating opinion or permissions without fully sounding out the views of all parties, promoting the interests of some individuals at the expense of others in the community, undertaking actions without concern for tribal lore are just some attributes of competitive individualism which weaken communal undertakings.
22 Writing in 1966, Moorhead records that "… there are still full-blood blooded aborigines to be found in the centre of Australia and in the far north…", op cit, 1966, p. 177.
23 Ibid, p. 169. It may prove instructive to compare this reaction of Aboriginal peoples to that of squatters who found that their belief that they owned the freehold of runs that they had taken on was utterly unfounded.
24 Amberlin Kwaymullvia: "Seeing the Light: Aboriginal Law, Learning and Sustainable Living in Country", *Indigenous Law Bulletin*, (2005), Vol 27, No 6.
25 See Attwood, op cit, 2020, pp. 15–25 for a discussion of the issues involved.
26 Ibid, p. 20 states "… it suggests that the government claimed possession on the basis of both *discovery* and *possession.*"
27 In making land grants the Crown reserved to itself the right to timber for naval repairs. See Governor Phillip's Instructions, 25 April 1787, Historical Records of Australia, p. 20.
28 Land title registration is discussed later when the Torrens System is considered.
29 Unlike banks founded under the English Common Law, the Bank of New South Wales was permitted to lend against the security of land titles from its inception in 1817. No doubt cunning bankers and their attendant lawyers found ways to circumvent the prohibition for valued customers. But it was at least another four decades before such a practice became commonplace among banks incorporated in England and operating in Australian colonies.
30 5&6 Vict, c. 36 (22 June 1842). This legislation is entitled in a variety of ways by different authors. For example, it has been variously referred to as The Australian Colonies: Waste Lands Act 1842, The Waste Lands Act 1842 and The Sale of Waste Lands Act 1842. A text can be found under the title of Australian Colonies, Waster Lands Act 1842 5&6 Vict c36 at

digitalcollections.qut.edu.au/4668/. For the purpose of this legislation Australian Colonies meant New South Wales, Van Diemen's Land, South Australia, Western Australia and New Zealand.

31 See Jamie Dalziel: "Pastoral Leases in the Northern Territory and the Reservation of Aboriginal Rights, 1863–1931, *UNSW Law Journal*, Volume 22 (2), 1999, pp 462–505 and Daryle Rigney, Steve Hemming and Shaun Berg: "Letters Patent, Native Title and the Crown in South Australia", Chapter 11, pp. 161–178 in Martin Hinton, Daryle Rigney and Elliott Johnston eds: *Indigenous Australians and the Law*, 2 Edition, London, Routledge-Cavendish, 2008.

32 Henry Reynolds and Jamie Dalziel: "Aborigines and Pastoral Leases—Imperial and Colonial Policy 1826–1855", *UNSW Law Journal*, Volume 19 (2), 1996, p. 338.

33 On 10 January 1840, The Colonial Land and Emigration Commission was created initially to improve the conditions under which single unaccompanied women could be conveyed to the colonies. Sometime in 1846, the principal Commissioners were, in addition, required to report annually on all colonial laws and upon the management of colonial land and emigration. The Commission finally ceased in 1877 but there is no clear evidence that its work influenced the course of the Crown's management of New Zealand land.

34 9&10 Victoria, c 104. Hickford, op cit, 2016, p. 200 opines that the 1842 Act remained in force in New Zealand until sometime in 1847.

35 These leases are likely to contain details of the legal properties of the Crown land leased in the Timber Creek district. I have not been able to consult copies of them. Thus, the information they may contain does not form part of this work.

36 Griffiths v Northern Territory of Australia (No 3)[2016] FCA 900, 24 August 2016, 14.

37 The most obvious examples are the administrative structures set out in the Native Land Act 1873 many of which were never put in place by the Native Land Court.

38 In English Common Law a company is deemed to have all rights and obligations of a natural person. For the purposes of Common Law "natural person" may mean a body corporate, an institution or a voluntary society as well as an individual. For the purposes of this book we adopt this convention without comment.

39 Thermal Springs District Act 1881 placed the district under Māori trusteeship.

40 Lake Waikaremoana Act 1971 made the lakebed Māori freehold land.

41 Te Awa Tupua (Whanganui River Claims Settlement) Act 2017 made the river a natural person.

42 Waitangi Tribunal: "Muriwhenua Fishing Report", Wellington, Waitangi Tribunal, 1988, p. 46.

43 Sir Eddie Durie CJ (1940-) was the first Māori to be appointed a judge and was Chair of the Waitangi Tribunal.

44 E T Durie: "Custom Law", Wellington, Waitangi Tribunal, January 1994, p 91. Reprinted by Treaty of Waitangi Research Unit, University of Victoria, Wellington, May 2013. Accessed at www.wgtn.ac.nz/stout-centre/research-units/towru/publications/Custom-Law.pdf.

45 Ibid, p. 91.

46 Hapu means "Section of a large tribe, clan, secondary tribe." See Williams, op cit,1957. It is often composed of closely related people and is often regarded as the level in Māori society within which decisions about day-to-day management of land were made.

47 David V Williams: "'Te Kooti tango whenua': The Native Land Court 1864–1909", Wellington, Huia, 1999, p. 142. By contrast, it was reported by Stuff, 1 May 2010, that the then Prime Minister, John Key, rejected, at the last minute, an agreement with Tuhoe to vest ownership of Urewera National Park in the tribe.

48 This complexity was broadly recognised by McLean when testifying to the Waikato Committee in August 1860. For example, when asked to describe the tribal right to transfer land McLean said: "It varies so much in different parts of the country, I should wish to know what particular part of the country you refer to, as the custom which prevails in one place did not in another." See *AJHR*, 1890, G-1, p. 2. It seems that the Pākehā members of the Waikato Committee wrongly believed that McLean was prevaricating.

49 The Native Lands Act 1873 is a possible but flawed exception. It was intended to encourage hapu to make decisions about land ownership by themselves without intervention of the Native Land Court and to employ the Court to register the results of their deliberations. For a number of reasons, it failed in these aims.

50 For example Francis Dart Fenton: "Observations on the State of the Aboriginal Inhabitants of New Zealand" http://www.enzb.auckland.ac.nz/document/?wid=1742&page=0&action= argued that Māori land was analogous to English commons before enclosure while James Mackay: "Our Dealings with Māori Lands …" draws an analogy between the behaviour of Māori and that of Highland Scots before the Clearances.

51 See James Bellich: *Making Peoples: A History of the New Zealanders From Polynesian Settlement to the End of the 19th century*, Auckland, Allen Lane The Penguin Press,1996, pp. 224–228 who suggests that this state of affairs lasted well into the second half of the 19th century in some parts of the North Island. Bellich states: "By 1861, 100,000 Pākehā heavily outnumbered 60,000 Māori. But three-quarters of these Pākehā were in Auckland, Wellington and the South Island, together with something like a sixth of Māori. Elsewhere, in main Māoridom, 50,000 Māori interacted with 25,000 Pākehā. Here, Māori had the power to impose their definition of consent, or at least to force Pākehā to negotiate with it, and to indicate clearly to posterity what it was." p. 228.

52 I distinguish "te Tiriti o Waitangi" the Māori language version of the Treaty of Waitangi, which was the version that most people signed from the English language version which nowadays we term "The Treaty of Waitangi". In this work I refer respectively to "te Tiriti" and "The Treaty".

53 See Alan Ward: "Alienation Rights in Traditional Māori Culture: A Comment", *The Journal of the Polynesian Society*, Vol 95 (1986), No 2, pp 259–266, p. 259.

54 To some extent this lack of a coming-together, except in the limited circumstances already noted, was the direct result of the flood of legislation about Māori land passed by the settler-dominated Parliament from 1862 onwards which set an unyielding frame around any political discussion of the matter.

55 Brent Layton: "Alienation Rights in Traditional Māori Society: A Reconsideration", *The Journal of the Polynesian Society*, Vol 93 (1984), No 4, pp 423–440, pp 424–425.

56 Stripped to its essentials a contract must include at least three elements, all agreed in the absence of coercion: namely, an offer of supply, an acceptance of delivery and a consideration.

57 Hickford makes a similar point when he states: "Deeds of purchase were used to quiet not only the proprietary interests in territory which Māori politics might claim but also the normative indigenous authority or jurisdiction to determine how such resources might be allocated and to whom." See Mark Hickford: "'This Intricate Question'—Some Reflections on Māori Property Rights, Custom and Constitutionalism in the 1840s", Paper presented to Prato Symposium, 20–23 April 2009, www.ched.uq.edu.au, p. 1 accessed 5 September 2017.

58 It is difficult to describe, in English, the interactions between Māori and Pākehā that occurred and the continuing arrangements that resulted, without employing the vocabulary of trade, exchange or market. Yet this Pākehā usage emphasises the market-related commercial dimension of the relationship between Pākehā and hapu, even when such a connotation was neither intended nor understood by Māori. Hence, the coming of the Common Law, cast the hosting of Pākehā in Māori communities into the adversarial court procedures, which, in many cases, ultimately, fundamentally altered the relationship that was originally established and which began the process by which pākehā came to occupy the land.

59 William Colenso: "On the Māori Races of New Zealand", Christchurch, New Zealand Exhibition Ethnology, 1865 reprinted by Scholar's Choice, Milton Keynes, Lightning Source, n.d. Colenso denies that the collective sale of land was traditional Māori practice. At pages 32–33, when speaking of early Pākehā purchasers of Māori land he states: "Although the foreign transferees (not knowing the native custom,) often wished others being co-proprietors to sign the document of transfer; and this, bye-and-bye, came to be looked upon as New Zealand

custom; whence came the modern belief that *all* must unite in a sale; and thence it followed, that one could not sell his own land! But such is not of New Zealand origin." It is noteworthy that McLean employed, to great effect, the creation of land buying events between 1846 and 1853 when he presided over the purchase of half the country.

60   Francis Dart Fenton (1820/1825–1898) was apprenticed to his uncle's solicitors' office in Huddersfield. He arrived in New Zealand in 1850 and squatted on Māori land near the mouth of the Waikato River not far from Maunsell's mission at Maraetai. Governor Grey appointed him clerk at the Registry of Deeds in 1851. He subsequently served as Native Secretary in 1856, Resident Magistrate in Waipa and Waikato 1857–1858, assistant law officer in Auckland 1858–1862, Crown Law Officer 1862–1865, and Chief Justice of the Native Land Court 1865 until he retired in 1882.

61   This is not to argue that the Native Land Court provided just outcomes. Like all courts, it was hostage to all manner of manipulation because Fenton CJ refused to hold hearings close to the location of claims, declined to accept as evidence information and testimony which was not laid formally before the Court and did not permit title to Māori land to be vested in the tribe, insisting, instead, that the ten people included on the crown grant were beneficial owners of the land in question. Thus, there were considerable incentives for plausible-enough witnesses to tailor their testimony for their own and their employers' purposes and for potential purchasers and their agents to exploit Māori who were often forced to spend considerable periods away from home waiting upon the Court. It should be noted that Boast, op cit, 2016 has questioned this assessment and has argued that the proceedings of the Native Land Court were much more flexible and pragmatic than many of its critics have stated.

62   In recent years, Boast has argued that the Native Land Court was much more flexible in accommodating Māori points of view than had previously been thought. He bases his conclusion on an extensive analysis of the records of cases brought before the Native Land Court. See Richard Boast: "Native Land Court 1862–1887: A Historical Study, Cases and Commentary", Wellington, Bookers, 2013; "The Native Land Court Volume 2 1888–1909: A Historical Study, Cases and Commentary", Wellington, Thomson Reuters, 2015 and "The Native/Māori Land Court Volume 3 1910–1953: Collectivism, Land Development and the Law", Wellington, Thomson Reuters, 2019.

63   This assessment is based upon a summary of cases contained in Fenton, op cit, 1879/1994.

64   Fenton, ibid, 1879/1994 p. 19 states: "It would be highly prejudicial to allow the tribal tenure to grow up and affect land that has once been clothed in lawful title, recognised and understood by the ordinary laws of the country. Instead of subordinating English tenures to Māori customs, it will be the duty of the Court, in administering this Act [the Native Land Act 1865], to cause as rapid an introduction amongst the Māoris, not only of English tenures, but of English rules of descent, as can be secured without violently shocking Māori prejudices."

65   The so-called hungry months usually occurred in late Spring when all the produce stored for winter had been consumed but before the early crops of the new season could be harvested. A long winter followed by a wet, cold spring could mean starvation for many. Since World War II, these risks have been increasingly countered in rich countries by internationally-sourced supplies of food, improved food preservation techniques and sophisticated storage facilities.

66   The upbringing of Chief Land Purchase Commissioner Donald McLean appears to have been adversely affected by such landlordism. McLean was born in Tiree, Inner Hebrides, in October 1820. According to Farquer, op cit, 2007, pp. 9–10 McLean's father was dispossessed of his farm and moved to Argyll. McLean was cared for by a local minister and afterwards by his uncle who was also a Presbyterian minister. He sailed for Australia in 1838 and arrived in New Zealand in early 1840. It is not known how this fact may have influenced his later actions.

67   Here the New Zealand Company includes a number of companies and associations which it spawned. They include the Plymouth Company, The Second Colony (Nelson), the Colony of New Edinburgh (Dunedin) and the Canterbury Association.

68 Normanby instructed Hobson as follows: "… until they [i.e. the aborigines] can be brought within the pale of civilised life, and trained in the adoption of its habits, they must be carefully defended in the observance of their own customs, so far as these are compatible with the universal maxims of humanity and morals. But the savage practices of human sacrifice and cannibalism must be promptly and decisively interdicted….". See McNab, op cit, 1908, p. 735. Neither Hobson nor Fitzroy was provided with the resources to defend "desirable" Māori customs or "interdict" undesirable ones. It remains a matter of serious debate whether this such carelessness represented ignorance or design within the Colonial Office.

69 Hickford quotes from a minute by James Stephen casting doubt upon the uniform applicability of American jurisprudence to all British colonies in general and to Māori in particular. See Mark Hickford: "'Vague Native Rights to Land': British Imperial Policy on Native Title and Custom in New Zealand 1837–53", *Victoria University of Wellington Legal Research Papers,* Volume 6, Issue 31, 2016, Paper No 149/2016, pp. 183–184.

70 Ann Parsonen: "Land and Conflict in Taranaki, 1839–59: Revision of Report No 1 to the Waitangi Tribunal "The Purchase of Māori Land in Taranaki, 1839–59"", Wai 143, November 1991, reports at page 124, footnote 254, that on January 1855 the surveyor Rogan wrote to McLean stating that: "… owing principally to the Natives adhering to their respective claims to the land … it is in most cases impossible to survey the different allotments so as to make them come to certain Māori land marks."

71 The use of the term "quieted" is a striking feature of correspondence during the colonisation process. In practice, it did not mean that the Common Law relating to land would be amended so that the communal values held by Māori could be accommodated. Rather, it meant that Māori were not, for whatever reason, expected to object to the insertion of the facts of individual ownership of land into their lives.

72 Many of the plans of New Zealand settlements and the sections they contained were drawn in London without the benefit of accurate survey data. See Judith Bassett: *The Pākehā Invasion 1840–1860,* Chapter Two, pp 39–56, in Judith Binney, Judith Bassett and Erik Olssen: *The People and the Land, Te Tangata me Te Whenua: An Illustrated History of New Zealand 1820–1920,* Wellington, Bridget Williams Books, 1995. At p. 41 Bassett provides a reproduction of an undated plan of the City of Wellington which has a non-existent river or canal flowing along Kent Terrace towards a barge basin (presumably now occupied by the Bain Reserve) upon which steamships appear to be plying for trade.

73 The precise timing of the change in official opinion about Māori ownership of land is not precisely known. It seems that Lord John Russell, who was appointed Secretary of State for War and the Colonies in September 1839, inclined to this view by the time he issued the Letters Patent in November 1840.

74 Official Colonial Office views about the ownership of land in New Zealand changed radically between 1838 and 1846 and increasingly conformed to the views of John Locke about general ownership of property.

75 Australian land was regarded as being without proprietors. It was, therefore, regarded as *terra nullius* (although the term does not appear to have been coined until much later in the 19th century).

76 We have coined Pre-Primary Market as the first stage in this process and Primary Market as the second stage.

77 For a very thorough account see Rosemarie V. Tonk: "The First New Zealand land commissions 1840–1845", MA Thesis, University of Canterbury, May 1986, downloaded from https://ir.canterbury.ac.nz/handle/10092/7720 on 6 March 2019.

78 By the New Zealand Land Claims Act, 1840.

79 Fisher resigned 25 June 1841 having been provisionally appointed as attorney general. (Tonk, op cit, 1986, pp. 52–53 suggests that he found trying the rigours of conducting his commission

entirely under canvas.) Richmond resigned in July 1843 on becoming Chief Police Magistrate of the Southern District.

80 During that time, the Commission made 1,049 enquiries. It allowed 490 claims and disallowed 241. A very large number of claims were not argued before the commissioners and so dismissed.

81 When reporting to Governor Fitzroy on the New Zealand Company's claim to the Nelson District on 31 March 1845 Spain set out what he called the principle that "… mere conquest, unsupported by actual and permanent occupation … bestows no title on the invaders." This view was particularly serendipitous for settler interests given that the entire Nelson province was under the suzreignty of Te Rauperaha (which he had already asserted by means of deadly force at Tuamarina) because it meant it was legally valid to ignore his claims to the land.

82 Spain, in particular, appears to have taken considerable pains to ensure that these conditions were met in the dealings of the New Zealand Company.

83 It should be noted that the openness of the presumed market was quite limited. Commissioners do not appear to have required that the original sale should have been subject to competition among prospective purchasers. Moreover, it also appears that Māori were not able to make claims before the commissions.

84 Adams, op cit, 1977, p. 188 states that Earl Grey "… had to abandon his doctrinaire views in the face of the recalcitrant reality that the Māoris did own 'waste' lands in New Zealand, believed that their ownership had been guaranteed by the Treaty of Waitangi, and would resist any attempt to deprive them of it." This appears to be too generous an assessment of the good faith of Governor Grey, who manipulated the Earl into acquiescing to this position.

85 In this respect, Governor Grey's approach matched the political realities encountered by Earl Grey.

86 So misleading were these reports from Grey that his successor Gore-Browne was surprised by the inaccuracy of the briefings about the state of affairs in New Zealand that he received from the Colonial Office.

87 It is very debateable how much of Governor Grey's despatches were taken at face value. Colonial Office officials often commented disparagingly upon Governor Grey's despatches. All the while Governor Grey could be presented as successful there was no public attempt to correct his falsehoods.

88 It is estimated by Pool, op cit, 1991, Table 5.2, p. 76 that in 1857–1858 the total Māori population numbered 61,500. Jeanine Graham: *Settler Society* Chapter 5, pp 112—140 in Geoffrey W. Rice ed: *The Oxford History of New Zealand* 2 Edition, Auckland, Oxford University Press, 1996, estimates that settlers numbered 26,707 in 1851 and 99,021 in 1861 (see Table 1, p. 117).

89 Maurice Ormsby points out quite correctly that New Zealand Common Law is English customary law which has come to incorporate elements of Māori customary practice. The term "narrow legalism" refers to the manner in which colonial judges often chose to interpret statutory law during the period in question.

90 The architect of this policy was Francis Dart Fenton.

91 It is important to recall the legal distinction between the title to an estate in land and ownership of the land itself. The title to an estate in land is merely a claim to the uses (e.g or stream of benefits) which a piece of land can yield. An estate can be leased to someone who can then work the land. By contrast, ownership of land means command of the ability to dispose of the land in question. In feudal times, the sovereign owned the land but granted titles to it in a fief or fee to subordinate lords on the understanding that services were due to be rendered. Now, in New Zealand, titles in land are generally in fee simple which means that no services are owed to the sovereign or crown for the use of land in question. See Appendix 2 for a more detailed discussion.

92 Such practices appear to be a universal feature of colonisation. They were greeted with trepidation by Colonial Office officials in the 1830s who were well aware of the depredations suffered by Indian Nations in North America. See Angie Debo: *A History of the Indians of the*

United States, London, Folio Society, 2003, especially pp. 126–127.
93 Much later, in 1873, a Commission of Inquiry, chaired by C W Richmond J, examined these same practices in the Hawkes Bay. The Commission found no evidence of fraud. See *Appendices to the Journals of the House of Representatives,* 1873, G-7, "Report of the Hawkes Bay Native Land Alienation Commission".
94 The omission of cultural factors meant that some claimants were able to fashion their evidence to the Court to their own advantage. It is not known how common this was.
95 Attachment to a letter sent in reply to a complaint addressed to Gipps by a number of Wellington settlers who objected to the conduct of the first sale of town allotments in Auckland on 19 and 20 April 1841. See *The New Zealand Journal,* Vol 2, London, Saturday, September 4, 1841, pp 222–223,
96 In the days before public transport it was common to encounter substantial and grandly-appointed dwellings in close proximity to the smaller residences of the servants and others who serviced the whims and caprices of their richer neighbours. So far as is known, the last remaining enclave of such a socially-mixed inner-city suburb, dating from the early Victorian era, was located in Tonks Avenue, Wellington and was dismembered in the early 21st century in order to make room for the so-called motorway to the south and east of the Terrace Tunnel. A different reminder of the same social juxtaposition can be found in Nelson where King Street, which contains many small cottages, is located close to a number of large, old dwellings adjacent to the south of the city centre.
97 Kate Lepper correctly points out that this pricing calculation makes purchase of such lots risky for low-paid people. However, since the concession was supposed to be available only to relatively senior officials who were relatively well-paid, the risk was presumably relatively well-contained within settler society.
98 It is of course possible that the hypothesis of sharp behaviour by Cooper, Mathew and Shortland could be tested by an investigation of their private affairs. It is not known if such examinations have been attempted.
99 R C J Stone: *From Tamaki-Makau-Rau to Auckland,* Auckland, Auckland University Press, 2001, p. 249.
100 Michael Bassett: *The Mother of All Departments: The History of the Department of Internal Affairs,* Auckland, Auckland University Press, 1997, p. 20
101 This fact was recognised by Gipps who re-issued the original auction notice because of the uncertain circulation of the *Government Gazette* in New Zealand.
102 S M D Martin: *New Zealand in a Series of Letters,* op cit, nd. Letter VII, dated January 1842, pp 126–128 provides a description of the conduct of the sale of town and suburban allotments in 1841 in which he accuses Shortland, in particular, but also Cooper and Mathew, of conspiring to organise "a job" on the sale for their collective personal benefit. This accusation has been repeated many times since, apparently without careful examination of the available evidence. He states that some 6 acres of town allotments were reserved from the sale by officials, according to Gipps's instructions, comprising the most sought-after holdings. He also states that Hobson subsequently reduced the selections of officials "to something like the proper quantity". He complains that competition from officials in the public auction pushed up prices of non-reserved selections which led to widespread subdivision by their new owners. He suggests that Shortland was bribed by a Mr Porter to be appointed to the Legislative Council. Finally, he states that he suspects that Cooper speculated "in these purchases [of land] with the revenues of the Colony then in his keeping". Similar accusations, albeit less precisely described and more rhetorically expressed, were contained in a letter to Gipps written by a bevy of Port Nicholson settlers and published in *The New Zealand Journal,* Vol 2, p. 222, on 4 September 1841. These same accusations were placed before the House of Commons Select Committee considering New Zealand affairs in 1844 by Samuel Brodie. This Select Committee was heavily supported by the New Zealand Company.

103 Bassett, op cit, 1997, p. 20.
104 Mackay, Alexander, op cit, "No 20—Lord John Russell to Governor Hobson 9 December 1840". Accessed at nzetc.victoria.ac.nz/tm/scholarly/tei-Mac01Comp-t1-t5-g1-t2-g1-t20html.
105 See New South Wales Government Gazette, Issue 57, 16 September 1840, pp 911–912.
106 New South Wales Government Gazette, Issue 23, 23 March 1841, p. 417.
107 Department of Lands and Survey: "Register of Sales of Crown Land 1841–1850", National Archives, ANWN 8889, W5280/22. Gipps's instructions envisaged that land to be auctioned be surveyed prior to sale. This meant that sales of Crown land were determined by the capacities that the Surveyor General could command. Hence, it is likely that sales could only be held at a rate of roughly five per year during this time.
108 Compiled from ibid, various pages.
109 Butlin, op cit, 1961, p.90.
110 Patricia Burns: *Fatal Success: A History of the New Zealand Company*, Auckland, Heineman Reed, 1989, pp 248–254.
111 See Lords Commissioners of the Admiralty, op cit, 1806.
112 McLintock, op cit, 1958, p. 145.
113 FitzRoy's arrival is variously put at the 23 or 26 December.
114 Fitzroy was appointed to succeed Hobson in "spring" 1843 and his family departed from Torbay on the *Bangalore* on 8 July 1843. John and Mary Gribbin: *FitzRoy: The Remarkable Story of Darwin's Captain and the Invention of the Weather Forecast*, London, Headline Book Publishing, 2003, pp 209–210 and p. 213. It is not known if anyone has discussed what might have been had FitzRoy arrived in New Zealand earlier than he did.
115 McLintock, op cit, 1958, pp. 154–155 reports that salary arrears and other contingencies amounted to £9,000 and current revenue amounted to two thirds of expenditure. Attempts to borrow from local banks were met with demands for interest yields of 12 to 15%.
116 Given the high level of dependence on land sales as a source of Colonial Government revenue, it is all the more surprising that the Civil List did not include recognition of a person expert in concluding sales of land.
117 Hobson, Shortland and Fitzroy were experienced officers of the Royal Navy. They would have been used to drafting and negotiating such bills, without specific authority or detailed supervision, to pay for works and stores purchased in overseas locations, often beyond the legal protection of the British Empire. The procedures for doing this are set out in various editions of "Regulations and Instructions Relating to His Majesty's Service at Sea Established by His Majesty in Council" issued to Masters aboard all naval vessels in commission. At length, the UK Treasury did meet the obligations entered into by them on behalf of the UK Government.
118 Much research remains to be done on the early history of New Zealand's public finances. On the basis of a quick and unsystematic perusal of early Blue Books held by Archives New Zealand it appears that no fixed accrual rules were employed by the compilers of the accounts of the Crown Colony Government. Thus, in the early 1840s, it was common for the same item of revenue to be counted in more than one year and some expenditures were reported in years subsequent to the years in which they were incurred, apparently at the whim of the compilers. The result was that the accounts often presented a falsely optimistic picture. This may account for the reluctance with which the UK Government greeted colonial demands for more adequate finance from the UK Treasury.
119 Gribbin and Gribbin, op cit, 2003, pp 209–210.
120 See Rose Daamen: "The Crown's Right of Pre-emption and FitzRoy's Waiver Purchases", Rangahaua Whanui Theme D, Wellington, Waitangi Tribunal, August 1998, p. 57.
121 Presumably, this was to safeguard the profits from land jobbing that the Colonial Office relied upon to meet the costs of operating the colony of New Zealand.
122 Daamen, op cit, 1998, p. 61.
123 A H McLintock: "Crown Colony Government in New Zealand", Wellington, Government

Printer, 1958, pp 153–154 calls the New Zealand government "bankrupt" (phraseology echoed by Littlewood, op cit, 2019) and notes that investment funds had dried up and with that the supply of currency, immigration had declined following the Wairau Affair and there was a serious decline in customs revenue due to the decline in trade volumes (the government finances were highly dependent on the proceeds from customs duties). Public servants' salaries were in arrears. Fitzroy had been expressly forbidden to issue Treasury Bills or to reduce the civil list.

124 Ibid pp. 153 ff describes a number of instances of malfescence among leading officials.
125 When approached, the manager of the Union Bank in Auckland offered to lend the colonial administration £2,000 at 12.5% p.a. on the security of the colony's Imperial grant-in-aid of £7,545. See J Hight and H D Bamford: *The Constitutional History and Law of New Zealand*, Wellington, Whitcombe and Tombs, 1914, pp. 175–176. See Fitzroy, op cit, 1846/1997, p. 25; John and Mary Gribbin: *FitzRoy: The Remarkable Story of Darwin's Captain and the Invention of the Weather Forecast*, London, Review, 2003, p. 219.
126 Brodie, op cit, 1845/1997, p. 88.
127 E Wilson Wilson, op cit, 1935, p. 138.
128 Ibid, pp. 158–159.
129 Ibid, p. 159. Here McLintock, op cit, 1958 suggests around 100,000 acres were sold under the terms of licences issued under these proclamations.
130 Quoted by Jonathan Adams: "Governor FitzRoy's Debentures and their Role in his Recall", *New Zealand Journal of History*, (1986), Vol. 20, No 1, pp 44–63 at p. 51.
131 It should be noted that he encountered the Nelson and Wellington colonists in the aftermath of the Wairau Affray and faced the largely negative sentiment among them attributed to Acting Governor Shortland. Many Māori also expressed concerns about the decline in land purchasing.
132 When a currency is made legal tender, it cannot be refused to be accepted as payment.
133 The UK Government acceded to this policy with proviso that the debentures be redeemed as soon as possible.
134 McLintock, op cit, 1958, p 157.
135 It seems likely that a rigorous audit would have revealed that at this time the New Zealand Company was being operated while insolvent.
136 University of Ireland: "Parliamentary Papers, Volume 33, Papers Relative to New Zealand", Shannon, Irish University Press, 1969, pp 43–45; Copy of Minutes of a Meeting of Native Chiefs, by appointment, at Government House, on Tuesday, 26 March 1844. Downloaded from https://books.google.co.nz/books?id=_GwSAAAAYAAJ&pg=PA2&Ipg=PA2&dg=Fitzroy%27s+Proclamation+on+pre-emption+March+1844&so on 7 March 2019.
137 Settler interests were quick to assert that the second Proclamation was widely ignored an accusation which loomed large in the lobbying that led to Fitzroy's recall by the Secretary of State for War and the Colonies.
138 For example, in theory, at least, he might have issued titles in terms of leases to which a variety of terms such as deferred payment and conditions like time limits or geographical boundaries could have been attached.
139 In consenting, the Governor was, in practice, issuing the prospective purchaser with a short-term licence of occupation à la Gipps.
140 So far as is known this is the only instance in New Zealand that the crown or purchasers met survey costs according to the custom common in the Australian colonies.
141 Hight and Bamford, op cit, 1914, p. 225.
142 See Fenton, op cit, 1879/1994, p. 81.
143 Prior to his being appointed Governor of New Zealand Fitzroy was Tory MP for Durham. Can his treatment by the UK Government be related to differences with liberal Whigs who peopled the core of the Cabinet?
144 Fitzroy's knowledge that he was to be replaced without a replacement to hand meant that he was forced to postpone preparations for a planned offensive against Kawiti and Heke. See Ian

Wards: "The Shadow of the Land: A Study of British Policy and Racial Conflict in New Zealand 1832–1852", Wellington, Government Printer, 1968, p. 190.

145 "Report of a Board Appointed by His Excellency the Governor to Enquire into and Report upon the State of Native Affairs", Votes and Proceedings of the House of Representatives, 1856, Session 1, transmitted 9 July 1856.

146 Donald McLean is a notable exception to this tendency among Pākehā.

147 Carwyn James: "From Whitehall to Waikato—Kingitanga and the interaction of indigenous and settler constitutionalism", Chapter 6, pp. 132–148 in Brad Patterson, Richard S Hill and Kathryn Patterson eds: *After The Treaty: The settler state, race relations and exercise of power in colonial New Zealand*, Wellington, Steele Roberts, 2016, p.135.

148 The Alabama Commission was set up to settle claims for damages by Great Britain and the USA to each other as a consequence of actions by both governments during the American Civil War. The Commission was named after the CSS *Alabama* which was a commerce raider built for the Confederate Navy by Laird's of Birkenhead but armed and outfitted in the Azores. Between August 1862 and June 1864, she attacked Union vessels throughout the world resulting in claims for losses and damages by affected shippers and shipowners. The resulting arbitration was incorporated into the Treaty of Washington 1871.

149 FD Fenton: "Mana", *AJHR*, 1890, G-1, p. 15.

150 Extract from Shortland's "Mythology", ibid, p. 15.

151 Angela Ballara: *Iwi: The dynamics of Māori tribal organisation from c. 1769 to c. 1945*, Wellington, Victoria University Press, 1998, p. 227 states: "Hapu remained the primary political, economic and social unit of Māori society into the 20th century even after general Māori acceptance of tribes as an alternative representative body in some circumstances."

152 Ibid, p. 81.

153 As we will see, this approach to some aspects of this significant gap in our knowledge of the international economic system during the first 60 years of the 19th century and in this chapter make some tentative attempts to fill it. Māori land ownership underlay the re-drafting of the Native Lands Act which McLean commissioned and oversaw in 1873.

154 Ibid, pp 81–82.

155 Ibid, p. 219.

156 Firth, op cit, 1973, p. 378.

157 Waitangi Tribunal: "Report of The Waitangi Tribunal on the Muriwhenua Fishing Claim (Wai 22), Wellington, Department of Justice, 1988, p. p. 37. The Report contains references to the sources quoted.

158 It should be recalled that the idea of "rights" is a product of 18th century Pākehā thinking. It is not known how far it had penetrated into Māoridom.

159 *AJHR*, 1890, G-1, p. 2

160 Ibid.

161 Walter Brodie: *Remarks on the Past and Present State of New Zealand, Its Government, Capabilities and Prospects with a Statement of the Question of Land Claims and Remarks on the New Zealand Land Company; Also a Description (Never Before Published) of its Indigenous Exports, and Hints on Emigration, the Result of Five Years' Residence in the Colony*, London, Whittaker and Co, 1845, Facsimile Edition, Christchurch, Kiwi Publishers, 1997, p.71.

162 Joe Williams: "Not Ceded But Redistributed", pp 190–197 in Renwick ed, op cit, 1991. At pp. 193–194 Williams argues: "… from the Māori perspective, whatever was given up [in signing te Tiriti], certain very important rights and powers *viz* title to the tribal estate, and tino rangatiratanga over it, were not. If that is right then any claim by the Crown in right of New Zealand to absolute and unfettered sovereignty is a claim that we stole it fair and square, and we are not going to give it back."

163 Since the early 1990s, a number of relatively substantial settlements have been concluded between iwi and the crown. They include Waikato Raupatu Claims Settlement Act, 1995;

Ngai Tahu Claims Settlement Act, 1999; and Ngati Awa Claims Settlement Act, 2005. These settlements are all omnibus arrangements providing recompense for a number of grievances. They are not wholly aimed at redressing the issue of the inadequate initial consideration paid for land. Invariably, they are worded so as to avoid posing the question about the validity of the doctrine of Aboriginal title

CHAPTER 5

START OF AN AUSTRALASIAN BANKING INDUSTRY

This Chapter shows how a quantity of money came to stand for the price of a piece of land in Australia and New Zealand. It describes the steps by which the traditional "business of banking" became the foundation and source of debt-based currency. By this development a monetary equivalent of an estate in land was created.

The colonial monetary system was based on traditional English forms of banking. There was only one short-lived attempt by the British Government to impose its own monetary relations in the form of the Colonial Bank of Issue which operated in New Zealand in the early 1850s. For the most part, monetary affairs were left to private enterprise in the form of colonial banks established in London and the Bank of England which was privately owned by mostly Whig shareholders and was not nationalised by the British Government until 1946.

Money Commodities and Monetary Institutions

In the make-believe world of economic theory, money is anything that is widely and simultaneously accepted as a medium of exchange, a store of value, a unit of account and a method of deferred payment.[1] But, this is an ideal type that is rarely observed at all times and in all places. Actual monetary systems consist of a patchwork of partial monies which only serve some of these functions at a particular time and place, or serve all of them at some times or in some places but not at or in others. Partial monies can function within particular regions, or among members of social sets, or for making particular transactions. For example, sales of racehorses in the UK are conducted in terms of guineas. A system encompassing many partial monies may arise in the course of economic interaction, by government intervention or by force of monopoly or social power.

   A monetary system comprises not only monetary commodities but also monetary institutions. Monetary institutions are not just organisations, like banks, but also include widely-held beliefs and expectations like sterling is as "good as gold". There is little disagreement about the existence and the importance of these organisations and beliefs. But by what they mean in practice, where they arose and how they evolve remains shrouded in mystery.[2] It is very widely acknowledged that money is widely accepted but there is no single, coherent explanation of why this is so. Just as land ownership in British colonies is founded on the mystery of the crown, so British money rests upon the mystery of its acceptability.

The monetary systems of Australasia are portrayed in this book as bank-centred. But, different aspects of them developed at different times. The serendipitous importation and circulation of currency in the early days of New South Wales has already been described. In particular, the importance of the role played by the Commissariat Store has been emphasised in introducing a reliable currency in the form of Store Receipts, buying the produce of farms and providing access to international currency through retiring its Store Receipts for bills on the UK Treasury. Yet even this arrangement required occasional augmentation in the form of importation of silver coinage. In New Zealand, during its pre-colonial era, there was promiscuous importation of coins and some use of trade bills drawn on Sydney traders and occasionally London bankers.

But it is not possible to describe the monetary arrangements of Australasia at this time in terms of monetary system or systems. The companies involved appear to have concerned themselves with bilateral transactions with customers. There appear to have been no rules of conduct agreed between banks except those negotiated in London. There is no evidence of a centralising tendency meaning a set of forces acting to cohere the various monetary agents into a sustainable set of relationships. But it seems certain that in both the environs of Sydney and the Bay of Islands in the North Island of New Zealand some people did have access to money commodities most of which were originally created by banks, many of which were located overseas.

There were also many non-bank monetary instruments which are not the result of banking processes but which are known to serve as currency in some circumstances. Such moneys generally arise in the course of domestic trade, beneath the notice of officials concerned with influencing the economic development of countries or regulating commerce. For this reason they have largely gone undescribed and unmeasured. For example, IOUs of well-known traders or merchants can act as partial monies. As a result, how such money commodities work, the nature of the institutions which support their introduction and use, why they occur or how widespread in society their impact spreads are not known. It is quite impossible to judge with any accuracy how important these partial moneys were in the development of the domestic Australasian or the nineteenth century international monetary systems. Nevertheless, during the last half of the 19th century an extremely active sector of non-bank financial institutions including land companies, stock and station agents and mercantile companies emerged unaccompanied by systematic reporting. In addition, the so-called petty banking practices, derided by Governor Macquarie, seem to have persisted well into the 20th century in the form of shop credit, trade tokens, locally-circulated IOUs or traders' notes all without benefit of accurate description or measurement. For this reason, it is not possible to extend the discussion contained in this book to consideration of non-bank moneys and their absence from this book cannot be taken as evidence of their unimportance.

BANKING IN AUSTRALIA

In the 19th century, especially in the British Empire, money was intimately related to the operations of privately-owned banking companies. The circulation of notes and coin was largely initiated and overseen by private banks. Chequing facilities organised by those same banks were the dominant form of currency by the end of the century and it was possible to transfer credit to anyone, anywhere through the London banking system. Those same companies and their associates, usually head-quartered in London, organised and dispensed large aggregations of international capital that ebbed and flowed between countries. An intricate web of specialist financiers spread risks as widely as possible in both time and space between and among debtors and creditors. Through this banking-based system working people were paid, trade was financed, land was bought and sold and lending and borrowing were made possible in the Australasian colonies.

But banks do not just happen; they are created and then, once established, managed so that they survive. In the early 19th century, most banks were founded so that their members or shareholders could make profits by creating, buying and selling financial instruments. The most important activities were issue of bank notes, buying and selling bills of exchange and accepting deposits. In these ways banks provided an acceptable means of exchange to their customers by performing transactions with other banks. For example, if a person A with an account in bank Y wishes to pay another person B who holds an account with bank Z, she will instruct bank Y to draw on her account and present the money as a deposit in B's account at bank Z. Even such simple transactions provide both banks with valuable information; both banks involved learn about each other's procedures, efficiency and honesty and gather valuable knowledge about each other's customers. This information forms the bulk of a banker's expertise.

Such expertise is used in the mysterious and highly secretive processes which lead eventually to wide acceptability. The processes require that both banks trust each other which, in turn, assumes considerable knowledge of each other's business. Even in the above transaction, both banks must accept without question that:

- The documentation attached to a transaction accurately describes its entire extent and character.
- Neither bank will fail while the transaction is being conducted.
- Record keeping will be timely and accurate.
- Both banks have the wherewithal to complete their parts in the transaction.
- Each bank knows enough about its customer's affairs to be able to vouch for them.

Once a bank can perform simple transactions without question it is possible for it to orchestrate more complex deals which enable funds to be created and to be transferred through time and space. No matter how complex such transactions become they are all assembled from simple building blocks including the bill of exchange system, bank transactions (i.e. forming deposits and creating credit), facilitating sales and purchase at future dates (i.e. forward trading) and buying and selling options to buy or sell (i.e options trading). Such increasing complexity means that different risks and uncertainties are encountered which must be carefully understood and managed if the bank is to survive.

In the early years of the 19th century banks could only legally operate by Royal Prerogative under a Charter.[3] At that time, all companies were regarded with official suspicion to the point that their activities were highly constrained. Most companies were partnerships or consortia the members of which faced the prospect of unlimited liability for losses incurred by the businesses they owned. The reason for this was a history of companies being formed for speculative purposes (such as investment in tulips or canals) and quickly becoming bankrupt.

The first two banks in New South Wales, the Bank of New South Wales, founded in 1817 and heavily supported by the colonial government, and the Bank of Van Diemen's Land (established 1823) were exceptional because they both openly encouraged shareholders to believe that their liability for losses incurred by the bank were limited to the face value of the shares that they owned (i.e. limited liability) In neither case was this true. Furthermore, this falsehood was a supposition that successive Governors of New South Wales (Governors Macquarie and Brisbane) did little to correct for fear of the loss of business confidence that news of their shareholders' unlimited liability may cause. In fact, both banks operating in Australia, before 1825 were legally partnerships which meant the liabilities for losses faced individually and collectively by shareholders were in fact unlimited. This property was thought to encourage probity and avoidance of risk on the part of bank managers.

As a rule of thumb, irrespective of the level of government support they enjoyed, privately-owned banking organisations could not hope to survive in Australasia unless two conditions were satisfied. First, they required a large enough customer base formed principally by relatively prosperous free settlers and second, they required the benefit of a joint stock association of shareholders.[4] Neither condition was fulfilled until the mid-1820s. At that time, free settlers started to form a tempting customer base for banking business and in 1826 the Country Banks Act became law.[5] This allowed joint-stock banks with six or more shareholders to issue notes but not within 65 miles of London. It was under this legislation that a number of so-called Anglo-Australian banks[6] were formed. Many prospered by lending to wool-growing squatters during the 1830s and early 1840s. In addition, the charter of the Bank of New South Wales permitted the bank to make loans secured by mortgage provided they were not made for a period of longer than 12 months and the total incurred did not exceed one-fifth of the Bank's paid-up capital.[7]

None of this lending activity necessarily involved lending on the security of real estate (i.e. on mortgage). Pastoral expansion initially in New South Wales and later in Victoria and South Australia was reliant on pasturing crown land over which a proprietor held a licence to occupy. She had no security in the land to pledge to a potential lender. But, in any case, there was little need for pastoralists to borrow on mortgage for land purchase. Most banks seem to have made loans to wool-growers secured by liens on the proceeds of future wool sales or, more commonly, on the security of the value of livestock. By 1850, in Australia registered liens on wool and registered mortgages on stock amounted to respective totals of £101,151 and £343,047.[8]

Between 1826 and 1841, a further 18 banks were established in Australia as follows:

FOUNDATION DATE	BANK
1826	Bank of Australia
1828	Cornwall Bank
	Derwent Bank
1829	Commercial Bank of Tasmania
1834	Commercial Bank of Sydney
	Tamar Bank
1835	Bathurst Bank
	Bank of Australasia (merged with Cornwall Bank 1835; Bank of Western Australia 1837)
1836	Bank of South Australia
1837	Bank of Western Australia
	Union Bank of Australia (merged with Tamar Bank 1837; Bathurst Bank 1840; Archer Gilles 1840; Bank of South Australia 1892)
1839	Sydney Bank
	Port Phillip Bank
	Australian Trust Company
	British Colonial Bank and Loan Company
1840	Archers Gilles
	Scottish Australian Investment Company
	Colonial Bank
1841	Western Australia Bank

This rash of bank formation was in response to the growing economic importance of wool exports resulting from the spread of squatting beyond the Nineteen Counties of New South Wales. In addition to dealing in bills of exchange, many banks lent on the security of a mortgage on stock or a lien on produce. However, during the 1840s, the Australian economy was plagued by persistent recession as export prices then land prices fell.[9] By 1841, five of the above banks were incorporated into either the Bank of Australasia or the Union Bank of Australia. Moreover, the Colonial Bank, the Bank of Australia, Sydney Bank and Port Phillip Bank were defunct by the end of 1843 and the Derwent Bank closed in 1849.[10]

By 1850, the estimated non-indigenous population of Australia was 405,356 and in another five years it was 793,260.[11] Economic prospects were radically altered in 1851 with the discovery of gold at Bathurst in May followed by fields along the western slopes of the Blue Mountains, and the rich field of Clunes, Anderson's Creek, Ballarat and Bendigo. In less than a year, gold became Australia's "richest industry".[12] Banks found it very profitable to purchase raw gold either on the goldfields with their own notes and depository receipts or through agents acting on commission and to export refined gold in the form of bars and ingots to London. Consequently, these discoveries encouraged the formation of another eight banks over the next six years or so. They were:

FOUNDATION DATE	BANK
1852	English Scottish and Australian Bank
	London Chartered Bank of Australia
1853	Australian Joint Stock Bank
	Bank of Victoria
	Bank of Tasmania
	Bendigo Bank
1856	Colonial Bank of Australasia
1858	National Bank of Australasia
	Over the following 15 years another seven banks were established as follows:
1862	Melbourne Banking Company
1863	City of Sydney Bank
1865	Ballarat Banking Company
	Bank of Adelaide
1866	Commercial Bank of Australia
1869	Mercantile Bank of Sydney
1872	Queensland National Bank
1873	Australia and European Bank

These banks operated independently until a spate of mergers occurred in the 1920s. By 1961, Butlin records that there were only 7 trading banks operating in Australia of which only three also had branches in New Zealand.[13] Thus, in Australia and New Zealand, by the mid-1870s the main elements of the banking industry had been set in place.

Nevertheless, evidence of the emergence of a banking system remains sparse. Butlin reports that an organisation called the Associated Banks of Victoria "grew out of joint action in the 'fifties and 'sixties, especially in connection with government loans".[14] In 1875, Australian banks in London formed an association and The Associated Banks of Victoria was formally constituted in 1877 without the Bank of New South Wales.[15] In the absence of a central bank, the Associated Banks acted in a concerted albeit often reluctant fashion to make loans to member banks in difficulties, to guarantee payment of outstanding notes issued by failed banks and, later, to organise centralised clearing of cheques and other bills. But it is not known with certainty how far other kinds of cooperation extended nor whether or not Butlin is correct in stating that cooperation between banks did not occur in other Australian colonies.

**INTERNATIONAL MONETARY INSTITUTIONS
1844 ONWARDS**

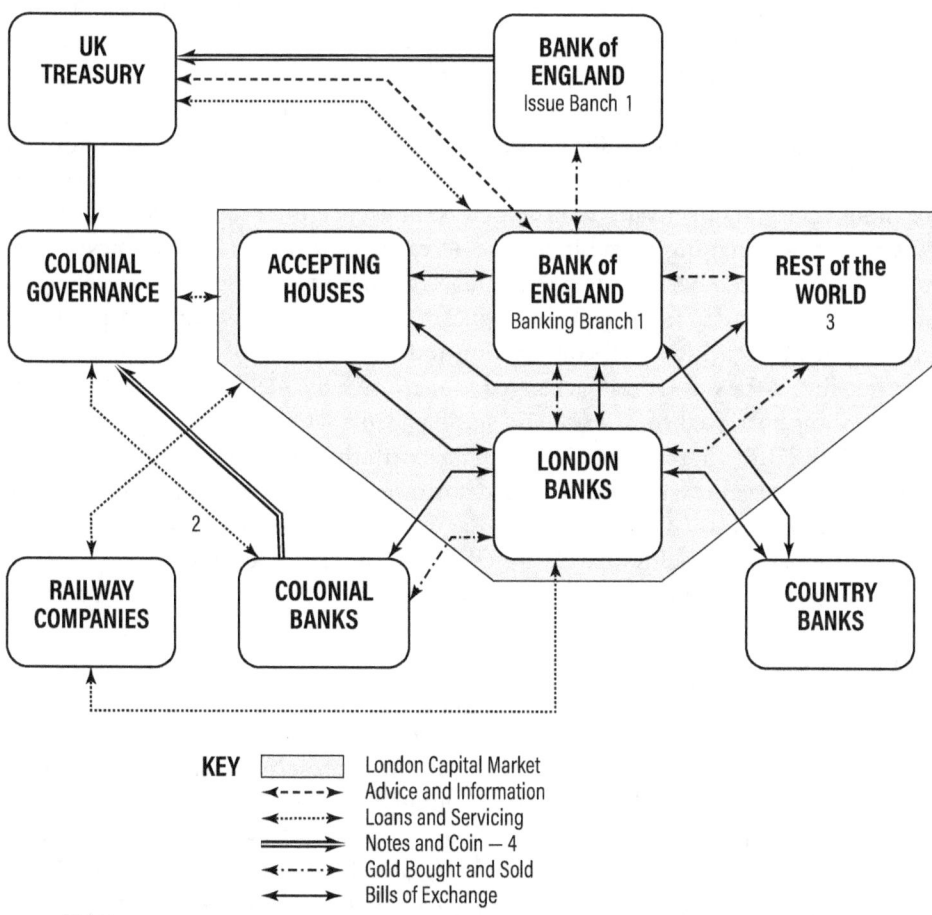

Notes
1. The Bank of England was divided into two branches by the Bank Charter Act 1844
2. Long-term borrowing by railway companies began as short-dated bills of exchange issued serially by individual banks but eventually developed into long dated securities issued to syndicates of lenders
3. Institutions domiciled in the Rest of the World participated in the London Capital Market as needs and opportunities arose. Only after 1870 did central banks formally involve themselves.
4. By the Bank Charter Act 1844 note issue by the Bank of England was limited to the sum of the bank's gold holdings plus £14 million secured against UK Government stock - the so-called Fiduciary Issue

Nevertheless, I doubt that Butlin's assessment, which was made in 1961, remains accurate. In both Australia and New Zealand there is documentary evidence of collusive behaviour between banks over a long period. In 1986, Butlin[16] records a bank conference in Sydney in February 1852 at which it was decided to suspend advances against gold shipments. It should also be recalled that banks operating in New Zealand (including the Bank of New South Wales) concluded a cartel agreement in early 1868[17] and that the Chairman of the National Bank of New Zealand reported collusive behaviours towards his bank at the 1874 Annual Meeting.[18] Presumably these were orchestrated by the association of Australian banks in London, of which the Bank of New Zealand represented by Thomas Russell appears to have been an active member. A full account of the long history of the cartelisation of Australasian banking deserves much further research. For the moment we shall be concerned with describing its main features and impacts.

In the 1850s and 1860s, the demands for capital expenditure by the wool industry greatly enlarged the demand for loans. This was because wool production could no longer be based upon a business strategy based around occupancy of very large areas of virgin land held under various forms of lease or licence-to-occupy. In large part, this was because as squatting spread it became necessary to fence holdings to prevent loss of stock to disease, other stations or wild dogs. It also became increasingly necessary to improve pasture and to secure reliable supplies of water. Thus, major capital expenditure was required for fencing, water conservation and improvement of pasture. In addition, the breeding stock was radically changed to increase wool yield. Much of the capital required was borrowed from stock and station agents which were, in turn, financed by the banks. This approach was in accordance with the banking practice of placing a merchant between the bank and its landed borrowers. In addition, a succession of legislation beginning in 1861 to encourage closer occupation and wider ownership of land meant that many leaseholds were converted into freehold with a consequent increase in borrowings for land purchase by former squatters.

Bank Management

Until the late 1860s, the shareholders of a joint-stock bank could not enjoy the advantages of limited liability unless the promoters of the bank received the benefit of the Royal Prerogative to grant it to them. Normally, this meant, in practice, that the bank had to be incorporated by Royal Charter,[19] although it could also be incorporated by Act of the English Parliament.[20] It is true that the Bank of New South Wales and the Bank of Australia both traded under charters, granted by the Governor of New South Wales, which purported to grant them limited liability from their inception. But in both cases the charters were ruled by the Colonial Secretary to be of no legal effect. Thus, both the Bank of New South Wales and the Bank of Australia were legal partnerships of proprietors who were responsible individually and severally for any losses that the bank may incur.[21] Polite Sydney society remained carefully silent about this fact well into the 1820s for fear of instilling panic in the hearts of bank depositors. By the late 1820s, however, the demand for banking services was growing rapidly among settlers and the companies that served them in Australia. But increasing the scale of banks was often difficult and expensive.

Partnerships, like banks, could only increase their equity base by taking in new partners or increasing subscriptions from existing partners. Either course of action would mean that a new partnership to replace the existing firm would have to be entered into. This involved seeking a new Royal Charter or Royal Assent for a new Act of Parliament both of which were costly and time-consuming. By 1830, the legal impediments to bank expansion were thought to be restraining colonial development among British colonies.

In 1830, the Board of Trade, when faced with a proposal for a chartered bank in Mauritius, drafted regulations which aimed to relax the current restraints. They set out three principles[22]:

1. *A real bills definition of banking:* "… the funds of the bank should not be employed in Loans or advances upon Land or other property not readily convertible into money … but be confined to Advances upon Commercial paper or Government securities and general dealings in Money and Bills of Exchange."
2. *Double liability* for shareholders to provide protection for the creditors of the bank, including the innocent banknote-accepting public.
3. *Financial reporting* to shareholders and government.

These principles were incorporated into the Royal Charter that was finally granted to the Bank of Australasia on 21 May 1835. On that date, it became the only joint-stock bank in Australasia actually advantaged with limited liability. Its shares could be readily traded with the result that its ownership structure could adapt to changing circumstances without the expense of time and money needed to dissolve and re-form the business. This brought the added potential advantage of continuous share quotations which, in theory, should provide some guide to how well the business is being run.

The Royal Charter of the Bank of Australasia formed the foundation for all those that followed. It contained the following provisions:

1. The bank could not commence business until the capital was fully subscribed and at least half paid up.
2. The bank's total debts must not exceed three times the paid-up capital plus deposits.
3. Notes must be payable on demand at the principal office and the issuing branch.
4. The Charter would terminate if cash payments were terminated for six days in a row or for a total of sixty days in a year.
5. Personal liability of shareholders was limited to double their subscriptions.
6. The bank must not lend on paper bearing the name of a bank officer or director to a total greater than one-third of total loans.
7. Land or similar property must not be taken as security, the bank must not deal in property or other merchandise except to dispose of property taken for unpaid debts. The legitimate operations of banking were: "… advances upon commercial paper or government securities, and general dealing in money, bills of exchange, or bullion… ".[23]
8. Dividends must be paid out of realized profits.
9. Notes could be issued for £1, £2, £5 and higher, but not for fractions of a pound.
10. Weekly statements of assets and liabilities (as specified) to be sent from each colony to head office.
11. Half-yearly averages of these statements to be published in each colony and aggregated in London.

In 1840, the Treasury published "Regulations and Conditions for the Observance of which Provision should be made in the Charter or Legislative Enactment Relating to the Incorporation of Banking Companies in the Colonies"[24]. These regulations incorporated all the provisions of the Bank of Australasia Royal Charter with the following significant[25] additions:

- The company shall not hold shares in its own stock nor make advances on the security of these shares.
- No bye-law of the company shall be repugnant to its charter, act of incorporation or the laws of the country within it operates.
- The charter may provide for an increase in capital.
- Where shares are transferred in the period between the date of incorporation and the date of the start of business the responsibilities of the original shareholder will remain in place until at least six months after the transfer.
- Treasury recommends that the charter does not contain detailed instructions about the management of the bank or the business to be undertaken.

These Treasury Regulations governed, in theory at least, the formation of new banks in Australia and New Zealand from 1840 onwards. The framework is clearly evident in the form taken by the Bank of New South Wales Act 1850. But their immediate impact was relatively slight because so few new banks were floated before the early 1850s in Australia and early 1860s in New Zealand.

Nevertheless, once settlement in both countries began in earnest the restrictive provisions of the Regulations became immediately apparent. The colonisation project and so the wealth of both countries depended on the successful exploitation of land by the application of capital and labour both of which required financing by banks. The only bankable assets available were either a lien on the sale proceeds of the products of the current season or a mortgage on stock owned or on the land itself. All were contrary to the Treasury Regulations and Conditions. Thus, it became increasingly essential for bankers and other financiers to find ways of avoiding the Real Bills Doctrine so that land could be taken for security against lending to agricultural businesses.

The 1840 and 1846 Regulations and Conditions (see Appendix 7) which clearly stated that banks shall not lend on the security of land were of little effective impediment to this type of mortgage lending. This was because although lending on the security of land was forbidden it was accompanied by a crucial proviso that the bank might subsequently acquire property in settlement of a debt.[26] A variety of mechanisms were employed to ensure that it was possible to lend against land and stay within the letter of the law. One was for the bank to accept deposit of the title documents to land on one day and then, on a subsequent day, to create a mortgage deed using those documents; another was for the bank to lend to a separate[27] non-banking institution, such as a land company or stock and station agent, which could then make advances to landowners.

By the mid-1850s the attitude of the UK Treasury to company regulation was in the process of change. The Treasury and the Board of Trade in London had concluded that little was to be served by continuing to make it difficult to form limited liability companies. Their shared view was that the most satisfactory results would result if shareholders could make their own judgements about the present worth and future prospects of companies informed by reliable, timely and freely, publicly-available information. The result was a simplified procedure for company formation that was introduced in the New South Wales Limited Partnerships Act 1853 and the 1858 Companies Act. In addition, the latter Act reduced restriction upon the permitted activities of companies and, for example, allowed companies with limited liability to lend against the security of land. But banks and insurance companies were expressly excluded from these developments. For example, the 1853 Limited Partnerships Act states:

1. After passing of this Act limited partnerships may be formed for the transaction of Agricultural Mining Mercantile Mechanical Manufacturing or other business by any number of persons upon the terms and subject to the conditions and liabilities hereinafter prescribed. Provided that nothing herein shall authorize any such partnership for the purpose of either Banking or Insurance.[28]

In similar vein, The Joint Stock Companies Act 1860 provided that:

2. This Act shall not apply to persons associated together for the purpose of banking and insurance.[29]

In 1862, the Companies Act was passed in the British Parliament which allowed any kind of business to be operated as a joint stock company with shareholder liability limited either by subscribed shares as yet unpaid or by guarantee (i.e. by undertaking to contribute a specified amount in the event of the winding up of the company).[30] Some have called it a significant de-regulation of company incorporation and have argued that this provision allowed some firms into unsustainable speculations which led directly to the Overend and Gurney Crisis of 1866.[31] It seems that banks, already established under charters, were slow to adopt the innovations in company law and avoided speculative enterprises although they could nor remain immune from their negative impacts.[32]

This legislation does not appear to have made its way into New Zealand statute. Instead, the General Assembly passed the British Companies Act in 1865. This legislation allowed all businesses legally incorporated in the UK to operate on a like-for-like basis in New Zealand. However, Section IX stated:

"Nothing in this Act contained shall be construed to authorize any Company incorporated as aforesaid to issue Bank Notes or Promissory Notes on demand within the Colony."[33]

As a consequence, we cannot argue that this particular change to Company Law led to an immediate sea-change in the development of the New Zealand and Australian monetary systems.

It is more likely that colonial banks were more immediately influenced by a well-concealed judgement of the Privy Council in London. In the late 1860s, the Privy Council ruled that a chartered bank was allowed to take possession of title to landed property only if that title had been acquired in the course of its banking business.[34] It seems that a borrower who fails to meet his obligations to the bank would be in breach of the conditions of supply under the Sale of Goods Act, notwithstanding existing banking law and regulation.[35] This was an important judgement. It invited banks to find ways around the prohibition on lending against landed security. Many took advantage of this judgement so that mortgage lending became an important aspect, if not a major part, of colonial banking.

In the 1860s, widespread abandonment of the charter-system of bank incorporation was another generation away and had to await the wholesale bank suspensions which occurred during the crises of the 1890s and the reformation of "new banks" from the ruins of the "old" in their aftermath.[36]

For much of the period until World War I, therefore, the chartered banks continued to operate within the frameworks laid down in their respective acts of parliament which were originally derived from Treasury regulations. This meant that because the charters were for a limited time (usually 21 years) they had to be renewed at regular intervals. For example, a Bank of New South Wales Act, was passed in 1850, 1870, 1886, 1905 and 1910. Each successive act appears to have repealed its predecessor and replaced the existing act with a virtually identical act which was designed to extend the existing charter for a further 21 years. The trading banks in Australia and New Zealand appear to have operated within similar legal frameworks until banking law was fundamentally altered during the 1980s.

BANKING IN NEW ZEALAND

In early 1840, there was no monetary system operating in New Zealand presumably because there was little or no need[37] for one. Most trade with Māori seems to have involved barter or cash on the nail. Most settlers paid for their land in England using their own existing banking arrangements; the money involved often never got as far as New Zealand. But if the colonisation project was to be successfully accomplished in New Zealand by introducing a market or markets for land, a monetary system of some sort had also to be introduced. Apart from some rare exceptions,[38] this crucial requirement was not understood by policy makers whether in the UK, New South Wales or New Zealand.

Neither Phillip nor Hobson arrived in Australasia with any tools with which they might have constructed a monetary system. For some reason, no-one had thought it a desirable let alone a necessary part of policy. Perhaps this might be excused in the case of New South Wales which was intended to be a prison and, as Butlin has pointed out, prisons do not need money.[39] Yet, in New Zealand, Hobson and his successors were expected to be able to buy land from Māori at a low price for gold-backed currency (i.e. "ready money") and sell at a profit to would-be settlers.[40] Both purchase and sale were presumed to involve the use of money and was also central to the design of Edward Gibbon Wakefield's proposal for colonisation because it:

> "… would supply the desideratum so anxiously sought by the Parliamentary Emigration Committee; namely, a means of conducting the emigration of paupers from Britain, *without any expense to the country.*"[41] (Italics in original.)

Colonial Office officials argued that the resulting profit would be sufficient to finance setting up and running the colonial government so that there would be minimal further calls on the UK Treasury. It appears that, insofar as it existed in 1840, the British Government's conception of New Zealand monetary relations involving non-indigenous people were totally encompassed within a closed, self-contained system centring on the New Zealand colonial treasury and including the UK Treasury and Sydney banks.[42]

If precious little prior consideration had been given to the organisation of monetary relations in colonial New Zealand, then it appears that no-one gave even a passing thought to the general monetisation of economic relations with Māori.[43] The eventual use of money by Māori appears to have been regarded as some type of natural outgrowth of colonial economic development among non-indigenous people.[44] Virtually nothing, except anecdotes exist about the use of bank notes, promissory notes, coins and bills by Māori or Aboriginal Peoples and the social and economic relationships this entailed at this time. It is recorded that, by the end of the 1840s, Māori were actively involved in trade with Auckland, Sydney and California. We also know, that from 1844 onwards, McLean, when negotiating for land in the Hawkes Bay and Wairarapa, carried with him large quantities of gold and silver coin in small cloth bags which, on successful conclusion of a sale, were distributed by senior chiefs to the various hapu consenting to the purchase. Kemp's purchase of the South Island of New Zealand also appears to have been settled in several instalments of gold coins over several years. But none of this amounts to evidence of a monetary system operating in New Zealand. Rather, in the absence of evidence of the existence of monetary institutions, it indicates merely that sterling currency was a kind of partial money sometimes used in the exchange of land.

Let us recall what did not exist in 1840. There was no tax system except collection of customs duties.[45] There was no mint.[46] There was no system of government expenditure and revenue collection and no coherent system of accounting for them. There was no gold production. Communications were primitive. There were no newspapers. Universal education was unheard of. It is likely that many transactions were in the form of barter or gift and currency was employed only when absolutely required as part of the transaction. Most important of all, until 1845, there was no Commissariat operating in New Zealand as there was in New South Wales.

Just as in the early days of the colonisation of New South Wales, in 1840, a number of individual monetary expedients were employed in New Zealand, isolated from each other. Even with the benefit of hindsight, they cannot readily be fitted into a coherent system of relationships and institutions. There was the stock of £2,000 worth of gold coins advanced from the New South Wales treasury and brought to New Zealand by George Cooper, New Zealand's first Colonial Treasurer.[47] Hobson's salary was paid in London because that was where he was recruited. The salaries of his officials were paid via the government of New South Wales. During 1840 to 1845, from time-to-time Hobson, Shortland and Fitzroy issued bills drawn on the UK Treasury which were honoured but only after considerable objection from the Secretary of State and after much delay. Some settlers imported currency with them. Gold and silver currency in a variety of forms was received from masters of visiting vessels in return for harbourage, victuals, raw materials and refitting. There was a branch of the Union Bank of Australia in Wellington from early 1840.[48] There was the New Zealand Banking Company founded in Kororareka in September 1840.[49] There were banks in Sydney and London which accommodated some settlers. There were local merchants who provided credit by means of bills of exchange or currency by issuing promissory notes. Some individuals, like Algernon Tollemarche and his nephew, Donald Sinclair[50], made loans on the security of mortgages on real estate. In 1840, even collectively these elements could not be realistically regarded as forming a coherent monetary system.

New Zealand is unusual because the costs of its colonisation had to be extracted, by one means or another, from a people most of whom did not ordinarily use money (i.e. Māori) and from another group many of whom did (i.e. non-indigenous people).[51] (For these reasons, the only forms of taxation which could, in practice, be applied were duties on customs and excise and harbour dues.) Yet, no thought about, or enquiry into, the question of how this transfer of costs was to be achieved in practice, appears to have occurred during the lengthy, confused and often abusive discussions from which colonisation of New Zealand emerged from early 19th century English politics.

Wakefield's nostrum was attractive to the British Government because at last it seemed it could avoid the costs which had attended past attempts to establish colonies and to hold them together in the British Empire. Colonies supplied raw materials and purchased finished goods "Made in England".[52] In the early 19th century, the declining role of trade as the mortar securing the joints between British colonies was replaced by flows of money and capital managed by London banks, which massively increased in scale and scope. Increasingly, the glue that held the British Empire together was the pattern of capital flows into and out of the London capital and money markets thus giving birth to a garbled version of Wakefield's idea of a self-funding empire.

Colonial Office Policies

Of all the agencies of state power commanded by the UK Government in the 1830s, the Colonial Office was by no means the least capable of envisaging future contingencies and of providing for their effective remedy. Nevertheless, despite its clearly enunciated plans to finance the colonisation of New Zealand by the crown's jobbing in Māori land, the Colonial Office made no attempt in 1840 to facilitate the buying and selling of land upon which the financial success of its strategy largely depended. Moreover, there appears to have been no attempt to formulate an alternative strategy to replace the original one should it prove unsuccessful.

It was not until 1846, when Earl Grey, then, Secretary of State for War and the Colonies, strongly recommended to Governor Grey that he set up a Colonial Bank of Issue, that the Colonial Office clearly indicates the necessity of such an initiative and, by implication, advertised the policy vacuum in New Zealand created by officials' reliance on wishful thinking over the preceding decade. It is an indication of Governor Grey's lack of commitment to the matter that the Colonial Bank of Issue did not open for business until 1850.

The reasons for this lack of official action are, at this distance, impossible to fathom with any accuracy. It is possible that Colonial Office officials simply did not regard the matter of sufficient concern, given the varying pressures of work they faced. Their predilection may have been to stand aside to allow private enterprise to provide a currency system and there was some evidence to support a belief in the potential effectiveness of this course of inaction. For example, Bedford states:

> "The earliest reference to banking in New Zealand is contained in a prospectus issued in January 1839 by Mr John Crawford a Solicitor of Paisley Scotland. He endeavoured to found a New Zealand Bank and Colonisation Company...."[53]

Moreover, banks were already active in both Sydney and Tasmania and the New Zealand Company was closely associated with financial interests in the City of London. Finally, in 1840, a consortium of prominent Bay of Island traders and Sydney merchants founded the New Zealand Banking Company with its sole branch in Kororareka.

In the commercial reality of New Zealand in 1840, the fundamental failure of a policy based on trying to sell land by auction without regard to the way that buyers might pay for it[54] quickly became evident in Auckland between 1841 and 1844.[55] Very few sections were sold by the crown despite its holding repeated land auctions. In retrospect, we can see that by late-1841 it was clear that the future financing of the New Zealand state by jobbing Māori land[56] was unsustainable unless the Colonial Government could muster a way of fostering a high chance of capital gains. Yet, neither Governor Hobson nor Acting Governor Shortland sought to change the financial foundations of the New Zealand state. The story of money in New Zealand until the early 1860s is largely confined to the indispensable work of Bedford and Butlin both of whom relied heavily upon bank records for their information.[57]

There were private initiatives to provide finance for land purchase and occasional references to the financing of land purchase by means of co-operative ventures similar to credit unions. So far, I have been able to find no reference to such a development occurring before the 1860s. For example, in her account of *A Crowded Thorndon Cottage* Beverley Randall states that in 1865 when seeking to buy land on which to build:

> "William [Randall] did not have the £75 the owner wanted. He and Sarah had saved £25 but a £50 mortgage had to be arranged with the *Land on Deferred Payment Society.*"[58]

It is possible that this society was associated with the Wellington Provincial Government's sales of crown land or possibly connected with the Exclusive Brethren to which the Randalls belonged. It is known, however, that, in 1876, Joseph Sowry was given permission to form the Woodville Small Farm Association to take up 2500 acres of land under the Hawkes Bay Provincial Council's deferred payment scheme.[59] More recently, McAloon has found evidence in the land registers of considerable mortgage lending by non-bank entities such as the Rhodes siblings.[60] Finally, Arnold states that the land sold to the Woodville Small Farm Association by the Hawkes Bay Provincial Government was priced at £1 per acre with seven years to pay at the rate of 9d per acre per quarter.[61]

By 1870, the practice of lending of significant sums over lengthy periods on the security of a mortgage on land was well-established in New Zealand and may have been introduced into the colony by early settlers. It is possible that prospective borrowers knew better than to seek long-term accommodation from the branches of country banks that were, by then, opening all over England.[62] But even with the introduction of joint-stock banking their shareholders continued to shoulder unlimited liability and the country banks were not equipped to accept the risks inherent in lending over many years secured by a mortgage on land. Thus, while a local businessman might well seek to negotiate bills at a country branch, if longer term finance were required it was usual to approach a local magnate, whose sources of funds came from long-term assets which enabled her or him to lend on mortgage into the medium-term. This would occur, for instance, if the sources of funds for lending have a maturity which is similar to that of the lending undertaken. An example would be rents from long-term tenancies the terms of which are regularly reviewed as appears to be the case of Hon. Algernon Tollemache. In that case, there would be a relatively small mismatch between the maturities of lending undertaken and of the longevity of income sources. Such a lender is much less exposed to the risk of losses because of sudden rises in short-term interest rates or falls in land prices than if she employed much shorter-dated sources of funds to fund the same long-term mortgages.

Little is known about such banking activities in colonial New Zealand. Fortunately, a source has come to light which throws a different light on monetary events in the 1850s. Professor Sue Middleton has provided me with access to copies of private letters written in New Zealand by Hon Algernon Tollemache MP[63] to his brother Frederick in the UK. Algernon Tollemache was an active[64] financier of settlers during the first 40 years of colonisation. His letters describe some of the lending he undertook.[65] Further light has been shed by McAloon who has analysed the registers of mortgages in the Canterbury Branch of Archives New Zealand. He concentrated on the largest mortgages made after 1870 which mean that very little is known about smaller loans made in other parts of the country.

The extent of lending by wealthy magnates in colonial New Zealand may have been very significant. Tollemache wrote on a number of occasions that he lent on mortgage for seven years and 10% per annum. He also reported on 1 February 1854: "My income in New Zealand is £1387 a year and it will every year increase".[66] Tollemache provided very significant finance to leading Hawkes Bay pastoralists Henry Russell and Donald McLean, to Māori *rangatira* including Te Hapuku and to a number of entrepreneurs in Nelson and Wellington.[67]

Until the mid-1850s, banks remained small and insignificant providers of finance for land acquisition. The New Zealand Banking Company moved its operations to Auckland when the capital was moved there in 1842. It did not attract large-scale business and ceased trading in 1845 and it was not until 1850 that all its debts were finally settled. The Union Bank of Australia opened in Wellington in 1840[68], in Nelson in 1842 (closed between 1848 and 1852), in Auckland in 1848 at which point it became the colonial Government's bank, in Lyttleton in 1855, in Dunedin in 1857 and in Christchurch in 1858 where it established its New Zealand headquarters. The Union

Bank appears to have deliberately retrenched its operations in New Zealand until the early 1850s. Bedford summarised the situation as follows:

> "The Directors of the Union Bank did not, however, discriminate between the condition in New Zealand and New South Wales, but in excess of distrust withdrew all available funds from the colonies to London."[69]

In accordance with this strategy the Nelson branch was closed in 1848 and the scope of those that remained (Auckland and Wellington) limited to that of exchange agencies.[70] As a consequence, private financiers, like Tollemache, were able to take advantage of the absence of local commercially-organised lending. They do not appear to have publicly advertised but relied heavily on personal relationships.[71] Tollemache also maintained deposits with merchants such as Fell in Nelson.[72]

FitzRoy's Financial Innovations

During the early 1840s, the supply of currency and other forms of money to New Zealand was practically non-existent. Both Governor Hobson and Acting-Governor Shortland experimented with the issue of bills drawn on the UK Treasury. But the grant-in-aid supplied by the British Government was always inadequate to meet the expenses of colonial administration as set out in the Civil List. In addition, Diamond states that the Colonial Office, in a fit of disordered optimism, ordered that Hobson repay a debt of £44,000 plus all local demands incurred by Governor Gipps in assisting the New South Wales immigration fund.[73] In the absence of a coherent system of taxation all the Colonial Office could suggest was to cut staff which was in direct contradiction to the instructions of Colonial Secretaries to maintain the existing Civil List. Thus, rudderless the New Zealand colonial government drifted into financial deficit.

Upon his installation in December 1843, Governor FitzRoy was faced with leading a colonial government which was effectively bankrupt.[74] Revenue from land sales was negligible and there was no readily accessible medium of exchange. We have already seen that FitzRoy experimented with suspending the crown's right of pre-emption with but limited success. He also made a number of financial innovations designed to make currency more easily available.

FitzRoy found that Auckland residents had no access to a universally accepted means of exchange because gold and silver currency had drained out of the colony to overseas and was not replenished by export earnings. In a society of any complexity the lack of a medium of exchange is a major impediment to social interaction of all kinds, not just commerce. Hence, unless some kind of substitute could be invented there was a risk that settlement in Auckland would have become severely curtailed or even abandoned. Apparently, unbeknownst to FitzRoy a similar lack of currency was bedevilling Nelson at much the same time.

FitzRoy, on his own initiative, undertook two financial innovations which eventually played a significant part in his recall. First, he issued bills drawn on the UK Treasury to meet the shortfall in the colonial government budget. In doing so he was merely doing what any Captain of the Royal Navy would do when faced with a bill for repairs or re-fitting in a foreign port.[75] But his second financial innovation was less orthodox. FitzRoy issued debentures[76] in relatively small denominations and persuaded the Legislative Council to designate them legal tender. In doing so, he anticipated, by more than a century, the issuance of legal tender currency with no backing other than the name of the UK Government.[77] In other words, in his desperation, he hit upon the very form of specie-less legal tender which has been issued by most governments in the world since World War II. With the benefit of hindsight, it now seems that by providing a ready supply of liquidity, however imperfect, FitzRoy helped ensure the survival of Auckland through the deep Australian recession of 1842–1844.[78] On his appointment, Governor Grey was instructed to redeem FitzRoy's notes using a supply of specie he had been granted and was then encouraged to found a bank of issue for which a further supply of gold and silver coinage had to be found.

Colonial Bank of Issue

Earl Grey, Secretary of State for War and the Colonies, considered that a reliable currency was a public benefit which should be available to everyone.[79] He was evidently aware of many of the weaknesses incorporated into FitzRoy's attempt to issue paper currency as legal tender in New Zealand. But the resulting organisation was hampered by instructions which appear to have had their origins in, and subsequent lobbying in London by, the Union Bank of Australia. These conditions included forcing the proposed bank of issue to keep a large reserve in coin which earned no interest and to invest heavily in low-yield British Government stock.[80] The inevitable result was that the Colonial Bank of Issue eventually became loss-making thus providing a reason for Prime Minister Stafford to propose its winding-up in 1856.

Earl Grey sought to address the weak foundations of the colonial currency system by bringing the Colonial Bank of Issue within the ambit of supervision and control of the UK Treasury through the agency of the Commissariat that had been serving the British Army in New Zealand since 1845.[81] It administered the Military Chest[82], which, Taylor states, was "… a source of funds for military and other specified government purposes in foreign stations."[83] Thus, by involving the Commissariat in the Colonial Bank of Issue via transactions through the Military Chest, Earl Grey brought the bank into the financial systems of the UK Treasury by which the finances of the British Empire were managed.[84] Thus, before 1860, New Zealand was enmeshed in the financial arrangements of the British Empire through two mechanisms. The first was through private banks financing trade bills and the second resulted from the colonial government's financing activities in London. It was envisaged that funds received by the Colonial Bank of Issue but which were unlikely to be needed for the purpose of exchange into notes would be deposited with the Commissary and would be evidenced by a certificate issued by the Commissary. That certificate would then be conveyed to London and public securities would be issued by the Treasury to the amount stated to the credit of the colony. The Colonial Government was permitted to draw on this balance if it became necessary to raise gold and silver coinage. The bank was also permitted to seek advances of cash from the Commissary which were then to be repaid by deductions from the investments previously made. Finally, the Secretary of State arranged for the engraving and printing of banknotes in the UK.[85]

The Colonial Bank of Issue was inaugurated on 16 October 1847 [86] but did not begin operations until 1850[87] and did little business until it was given a monopoly over note issue in October 1852.[88] The total amount of its notes outstanding eventually grew to £40,000 in 1856 when the Colonial Government decided that the bank was draining the colony of funds which could be more advantageously used for economic development initiated by non-indigenous settlers. This was, it was argued, because the costs of running the bank were greater than the interest it received on the investments in public securities made in London on its behalf. It was also pointed out that the need to keep a third of its assets in cash limited its ability to make profits out of advances. Finally, it was asserted that the bank could not adjust the colonial money supply to meet New Zealand trading conditions.[89] On 29 July 1856, the Colonial Bank of Issue was wound up.[90] and the Union Bank was commissioned to retire the bank's outstanding note issue. For this task the Union Bank was granted £15,000 in cash and £25,000 in debentures.[91]

The Colonial Bank of Issue linked the New Zealand economy to that of the monetary system of the British Empire in a very circumscribed way. The bank's operations were "confined to the issuing of bank notes for cash, and to the payment of such notes in cash on demand." [92] The bank, thus, gave potential customers a choice between holding its notes, which were guaranteed by the British Government, or holding cash (i.e. gold or silver coin and Bank of England notes), which were also guaranteed by the British Government. It was unable, therefore, to make advances and take deposits from the general public or to trade in or discount trade bills. Thus, unlike its direct competitor in New Zealand, the Union Bank of Australia, it was unable to create currency through its own banking operations. Moreover, notes were to be expressed in pounds sterling[93] and could not be issued in fractions of a pound.[94] Apart from the saving in weight of carrying a given amount of currency in the form of notes rather than coin, it is hard to understand the advantages that were conferred to its customers by the services it offered. Confined in this way, the Colonial Bank of Issue merely offered a bank note alternative to holding cash. The only way that the bank's note issue could be increased was as a result of an exogenously-determined inflow into New Zealand of gold or silver legal tender or UK Government bills (i.e. Treasury Bills) exchanged for bank notes.

Even then the bank was heavily circumscribed. One-third of all cash received in exchange for its notes had to be held in cash. The remainder was to be entrusted to the Commissary to be invested in public securities in London. Thus, users of the Colonial Bank of Issue were, in practice, lending to the UK Government either by indirectly investing the UK Government debt or by accepting UK Government issued coinage. The colonial Government was permitted to seek advances of specie from the Commissary or draw on the UK Treasury up to a maximum of the value of the bank's holdings of public securities. Hence, in conducting such an operation the colonial government was withdrawing a deposit which the bank had previously made at the UK Treasury. It is not known to what extent, if any, this facility was employed during the lifetime of the bank.

Banking Developments

The Oriental Banking Corporation opened for business in Auckland and Wellington in 1856.[95] Immediately, it tried to compete for customers by offering interest on current accounts and agreeing to take 12-month bills secured by mortgages. The Union Bank reacted by paying interest on deposits to which the Oriental responded by opening branches in Dunedin and Invercargill. Butlin argues that in the late 1850s and early 1860s the Oriental was trying to cultivate New Zealand as a source of deposits and a place to make exchange profits in order to finance its operations in Australia.[96]

But Butlin's interpretation of the Oriental strategy may be more a reflection of the Union Bank's actions than an accurate description of the Oriental's behaviour. The Oriental was regarded at the time as the leading exchange bank in Asia and its extension into New Zealand was part of a rapid increase in branches throughout the Southern Hemisphere and Asia that it undertook from the mid-1850s onwards. It is also perhaps possible that the Oriental's strategy foreshadowed that of Overend Gurney[97] of using short-term bill trading to fund longer-term mortgage lending. In any case, the profits from dealing in bills of exchange that the Oriental expected did not materialise and its branches were taken over by the Bank of New South Wales in 1861.

The obstructive tactics of the Union Bank failed to prevent a number of successful new entrants into the New Zealand finance industry at the same time. In March 1847, March 1857 and March 1861, Butlin[98] estimated that the extent of the Union Bank's business in New Zealand was as follows:

	1847	1857	1861
Note Issue (£)	n.a.	33,406[99]	105,595
Deposits (£)	22,178	321,769	619,352
Coin (£)	n.a.	95,266	149,291
Advances (£)	23,601	264,495	641,208

n.a. Not Available

The rapid growth of Union Bank advances between 1857 and 1861 was the result of the Bank's lending to Canterbury squatters. In this, it was greatly assisted by the passage on 3 June 1858 of the Wool and Oil Securities Act. This Act allowed bank advances to be made (and registered) to sheep and whaling stations on the security of receiving the next clip of wool or of oil and bone secured in the next whaling season. This legislation effectively removed many impediments to banks' lending on the security of land in New Zealand. However, the legislation did not amend the way that banks were to provide assurance against the risks of undertaking such lending.

In the early 1860s, New Zealand was on the threshold of an economic expansion which conveyed the society to a position among the richest countries of the world within the next half century. During that time a full-blown monetary system developed which was intimately connected to the very heart of the Gold Exchange Standard. Those developments were built upon a system which was originally designed for the banking needs of the English countryside in the form of the Country Banks Act 1826. For the present, I shall leave to one side how this dramatic transformation occurred because it is first necessary to describe how New Zealand found it necessary to construct its own system of legislation to govern the ownership and sale of Māori land. This was a process that was unnecessary in Australia because the crown had already asserted its ownership of the entire continent.

Chapter Notes

1. In effect, economics most commonly defines money as "money is what money does" to which a number of luminous and explanatory metaphors, similes or analogies can be added. This body of theory originated in Joseph Harris: *An Essay Upon Money and Coins*, London, Hawkins, 1757–1758 and Francis Walker: *Political Economy*, New York, H Holt, 1884.
2. See James Buchan: "Frozen Desire: An Inquiry into the Meaning of Money", London, Pinter, 1997.
3. The charter which Macquarie granted the Bank of New South Wales in 1817 was repudiated by Lord Bathurst the Secretary of State for War and the Colonies but Macquarie effectively neglected to report on the Bank of New South Wales until the Bank has been in existence for more than three years. By that time, it had become firmly established in Sydney commercial circles.
4. Joint stock ownership means that shareholders own a business in proportion to the shares that they own. The liability of shareholders may or may not be limited by the contribution each shareholder has made to the capital of the business. The main advantage of joint stock ownership has over a partnership is that the ownership structure of an organisation can be changed through sale and purchase of shares; in the case of a partnership, by contrast, in order to change ownership the original partnership must first be dissolved and a new one formed to take its place. Such a process is costly and potentially disruptive to the trust with the business is held.
5. Under the Country Banks Act 1826 shareholder liability remained unlimited.
6. Anglo-Australian banks is a term coined by S J Butlin. By it, he meant banks incorporated in the UK in order to offer banking services in Australia and New Zealand. Most were headquartered in large towns in the English regions with an active foreign trading base such as Birmingham, Bristol, Exeter, Liverpool or Norwich. All had London branches (often termed the headquarters branch) which could not issue notes and so adopted a coordinating role such as housing Board meetings and negotiating loans and bills of exchange with the London Discount Market. Both the Bank of Australasia and the Union Bank of Australia can be classed as Anglo-Australian.
7. Holder, op cit, 1970, p. 16.
8. The Derwent Bank in the late 1830s developed a method of facilitating direct lending between lenders in Great Britain and land-owning borrowers in Tasmania. While this circumvented the prohibitions against a bank lending against mortgage security it nevertheless collapsed when borrowers could no longer meet their obligations as wool prices dropped in the early 1840s.
9. S J Butlin, op cit, 1961, Chapter 7, pp. 90–118.
10. Ibid, p. 3 and p. 91.
11. Australian Bureau of Statistics: Australian Historical Population Statistics 2019, Table 1.1. Estimates do not include Aboriginal peoples or residents of Jervis Bay or Other Territories.
12. Ibid, p. 119.
13. Butlin, op cit, 1961, pp. 377–8.

14 Ibid, p. 234.
15 Ibid, p. 235.
16 S J Butlin: *The Australian Monetary System 1851–1914*, edited by Judith F Butlin, Canberra, Reserve Bank of Australia, 1986, pp. 8–9.
17 Sinclair and Mandle, op cit, 1961, Appendix II, The Banking Agreement of 1868, pp. 235–236.
18 Hawke, op cit, 1997, p. 7.
19 S J Butlin, op cit, 1970, p. 11–12.
20 See Ronald A Shearer: "Imperial Regulation and the Constitution of Early Canadian Banking", paper presented to a conference of The Canadian Network for Economic History, held at Queen's University, Kingston, April 2005.
21 This was a great restriction on the growth of banking. For example, when the City of Glasgow Bank collapsed in 1867 many shareholders were forced into bankruptcy because they could not pay the calls on their personal resources arising from the debts the bank had accumulated.
22 Shearer, op cit, 2005, p. 6.
23 S J Butlin, op cit, 1961, pp. 25–26.
24 For a full text of the 1840 Regulations and Conditions, which applied to New South Wales and New Zealand at the time of their promulgation, see Shearer, op cit, 2005, pp. 33–36. To see the text of the Regulations and Conditions revised in 1846 see "Incorporation of Banking Companies", *The Melbourne Argus,* Friday 28 May 1847, p. 4. trove.nla.gov.au/newspaper/article/4761607. Accessed 20 June 2021. A copy was not sent to the New Zealand colonial administration in 1840 because New Zealand was still a part of New South Wales. Only when the 1846 version was available was New Zealand included in the circulation list.
25 Shearer's text of the Treasury regulations contains 17 sections plus a *pro forma* reporting framework while Butlin's copy of the Bank of Australasia charter has 11 sections and no *pro forma* reporting framework. It is not known which version is authentic.
26 S J Butlin, op cit, 1986, p. 94.
27 It should be recalled that the degree of separation varied between companies. However, separation does not seem to have been actively policed let alone enforced.
28 See www.austlii.edu.au/cgi-bin/viewdb//au/legis/nsw/num_act/lpa1853n9264/. Accessed 21 June 2021.
29 See www.nzlii.org.nz/legis/hist_act/jsca186024n/1860n13353/. Accessed 23 June 2021.
30 The Companies Act 1862, (25 & 26 Vict c.89), Section 7. See https://law-platform.jp/refs/uk_1862cap89. Consulted 23 June 2021.
31 Davis Foucaud: "The Impact of the Companies Act 1862 Extending Limited Liability in the Banking and Financial Sector in the English Crisis of 1866", *Revue Economique,* Volume 62, Issue 5, 2011, pp. 867–897.
32 Ibid, p. VIII.
33 See www.nzlii.org/nz/legis/hist_act/bca186529v1865n9305/. Accessed 25 June 2021. Presumably, this Section was included to prevent a rapid influx of British-based banks into New Zealand presumably to reduce competition with the Bank of New Zealand.
34 N M Chappell: *New Zealand Banker's Hundred: A History of the Bank of New Zealand 1861 – 1961,* Wellington, Bank of New Zealand, 1961, p. 75 states: "… there was a question of whether banks had a valid claim to any land that came into their hands. Following a Privy Council decision in the early 1870's that such a claim was valid, banks in both Australia and New Zealand were soon to enter freely into this type of business…"
35 The precise date at which the Judicial Committee of the Privy Council made this ruling is unclear. In a judgement delivered on 30 June 1870 their Lordships ruled in the case of Bank of Australasia vs Cherry. Cherry claimed that the bank could not take possession of land he had pledged under a mortgage because under the Treasury Regulations banks were not allowed to lend against land. They ruled that notwithstanding any legislation there was a "good and valid debt between the bank and the customer" and "that the bank had a right to stipulate for and

take the security". See Privy Council Papers reference 1792_1312. www.bailji.org/uk/cases/ukpc/1870/1870.27.html.

36 Butlin, op cit, 1986, pp. 94–97.

37 Recognition of the advantages of access to unified monetary system is not natural. In a society in which alternative uses of resources and social relations are relatively fixed the need for a means of payment, store of value, unit of account and a method of deferred payment are not obvious and their introduction may impose risks or transactions and waiting costs. Only when there is a widespread demand for changes in productive relations and the risks that result does the lack of an acceptable money start to materially reduce economic and social opportunities.

38 People who *at the time of colonisation* recognised the importance of a workable monetary system included Governors Phillip and Macquarie, John Crawford, Edward Gibbon Wakefield and the Board of the Union Bank of Australia and the Court of the New Zealand Company.

39 This is of course not true. Modern prisons contain inmates who actively trade in a variety of goods and services for which they require access to currency. There seems to be no reason to suppose the primitive structure of the Sydney penal colony was any different in this respect. Hence, I conclude that the absence of monetary institutions from New South Wales must have been the result of deliberate policy the reasons for which have yet to emerge.

40 Normanby's instructions to Hobson make this clear. For example, "Having … obviated the dangers of the acquisition of large tracts of Country by mere Landjobbers, it will be you duty to obtain by fair and equal contracts with the Natives, the Cession to the Crown of such Waste Lands as may be progressively required for the occupation of Settlers resorting to New Zealand. … The resales of the first purchases that may be made, will provide the Funds necessary for future acquisitions; and, beyond the original investment of a comparatively small sum of money, no other resource will be necessary for this purpose. I thus assume that the price to be paid to the Natives by the local Govt will bear an exceedingly small proportion to the price for which the same Lands will be resold by the Govt to the Settlers." McIntyre and Gardner, op cit, 1979, pp 13–14.

41 M F Lloyd Pritchard: *The Collected Works of Edward Gibbon Wakefield*, Glasgow and London, Collins, 1968, Appendix Outline of a System of Colonization, p.179.

42 The paucity of confirmatory evidence for this conjecture cannot be over-emphasised. Much research into monetary relationships in different localities in early colonial New Zealand remains to be done. Local history might be the most appropriate home for such studies.

43 Despite the pioneering efforts of the late David Shepherd and the late Jan Whitwell the monetary history of New Zealand has been shamefully ignored by New Zealand economists and historians alike. So far as is known, there are no studies about the monetisation of New Zealand economy and society. Yet, many anecdotes about partial moneys taking different forms operating in different times and different places have been recorded over the years.

44 Some settlers regarded the spread of monetary relations within Māoridom to be part of progress towards higher forms of civilisation, if it occurred to them to reflect upon the matter. For example, much later, many senior chiefs became customers of the Bank of New Zealand.

45 Hobson brought with him George Cooper as Colonial Treasurer and Collector of Customs. Prior to that, Māori chiefs were in the habit of charging visiting vessels for harbourage.

46 A mint still (2025) does not operate in New Zealand.

47 Malcolm McKinnon: *Treasury, The New Zealand Treasury 1840–2000*, Auckland, Auckland University Press, 2003, p. 25. A further £3,000 was credited to the New Zealand Treasury at the Bank of Australasia in Sydney.

48 By agreement between the Court of Directors of the New Zealand Company and the London Board of the Union Bank the officers and equipment of the bank were transported free of charge in Company vessels.

49 Based on an offer of £7,000 worth of shares. Half the capital of the bank was subscribed in Sydney where the company was registered. The manager was Alexander Kennedy and the

directors were Gilbert Mair, Edward Williams, Henry Thompson, James Clendon, Daniel Pollen, John Scott, William Mayhew and Philo Perry.

50 Sinclair was the nephew of Algernon Tollemarche and acted as the latter's agent in New Zealand.

51 In North America, during the 17th and 18th centuries, the English had encountered so-called Indian "tribes". However, these "tribes" were allowed to function according to their own traditional practices, largely separate from the English settlers in the plantations who grew North American products for export to England. Hence, the question of how the Indian economy was to be monetised was not posed.

52 This also had the effect of providing, in the form of an active merchant marine, a ready-made training ground for seamen who could potentially be recruited, by fair means or foul, by the Royal Navy.

53 Bedford (ed), op. cit, 1916, p. 33. The venture apparently failed for lack of interest.

54 It is remarkable that Crawford had already confronted this problem. According to Bedford, ibid, p. 35 Crawford's prospectus for a New Zealand Banking and Colonisation Company stated: "Colonisation could be promoted successfully only when supported by the aid of monetary facilities such as banks and loan companies are able to afford." Despite the perceptiveness of its sponsors it seems that this company never became a working reality.

55 This was a time of slump in Australia. See Butlin, op cit, 1961, Chapter 7, pp. 90–118.

56 This model of colonial finance was originally proposed by Gibbon Wakefield in "A Letter from Sydney" originally published in London about 1829. Wakefield claimed that it offered "… a means of conducting the emigration of paupers from Britain, *without any expense to the country.*" See MF Lloyd Prichard, ed.: "The Collected Works of Edward Gibbon Wakefield", Glasgow, Collins, 1968, p. 179.

57 Most monetary history has been based on bank archives and official records. The shortcoming of such records is that private archives and records are usually kept because someone in authority wants posterity to read them. The documents they contain are normally carefully screened (sometimes repeatedly) to ensure that researchers reach conclusions that the depositors of documents desire and are steered away from undesired ones. The result is that private archives held by banks and other companies may be an unreliable source of New Zealand monetary history and great circumspection must always accompany their use.

58 Beverley Randall: *A Crowded Thorndon Cottage: The Story of William & Sarah Randall and their ten children*, Wellington, Gondwanaland Press, 1992, p. 29. It has not been possible to trace and detailed information about this apparently co-operative society.

59 Rollo Arnold: *The Farthest Promised Land—English Villagers, New Zealand Immigrants of the 1870s*, Wellington, Victoria University Press, 1981, pp. 315–317. It is worth remarking that in 1871 and 1872 Sowry approached the Hawkes Bay Provincial Government on behalf of a local branch of the Rechabite Lodge proposing a similar scheme. Hence, it is possible that the early roots of this type of lending can be discerned in the activities of Friendly Societies as well as Credit Unions and local small farm associations.

60 Tollemache wrote from Wellington on 12 November 1852: "On October 1 last I lent the £1000 mentioned in former letters on two mortgages for 7 years certain at 10 percent interest on properties in this settlement. I have now therefore lent on mortgage £800 at Nelson and £1000 here on the above terms. I have promised to lend £200 to one of the parties at Nelson who has already given me a mortgage on his property. These are all registered according to the Ordinance here and are quite secure." Investigation of whether or not registers of mortgages mentioned by Tollemache still (in 2019) exist would take this study into new uncharted fields which are out of its present scope. It seems that Tollemarche relied upon rents on his London properties let on long leases as a source of funds. He also seems to have taken advantage of contacts he formed with the staff of Ham House where he lived for many years.

61 Arnold, op cit, 1981, p.316. Arnold is at pains to emphasise that successful settlement of assisted immigrants in the 1870s depended on the active support of provincial governments through

provision of supplies, infrastructure and waged work.
62. Roger Outing: "An Introduction to English Banking History" britishmuseum.org/researcg/publications/online_research_catalogues/paper_money/paper_money_of_england_wales/English_banking_history.aspx. Outing states that: "By the 1820s, every town of substance had its own local bank with its own banknote issues."
63. Hon Algernon Tollemache 24 September 1805 – 16 January 1892 was the youngest son of Lord Huntingtower proprietor of Ham House near Richmond. He sat as MP for Grantham 1832–1837.
64. Tollemache was in New Zealand from 1849 to 1855, 1860 to 1865 and 1870 to 1876.
65. Tollemache also seems to have a low regard for New Zealand business ethics because in the course of the correspondence on 1 February 1854 he warned his brother: "Take my advice and do not consent to be either a Trustee or Director of any banking co[mpany] connected with New Zealand. I have a very poor opinion of the honesty of most persons in the colonies when dealing with absent parties. It appears to me to be considered quite right and fair to cheat them in every way. In becoming a Director you must trust parties you know nothing of and you must also become answerable for all their acts.—Have nothing to do with it."
66. £1,387 a year represents something over $350,000 per annum in terms of today's dollars. There does not appear to have been any attempt to investigate whether Tollemache ever financed McLean's land purchasing on behalf of the colonial government. It is noteworthy that Tollemache records that he took the trouble to register his debts wherever possible.
67. See Alan Ward, "McLean, Donald", *Dictionary of New Zealand Biography*, first published in 1990. *Te Ara—the Encyclopaedia of New Zealand*, https://teara.govt.nz/en/biographies/1m38/mcleanl-donald (accessed 30 September 2019) and Mary Boyd, "Russell, Henry Robert", *Dictionary of New Zealand Biography*, first published in 1990. *Te Ara—the Encyclopaedia of New Zealand*, https://teara.govt.nz/en/biographies/2r32/russell-henry-robert (accessed 30 September 2019)
68. Famously, the manager of the Union Bank in Wellington, Mr J Smith, arrived on the Petone foreshore sitting upon the bank's safe, which weighed more than two tons and was being rafted ashore from the *Glenbervie* that had arrived in Wellington Harbour on 7 March 1840.
69. Bedford, op cit, 1916, p. 52. By this statement, Bedford presumably meant that the business of these branches was confined largely to the negotiation and discounting of bills of exchange.
70. Nelson was one of the many places in which local merchants issued notes for customers. These notes circulated in the local community in place of currency albeit sometimes at a discount. The role of these local, commercially-created monies has been largely neglected by historians. Their relative importance and their influence on the course of the economic development of the colony is largely unknown.
71. For example, Tollemache was a close friend of Donald McLean and oversaw the education of McLean's son in England.
72. This outcome bore particularly heavily upon Māori who presumably would have had few contacts with non-bank financiers and whose only recourse to finance for development of their land was the Colonial Government. Before Governor Grey took office the government was barely able to fund its own operations let alone promote agricultural or industrial development of non-indigenous people and Māori.
73. Marion Diamond: "Most Injudicious … Most Injurious" The Royal Bank of Australia's Loan to the New Zealand Government, 1842", *New Zealand Journal of History*, (1986), Vol 20, No 1, pp. 64–72, p. 64.
74. It appears that FitzRoy arrived in Auckland having been misled into believing that the Colonial Government was in a strong financial position. In fact, in early 1844, the colony was already £24,000 in debt and had an estimated prospective income of only £20,000 per annum. See John and Mary Gribben: *FitzRoy: The Remarkable Story of Darwin's Captain and the Invention of the Weather Forecast*, London, ALSOHeadline Publishing, 2003, p. 223.

75   This action was severely frowned upon by the Colonial Office in London since Fitzroy was considered to have disobeyed his instructions. Nevertheless, the UK Treasury eventually honoured the bills that Fitzroy drew on it as it did the bills drawn by Hobson and Shortland before him but not before rumours of their repudiation echoed around Sydney and London

76   The debentures issued by Governor FitzRoy carried no rate of interest and no maturity date. They were, in effect, issued against a promise to pay. The value of this promise rested upon the value of the name of the Colonial Government which was widely believed to be incapable of meeting its obligations from its ordinary revenues such as import duties or excises.

77   In the event, the FitzRoy currency traded at a discount to specie. In part, this was because holders of the notes did not sufficiently trust the name of the colonial government and were much against FitzRoy's policies towards Māori. The main reason for their discount against specie was that the notes were easy to forge and were printed on poor quality paper so making them vulnerable to damage. In the long run, the key weakness was that FitzRoy had neglected to provide for a coherent way of ensuring that the stock of currency could be maintained by means of its periodic withdrawal and re-issue.

78   See Ken Matthews: "The legal history of money in New Zealand", *Reserve Bank of New Zealand Bulletin,* Vol. 66, No. 1, March 2003, pp. 40–49. Another factor is the influx of Imperial troops and the Commissariat payments that accompanied them into Wellington in the aftermath Wairau Incident.

79   Earl Grey shared with Peel the importance accorded to the reliable issue of bank notes for economic development. It was this belief that lay behind many of the provisions of Peel's Acts after 1818 and the Bank Charter Act 1844. The spread of chequeing facilities meant that bank notes were not as important to the working of the monetary system as the UK Government believed. However, provision of sound currency could do little harm and even some good, albeit the benefits were confined largely to the wealthy.

80   Butlin, op cit, 1961, p. 161 records that the Union Bank of Australia made representations to the Colonial Office and succeeded in having the proportion of total assets of the Colonial Bank of Issue held in a coin reserve or low-yielding British government bonds raised from the 25%, originally envisaged, to one-third. Governor Grey made the Union Bank note issue illegal in October 1852. However, the Colonial Bank of Issue was a drain of the Colonial Government finances. The Colonial Bank of Issue was wound up in 1856 and the Union Bank was given the task of withdrawing the Colonial Bank of Issue's outstanding note issue and replacing it with its own.

81   Richard J Taylor: "British Logistics in the New Zealand Wars, 1845–66", unpublished PhD thesis, Massey University, 2004, p. 36. Taylor argues that logistical deficiencies were to blame for many casualties and deaths during the Crimea War 1854–56 which led to the creation of a Commissariat Staff Corps, greatly increased staff and reform of commissariat procedures.

82   Until the 1830s, the cash operations of the UK Treasury were under the day-to-day control of three tellers each of whom had the custody of iron chests with multiple locks the keys to which were held by several persons. A given chest could only be opened when all keyholders agreed that it should. Presumably this system was the origin of the term "Tin Box Accounting" and the term "Military Chest" is a hang-over from this system.

83   Taylor, op cit, 2004, p. 36. It should be recalled that the official position of the Minister responsible for the colonies was the Secretary of State for *War* and the Colonies thus giving the authority to include this new responsibility.

84   "Despatch from Earl Grey to Governor Grey on the Colonial Bank of Issue", *New Zealander,* Vol 4, Issue 312, 26 May 1849, downloaded from https://paperspast.natlib.nz/newspapers/NZ184905.26.2.6 28 March 2019.

85   Ibid.

86   Ordinance Session VIII, No XVI. This Ordinance limited the Union Bank's issue of currency to the mean outstanding of the two years preceding the passage of the Ordinance.

87 Butlin, op cit, 1961, p. 161 states: "The ordinance required Royal assent, and note forms had to be obtained from England, so that the bank did not open until June 1850."
88 This was the date that the Colonial Government legislated to remove the Union Bank of Australia's right to issue bank notes in the Bank Paper Currency Act 1856.
89 Butlin, op cit, 1961, p. 161.
90 New Zealand Colonial Bank of Issue Winding-Up Act 1856.
91 Butlin, op. cit., 1961, pp 161–162.
92 Ordinance Session VIII, No XVI, Section 7.
93 Ibid, Section 10.
94 Ibid, Section 14.
95 The Oriental Banking Corporation was the largest exchange bank in Asia and expanded rapidly in the 1850s. Its entry into New Zealand was part of this expansion.
96 Butlin, op cit, 1961, pp.162–163.
97 Overend Gurney was a very large an influential acceptance house. Its main business was to accept bills for a small consideration to make them more acceptable to discounting banks. In 1825 it rescued the Bank of England. After 1858, when Overend left the firm, it began to use short-term funds to invest in long-term investments like railways. It collapsed in 1867.
98 Ibid, p. 157 and 166.
99 When the Union Bank of Australia was employed by the colonial government to withdraw the notes issued by the Colonial Bank of Issue it is believed that its note issue was in excess of £40,000. See Butlin, op cit, p 161. Bedford, op cit, 1916, p. 118 reports that the note issue of the Colonial Bank of Issue on June 1854 was £40,323.

CHAPTER 6

AUSTRALASIA AND THE DEVELOPING GOLD STANDARD

This Chapter shows that the colonisation of Australasia took place with the full contribution of the international monetary system of the day. This was not the automatic Gold Standard celebrated in economic theory but a halting version of it still exposed to structural faults. This chapter outlines some aspects of a significant gap in knowledge of the international economic system during the first sixty years of the 19th century and makes some tentative attempts to fill it.

By the 1860s, Britain's colonies were founded within, and held together by, a framework of international payments and receipts centred upon the London money and capital markets. No doubt Colonial Office officials and officers serving in the colonies did not question the existence of this framework when making policy even to the extent of attributing the existence of the British Empire to the power and influence of the Royal Family. This would account for the fact that they appear to have given little or no thought to how potential settlers would pay for their colonial land holdings or find the capital required to make them productive. This financial framework became known as the gold standard system but only with the benefit of hindsight and with the aid of much wishful thinking. The way it actually worked is by no means clear.[1]

Economists do not agree when the gold standard system began. Globally, it did not exist before 1880 when the USA abandoned a bi-metallic standard in favour of gold. Some have asserted that the gold standard was established by the 1844 Bank Charter Act and yet others point to the start of the gold standard as the late 1810s and early 1820s when the Bank of England became prepared to guarantee a price of £3–17s-101/2d per troy ounce of gold 95% pure. Finally, Eichengreen argues that Great Britain adopted:

"… a *de facto* gold standard from 1717, when Sir Isaac Newton, then Master of the Mint, set too high a silver price for the gold guinea."[2]

Which date we chose to adopt matters very little for our narrative but the very existence of this disagreement indicates that:

❖ The gold standard system is not precisely defined as a single entity or set of processes; and
❖ The full-blown gold standard evolved over 160 years as a result of a number of choices taken in a number of countries over a long time.

Much research is required before we can be sure that it is accurate to argue that the colony of New Zealand was, from its inception, part of the Gold Standard as traditionally described. Indeed, we shall see that it was probably only after 1907 that the accuracy of that proposition can be reasonably well-established. This high-point of the Gold Standard in Australia and New Zealand lasted only until 1916 when the Bank of New Zealand announced that it would accept gold certificates rather than physical gold in settlement of inter-bank imbalances on the Wellington clearing system.[3]

Holding the British Empire Together

During the Long Nineteenth Century, most influential English politicians believed that money consisted solely of the gold-backed currency which Parliament had determined in 1816 and 1819 would be legal tender. There was apparently no understanding that the monetary networks that had developed informally during the 17th and 18th centuries, under the indirect oversight of the Bank of England, created widely accepted means of exchange and stores of value. These often family-based networks created currency that was publicly-accepted, at least locally.[4] Thus, even in 1816, other sources of currency existed apart from legal tender. They included bank notes, trade tokens and portable tally records; the manufacture and distribution of all was largely beyond the direct control of the Government.

Sir Robert Peel (1788–1850) was a Tory MP from 1809 until his death. He was twice Prime Minister and his Government passed the Bank Charter Act 1844. In 1819, he was appointed Chair of the Bullion Committee which plotted the course by which Great Britain would resume cash payments after the restrictions imposed during the French Wars. The result was the Resumption of Cash Payments Act 1819 which specified a gold price of £3 –17s – 10 1/2d per troy ounce of gold 95% fine. Peel believed that the stock of currency defined as bank notes and minted coin in circulation required careful control. This would be best achieved when the stock of notes and coin is kept in close relation with the amount of gold held by the Government. To this end his government passed the Bank Charter Act 1844 which endeavoured to bring this discipline to the monetary system of Great Britain under the leadership of the Bank of England.

Peel's monetary reforms[5] were doomed to failure because, although they succeeded in controlling the supply of gold-backed legal tender, they had no direct effect on the variety of other, widely circulated moneys that were not legal tender. Indeed, it might be argued that by directing regulatory attention towards the monetary circuits presided over by the Bank of England they allowed a wide variety of monetary instruments to develop in the policy vacuum created by neglect of the wider reality.

The Glorious Revolution and the Bill of Rights which was associated with it meant that inevitably England, and later Great Britain, became embroiled, on behalf of the newly acquired Royal Family, in a series of wars on the continent of Europe.[6] By its Royal

Charter, the Bank of England was permitted to buy and sell debt instruments.[7] This meant that the Bank[8] became central to the UK Government's borrowing operations during the 18th century which, in turn, were central to its ability to pursue a succession of foreign wars, meeting the costs of warfare faced by allies and the associated costs of arming and re-arming of the Royal Navy.[9] It also meant that the Bank of England was heavily involved in the management of gold-backed legal tender including the export and import of specie.[10]

At the same time, the Bank's ability to trade in debt securities developed in a number of ways in response to financial innovation of its banking clients. Even in the 18th century it is likely that the most common means of settling large debts was by means of banker's paper.[11] Legal tender, like Bank notes and gold-backed coins, was being superseded by the use of financial instruments issued by banks in the form of bills, drafts, letters of credit and promissory notes. Often, these instruments were issued by so-called country banks or merchants and circulated in a relatively narrow geographical area or social space. In that case, they were faced with the uncertainty that local circumstances, such as a drought or disease or even gambling losses by a local magnate could undermine the basis on which that paper had been created and accepted by local networks. This could occur even if the institutions or families concerned had access to highly effective methods of collecting and processing appropriate information. At the same time, the scale of risks increased as the scope of the British domestic economy widened to include international transactions such as the development of North American and West Indian plantations based on slavery or indentured labour.[12]

During the 18th century, local banks managed these risks in broadly three ways. First, they became customers of the Bank of England and other London-based banks. This meant that they could assure themselves of a ready source of liquidity to meet their obligations in almost any circumstance by accessing the London Discount Market. Increasingly,[13] by reason of its close association with successive Whig administrations, the Bank of England became the bankers' bank. Second, they were absorbed into other banks which had a broader reach into other regions, other industries or other countries so that local risks (such as drought-induced crop failure or individual bankruptcy) could be spread over a wider variety of monetary flows. Third, they developed sources of information about the risks they were taking and deployed that information to manage their businesses. As risk became more complex this led some firms to specialise in particular aspects of the business of banking. But at no stage in these developments was there discussion in official circles of the possible impacts on systemic risk.

1825 Crisis and Financial System Development

During the early 1820s, the Bank of England was unwilling to hold sufficient gold reserves to forestall a major liquidity crisis. Gold represented a deadweight on the Bank's balance sheet because it yielded no interest, was costly to store and safeguard and was bought and sold at a fixed price at the Bank of England. Large holdings of gold were, therefore, contrary to the Bank's overall business aim of earning profits for its private shareholders.[14] Hence, during the period before the 1825 Crisis, the Bank of England displayed a marked eagerness to reduce its holdings of gold and to increase its investments in interest-bearing securities despite clear signs of growing financial instability. This want of a clear commitment to maintaining the stability of the financial system meant that increasingly private banks came to rely upon rediscounting[15] commercial bills whenever they required liquidity and became increasingly reluctant to draw on their gold reserves held on deposit at the Bank of England. Instead, London banks started to lend at call to bill brokers, which then began to trade in bills on their own account. Overend Gurney and Co, a very large bill broker, played a major part in ensuring that the London money market continued to function in 1825. It did this by affording short-term accommodation to all comers[16] (including the Bank of England) so that trading could continue.

In the aftermath of the 1825 Crisis at the Bank of England Lord Liverpool's Tory Government sought to change the legal framework within which banking companies, if not the banking industry,[17] operated. The Government enacted the Country Bankers Act in 1826.[18] This Act permitted country banks located outside a 65-mile radius of London to freely issue bank notes and to become joint-stock banks with unlimited liability, provided they had more than six partners and had freely-traded shares. At the same time, the Bank of England was permitted to open branches, which it did in a number of leading towns[19]. Neal argues that many of these country banks became branches of joint-stock banks headquartered in London. They, therefore, ceased to be linked together solely by bi-lateral correspondent arrangements. In time, London headquarters ceased to perform banking functions and:

> "[i]… ts role was to process and diffuse information to the various branch offices located beyond the 65-mile radius from London."[20]

Indeed, Newton and Cottrell report that Boards of Directors often concerned themselves only with decisions about loans; decisions about discounts were left largely to local managers.[21]

It seems that Tory governments regarded the Bank of England as a Whiggish and monopolistic institution. By forcing it into branch banking the Government was attempting to expose the Bank to competition from other privately-owned banks[22]. Of necessity, the Bank of England introduced its own system of making payments between its branches. This meant that a country bank with an account at a branch of the Bank of England could make payments to, and receive payments from, another similarly-equipped bank in another part of the country. Indeed, a local bank could place bills with a London bill broker with instructions to pay any proceeds into the appropriate account at the Bank of England. Neal concludes that:

> "… the branches of the Bank of England greatly improved the payment mechanism that underlay the smooth functioning of the bill market."[23]

At the same time, the Bank of England forewent opportunities to discount any but very short-term and highest quality bills approved in London or to charge commissions on discounting. Hence, rather than ensuring that highly competitive conditions existed in local banking circles, the Bank of England actively took steps to preserve existing local banking relationships and margins. The simpler payments mechanism via the Bank of England and the nurturing of local bill markets served to enhance the liquidity of commercial bills in general. This, in turn, helped secure the places of country banks in their local markets. In 1830, the Bank of England opened facilities for re-discounting to bill brokers thus providing them with another source of liquidity independent of the private London banks.

By the early 1830s, therefore, a coherent monetary system had emerged in England. It was a system which emerged from a series of incremental changes put in place in response to opportunities for profit. Private London banks had become heavily involved in dealing in commercial bills by which lending and liquidity were distributed throughout the English monetary system. Some have argued that this meant that the English system took on many of the characteristics of the 18th century system of Scottish banking. This was particularly so after the formation, in the 1850s, of a national clearing house for cheques.

Crown Colonies

Shortages of currency occurred quite frequently in the early years of New South Wales. Supplies of ready money and legal tender ceased and were supplemented, if not replaced, by locally-issued promissory notes. (Similar shortages were reported in Nelson before 1844.) Despite these deficiencies in colonial monetary systems Ripon's Rules were introduced 1831 to govern sales of crown land. They specified that payment was to be 10% of the purchase price on the fall of the hammer and the remainder paid within one calendar month.[24] In the case of the Australasian colonies these sums were to be tendered at the colonial treasury either in Sydney or in Auckland either in the form of "ready money" or in bills drawn on Sydney banks. This implies that Governors Bourke, Gipps and Hobson and their officials took for granted the existence of, and access to, some kind of monetary system that effectively facilitated the making of crown transactions in South Australia, New South Wales and New Zealand. In New South Wales, for example, the Bank of New South Wales was founded in 1817. It was followed by the Bank of Van Diemen's Land in 1823 and by 24 others before the end of 1839.[25] Of these, nine failed during the slump of the 1840s.

Due to the absence of monetary data for New Zealand in the 1840s it not possible to precisely describe monetary conditions.[26] The Union Bank of Australia opened branches in New Zealand by arrangement with the New Zealand Company. In addition, the Banking Company of New Zealand survived only until 1845.[27] We know that the colonial government held an account at the Auckland branch of the Union Bank of Australia which was not opened before January 1848.[28] It was not until 1847 that the Auckland Savings Bank commenced business. We are told by contemporary observers[29] that the first sale of town allotments in Auckland was heavily influenced by purchases by so-called "Sydney Speculators". We also know that, in subsequent years, apart from proceeds of land sales, the main source of New Zealand government revenue was customs duties. We know that from time-to-time currency ceased to exist in the early 1840s in New Zealand to the point that FitzRoy issued debentures as legal tender in 1844.[30] It seems appropriate to assume that the term "ready money" inserted in colonial regulations means UK legal tender.[31]

Together, these suggest that the New Zealand Government was involved in a system of monetary relationships in which Sydney-based banks were of importance. But prior to the development of export industries, these monetary relationships could only be maintained by means of capital injections from outside, presumably originating in the UK Government, accompanying settlers from the UK, or sourced from Sydney or elsewhere to finance speculation in land. None of these sources was consistently available and at some times, such as during 1843–1844, none were. There is no evidence that domestic bank advances were a consistent source of deposit creation or that indigenous financial institutions were sufficiently well-capitalised to sustain a substantial private note issue. So, when less liquidity was imported because fewer exports were sold, local trade using legal tender was heavily constrained and sometimes effectively ceased. It seems, therefore, that many of the features of the monetary system that emerged after 1840 were only intermittently in evidence.

Moreover, in the early 1840s, the colonial monetary systems were but loosely and indirectly related to the operations of the Bank of England via Colonial Office Grant-in-Aid and Commissariat payments from the UK Treasury, assistance from the colony of New South Wales and the operations of Sydney banks. Already by 1840 the New South Wales economy was growing rapidly as wool exports rose. Wool growers were in receipt of substantial inflows of currency which occurred presumably as bills of exchange on overseas importers were discounted of paid on maturity. The New South Wales banks would, therefore, receive these funds, presumably in the form of gold and silver coins, which could be drawn on branches in Australia by wool growers. Thus, the local money supply would increase and with it domestic colonial spending. When exports fell as they did in the mid 1840s the opposite would occur.

But wool growers had few assets. They squatted on crown land for which they paid little or no rent and, in the 1840s, made few improvements such as fencing or irrigation. Wool prices began to fall in the late 1830s and the profitability of their operations was reduced as less productive land was increasingly occupied. Loans at existing lending rates became more difficult to service and new loans, often from mortgagors in London[32], became harder to obtain. It was usual for squatters to pay wages annually "by order" on a bank or merchant. Squatters delayed settling wage orders which meant that banks and merchants increasingly refused to accept them. Workers' incomes fell or were delayed and liquidity was constrained. In 1843–1844 a general economic downturn occurred, unemployment was significant and sales of land by the crown virtually ceased. The only bankable[33] asset owned by wool growers was their stock and the wool and tallow it produced. In 1843 the New South Wales Legislative Council made it possible for mortgages on stock and liens on wool clips to be registered. Butlin[34] regards this innovation as a major contribution to the recovery from the 1840s slump and a significant contribution to the future finance of Australasian agriculture.

It was into this general system that the New Zealand pre-colonial economy had been gradually insinuated for more than 40 years and to which it was formally introduced in 1840. The extension of the boundaries of the colony of New South Wales to include New Zealand meant that all commercial regulation including that related to banking, insurance and land ownership immediately applied to the new territory. Hence, until New Zealand was established as a separate colony, if justified by commercial realities it would have been possible for existing Sydney-based financial practices to have taken root. That they did not is probably because there were few commercial lending opportunities in New Zealand that compared favourably with those on offer in New South Wales. It is also likely that the lending policies of the Union Bank of Australia in New Zealand were dictated by the Board of Directors in London who would have had little reason to separate New South Wales from New Zealand. Indeed, lack of reliable timely information would probably mean that relatively low risk activities such as discounting and issue of bills of exchange would dominate the Union Bank balance sheet. Only as extensive wool growing developed on the South Island in the 1850s did wool exports start to grow. For this reason, it was logical for the Union Bank to eventually establish its headquarters in Christchurch.

In the early 1840s, when the risk of the absence of liquidity was ever-present, the Union Bank maintained shareholders' funds that were high by modern standards. It also severely limited accommodation and charged penal rates of interest for highly risky[35] loans (as FitzRoy discovered). In Australia, in the 1840s, in order to circumvent the restrictions on lending on real estate, the Union Bank began to make advances secured by liens on the wool clip and to offer mortgages on sheep and cattle. It is not clear when these innovations were introduced by the Union Bank of Australia to New Zealand bank customers.

So far as the crown was concerned, the monetary system, when it was in operation, was limited in extent to Sydney and internal trade principally around Auckland. When New Zealand owed more to the rest of the world than it was owed, gold currency (presumably in the form of sovereigns) was physically exported to Sydney to meet the shortfall. This led to the periodic absence of ready money for use in local trade. Sometimes local merchants would attempt to fill the vacuum by issuing their own notes which circulated from hand-to-hand for a time. Over the next 20 years, notes were issued[36] from time-to-time locally by merchants in Auckland, Wellington, Nelson and Dunedin. The gold that was exported then became a receipt of the Union Bank in Sydney which could be used to offset the same imbalance on its accounts in London.

New Zealand Company Colonies
Turnbull, writing in 1959, concluded that the New Zealand Company oversaw a lottery in entirely synthetic claims on land selections (called land orders) which, when they were created, had no foundation in the underlying physical or legal reality of actual allotments of land in New Zealand (see Chapter 7 for a description of the lottery for Land Orders.). It did this because it tried to convince purchasers who would never settle in the colony to buy claims to land, sight unseen. Turnbull wrote:

"The lottery was a perfect device for encouraging the sale of "shares"[37]; it took

> no account whatever of the use to which land would be put in the settlement, except to encourage colonists to gamble with it."[38]

and:

> "Nearly all colonists assumed that their earnings would be supplemented or their fortunes made by the rent and sale of land, and for a while in Wellington the lucky holders of early choices from the lottery were not far wrong in their expectations."[39]

The requirements of a monetary system to serve the needs of participants in a lottery are rudimentary compared with those needed to serve the more complex functions of trade, production, distribution and accumulation. Hence, non-indigenous settlers, living in the New Zealand Company settlements, appear to have had access to somewhat different monetary mechanisms from those brought into existence under the Crown in Auckland or Sydney.

Again, we know very little about the nature of the monetary system that operated in the colonies of the New Zealand Company. The Directors of the New Zealand Company were drawn from among the elite of the City of London.[40] In 1848, the Court of Directors of the New Zealand Company consisted of a Deputy Governor, Hon Francis Baring MP and 20 Directors among whom were seven MPs. Despite the collective repute of its directors (or perhaps because of it) it seems probable that, by that time, the Company had been trading in insolvency for four or five years.

In August 1839, the New Zealand Company negotiated, an agreement with the Union Bank of Australia.[41] The New Zealand Company agreed to conduct all its business through the Union Bank and to nominate three emigrants acceptable to the Bank as local directors. The Bank undertook to open a branch in the Company's settlement (Port Nicholson), to issue notes and to ship specie for local use. Deposits would be accepted and paid either in notes or in drafts on London or Australian branches of the Bank. Customers within New Zealand were, therefore, directly linked through mechanisms in the London discount market. A further branch was opened in Nelson in 1842 but was closed in 1848. The New Zealand Company quickly became a significant borrower at the Bank but poor economic prospects and the difficulty with which the New Zealand Company paid its debts meant that a branch was not opened in Auckland until January 1848.

Under the terms of the land order lottery run by the New Zealand Company, most land was paid for in the UK within the English or Scottish banking systems and was employed by the New Zealand Company to meet its own obligations which also fell largely in the UK[42]. The Union Bank of Australia set up branches in Wellington and later Nelson. At various times in 1842 and 1843 currency could not be obtained in any of the New Zealand Company colonies. A few merchants[43] issued their own promissory notes in an attempt to facilitate trade. We know that well-to-do settlers used drafts and bills on their bankers in London to settle accounts in Wellington and Nelson despite having to pay usurious rates of interest. Unfortunately, I have been unable to find evidence to help assess the relative importance of these factors. But taken together they indicate that the monetary system operating in the Company colonies, insofar as it existed, operated externally to New Zealand; most business transactions occurred in London.

In the Company settlements, as with the crown colony monetary system, central roles were played by chartered banks. But in the case of the New Zealand Company settlements the important decisions were made in London, not in Sydney.[44] It seems likely that any imbalances were adjusted by the New Zealand Company in London rather than through Sydney banks and it appears that currency was physically exported or bills negotiated from time-to-time to meet colonial obligations.

Links between the crown colony monetary system and that of the New Zealand Company colonies did not quickly emerge. Nevertheless, some measure of unification began to occur as a result of unplanned circumstances as follows:

a) when the crown deployed military resources in Wellington in the aftermath of the Wairau Massacre or in the Hutt Valley in pursuit of Te Rauparaha and Rangihaeta;
b) when Kemp and Mantel were sent to purchase Ngai Tahu lands in the South Island; and
c) when the colony was forced to accept the cost of the UK Government's bailout of the New Zealand Company.

In January 1848 the Union Bank opened a branch in Auckland.

Colonial Bank of Issue

In 1847, the Colonial Office encouraged Governor Grey to open a note issue bank to challenge the Union Bank's monopoly.[45] In 1847, Earl Grey instructed Governor Grey effectively to use the UK Bank Charter Act 1844 as a recommendation rather than an instruction. His view was that there was no need to so severely limit colonial banks because they faced different demands and different risks from banks in London. His views were more a reflection of the Currency School[46] than the Banking School which inspired English legislation.[47] Earl Grey, therefore, believed that the volume of bank notes was largely a result of people's preferences and not of banks pressing unwilling customers to accept them. He argued, nevertheless, that acceptors of bank notes were entitled to the protection of the state and for this reason encouraged Governor Grey to set up a Colonial Bank of Issue under the control of, and guaranteed by, the New Zealand Government.

In England it came to be accepted that banks were largely concerned with discounting and re-discounting bills of exchange. Yet, this view ignored the fact that, for the majority of settlers, the entire colonial enterprise centred on the ownership and development of land for which long-term debt was an essential input. It meant that New Zealand banks were forced to find alternative ways of financing the growth and development of the New Zealand economy. A number of ways were devised to avoid the provision against bank lending on the security of real estate. They included founding non-bank mortgage companies which the banks then financed through short-dated commercial paper and overdrafts at call; so-called cash credits which was lending based on an assessment by each bank of the personal worth and trustworthiness of the customer; liens on produce which enabled lending against the eventual proceeds of production to take place; or stock mortgages on the sheep and cattle maintained on the farms. But the most important avenue to facilitate lending was to make commercial loans to merchants, like Dalgety's, the National Mortgage and Agency Co. and the New Zealand Loan and Mercantile Agency Co., which then provided finance to the farmers. These were hardly thought of in 1860 and their full flowering is part of the story of the 1870s and 1880s.

We have already noted that the Colonial Bank of Issue's operations were so circumscribed that the bank acted as "drain" on the finances of the colonial government and was closed in October 1856.

Banking Regulation

The Legislative Council passed an Ordinance in 1851 which came to be known as the Bank Charters Act 1851.[48] At the time, no bank could be set up as a joint stock company with limited liability and all had to receive a charter by Act of Parliament before operations could commence. The Bank Charters Act 1851 set out 12 conditions which every bank charter must contain:

1. Total capital must be specified and all capital must be subscribed within eighteen months from the date of the charter.
2. "The bank shall not commence business until the whole of the capital is subscribed and a moiety at least is paid up".
3. The capital shall be paid up within 4 years of the charter date.
4. Debts and engagements shall not exceed three times the paid-up capital plus deposits in specie and Government stock.
5. Suspension of specie payments on demand for more than 60 days within any one year means that the charter is forfeited.
6. If the bank's assets are insufficient to meet its engagements shareholders are responsible for an amount that is twice that of their subscribed shares.
7. The bank cannot hold shares in its own stock and may not make advances on the security of those shares.
8. Discounts or advances to a single Director may not be more than one-third of all advances and discounts.
9. "The Company shall not advance money on security of lands or ships or on pledge of merchandise, nor hold land or houses except for the transaction of business, nor own ships, nor be engaged in trade except as dealers in bullion or bills of exchange, but shall confine its transactions to discounting commercial paper negotiable securities and other legitimate banking business."
10. "The dividends to shareholders shall be made out of profits only, and not out of the capital of the Company."
11. Statements of assets and liabilities to be published in prescribed ways at prescribed times.
12. All charters are to be subject to such conditions as may be prescribed by the Secretary of State.

Condition 9 is particularly noteworthy. On the face of it, it contains an absolute prohibition bank lending secured against the security of landed estates, ships and pledges of merchandise. Morever, banks were forbidden to own land, houses or ships "except for the transaction of business." However, we shall see that, in time, these six words provided more than sufficient legal leeway for banks to ignore Condition 9.

These regulations were often revised but, in essence, remained in force in New Zealand until the 1980s when the last private banking Act of Parliament was passed and a new system of banks registered at the Reserve Bank of New Zealand took its place.[49] The charters tried to ensure that banks did not lend for the purchase of land, buildings and ships because such lending was regarded as risky, long-term and highly illiquid.[50] Yet, the main reason for introducing banking to Australia and New Zealand was to finance settlers onto the land, assist them to develop the land they bought and to help them export the produce their farms yielded. All these purposes had two characteristics in common; namely, the returns to all are necessarily long-term and the export markets for the products were already readily available albeit beyond the control of domestic producers. Thus, this Ordinance ran directly counter to the fundamental purpose of settler colonial enterprise. It was, therefore, just a question of time before bankers found expedients to find ways around Regulation 9 and yet more time before those expedients ate at the very heart of the Australasian banking system.

One reason was that the methods employed to circumvent this regulation were hardly likely to actually reduce risks faced by bankers. For example, the Bank of New South Wales sought to interpose a reliable and well-heeled merchant between itself and its farmer customers.[51] But in a general downturn in agricultural prices all, including merchants dealing in agricultural produce and supplying settlers, would suffer. Hence, this expedient was unlikely to afford the bank relief or make the assets it held more liquid. Indeed, because the banking risks were affected by another independent organisation, the arrangement introduced new risks which could not be directly managed by the bank.

The phrase "business of banking" was introduced into colonial jurisprudence at this juncture but remains as undefined now as it was then. In the 1840s, "the business of banking" was often understood to be confined to issuing, accepting, discounting and trading in short-term securities of no longer than 90 days maturity, buying and selling gold bullion as a broker, accepting deposits and making advances. But even as the phrase was originally coined it was becoming increasingly obsolete. By the 1840s, banks in London commonly lent for longer maturities than 90 days, they held gold and loan securities on their own accounts and they lent gold to customers.[52] Cheques had become a major source of business and overdrafts advanced on chequing accounts enabled large-scale deposit creation.[53]

In New Zealand, competition emerged in other aspects of banking. Encouraged by the growth of the wool industry, which was an industry it understood from its experience in Australia, the Union Bank opened an agency in Lyttleton in 1851, re-opened the Nelson branch in 1853, opened an agency in Christchurch (1856), a branch in Dunedin (1856) and an agency in Napier (1858). All of these branches aimed to service the growing demand for finance from wool growers. The Oriental Bank opened branches in Dunedin in April 1856 and in Auckland in August 1857. The Oriental tried to attract customers from the Union Bank by offering interest on current and deposit accounts and by undercutting exchange rates. It also discounted twelve-month bills secured by mortgages on real property. The Oriental opened branches in Dunedin and Invercargill before its business was eventually taken over by the Bank of New South Wales in June 1861.

It appears that both variants of the earliest New Zealand monetary system were bank-based. Neither early development was connected to the other except at long remove via the bill payments system of the London money market.[54] They share a serious weakness. Both appear to have been largely mechanisms by which, in the absence of substantial and sustained export receipts and the accumulation of savings that they generated, capital flows were dispensed through the New Zealand colony. Their existence largely depended on the existence of significant inflows of capital and other remittances into New Zealand.[55] When these ceased, notes and coin ceased to circulate.

Australian Financial Relationships

The banking industry in Australia was just as fragmentary as monetary relations in New Zealand. But the reasons for the absence of system were different. During the 1830s, the banking industry grew rapidly in New South Wales impelled by increased free emigration and a boom in wool production accompanied by a rise in export prices. By 1840, at least twelve banks were operating in Sydney. The largest were Bank of New South Wales, the Bank of Australia, the Bank of Australasia and the Union Bank of Australia. The larger merchants also engaged in banking. Banks were also operating in Tasmania and South Australia.

During the 1840s the New South Wales economy underwent a sharp trade cycle depression which resulted in a fall in wool prices. The slump began in 1841 and lasted until late 1844. A number of Australian-based banks closed including the Bank of Australia, Archers Gillies and the Bathurst Bank. Of these, the failure of the Bank of Australia was most disruptive. The Bank of Australia failed because it held large quantities of unpaid bills of Hughes and Hoskins, a large merchant, and of JT Hughes. The Bank of Australia obtained assistance from the Bank of Australasia and, more reluctantly, from the Union Bank of Australia. But the debt involved was disputed. After two trials and a hearing of the Privy Council the Bank of Australasia was awarded debt, interest and costs. The dispute was eventually settled (with the aid of proceeds of a lottery of Bank of Australia properties) in July 1851.

Both Butlin and Holder judged that banks remained very reluctant to lend on the security of real property. But Butlin states that in some cases:

"… what was legally the collateral security was in fact the basis of the loan."[56]

It appears that intending borrowers were asked to enter into an arrangement by which a mortgage upon landed property was pledged as collateral security for banking transactions. Alternatively, "secure accounts" were entered into through which discounts and credits were provided by the bank and the borrower executed a mortgage to trustees acting on behalf of the bank. It is not known how common such arrangements became. Nevertheless, banks appear to usually leave mortgage lending to insurance companies, solicitors with trust funds or a number of land companies founded in London.

Loans secured against real property were also made possible by innovations in the 1840s. During 1843, it became possible to register liens on growing wool and mortgages on stock. But banks preferred to finance merchants engaged in this kind of lending. The impact of these innovations is difficult to judge because a number of existing loans were recast onto this new basis. For much of the period before 1850 Australian-based banks did not offer foreign exchange facilities, which were left to the so-called Anglo-banks.[57] But even by 1845 the Commercial Bank of Sydney and the Bank of New South Wales had negotiated agency arrangements with overseas banks to settle export bills. By this time the Commissariat was probably a minor participant in the Australian foreign exchange business.

Before gold was discovered in 1851, the leading banks displayed relatively subdued growth. In New South Wales, the salient features were;

	Bank of Australasia	Union Bank of Australia	Bank of New South Wales	Commercial Banking Co of Sydney
Notes:				
March 1842	52,034	27,259	27,015	52,482
March 1849	79,561	90,369	34,519	31,226
Deposits:				
March 1842	245,530	167,549	220,977	189,510
March 1849	345,782	412,070	225,767	152,735
Loans:				
March 1842	621,440	446,572	376,945	400,846
March 1849	779,241	467,159	325,794	152,567
Cash:				
March 1842	123,935	138,026	84,008	82,862
March 1849	146,775	245,611	157,565	90,958

Source: Butlin, op cit, 1961, p.110

There are differences between the Anglo-Banks and the Australian-based institutions. First, the Anglo-Banks were larger than the others especially in note issue and loans. This may be a reflection of the relative trust placed in them by customers or because they had formed more effective branch networks. Second, loans of Anglo-Banks rose between 1842 and 1849 whereas those of Australian-based banks declined. Third, the cautious policies of the Union Bank of Australia stand out. It was noteworthy for its large holdings of cash and very conservative lending.

There is very little evidence of concerted action among banks at this time. The Union Bank of Australia only very reluctantly agreed to join the Bank of Australasia in assisting the Bank of Australia and that reluctant agreement extended only to an advance of £10,000. In addition, the same bank only reluctantly agreed to contribute a small share of the assistance afforded to the Derwent Bank. In 1842 and 1843 attempts to agree to not pay interest on current accounts and to reduce discount rates came to nothing.

Inherent Instability

The monetary system that was established in Australia and New Zealand in the 1840s was inherently unsustainable. When capital flowed freely into Australia and New Zealand in the form of overseas borrowing[58], private capital transfers or military spending the systems grew and prospered. It was during those times we would expect to find that the use of monetary instruments would grow and become more common. When these sources of capital declined, however, the monetary systems[59] fell into decay and currency ceased to be available for day-to-day transactions. In those circumstances, bills went unpaid, wages and salaries went into arrears, alternatives to legal tender emerged and some people withdrew, at least partially, from engaging in commerce.

Currency was drained from Australia and New Zealand in this way because of the working of the international financial system of the early 1840s. That system brought together many banks in widely separated parts of the world but only in a semblance of coherence. It permitted payments to be made and received, it allowed debt to be incurred by one country to borrowers in others and it permitted information about potential risks and rewards to be distributed internationally. But it only existed so far as systems of banks existed. Thus, when the Union Bank, for example had net obligations to other banks in another country it had few opportunities to offset them through bills of exchange because neither Australia nor New Zealand had an active banking system. Consequently, the Union Bank met its net obligations to overseas by exporting gold-backed currency.[60] It did so because, in the absence of sustained New Zealand export revenues, it could not consistently access the bills of exchange mechanisms which would obviate the physical conveyance of gold currency. Thus, a bank-based system incorporating a bills of exchange mechanism could not be developed until wool exports from Nelson, Canterbury and Otago, which British importers paid for in sterling, became significant as the 1850s wore on. Butlin describes the opposite case when the Union Bank started to issue export bills for collection in London. The London Board assumed that export bills could be freely purchased in Sydney and sent £30,000 in gold coins to Sydney with instructions to make further purchases. The local management could not comply because suitable bills were not available.[61]

The different character of the monetary systems which developed in the 1840s was the result of poor communications within New Zealand and quite distinct economic priorities. Indeed, Morrell[62] characterises the state of New Zealand in the 1840s as a series of distinct and separate settlements which were, in many respects, more closely related to New South Wales or England than to each other. Indeed, he describes the provinces as "… in great measure self-sufficient".[63] Hence, even if banks had been in existence, it would probably have been necessary to manage each branch of a given banking company independently of each other. In other words, in the absence of inflows of funds from outside sources each settlement would have had to generate internally the savings needed to allow bank accommodation to occur.[64]

1840s system

The absence of a monetary system from New Zealand in the 1840s is all the more surprising because Governor FitzRoy experimented with an entirely debt-based money during 1844 to 1846. If introduced and managed with determination and discipline such a system could have papered over many of the cracks which made New Zealand monetary relations so patchy at that time. Indeed, with sufficient care it is conceivable that a monetary system could have emerged from FitzRoy's initiative that would have short cut the diversion into the Gold Standard and its unstable aftermath that Australia and New Zealand underwent during the second half of the nineteenth and the first half of the twentieth centuries. But such was the fraught state of Auckland politics and the shock of Colonial Office officials that FitzRoy was not allowed sufficient patience to enable his experiment to be brought into full operation.

The diagram on page 157 illustrates the flows of funds involved in the purchase of land in Austalasia by early 1850. It is simplified by omitting three features of the colonial transactions system known to exist in the 1840s. First, it leaves out the transactions involving trade in goods and services whether from overseas or within the country. This is an important omission because the finances of the colonial governments were heavily reliant on income from duties and charges which both Māori and New Zealand settlers paid. Second, of less importance perhaps, is the assumption that Māori did not avail themselves of the services of the Union Bank of Australia or other financiers to any great extent. Third, it is assumed that absentee landowning was much more prevalent in New Zealand Company settlements than in New South Wales. The reason for this is that the activities of Sydney-based speculators appear to have been confined to the very early sales of sections in Auckland.

The above description is a simplification used to highlight the close connections between the New Zealand Company, its client landowners (whether absentee or settlers) and the London banking system. The New Zealand Company designed its system of selling land in New Zealand to assist absentee owners to purchase land. Thus, sales took place through the sale, in London, of transferrable rights to select land when it became available called a Land Orders.[65] These rights became the subject of trading both in the UK and New Zealand. However, owning a right to a place in a queue to select land was not the same thing as owning a title to a landed estate. Thus, many who held valid land orders were forced to wait considerable periods before they could access the land they thought that they already owned. While waiting, many consumed the capital they brought with them. Some even sold their land orders for ready cash to other settlers in New Zealand. Thus, it was possible for people with ready capital to accumulate considerable estates in the New Zealand Company settlements. But this also meant that capital which could have been employed in land improvement was, instead, often fully committed to land purchase.

Elsewhere, the promise of using the profits from land sales to finance the colonial administration proved illusory. Apart from the first two auctions of Auckland town suburban sections in April and September 1841, the majority of lots put up for sale by the crown before mid-1844 were left unsold. In large part, this was due to a severe recession in Australia, which, partly as a result of bank decisions,[66] spread to New Zealand. As a result, a significant deficit developed between the government's spending and its revenue. Normally, such a shortfall would be financed by the government's banker (i.e. the Union Bank of Australia) but the assistance that the bank felt able to make available was nugatory when compared to the Colonial Government's needs. It was also expensive. This gap was largely ignored by Hobson and Shortland and financed by unauthorised borrowing and money issue by FitzRoy.

It is clear that the financial model which is implicit in Normanby's instructions would always prove unviable in the face of a serious downturn in trade. The creation of a self-sustaining colonies in Australia and New Zealand required a financial contribution from the UK Treasury sufficient to supply the wherewithal to purchase goods and services until government revenues grew sufficiently to make borrowing unnecessary. Funding to this necessary extent was never made available until Governor Grey's time. But by then, trading conditions had improved and so had the finances of the colonial government.

Gold Flows in the Early 1840s

In the early 1840s, gold only came to New Zealand from overseas.[67] In this respect, New Zealand was in a similar position to that of first two decades of the Australian colonies. So far as the crown was concerned, this inflow took the form of payment for land financed by capital imports by settlers or agents acting on behalf of absentee landowners and by grants and loans from the UK Treasury. There was also Grant-in-Aid and Commissariat payments from the UK Treasury and occasional loans from the Colony of New South Wales. There were but a few advances and discounts to the colonial government. The New Zealand Company relied upon payments in gold from settlers and absentee landowners and upon the ability to draw on credit from its bankers. But, by 1844, its credit was all but exhausted and a rescue had to be organised by the Colonial Secretary in the form of a "loan" of £268,000 in 1847.[68]

Local legal tender in New Zealand was sterling which in practice meant gold sovereigns and silver. New Zealand has never maintained a mint so all the currency circulating in New Zealand[69] has always been imported whether from the UK or Australia. In the absence of sustained domestic production of gold or of a ready supply of gold payments for goods and services exported or of ever more eager potential owners of New Zealand land the above system was bound sooner or later to run out of gold currency. This occurred periodically during the first twenty years of the colony and led to local merchants issuing their own notes to supplement the lack of ready cash. Hence, far from reducing liquidity as required under the classical gold standard when gold is exported and not replaced it is likely that the net export of gold led to an increase in local currency, although not in the form of legal tender.

It is also believed that Māori sustained considerable foreign trade during the early years of colonial New Zealand. Insofar as this resulted in an export surplus it would have reduced the overall need to import gold. It also seems that few Māori enjoyed access to banking facilities. Hence, it remains unclear how these enterprises, which engaged in foreign trade, were linked to the international payments system that centred on the Bank of England. It is possible that the proceeds from exports were hoarded or saved or spent on imports.

Although these possible components of a monetary system can be identified much research is required before a coherent picture of how New South Wales and New Zealand fitted into the international financial system in the 1840s can be presented. We do not know how far they were linked together (for example, by management of financial assets and liabilities). Little is known about the relative importance of the flows that can be identified and whether there are significant flows missing from the picture deduced. Finally, we are unsure about how the various flows interacted with each other either to being about smooth adjustment or explosive disequilibrium.

In order to precisely address these questions I offer an outline sketch of the main working components of the late 1840s gold standard and the relationships they shared with each other. In doing so, I am much assisted by the fact that in April and October 1847 there were two major financial crises in London which resulted in considerable official enquiry at the time and much subsequent investigation.[70] However, my sketch indicates only the main features of the gold standard system in the early stages of its life in order to identify the most important sources of change and innovation within it. It does not pretend to be a complete working model of the system that then existed.

At the outset, the legislative setting should be recalled. First, apart from the Bank of New South Wales, all banks operating during 1847 in New South Wales and New Zealand were chartered under the Country Banking Act 1826 and were heavily reliant upon the London discount market for supplies of liquid assets. This meant that they were always at pains to ensure that they carried a positive balance of liquid assets (mostly cash on hand and call deposits with other banks) in London.[71] The balance was kept as small as possible because it yielded little or no interest. As the 1830s wore on, and particularly during the depression of the 1840s, these so-called London Funds appear to have grown in importance and became the central indicator of the soundness of bank management. Second, the Bank Charter Act 1844 split the privately-owned Bank of England into two departments; the Issue Department which issued sterling and the Banking Department which conducted banking relationships.

It is also important to remember the economic situation. In the late 1840s, neither New South Wales nor New Zealand supplied significant quantities of gold, the development of wool exports from New South Wales was significant but barely begun in New Zealand and foreign borrowing by the Australasian colonies had yet to reach high levels. Finally, we must not forget the extremely rudimentary nature of the colonial monetary systems. There was no single organised cheque or bills clearing system and all inter-bank lending seems to have taken place by *ad hoc* arrangements[72] negotiated bi-laterally between banks' boards of directors rather than through bargaining in an open market.

We can imagine the nature of the coordinating forces which this system could bring to bear by describing how a significant level of outflows might impact the system. For the purpose of illustration, we assume that the London banking system faces increased demands for liquidity because of a combination of:

- outflows of capital due to increased borrowing from overseas, sizeable overseas payments on account of debt service,
- large calls by widely-sold stocks such as those of railway companies, and
- calls to meet import bills.

This combination of outflows of liquidity could not be readily met by raising more deposits at current interest rates. It would predominantly lead to a reduction in cash reserves and increased demands by banks to re-discount bills of exchange. Short term interest rates will rise and so give rise to more profitable discounting opportunities than before. The Bank of England will seek to enhance its profitability by engaging in more discounting business at higher rates of discount. The same will be true of all banks with available funds in the form of liquid reserves. Nevertheless, the ratio of discounts to reserves in the Banking Department of the Bank of England[73] will rise which will further raise discount rates on the London discount market. All banks will become sparing about making discounts so as to carefully husband liquid reserves. Rises in the discounts to reserves ratio of the Banking Department are likely to eventually lead to the Bank of England refusing accommodation and, in so doing, precipitating a liquidity crisis. Lending between banks will then cease. While this is likely to reduce domestic spending on all goods and services whether produced at home or overseas, it does not mean that the economy is induced by progressive means to adjust to economic realities. The international financial system that was revealed by the 1847 Crisis stopped functioning when it came under this kind of liquidity pressure.

In the above thought experiment the Issue Department of the Bank of England is relatively unaffected by events in the London discount market. Importantly, in this system, the Bank of England is only able to issue notes convertible into gold against the fixed £14 million Fiduciary Issue and £-for-£ for any further gold on hand. In practice, the rise in interest rates is likely to lead to an influx of gold from overseas[74] and so support an increase in note issue. Unless the issue of Bank of England notes, fully convertible into gold, is separated from the purchase of gold by the Bank of England Issue Department, overall liquidity in the London money and capital markets is fixed. Eventually, in 1847, the British Government solved the problem by instructing the Bank of England to provide accommodation by means of discounts at 8% and by promising the Bank of England indemnity were it to breach the 1844 Bank Charter Act[75] by issuing a larger volume of banknotes than the £14 million Fiduciary Issue. Once it became known that the Bank of England would provide accommodation, albeit at high rates of discount, banks ceased to hoard currency and the scramble for cash disappeared. With that, the 1847 Crisis was over.

We might draw the following lessons from the above illustration:

1. Any international coordination that took place through the gold standard system immediately after 1844 occurred by means of the ordinary workings of the London discount market.
2. When this proved inadequate to assure the coherence of the sterling monetary system, the support of the British Government was drawn upon.
3. The system appears to take very little account of economic conditions in colonial countries. Hence, stabilisation of colonial economies was less a property of the gold standard and more a matter of chance.
4. The gold standard system was bound to change as innovations found their way onto the London money and capital markets and became reflected in the practice of colonial finance and land tenure.

Chapter Notes

1 The international monetary system in the 18th and 19th centuries was being transformed from systems which ensured that merchants were paid in full and on time for goods they bought and sold into a way of making the savings made in one society available to many others. Safely making this translation occur involved far-reaching innovations in information gathering, data processing and management systems. It also involved large investment of human and physical capital and financial wealth.
2 Barry Eichengreen (editor): *The Gold Standard in Theory and History*, New York, Methuen, 1985, p. 4.
3 See Chappell, op cit, 1961, p. 280 for a reproduction of an example of a settlement note.
4 Nowadays these are termed near-monies because, in normal circumstances, they function as if they were legal tender. The Currency School largely ignored the existence and changing character of these financial instruments.
5 Peel's Reforms is the term usually given to the activities of the Parliamentary Committee on Cash Payments which Sir Robert Peel chaired after August 1818. The committee considered the expediency of requiring the Bank of England to resume paying gold on demand for its notes. Peel's view was that it would be morally wrong to repay people who had lent to the Government in depreciated currency. Accordingly, the Committee recommended that large denomination notes should be progressively made convertible as follows: from February 1820 at £4–1s-0d the ounce, from October 1820 at £3–19s-6d the ounce then in May 1821 'at the ancient and permanent standard of value' of £3–17s-101/2d the ounce. All other notes were to become convertible at this value in May 1823. This is the date that many regard as the commencement of the Gold Standard.
6 To a large extent this was the result of the lengths to which the English Parliament had to go find a protestant successor to King William III and Queen Mary. Some say that more than fifty possibly legitimate candidates with claims to the English throne were discarded before the Hanoverian Succession was settled upon and established by the Bill of Rights in 1688. Each eliminated candidate was potentially a source of insurrection and most resided on the continent of Europe. For some time, therefore, the English people were suppressing, by military might and

	payment of pensions, claims to the throne on behalf of their adopted sovereign and his family and fighting the quarrels with other continental powers which the Hanoverians bequeathed them.
7	Debt instruments are written agreements between a borrower and a lender specifying the terms and conditions of the loan they have agreed.
8	The Bank of England was for much of the 18th, 19th and 20th centuries widely known simply as "The Bank".
9	Perhaps the most striking expenditure was to sheath the bottoms of British Men-o'-War in copper sheet so as to raise operating speeds and reduce the need for maintenance between 1779 and the early 1790s. This was said to cost £1,500 per vessel. However, this does not include the further cost of re-bolting the hulls of all vessels because of problems of electrolysis between the copper sheets and the iron bolts and nails previously installed.
10	Specie means gold and silver of a specified parity and weight taking the form of ingots or coin.
11	The term "bankers' paper" means an order in writing given by a bank to credit its holder with a specified amount of currency on a specified date.
12	The colonisation of the Americas was sponsored by British sovereigns. For example, in 1608, James I provided a Royal Charter to the London Company to colonise Virginia and personally invested in it. In this and similar ventures, he was joined, over the succeeding 150 years by his successors and other aristocrats who had grown rich from wool, mining, enclosures or the finance of smuggling and who sought new ways to invest their wealth.
13	Use of the word "increasingly" probably exaggerates the speed with which this development occurred. Providing liquidity to other banks at a time of crisis was usually not profitable to the shareholders of the Bank of England. It was something that the Bank of England tried to avoid. Thus, it was not until the last two decades of the 19th Century that the Bank of England, under considerable political pressure, started to take on the responsibility of acting as banker in last resort the London Money and Capiral Markets.
14	Another way of putting the choice is to say that shareholder priorities ran directly counter to the public duties of the Bank of England when discharging its implied responsibility to act as the bankers' bank. At a later time, this latter function became known as lender in the last resort and was not explicitly adopted by the Bank of England until 1847 when the Bank abandoned a fixed discount rate. Even then, it was not until the events of the 1880s and 1890s and, in particular, the Baring Crisis that the Bank began to be active as a lender of last resort. It might also be remarked that its reluctance to supply gold on demand meant that the so-called Gold Standard of the 1820s was neither as automatic in its operation nor as binding in the obligations it required from the institutions that were part of it as is commonly believed.
15	We have seen that banks were in the business of discounting, for cash, the bills held by their customers. A bank, having discounted bills, may find itself in need of liquidity before the date when it is due to receive the bill's full cash value. If so, that already-discounted bill may be offered for discount (or sale) to another bank such as the Bank of England. This process is called re-discounting and may be repeated many times before a given bill matures.
16	This came to be called acting as lender of last resort.
17	In the early 19th century banking, i.e. the undertaking of banking operations, went unregulated. The authorities were only concerned to ensure that banks, i.e. chartered banks, were governed in certain ways.
18	Lucy Newton and PJ Cottrell: "Joint-Stock Banking in the English Provinces 1826–1857", *Business and Economic History,* Vol 27, No 1, Fall 1998, pp. 115–128.
19	During 1828 and 1829, the Bank of England opened branches in the following English trading centres: Birmingham, Bristol, Exeter, Gloucester, Hull, Leeds, Liverpool, Manchester and Norwich. By 1832, most business, measured by volumes of discounts and notes outstanding, was conducted by the branches in Birmingham and Manchester. See Larry Neal: "The Financial Crisis of 1825 and the Restructuring of the British Financial System", *Review of the Federal Reserve Bank of St Louis,* May/June, 1998, pp. 53–76.

20   Ibid, p. 75.
21   Newton and Cottrell, op cit, 1998, p.121.
22   At this time, The Bank of England was privately owned and was not nationalised until 1946.
23   Neal, op cit, 1998, p. 73.
24   These terms were laid down by Gipps and had remained unchanged since Goderich decreed in 1831 that, henceforth, crown land was to be distributed by sales at auction.
25   See Butlin, op cit, 1968, Appendix II, pp. 575–576. No doubt the flurry in bank formation during the 1830s accompanied the rapid development of wool growing by squatters on land beyond the Nineteen Counties.
26   This despite the fact that data on New Zealand banking are relatively complete from the inception of the colony. However, these are data about chartered banks which do not include many of the non-bank forms of monetary relation upon which the colony appears to have relied in its early life.
27   Butlin, op cit, 1961, pp. 154–155.
28   Despite this relatively long-standing relationship FitzRoy found the bank unwilling to lend the New Zealand Government more than £5,000 and then only at rates of interest of between 12% and 15%. In this context it is worth recalling that as late as 1859 the Union Bank demanded that the colonial Government execute a lien on progress payments for the building of the Custom House in Auckland despite the fact that it held the account from which the payments would be made.
29   These may have been very biased. They included John Logan Campbell who complained that he could not afford a section on the corner of Shortland Street and Queen Street because of "Sydney speculators".
30   HD Bedford "The Monetary Difficulties of Early Colonisation in New Zealand", *The Economic Journal*, No 102, Jun 1916, pp 257–276.
31   In this context "ready money" means cash or its close equivalent denominated in sterling. This effectively means legal tender according to the Coinage Act 1816. It is perhaps conceivable that, in colonial contexts other meanings might be attached to the term. For example, we have already noted the emergence of the terms "currency" and "sterling" in Sydney. However, it is highly unlikely that a former Chancellor of the Exchequer, as Ripon was, would resort to such colonial nomenclature in drafting rules for auctioning crown land.
32   It was at this time that the Derwent Bank encountered difficulties. This bank had found way to circumvent prohibitions against lending on the security of land by arranging for its subscribers or depositors lending directly to the purchasers of colonial land.
33   An asset is bankable if it can be pledged by a borrower as security for a loan. In the 1840s, only a personal guarantee by an undoubted person, a lien on the wool clip or the amount of whale oil gathered in a season could be classed as bankable.
34   Butlin, op cit, 1968, p.345 states that by 1850: "The lien on wool and mortgage on stock were too precious for squatters to abandon them; they had come to stay." By the Wool and Oil Securities Act passed by the New Zealand General Assembly in 1858 similar security became available to lenders in New Zealand.
35   Before 1860, the Union Bank regarded lending to the Colonial Government in New Zealand as relatively high risk.
36   Evidence for this assertion is contained in private correspondence and trade advertising. So far as is known no systematic study of this phenomenon has been undertaken. For that reason, it is not known how common this practice was or even if the terms and conditions attached to the notes thus issued shared common features.
37   Land Orders were labelled shares in the publicity of the New Zealand Company. Presumably this was an attempt to divert, by verbal gymnastics, the attention of potential purchasers away from the lack of actual land to back its Land Orders.
38   Turnbull, op cit, 1959, p.16.
39   Ibid, p. 42.

40 See www.nzetc.victoria.ac.nz/tm/scholarly/tei-Stout63-t6-front-d3.html.
41 Butlin, op cit, 1961, Chapter 9 The First Bank in New Zealand, pp 153–172.
42 There were occasions in1843 and 1844 when the New Zealand Company in Nelson could not fulfil its promise to employ all emigrants on public works and sought to cut the rates of pay it offered. This was because it had not received sufficient funds from the Company in London, Insufficient capital had been imported to develop the available land and the labourers that had been transported to colony on free passages could not find employment. As a result, protests occurred, the town's voluntary defence associations were armed but the Government refused to station regular troops there. Eventually, in October 1844, the Company stopped altogether paying the wages that it had originally promised. See Hill, op cit, Part One, 1986, pp 208–212. See also Jared Davidson: *The History of a Riot*, Wellington, Bridget Williams Books, 2021.
43 Fell in Nelson and Jones in Dunedin were two such.
44 Apart from the Bank of New South Wales, the leading banks in Sydney were chartered in the UK and largely owned by British shareholders. Most were incorporated under the Country Bankers' Act 1826.
45 Despatch Earl Grey to Governor Grey dated February 1847. As a consequence, the Legislative Council passed an Ordinance to establish the Colonial Bank of Issue which was submitted to the Colonial Office for approval. The UK Treasury insisted that the specie backing of the note issue should be at least $33^1/_3$% and preferably 50% and the investments of the bank should be confined to UK Government stock rather than colonial loans as was originally envisaged.
46 The early 19th Century saw a major dispute in monetary economics. On the one hand were the Currency School which held that money consisted of anything which acted as a means of exchange and might take many forms depending on what was and was not generally acceptable. By contrast the Banking School held that money was neither more nor less than legal tender the total quantity of which could be controlled by regulating the gold reserves of banks.
47 Sinclair and Mandle, op cit, 1961, pp 28–32.
48 This Ordinance was "An Ordinance to authorize the Governor-in-Chief to grant Charters of Incorporation to Banking Companies" and dated 30 July 1851. This was a repetition of a similar measure enacted in the UK in 1840 with the exception of sections related to note issue. It was distinct form the Bank Charter Act 1841.
49 By the Reserve Bank of New Zealand Amendment Act 1986, the use of the word "bank", "banker" or "banking" in a company title was restricted to those organisations which had been duly registered by the Reserve Bank. This was part of a widespread de-regulation of the New Zealand financial sector.
50 Note that ships are considered difficult to sell (i.e. illiquid) because ownership may be held by many who have shares in the vessel or its cargo.
51 Sinclair and Mandle, op cit, 1961, p. 34.
52 It is true that very few UK banks, unlike their German counterparts, invested their own resources in company shares. The key ingredients to the Overend Gurney collapse in 1866 and Baring Crisis in 1890 was a policy of investing in long-dated securities, usually in the form of long-term government debt, using the resources raised in the short-term money market. This business strategy was precisely the one which Governor Grey's 1851 Ordinance was designed to prevent.
53 This method of creating currency was largely ignored in the debates which swirled around the reform of banking in the early 19th century. Well into the 1870s, when chequing facilities were an increasingly important source of liquidity, successive British Governments continued to cleave to the belief that by limiting the ability of banks to issue notes was a sure way of limiting the supply of money in the economy.
54 This did not necessarily mean that New Zealand was "on" the Gold Standard. See B C Ashwin: "Banking and Currency in New Zealand", *Economic Record*, November 1930, pp 188–204.
55 For example, Burns, op cit, 1989, p. 223 records time-honoured inconsistency between the

demands by settlers for "… loans on collateral which regular banking practice regarded as inadequate…" and the insistence of the Union Bank head office "… on the strictest professional standards in all respects…". As a result of these incompatible world views the Union Bank became the target of the New Zealand Company's wrath in 1848.

56 Butlin, op cit, 1968, p. 505.
57 An Anglo-bank is an institution operating predominantly in Australia and New Zealand but which was founded in the UK under UK legislation, with a head-quarters in London. Australian-based banks were established in Australia wherein their headquarters were located.
58 New Zealand did not issue publicly traded debt instruments until after conclusion of the 1856 Compact. Hence, any borrowing would have been the result of private initiatives à la Algernon Tollemache.
59 In New Zealand, during the 1840s it seems likely that monetary circuits were very limited in extent and perhaps relatively short-lived.
60 Such carriage was a risky and costly. It is not known how frequently such shipments of gold coin were undertaken in the early 1840s. If ever such data could be obtained it might indicate the extent of how partial banking relationships were in New Zealand at that time.
61 Butlin, op cit, 1961, p.112.
62 WP Morrell: *The Provincial System in New Zealand 1852–76*, Second (revised) edition, Christchurch, Whitcombe and Tombs, 1964, p. 22.
63 By this phrase Morrell is intending to convey the fact that each province was entirely reliant on its own talents, savings and customers for its survival and development. He does not mean to argue that a particular aspect of commercial life, such as bank branches, were invariably run sufficiently well to ensure that survival was universally achieved.
64 This realisation was, no doubt, the inspiration for the founding of local savings banks in many parts of New Zealand beginning in the 1850s in New Plymouth.
65 Rarely have securities been more misleadingly named. In many cases Land Orders were sold in London long before any land had been purchased let alone surveyed in New Zealand and the Land Order itself represented merely an option for the holder to take a place in the queue for selection. Land Orders represented a highly speculative form of investment the supply of which could be increased at will by the New Zealand Company.
66 For example, the directors of the Union Bank regarded New Zealand lending as somewhat more risky than that available in Australia and sought to increase the bank's holdings of highly liquid assets in London.
67 Falconer Larkworthy *Ninety-one Years: Being the reminiscences of a London banker*, London, Mills and Boon, 1929, p. 197 describes that, in 1855, the Melbourne mint melted gold dust "… into large or small wedges or ingots according to their intended destination—either England, India or China, the size, shape, surface colouring and markings suitable for one country not being adapted to the requirements of another."
68 The arrangement was concluded with Earl Grey. It consisted of a loan of £236,000 without interest to be repaid in three years in full. If, on the other hand, it was decided that the Company could not continue the loan would be remitted and, instead, the Government would buy all the Company's land in New Zealand at 5s per acre at a total cost of £268,000. It was this latter sum, reduced in negotiation to £200,000, that played a part in the 1856 Compact. See Burns, op cit, 1989, pp. 292–293.
69 This statement ignores the largely undocumented role played by circulation of privately-produced notes in New Zealand. Only during FitzRoy's governorship were such notes produced and circulated as legal tender by the Colonial Government. It has not proved possible to estimate the impact of these various innovations in currency issue.
70 See, for example, UK Parliament: "Report from the secret committee of the House of Lords appointed to inquire into the causes of the distress", Session 1, Vol 2. (0.50), 1857; Rudiger Dornbusch and Jacob A Frankel: "The Gold Standard and the Bank of England in the Crisis

of 1847", paper presented at "A Retrospective on the Classic al Gold Standard 1821–1931" Conference, Hilton Head Island, South Carolina, March 1982; Michael Anson, et al: "The Bank of England credit rationing during the crisis of 1847: frosted glass or raised eyebrows". Staff Working Paper Non 794, Bank of England, April 2019.

71 The so-called London Funds Mechanism is discussed at some length below. Butlin, op cit, 1988, p. 53 notes that the London Funds indicator emerged in the 1830s and 1840s. It became of greater importance towards then end of the 19th century as available liquid assets increased in range and volume and the London discount market with the Bank of England at its head increasingly actively managed the Gold Standard system of international payments.

72 For example, see Butlin's account of the various expedients suggested or employed over seven years resulting from the difficulties encountered by the Bank of Australia after 1843. Butlin, op cit, 1961, pp. 99–103.

73 By the Bank Charter Act 1844, the Bank of England was divided into the Issue Department and the Banking Department. The issue Department was concerned with note issue while the Banking Department conducted all the day-to-day transactions with the remainder of the banking system.

74 For a detailed discussion of how this comes about see Paul Einzig: *A Dynamic Theory of Forward Exchange*, London, Macmillan, 1967, pp. 192–193.

75 In a letter sent from No. 10 Downing Street on 25 October 1847 and signed by Lord John Russell, the Prime Minister, and Sir Charles Wood, Chancellor of the Exchequer.

CHAPTER 7

NEW ZEALAND LAND MARKETS

Here starts the distinct story of how land in New Zealand became commodified. It separates the initial stages of the process into a Pre-Primary Market and a Primary Market. The Pre-Primary Market was created so that the Government could obtain land from Māori and represents the means by which Crown Preemption provided in the Treaty of Te Triti O Waitangi took place. The Pre-Primary Market consisted of a sole monopoly buyer and many Māori sellers. The Primary Market for New Zealand land was the way in which estates in land were established and settlers could obtain those estates from the Government. A Pre-Primary Market for land never existed in Australia because Colonial Office officials (like Sir James Stephen) were not in post to insist that the land had to be first purchased from Aboriginal Peoples. However, obtaining land for sale was just the beginning of the problems faced by the independent state of New Zealand. It took the conclusion of the 1856 Compact to make the idea of a separate New Zealand comprehensible to the rest of the world.

Grey Re-engineers Crown Pre-Emption

FitzRoy's replacement as Governor, George Grey, arrived in Auckland on 14 November 1845 in the *Elphinstone,* a vessel of the Honourable East India Company, and became Governor four days' later. He was favoured with the promise of substantial financial and military resources, denied to FitzRoy, which he immediately mobilised to undermine FitzRoy's reputation while largely adopting his policies.[1]

Grey was instructed to reverse many of the policies which FitzRoy had initiated. In this, Grey's obedience was selective. He did reverse FitzRoy's attempt to permit (subject to a variety of conditions including his written permission) Māori to sell their land directly to Europeans. Governor Grey, presumably for the sake of consistency, proclaimed on 21 February 1846 that:

> "I, the Lieutenant-Governor, do hereby proclaim that I will in favour of the New Zealand Company, and of no other person whatsoever, waive the right of pre-emption of Her Majesty, Her Heirs and Successors, within such portion of the Northern and Middle Islands as are commonly known as the Company's districts."[2]

He also announced on 25 June 1846 that persons holding certificates under FitzRoy's proclamation had until 15 September 1846 to apply to the Surveyor General for a crown grant. On 16 November 1846, the Legislative Council passed the Land Claims Ordinance which reasserted the crown's pre-emptive right.[3]

Ordinance XIX of Session VII of the Legislative Council dated 16 November 1846 is important because for the first time, the crown right of pre-emption was defined in New Zealand law. Section 1 of Ordinance XIX states:

> "If any person shall, after the passage of this Ordinance, purchase or by writing or otherwise agree to purchase any estate or interest in land from any person of the Native race, or shall by writing, or otherwise agree with such a person for the purchase of the right of cutting timber or other trees, or of the right of mining, or of the right of pasturage, or for the use or occupation of land. And also if any person who shall not hold a licence from the Government for that purpose shall after the passing of this Ordinance be found using or occupying any land not comprised within a grant from the crown, either by depasturing sheep or cattle thereon, or by residing thereon, or by erecting any house or building thereon, or by clearing enclosing or cultivating any part thereof, or who shall be found without licence aforesaid to have cut timber or other trees thereon or have gotten any mineral therefrom. Every such person shall upon conviction of any of the offences hereinbefore mentioned, forfeit and pay any sum not less than five pounds nor more than one hundred pounds, to be recovered in a summary way. Provided that no person shall be convicted of any of the offences aforesaid except on the information or complaint of the Surveyor-General or of some other office duly authorised in that behalf by His Excellency the Governor."

The Ordinance of 16 November 1846 was more far-reaching than the "land purchase" that was mentioned in Article Two of the Treaty of Waitangi.

By Ordinance XIX the crown asserted a monopoly right over the use of all Māori land by non Māori (i.e. in practice Europeans). It appears, for the first time, to make illegal a number of activities, such as leasing of land to non-indigenous persons, which Māori commonly undertook. This Ordinance is, thus, the original source of the crown's right to mine, to lease pasture land and to issue licences to occupy. It was this broad meaning of crown pre-emption that was finally revoked by the Native Land Act 1862.

Governor Grey also spent much of 1846 disestablishing the Protectorate and Land Purchase Department under George Clarke and replacing it with a single-purpose Land Purchase Department run by Donald McLean.[4] Land purchase was placed under Governor Grey's personal supervision. For over 15 years, McLean was an important adviser to successive Governors on Native Affairs and exercised considerable freedom in negotiating purchases of land by the crown.

Ordinance XIX coupled to McLean's abilities in acquiring land forged the crown's pre-emptive right into a formidable weapon in the hands of a highly focussed organisation like the Land Purchase Department. It was made plain to Māori during negotiations for sale of land, that only the Governor could purchase land from them. Moreover, it was asserted that purchases and leases not sanctioned by the Governor were now illegal. Together, these provisions meant that when Māori entered into negotiations over the sale or lease of their land they could not call upon any alternative arrangements which might strengthen their bargaining position. Hence, Māori were placed in a position of either choosing to accept the Governor's terms or being unable to sell or lease to anyone else who the Governor declines to licence as an occupier. The Ordinance provided the Governor with control of the carrot of land sales and the stick of alternative tenures and usages. Thus, the power of the Governor's monopoly purchase position was significantly enhanced by Ordinance XIX and it remained firmly entrenched for much of the next 20 years.

Ordinance XIX encouraged the Land Purchase Department to adopt a "take it or leave it" attitude towards land transactions. This is most clearly seen in the cases of the huge crown purchases of the South Island. When the land which formed most of the Canterbury Province was "purchased" by Henry Tacy Kemp in July 1848, Kemp [5] set a niggardly price per acre that he was willing to meet, neglected to set aside reserves despite explicit promises to do so and failed to consult many senior rangatira (Māori chiefs) during the negotiations. In the case of the Wairau, the land was relinquished by Ngati Toa as a condition for the release of Te Rauperaha in 1847 who had been kidnapped and held captive without warrant or charge by Governor Grey. It was by such methods that virtually the entire South Island became crown lands by 1860.

In time, the willingness of the crown to ignore Māori concerns about the conduct of land transactions spilled over into other interactions between non-indigenous people and Māori. As the non-indigenous population grew to match that of Māori by the mid-1850s, some settlers started to assert their "rights" and working arrangements over land,[6] occupation became the subject of legal contract and litigation.[7] Rights of occupation obtained by "sale" were generally defined broadly which placed greater restraints on the behaviour of Māori than it did to the crown.[8] Hence, the effect of Ordinance XIX was to prevent the emergence of competition among potential occupiers of Māori land.[9] It was unashamedly pro-settler provided the Government could command sufficient money to continue to "purchase" and so quieten[10] Māori land in sufficient quantity to satisfy future demand for settlement. Moreover, the Ordinance, by eliminating potential competition for possession of Māori land, almost certainly reduced the price that the crown would have to pay to "purchase" it. In the next decade, Māori were often told by land purchase officers that they could either sell their land to the crown or to no-one.

Ultimately, the assertion of economic power by the crown encountered counter forces. For example, increasingly, some Māori chose not to sell land at all and formed themselves into so-called Land Leagues with varying longevity. Others sought to undermine the position of owners in common by using stratagems of their own. One such outcome of these conflicts was the First Taranaki War.

There were some differences between the situation in which Māori found themselves under Grey's Ordinance and that facing Australian Aboriginal Peoples. In New South Wales and Tasmania, the land that Aboriginal Peoples occupied could be freely granted by the crown without further ado. In New Zealand, Māori could sell their land at a price set by the Governor or not at all. The difference in outcome between the two native peoples was in practice very little. In Australia, Aboriginal Peoples received no capital transfer for the loss of the land they occupied; in New Zealand, Māori were paid a small proportion of what non-indigenous people settlers thought the land was worth. This difference might be summarised as a difference between *terra nullius,* on the one hand, and *terra next to nullius,* on the other.

In both Australia and New Zealand, settler development was at the expense of indigenous society and political power was closely related to the outward show of landed wealth. This meant that indigenous peoples were systematically denigrated. The disparities just happened to be much greater in the Australian colonies than in New Zealand. But they were just as general and just as permanent.

The crown's pre-emptive right of purchase remained in force until the Native Land Act 1862. Initially, McLean displayed great patience in approaching the subject of sale. But always presented the crown's offer as the only one available. All the while he would display bags of gold or silver coin before the hui assembled to discuss the sale of tribal land. By such means he and his fellow officers were able to acquire large swathes of the North Island between the mid-1840s and early 1850s. But without the backing of an efficient and effective bureaucracy and the determined political intransigence of the Governor, such personal methods could not be expected to keep pace with the rapid increase in emigration to New Zealand that took place in the 1850s. Corners were increasingly cut. Negotiations with Māori chiefs were often undertaken in secrecy away from the tribe, side payments were made surreptitiously, boundaries of blocks were not fully agreed, surveys remained unfinished and rangatira who opposed sale were circumvented.[11] Some Māori expressed dissatisfaction with the activities of the Land Purchase Department to the Government.[12] There is also evidence that some tried and failed to organise a Land League to resist sales of land in Taranaki.[13] Dissatisfaction with land purchase activities undermined Māori faith in te Tiriti as a protection for their ownership of their lands and so contributed, according to Wiremu Tamihana Tarapipipi, to the growth of Kingitanga.[14]

The stresses caused by the rapid demand for land was more pressing in New Zealand than in Australia. In New Zealand, the speed of land purchase by the colonial government set the limit of occupation but in Australia any perceived stress was relieved by squatting especially from the mid-1830s onwards. (It was, of course, theoretically possible to conceive of the British Government reducing the stresses imposed by non-indigenous immigration upon Māori society by limiting immigration into New Zealand, especially from the UK. But such a course seems not to have been considered by Colonial Office officials.) Those afforded assisted passages were selected to some extent before they left for the Antipodes.[15] Conceivably, it might also have been arranged by delaying the departure of emigrant ships by one pretext or another, a system of visas or entry permits or simply by raising the price of passages, to and from Australia and New Zealand, or by imposing a specific duty upon them. In time, both New Zealand[16] and Australia imposed crude, racially discriminatory methods especially against Chinese. New Zealand set out the maximum number that each ship calling in New Zealand could carry and charged each world-be Chinese immigrant a fee which had to be paid in cash before he could land. From time-to-time Australia relied upon so-called "literacy tests" and discriminatory taxation.[17] All such methods were contrary to the desire, particular of Australian colonies, to attract large populations in order to further economic development with the result that increasingly most emigrants from Europe sought to establish a future in the USA and Canada rather than Australia and New Zealand.

Representative Government

They were also inconsistent with the establishment of representative government in New Zealand which was imminent from 1846 onwards, although it seems that the few who were involved in domestic politics in Australia and New Zealand cared about that matter. Their concern appears to have been their own self-interest which was best served by biasing, in their favour, the competition for access to land.

In any case, it would have been contrary to the policy direction being followed by the British Government. From the late1830s, under the influence of the Durham Report on British North America colonial policy was directed towards the attainment of representative democracy. Durham explicitly recommended placing "… the internal government of the Colony in the hands of the colonists themselves".[18] In British North America (now called Canada), New South Wales and New Zealand this policy led to representative government being established in Nova Scotia, New Brunswick, Prince Edward Island and Newfoundland, New South Wales, Victoria, New Zealand, Tasmania, South Australia and Queensland between 1848 and 1856.

From 1846 onwards, settlers in a number of British colonies were increasingly active in pursuing representative government. In New Zealand, such campaigning was often part of the manoeverings against particular Governors, like FitzRoy, and was, in part, an expression of a belief among non-indigenous settlers that they had a right to own and control New Zealand in preference to Māori. In Australia, the apogee of this type of agitation for representative democracy was the erection by miners and destruction by militia of the stockade at Eureka, Victoria in 1854.

A constitution for New Zealand composed in London by the British Government was stillborn in 1846 largely because Governor Grey refused to implement it. Yet over the next three years he was active in promoting the emergence of a federalist model of government for New Zealand. This finally emerged as the Provincial System which was enshrined in the 1852 Constitution Act. With its implementation, and until the provinces were abolished in 1875, the place of the crown in the New Zealand land market was taken by Provincial Councils each with its own land legislation.

Early New Zealand Company Settlement

The New Zealand Company became the *de facto* agent of the British Government because of the agreement it concluded with Lord John Russell in 1841. Through it, the Company secured a crown grant for land in New Zealand at the rate of four acres for every £1[19] it could be shown to have spent on emigration.[20] Hence, although the Company had to submit its original purchases to the Spain Commission, provided the expenditure could be proved, it was always going to be granted land at that rate whatever Commissioner Spain may decide. Thus, the New Zealand Company was, almost from the outset of colonisation, in a very similar position to the crown in the Australian colonies because it could organise sales directly to settlers who could, potentially, apply for a crown grant for the land they purchased. Thus, the land markets in Wellington, New Plymouth and Nelson were effectively Primary Land Markets. In other words, they could be operated as if the purchases of land from Māori were legitimate even when their legality was contested.[21]

The contrast between the experience of the New Zealand Company and that of the South Australian Company is striking. Despite the contributions of Gibbon Wakefield to both colonial enterprises, the South Australian Company was much more long-lasting than the New Zealand Company. Both were private companies set up to make profits by selling land in the Antipodes to buyers in London. But, in 1834, unlike 1841, the British Government insisted that the South Australian Company could only send emigrants to South Australia when land to the value of £35,000 had been sold and a loan of £80,000 had been raised. When it proved that insufficient land could be sold at the proposed price of £2 per acre, George Fife Angas, a merchant enriched with money from the compensation he received from the loss of his the slaves on his Caribbean plantations, offered to set up a joint stock company to buy the land unsold by the British Government through the South Australian Colonisation Commissioners.[22] Angas acquired 102 lots of 135 acres each at 12s per acre plus the right to rent a further 220,160 acres of pasturage. In direct contrast with the New Zealand Company, therefore, colonists in South Australia could expect with certainty that good title to landed estates would be available to them

The terms and conditions of land purchase in the earliest New Zealand Company settlements of Wellington/Whanganui, New Plymouth and Nelson were different from those later applied to Canterbury and Otago. The latter two appear to have operated largely independently of the activities of the New Zealand Company, under whose auspices they were both originally founded. The South Australian Company was finally wound up on 17 March 1949. The New Zealand Company voted to relinquish its charters on 4 July 1850 an offer which was accepted on 13 July 1850. But due to wrangles over debts owing, the affairs of the Company were not finalised until 1857 and its final annual report is dated 27 May 1858.

Intending British purchasers of land in Wellington, Nelson and New Plymouth and, initially, New Edinburgh (Otago), whether they be settlers or speculators were charged a fixed price of £1 per acre for land in New Zealand. Sales commonly took place long before the New Zealand Land Company[23] had purchased the land it sold to settlers. For example, Burns states that on the basis of a prospectus dated 2 May 1839 the Company sold 99,999 acres and again on 30 July 1839 offered a further 50,000 acres for sale.[24] However, at the time of the transactions no-one knew whether or not the sections thus sold corresponded to actual pieces of land in New Zealand. It has subsequently emerged that at the time, the New Zealand Company did not own any land in New Zealand.[25]

Buyers were expected to participate in a complicated lottery for the right to a place in a notional queue to select land for purchase. This lottery was conducted in London and used four wheels operated by children.[26] The wheels were mounted vertically on axles and were constructed so that they could be loaded with cards which could be drawn without being seen from the outside. Each wheel was spun after each drawing. From the first wheel a card was drawn bearing the number on the register of applications for land, with the name of the purchaser (or, more precisely, punter). Then, the second child drew from his wheel a card inscribed Town Land with a number denoting the priority of choice. This was repeated for the third and fourth wheels from which priorities of choice of Accommodation[27] Land and Rural Land were respectively drawn. As a result of the lottery potential purchasers owned nothing more than options over a place in the queue to select three different classes of land. These options were called, deceptively enough, Land Orders.[28] The Land Orders were registered by the New Zealand Company in London which, in time, informed each settlement of their existence. In this way, each registered application for land was allocated a place in the notional queues formed by those wishing to select the various types of land that might eventually become available. This did not necessarily mean that land had already been defined by survey, nor that it was being sold, nor even that it was available to purchasers either by sale or selection. The option merely implied that if and when land should become open for selection by intending purchasers, the order in which selection of available lots would take place was known because it was already determined by the lottery for Land Orders. In more enlightened times this kind of deception would be regarded as systematic fraud and the Company and its Directors would become liable for severe penalties under criminal law.

The Land Orders or selection options so created were transferable[29] and do not appear to have had a maturity date.[30] They represented a manufactured (or so-called "synthetic") claim or security, which could be held, bought or sold, gifted or bequeathed independently of any decisions to settle in New Zealand. They were relatively low cost and their resale value was liable to rise and fall as news from New Zealand arrived in London. These characteristics made them an ideal vehicle for speculation (i.e. gambling). An active secondary market developed in these Land Orders, which was organised neither by the crown nor the New Zealand Company. New Zealand Company records reveal that many Land Orders were transferred between parties in England.[31] But it is not possible to know which of these transfers were the result of trading in Land Orders and which were gifts or bequests. Middleton[32] also reports that early in 1840 Donald Sinclair[33] sold five Wellington sections for 1300 guineas some of which were "low-numbered" (i.e. they represented places near the front of notional queues for selection choices).[34]

The Land Orders could only be redeemed at land sales within the various colonies in New Zealand. If an option holder (or his agent) turned out to be the only person selecting a given allotment, then he paid the price and the allotment was his under a crown grant. The amount that he had subscribed in London was counted towards the purchase price. If, however, two or more selectors with the same priority of choice selected a given allotment, then an auction was held among those selectors and the land was sold to the highest bidder.[35]

These processes imposed significant risks on would-be emigrants. For example, Brodie was adamantly opposed to them and wrote in 1845:

> "With regard to emigrants, the best advice I can give them who are about to emigrate is, that those who have capital *should not purchase any land whatever in England,* as they know not what they are buying; let them keep their money until they have seen the country. There are hundreds of emigrants in all colonies anxious to sell for ready money; and ready money will always command bargains."[36]

He further states:

> "A land order is a clog to freedom of action; it binds emigrants to a locality which they are soon compelled to admit is not the most advantageous: they cannot dispose of it, for others are in the same position, and they do not like to think the parchment for which they have paid so highly like a piece of waste paper; and yet what else has it been for the last five years?"[37]

Maintaining flexibility of action as a way of dealing with future risk was important because of the absence of an effective monetary system and capital market. Making unpropitious choices "sight unseen" could lead to heavy losses without alternative ways of reducing them. It was also emphasised by Dillon who, when writing to his mother on 16 January 1843, said:

> "I had almost forgot to write to you about a very essential thing. I left England without a letter of credit and the consequence is that I can get no money but at a great loss as of course the risk is great. Will you be so good as to arrange with Ronsom's that I should have one sent out as soon as possible? For the present, one on my annual income would do, as I do not wish to touch my capital till I see my way quite clearly, and yet I should like in case of a good opportunity offered to have some means of drawing."[38]

Dillon is, therefore, proposing to employ a letter of credit from his banker in London as an alternative to relying upon non-existent (or very expensive) banking facilities in New Zealand. This may have enabled him to negotiate lines of credit with suppliers or could have involved paying for merchandise or services in New Zealand by creating a bill drawn on his London bank under his letter of credit. His New Zealand supplier would then be able to cancel the debt by either selling the bill for cash to someone else or sending it to London for collection. Unfortunately, we do not know how prevalent this behaviour was nor how far it constrained the development of an open market in land in New Zealand during the 1840s and 1850s.

Although the New Zealand Company arranged for the Union Bank of Australia to open a branch in Wellington in 1840, there seems to be no evidence that the bank lent against the security of real property, such as land, to any significant degree at that time. Rather, it seems that a number of private financiers partially filled the gap left by the absence of meaningful banking facilities. They were unconstrained by banking law which only limited the activities of chartered and joint-stock banks, and they risked their capital without benefit of limited liability. These financiers, like Tollemache, supplied loans secured by first mortgage to settlers and merchants for the purposes of land purchase and investment in capital equipment.

Unfortunately, little or no research seems to have been conducted into this type of lending. Consequently, we have little idea about the true nature of the risks that were faced, the rewards that were earned, overall benefits and costs of the activities of these private financiers and who faced them and how effectively and efficiently the market for money operated in New Zealand at this time. Nevertheless, in the regions and within the social circles[39] in which they were active it seems likely that these financiers facilitated significant development of waste lands sold through auction.

Otago Terms and Conditions

On 1 July 1843, The New Zealand Company announced the terms and conditions for the sale of land[40] in the "Colony of New Edinburgh" now generally called Otago.[41] These were modelled on those employed in the sale of land in Nelson.

The Company proposed that, starting on 22 August 1843, it would offer 120,550 acres of selected land; 550 acres for the town, 20,000 acres of suburban lots and 100,000 acres of rural lots. Town lots were one quarter of an acre each, suburban lots were 10 acres each and rural lots were 50 acres each. The Company defined a "property" as one town lot plus one suburban lot plus one rural lot. 200 properties were reserved for the Company and a further 200 were reserved for the municipal corporation. The remaining 1,800 properties were offered for sale at £120 each. Applications for land had to be accompanied by a deposit of 10%, proof of payment of which was required before the application could be registered. The remainder of the purchase price had to be paid by a date to be nominated by the Company. Failure to meet this condition would mean loss of the deposit already paid. Full payment would entitle the applicant to three Land Orders for (a.) 50 acres of rural land, (b.) 10 acres of suburban land and (c.) one town lot. Land would be selected in order of priority determined by lottery, presumably by the method decribed above. The Company also assumed the right to reserve land should it "be necessary to reserve any number of allotments for sale to actual colonists". For its part, the Company undertook not to dispose of its lands at prices "which shall yield to the Company less than 10s. per acre" thus promising to place a floor below which land prices in the settlement could not fall.

By early 1843, the finances of the Company were in a state of incipient collapse[42], a state worsened by news of the Wairau Affair which burst the propaganda bubble that had been so assiduously inflated by the Company over the previous years. The Company unsuccessfully sought recompense and then a loan from the UK Government. Its bills were dishonoured and it was only by directors offering promissory notes (i.e. post-dated personal cheques) and the purchase of Company shares that the New Zealand Company was able to continue for a short time until its operations were suspended.[43] So uncertain was the title to land made available in New Edinburgh that was not until the end of November 1847 that its first settlers sailed. Indeed, it was not until the New Zealand

Company ceased to be effectively involved in the formation of the colony as a result of the terms of its agreement[44] with Lord Derby that the colonisation of the southern part of the South Island became possible.

Canterbury Terms and Conditions

Canterbury was also settled without material assistance of the New Zealand Company. Waste lands in the Province of Canterbury were divided into Town lands, Rural land and Pasturage.[45] The procedures for Town lands and Rural land were relatively simple.

The sites of towns were to be determined by the Provincial Council and proclaimed in the Government Gazette. Town lands were to be surveyed before sale and to be sold by public auction in sections. They were to be shown on a definitive map along with any public reserves. Town sections might be auctioned at the initiative of the Superintendent or upon application by "some person" (accompanied by a deposit of 10% of the upset price).[46] The highest bidder at the auction will be required to pay 10% of the purchase price immediately and the remainder within one week of sale. Once payment in full is received the purchaser will receive a licence to occupy which is transferrable by endorsement and which can be exchanged for a crown grant.

If the highest bidder fails to pay the deposit the section is to be immediately "put up for auction". If the purchase price is not met within one week the purchaser will forfeit the deposit and "all right or title to the land". In addition:

> "… the section may be sold to any person applying for the same for the price at which it was knocked down in the auction: and, if not sold, the section may be again put up to auction at any future sale."[47]

All rural land was to be open for sale in as near as possible rectangular blocks[48] of not less than 20 acres at 40 shillings per acre. Where possible all blocks should extend no more than half a mile from a "frontage line".[49] Bidders for rural allotments that formed part of land subject to a Pasturage License with Pre-emptive right could exercise their pre-emptive right upon payment of forty pounds for each section.

Upon payment of the purchase money the purchaser is to receive a license to occupy.[50] As soon as possible afterwards the land is to be surveyed by the Government Surveyor. If the land lies beyond the "surveyed districts", then the land is to be surveyed at the purchaser's expense by the Government Surveyor. The license to occupy is then to be adjusted in accordance with the surveyor's report. Once complete, the license to occupy can be exchanged for a crown grant.

Most land within the Province of Canterbury was occupied under transferable annual licenses granted by the Waste Lands Board for pasturage purposes. These licenses gave "no right to the soil or to the timber" and were subject to a "reasonable right of way". Such land was allocated on a first-come, first-served basis.[51] In making an application for occupation an applicant had to set out the boundaries of the run and to set out plans for its stocking. 120 acres were allowed for each head of "great cattle" (horned cattle, horses, mules and asses) and 20 acres per head of "small cattle" (sheep and their weaned offspring). Licenses were charged on a sliding scale. Runs containing less than

1,000 acres were charged at twenty shillings per hundred acres; runs of 1,000 acres but less than 5,000 acres at 2d per acre for the first 1,000 and 1d per acre thereafter. Runs 5,000 or more paid fees at 1/4d per acre for the first and second years, 1/2d for the third and fourth years and 3/4d per acre for the fifth and each subsequent year. There was, therefore, a significant incentive for applicants to seek to occupy blocks that were as large as possible.[52]

There was also some incentive for applicants for pasturage licenses to apply for fewer acres than they were, in fact, intending to squat upon. Not only would this reduce the stock that they had to agree to purchase[53] but also there was little chance of discovery given that the true extent of runs was not accurately surveyed and so would not be known to the authorities for some years to come. The Waste Lands Board presided over a system which was designed to impose pastoral farming throughout the hinterland of the Province as quickly as possible. There were penalties if the level of stock fell short of what the license applicant originally promised it would be. Regulation 53 stated:

> "If at any time during the first four years after the issue of the first license the quantity of stock for the run shall be less than that originally required, or during the next three years less than twice that amount, or during any subsequent period less than three times that amount, the Waste Lands Board may declare the whole or a portion of such run to be forfeited…"[54]

Thus, it would seem that provided squatting under license achieved rapid increases in stocking levels, with concomitant rises in wool production, the Waste Lands Board did not concern itself with who might be benefitting from the system.

All pasturage license holders[55] could apply for a right of pre-emption over portions of their runs. Again, this right applied on a sliding scale. For a run of not less than 1,000 acres and not more than 5,000 acres, it applied to a block of land comprising and circumadjacent to the homestead up to 6% of run acreage. For a run of 5,000 acres and over the allowance was over 250 acres of land comprising and circumadjacent to the homestead or principal station. In addition, a right of pre-emption could be obtained on all licensed land for all buildings, enclosures, plantations, cultivations or other improvements considered as qualifying by the Waste Lands Board plus 50 acres comprising and circumadjacent to lands occupied and improved.[56] By shrewd location of homesteads and other improvements it was possible for license holders to control access to water, shelter and other amenities so as to limit or forestall competition from others for the land that they occupied but did not own.[57]

Sales by Provincial Councils

On 4 March 1853, Governor Grey promulgated an Ordinance which set out General Land Regulations in the Colony of New Zealand.[58] These regulations came into effect at different times in different provinces[59]; they, therefore, did not apply to all of New Zealand at the same time. Moreover, they did not institute a single market for crown waste lands; for that, we have to wait another 39 years for the passage of the Land Act 1892. Furthermore, the regulations only applied to lands which had not been reserved to the Canterbury Association and the Otago Association. Thus, they did not apply to the very large acreages on the South Island which had been transferred to these colonising associations by the agreement between the British Government and the New Zealand Company. It was only by the 1856 Compact that the proceeds of sales of crown lands accrued to the various Provincial Councils.

Governor Grey divided the crown waste lands into town and suburban sections and those contained within Hundreds[60] and those which were not. Town and suburban sections were to be sold at auction (Section I.1.). Lands within hundreds were to be sold by auction (Section II.3.). The rights of pasturage were to be enjoyed by occupiers under a crown grant who might be pensioners in the service of New Zealand or "persons of the native or half-caste races" (Section II.6.). The quality of lands outside Hundreds were to be assessed and if found to be poor sold at 5s per acre in rectangular sections of between 80 and 640 acres (Sections III.8., 10.). Runholders were granted a right of pre-emption over between 10 and 80 acres for a homestead at the original purchase price (Section III.13.). The rules for auctions (Section V.20–24.) follow Ripon's Rules. Scrip issued in satisfaction for New Zealand Company land orders (Section VI.25.) could be used to buy land at the rate of £1 of scrip for the upset price or fixed price of one acre of rural land (Section VI.26.) except in hundreds proclaimed prior to 2 August 1851 and within the town of New Plymouth (Section VI.27.). The commencement of these regulations did not apply to the "Lands reserved to the Canterbury and Otago Associations" (Section X.31.).

The cause of regulatory unification was not furthered by the Waste Lands Act 1858. That Act forms the basis of all future legislation in this area because it states:

> "The several Acts, Ordinances and Regulations, specified in the Schedule of this Act,[61] are hereby declared to have been valid from the time of the passing and issuing thereof, and the said Acts, Ordinances and Regulations, and the Bills specified in the said Schedule shall with hereafter have the full force and effect of Law in the several Provinces to which they respectively relate …."[62]

In drafting the Act the Stafford Government did not attempt to consolidate existing law or make the regulation of crown waste lands consistent across all Provinces. Instead, it contented itself with supplying Provincial Governments with a retrospective assurance that whatever legal justification they may have employed when administering crown waste lands was perfectly legal. Hence, the law controlling the disposal of crown waste lands can only be summarised Province-by-Province.

Each Province passed its own Waste Lands Act. These acts contained a number of common features. All set up Waste Lands Boards to administer the crown waste lands, all set out general characteristics of sections, all required land to be publicly auctioned for which minimum public notice must be given, and all required a deposit of one-tenth of the purchase price payable at sale and the remainder payable one month thereafter. Reserves can be made by the Board for the following reasons:

- Districts proper to be constituted gold districts;
- Lines of internal communication by roads railways canals or otherwise;

- Drains around through or from swampy districts;
- Gravel pits and ballast quarries;
- Quays docks loading-places and the improvement of rivers and water-courses;
- Sites for common schools in which reading and writing in English arithmetic English grammar and geography shall be taught;
- Sites and endowments for evening schools in towns and villages and for public libraries and reading-rooms;
- Sites and endowments for hospitals infirmaries and other charitable institutions;
- Sites for scientific institutions mechanics institutes markets court houses prisons and other public edifices;
- Cemeteries;
- Places for the embellishment of towns for the health and recreation of the inhabitants thereof;
- And generally for any purpose of public profit advantage utility convenience or enjoyment.[63]

These expressions of public welfare are generally consistent with the view that crown lands were to be held by the Board primarily in trust for the common good, the enhancement of which was the first call on their use. Finally, one-twentieth of the land "of average value in every District"[64] is to be set apart and reserved as an endowment by the Board for educational purposes. Aside from these common features, the land regulations of each Province differed.

Auckland

In the Province of Auckland crown waste lands were classified into five categories:

- Town lands;
- Suburban lands;
- General country lands;
- Credit lands; and
- Land for special settlement.[65]

The Auckland Province was alone in selling crown waste lands on credit. Prior to 1 August 1860, any person 16 years[66] or over could apply to select between 40 and 80 acres of Credit Land.[67] A deposit of 1 shilling per acre gave access to a Land Order for the equivalent parcel of land.[68] Successful applicants were entitled to immediate occupation and to a five-year lease at sixpence per annum per acre. After five years' residence (i.e. erecting a house and clearing and tilling the land) the occupier is entitled to a crown grant on payment of the purchase price of 10 shillings per acre.[69] The impact of this measure is hard to assess. However, since the amount of land involved was relatively small, the facility was severely limited in time and the ability of a young person to raise the necessary deposit constrained it seems unlikely to have resulted in relatively poor people gaining access to land on which they could sustainably earn a living. Nevertheless, empirical investigation of this possible route into land ownership has yet to occur.

The Auckland legislation also contains a provision allowing Māori to buy back land under a crown grant that they had sold to the crown:

> "Whenever the title to any Native land shall have been extinguished, it shall be lawful for the Governor, within one month thereafter, to permit the Native sellers to purchase, at the rate of 10s. an acre, any portion of such land; and the same, when surveyed, may be conveyed by crown grant accordingly."[70]

Thus, it would seem that the original owners would be able to obtain a freehold title without the need to compete at an auction and with the Government meeting the costs of survey. As with Credit Land, the actual effect of this provision is difficult to estimate. However, given that 10s. per acre was regarded, at the time, as a relatively high price for General Country (i.e. non-agricultural) land in Auckland Province and that no reliable estimate of market value would be available to help guide the bids of prospective purchasers, it is likely that such purchases would be attended by a high degree of risk.

In addition, in districts such as Taranaki there were many potential interests from absentee Māori proprietors with whom agreement would be difficult but nonetheless required if the sale was to become widely recognised. It appears that when McLean experimented with such a scheme in Taranaki in the mid-1850s he met with some initial success.[71] This part of the Act was clearly an attempt to make retrospectively legal this aspect of McLean's land purchase policies.

Wellington

In addition to Grey's Proclamation, the Provincial Government of Wellington passed additional land regulations on 15 February 1855.[72] They provided for:

- Public notice by the Superintendent of districts to be opened for general purchase (Regulation 1.) and of auction sales (Regulation 14.).
- Reserves for sites of townships, town and suburban land, agricultural and small farm settlements and for "any other purpose of public advantage, safety, convenience, health or enjoyment" (Regulation 2.).
- Land for small farm settlement by an Association at the price of 10s per acre cash on sale with an additional reserve of one-third for common pasturage (Regulation 4–5.).
- Not more than one-thirtieth of public lands to be set aside for educational purposes (Regulation 7.).

In addition, the regulations contained restrictions on licensed occupation of public pasture lands[73] albeit much less prescriptive and onerous than were applied in the Provinces of Canterbury or Otago.[74] The system was administered by Land Commissioners appointed for each district. It provided for the issue of occupation licenses which had a tenure of 14 years costing £5 each and for annual rent at the following rates:

- For the first four years at one farthing per acre;
- For the next five years at one half-penny per acre; and
- For the remaining five years one penny per acre.

Occupiers were required to place one breeding ewe for every twenty acres and one cow for every 120 acres within 12 months of taking up a license. This level of stocking was to be maintained throughout the period of the license. License holders had the right of pre-emption over the 80 acres surrounding the homestead. Thus, holders of pasturage licenses obtained land at low cost and with minimal stocking requirements.

Nelson

Crown land in the Province of Nelson was administered according to two statutes both of which were reserved by the crown. The first, the Nelson Waste Lands Bill 1858, was reserved pending the pleasure of the Governor and the second, the Nelson Waste Lands Act 1863, was reserved pending Her Majesty's pleasure. I have been unable to discover why the Governor's and the Queen's pleasures was reserved and if or when those pleasures were ever signified.

We do know, however, that the Waste Lands Act 1858, passed by the General Assembly, gave retrospective approval for the 1858 Bill. Nevertheless, both pieces of legislation appear as part of the Land Act 1877 which incorporated provincial legislation and practice into national law until the 1892 Land Act. I have been unable to discover further details of any other relevant legislation that may have been passed during that time. I deduce that both measures were, between them, the legislative basis for the administration of crown lands in the Nelson Province for about 35 years despite the doubts initially attached to them.

Both the 1858 and the 1863 Act were to be administered by a WasteLands Board consisting of the Superintendent, the Commissioner for Crown Lands and the Speaker of the Provincial Council of whom any two formed a quorum.[75] Plainly the Nelson Provincial Council intended to keep the disposal of crown lands under strict and politically influential control. To the extent that a politically influential class of pastoralists emerged in Nelson (and in its ultimate off-shoot Marlborough) suggests that this policy was, in this narrow respect, successful. Indeed, large pastoral holdings were extended across the steep mountains which border the very limits of the City of Nelson. However, it is hard to judge how far the relative stagnation of Nelson which benefitted neither from Commissariat expenditure during the Land Wars nor any significant investment in communications infrastructure[76] during the Vogel Boom years was the result of this influence.[77]

Land was to be classified by the Board under four heads:

1. Town land being sites reserved for towns and villages
2. Suburban land being land in the neighbourhood of such sites
3. Mineral land being supposed to contain minerals of value
4. Rural land being all land not comprised in any of the foregoing classes....[78]

The upset price of Town, Suburban and Mineral land is to be fixed the Board[79] but the upset price of Rural land is also to be fixed by the Board at between five and forty shillings per acre[80]. Three officials ran the allocation of land and set its price.

Like the equivalent legislation for Auckland, the Nelson Waste Lands Act provided for the ability of Māori sellers of land to buy back some or all of the land they had sold and to hold it under an individual crown grant. Strikingly, however, this ability was racially restricted because by Section 38 of the Bill, Māori could not buy either town or suburban land.[81] This provision was confirmed in Section XXXIII of the Nelson Waste Lands Act 1863 as follows:

> "Whenever the title to any Native land shall have been extinguished it shall be lawful for the Superintendent within three months thereafter to permit any of the Natives who sold such land to the Government where an agreement to that effect was made at the time of such sale to purchase any portion of such lands being rural at a price to be assessed as hereinbefore provided and the same may be conveyed by crown grant accordingly."[82]

Thus, Māori were not allowed to buy back Town or Suburban land even if they were the original sellers to the Province.

The 1856 Compact

The lasting importance of the 1856 Compact has been ignored by many New Zealand historians.[83] Yet the Compact represents a cornerstone of the political foundations of New Zealand society. Indeed, the "Financial Settlement with the Provinces", which came to be known as the 1856 Compact, deeply embedded the close link between the disposal of land and Colonial Government finances. It also drew the Provinces of New Zealand into a close relationship with the London money and capital markets. Once established, these economic and financial links went largely unquestioned yet framed national politics in New Zealand at least until the 1930s.

The 1856 Compact was originally drafted by Henry Sewell and finally negotiated between Edward Stafford and the Provincial Governments.[84] Before its conclusion, the General Assembly was fundamentally divided over whether land and the proceeds of its sale were to be controlled by central or provincial government. The Constitution Act 1852 specified that elected Provincial Councils would be established but was silent about how those Provinces were to be funded. Further, by Section XIX the Provinces were prohibited from imposing customs duties or charges on shipping or from regulating currency. Moreover, that same Section made it unlawful for Superintendents and Provincial Councils to legislate so as to affect:

> "… Lands of the crown, or Lands to which the Title of the aboriginal native Owners has never been extinguished …" (Section XIX.10).

Thus, Provincial Councils could only administer land already sold under a crown grant. Nevertheless, in all the complexity of the 1852 Constitution, the Colonial Government continued to be the responsibility of the Governor, appointed by the Queen on the advice of the British Government, acting upon the advice of elected ministers and duly appointed officials. Not until December 1854 did the British Government concede "Responsible Government" to New Zealand.[85]

In August 1853, Governor Grey issued a number of circulars about the revenues that were to be managed by the Provinces. The land revenue (proceeds of land sales and leases) was charged with servicing the debt incurred by the colony in settling with the New Zealand Company[86], administration costs and payments for the purchase of Māori land. One half of the balance was to be paid to the Provinces. The other half was to be paid to the General Government for immigration purposes. However, should any Provincial Council be prepared to take charge of them, an appropriate part of the land revenue formerly controlled by the General Government would be transferred to the Province concerned. In addition, Collectors of Customs were instructed to pay two-thirds of the balance on customs revenue each week to provincial accounts. Quarterly adjustments between province and colony were intended to ensure that provincial receipts from this source were in accord with actual revenue and expenditure.

The first session of the General Assembly which convened on 24 May 1854 was characterised by unmanageable conflict between Provinces and leading politicians. Insofar as the squabbles were based on policy, two opposing camps can be identified. On the one hand were the Centralists who believed that the colonisation of New Zealand should primarily be the responsibility of the General Assembly. On the other, were the Provincialists (some of whom, especially from Wellington, were quite extreme) who held that the future of New Zealand should emerge solely from choices made by the Provinces. Despite a confused First Session of the House of Representative in which two executive committees were appointed then forced to resign, the General Assembly passed the Provincial Waste Lands Act (subject to reservation of the Queen's assent). This empowered the General Assembly to vest management of the crown Wastes and any revenues that may result in the hands of Superintendents and Councils of the Provinces in which they are located. Acting Governor Wynyard issued a circular on 17 October 1854 which reduced the provincial share of net customs revenue to one-half plus one-half of the land fund after deducting the charge for the New Zealand Company debt and survey costs.

But granting responsible government in December 1854 meant that this agreement was re-litigated when the General Assembly next met on 15 April 1856. Two ministries respectively headed by Sewell and Fox failed before a lasting government headed by Stafford took office on 2 June 1856. By 2 July 1856, Stafford had negotiated an agreement with the Provinces which became known as the 1856 Compact. It contained the following provisions:

- Agreement with the New Zealand Company to accept £200,000 in settlement of its outstanding claims for expenses of emigration, surveys, etc.;
- A loan of £500,000 to be guaranteed by the British Government;
- South Island Provinces to be responsible in equal proportions for interest at 4% plus a 2% annual sinking fund on the £200,000 to be paid to the New Zealand Company;
- Auckland to owe no part of the payment to the New Zealand Company;
- £180,000 of the remainder to be paid into a capital fund for the purchase of Māori land; Auckland liable for one-half, Wellington for three-tenths and New Plymouth for one fifth (except for the first £20,000 expended in the province);

- The land fund no longer to be used for land purchase;
- Apart from provided above the entire land fund becomes provincial revenue;
- Administration of lands is passed to Provincial Councils;
- Expenditure of the General Government to be a charge on customs revenue; and
- Three-eighths of gross customs receipts to be paid to the provinces.[87]

The 1856 Compact facilitated access of the New Zealand Government to the London Capital Market. A £500,000 loan was borrowed under a British Government guarantee lasting for 30 years by the New Zealand Loan Guarantee Act of 1857. It carried an interest rate of 4% p.a. The £200,000 owed to the New Zealand Company and a sinking fund of 2% was charged equally on the Provinces of Otago, Canterbury and Nelson. Auckland was retrospectively and prospectively forgiven any part of this charge. £180,000 of the remainder was allocated to Auckland (£90,000), Wellington (£54,000) and Taranaki (£36,000) to purchase Māori-held lands in the North Island. The General Government was allocated the entire customs revenue of which three-eigths was passed back to the Provinces. In addition, although apparently unadvertised, the General Government also took charge of the £120,000 remaining from the loan proceeds.

By means of this document Stafford set the general character of New Zealand Governments for some time to come. He ensured the financial strength of the General Government based on overseas borrowing and indirect taxation. He established a dependence on imported loan capital to cover deficiencies in domestic saving. He put in place the dependence of General Government finance on indirect taxation in the form of customs and excise duties. He engaged the self-interest of all the Provinces in gaining and maintaining access to the London Capital Market so that their policy differences and domestic rivalries were never driven so far as to threaten to undermine the country's Credit despite their never having been resolved. He avoided political opposition to direct taxes on income and wealth by not introducing them.

Despite the important political differences which made it necessary, the 1856 Compact was composed entirely of technical financial provisions. It encapsulated no great vision or lasting principle. It did not address how best to use the vast landed resources of the country to best advantage. It succeeded in ignoring the political differences in the General Assembly which made its birth so difficult. Nevertheless, it charted a course towards the future of provincial government in financial terms that was acquiesced in by all non-indigenous people represented in Parliament, although the benefits it provided were unequally distributed. This outcome was possible because a majority of provincial politicians valued their independence from central authority more than they sought to maximise the material wealth of their constituents.[88]

Some commentators[89] judge that this agreement favoured Canterbury, Nelson and Otago largely to the detriment of the North Island Provinces. This, it is argued, was because it was possible to rapidly secure occupants for the relatively open lands in the South which we made available to runholders on the relatively liberal terms outlined above. By contrast, North Island lands required expensive clearing before they could be brought into commercial production and, in any case, were still largely controlled by Māori. Hence, the North Island Provinces relinquished their share of the common land fund in return for access to loan finance.[90] Over the next 20 years, the short-comings of the 1856 Compact ate away the legitimacy of Provincial Government. By the mid-1870s, there were few who regretted the demise of Provincial Councils and Superintendents. Nevertheless, it was not until the 1894 Land Act that some measure of national conformability was imposed on systems for the disposal of crown waste lands.

Despite its weaknesses, the 1856 Compact succeeded in tightening the drawstring on the bag labelled "New Zealand" which contained six (soon to become 10) disparate settlements[91] each scrabbling for its own advantage. It did so by an arrangement that was largely financial in character. Nevertheless, each Province, dominated by non-Māori interests, maintained its own disparate visions and ambitions. The Compact did not address, let alone settle, these Provincial political differences through a widely accepted political bargain.

These political distinctions and animosities festered for lack of respectful attention, and, in the 1870s, expanded into the unmanageable incubus which led to the abolition of the provinces in 1876. But abolition of the provinces did not bring the underlying differences any closer to resolution. The national entity "New Zealand" did not arise in the concept of commonly-held culture; among non-indigenous people, at least, it was forged upon a common interest in whether or not land and money (and especially money from land) was to be gained or lost. Nevertheless, if there had been no 1856 Compact an apparently unified colony labelled "New Zealand" would not have come into being, when it did, and in the form it took. A coherent entity called "New Zealand", was formed in the process of borrowing in London. I have been unable to find out whether or not financial interests in the City of London exercised any influence over the form and content of 1856 Compact. But it is plain that Stafford's Compact defined a distinct entity "New Zealand" into a form which could raise long-term loans on the London Capital Market.

The existence of a distinct debtor entity labelled "New Zealand" was guaranteed by the British Government. It was highly regarded by London bankers to whom a British Government guarantee overrode any local political, social and economic differences. Immediately, New Zealand achieved a reputation as a country which always met its obligations in all circumstances. The original colonial relationship was altered into one between a lender and a debtor stretching over three decades.

But debt owed means that lenders have a source of power over a borrower. Banks which lent to New Zealand and which disagreed with the actions of the New Zealand Government can always bring the Government to heel through threats to future borrowing. In such subtle ways an accommodation is forged between the New Zealand Government and its bankers. That New Zealand has never defaulted on its debt obligations[92] has probably been at a real cost in terms of banker inspired austerity required to keep its reputation intact.

But over-arching all these considerations was the guarantee, by the British Government, of repayment of substantial overseas borrowing by the Colony of New Zealand. The negotiations conducted by Sewell in London which brought about this agreement and the debts incurred brought the colony definitively into the commercial and political ambit of the British Empire for the first time. In doing so, it demonstrated that the activities of the colonists were approved, facilitated and guaranteed by the most powerful nation in the world. It also meant that the English ruling class, through its instrument, the City of London and with the support of Her Majesty's Government, had a very significant interest in ensuring that settlers in New Zealand survived and prospered.

Nevertheless, in accepting the loan monies guaranteed by the Imperial Government, all future New Zealand Governments were inexorably drawn into a position in which they had to actively consider the impacts of choices they might contemplate upon the credit with which the Colony of New Zealand was viewed in the City of London. This was never a hard and fast set of notions. Indeed, it was rarely the subject of explicit statement in financial circles or between governments. Over the succeeding years, New Zealand Governments learned, by experience, to separate policies that were considered acceptable to English bankers from those that were not. If the colony followed unacceptable choices, then obstacles were placed in the way of raising future loans.

Hence, in the period from the 1856 Compact until at least World War I the direction of New Zealand social and economic development did not trespass beyond the "safety" of limits set by the consensus of financiers in the London Money and Capital Markets. A similar series of events occurred in Australia. The more Australian colonies and New Zealand borrowed and the greater the proportion of Australian and New Zealand productive assets that were foreign owned, the more pressing this imperative and the narrower the tightrope navigated by Australasian colonial economies became.

Chapter Notes

1. FitzRoy and his family finally left New Zealand in January 1846. In the intervening period since Governor Grey was installed, it seems that FitzRoy attempted, without obvious success, to provide advice to Grey, a fact which the latter later tried to deny. Grey spent the subsequent years adopting many of FitzRoy's policies while simultaneously advertising his predecessor's policy failures.
2. Submission by Bartley in the case of Charles Hunter McIntosh vs. John Jermyn Symonds, Supreme Court 4 May 1847, p.28, https://paperspast.natlib.govt.nz/newspapers/NZ18470508.2.8.
3. Hackshaw, pp 92–120 in Kawharu ed, op cit, 1989, p. 103.
4. Donald McLean was formerly a sub-Protector of Aborigines. Grey appointed him Chief Native Land Purchase Commissioner.
5. Henry Tacy Kemp purchased 13,551,400 acres for £2,000 which equates to roughly $0.07 per acre. Walter Mantell subsequently unilaterally reduced Māori reserves from the 10 acres per head originally promised by Kemp to 4 acres per head.
6. In the initial stages of colonisation many non-indigenous settlers occupied land controlled by Māori chiefs (Rangatira) who often requested use of equipment or services from the settler. While these were often called informal by settlers it is debatable how far this form of informality stretched in the hearts and minds of their Māori hosts.
7. Ann Parsonson: "The Pursuit of Mana", Chapter 6, pp. 140–167 in WH Oliver and Bridget Williams (editors): *The Oxford History of New Zealand*, Wellington, Oxford University Press, 1981.
8. It is noteworthy that Donald McLean, Chief Land Purchase Officer, along with leading members of Hawkes Bay squatocracy, accumulated considerable holdings of land leased from Māori owners without once being prosecuted on the information or complaint of the Surveyor-General. By contrast, Māori could use a successful transaction with the land purchase system as a way of asserting their own mana because it showed other potential claimants that the crown acknowledged them as "owners".
9. Proclamation XIX in installing a crown monopsony makes hollow any claim that the Pre-Primary Land Market in New Zealand was based around fair and open bargains between consenting parties.
10. Parsonson, op cit, 1981, p.151 has pointed out that on occasion Land Purchase officers declined to discuss the sale of land when offered by Māori located where there was a high risk of the settlers being subject to interference.
11. Ray Fargher: *The best man who ever served the crown? A Life of Donald McLean*, Wellington, Victoria University Press, 2007, pp 170 ff.
12. Ibid, p. 176.
13. Keith Sinclair: "Te Tikanga Pekeke: The Māori Anti-Landselling Movements in Taranaki 1849–59" pp 77–92 in Peter Munz ed: *The Feel of Truth: Essays in New Zealand and Pacific History: Presented to FLW Wood and JC Beaglehole on the occasion of their retirement*, Wellington, AH and AW Reed, 1969.
14. Stokes, op cit, 2002, pp 177–180
15. Blainey, op cit, 2014, p. 59 states that "… the young were preferred over the old, the fit over the unfit, the skilled tradesman over the labourer, the British over foreigners, and often to correct the shortage of women, the female over the male."
16. When New Zealand introduced an old age pension in 1898 Chinese people were specifically denied access to it. Section 64(4) of the Old-age pension Act 1898 states that "Chinese and other Asiatics, whether naturalised or not" could not be paid the Old-age pension even if they qualified to receive it.

17 See Crowley, op cit, 1980, Vol 3, pp. 19–21.
18 See Gerald M Craig (editor): "Lord Durham's Report: An Abridgement of Report on the Affairs of British North America by Lord Durham", Toronto, McClelland and Stewart, 1968, p. 141.
19 This is the equivalent of the standard upset price set by the Colonial Office in its Rules and Regulations of 5/ – per acre.
20 Although this is consistent with the standard upset price contained in Colonial Office Rules and Regulations it is in stark contrast to the 0.07d per acre paid to the South Island of New Zealand under the Kemp Purchase.
21 The arguments continue to the present. For example, in August 2023, the Supreme Court heard a plea from tribes in the Nelson area for redress resulting from the New Zealand Company failing to honour its part of the purchase of lands in the Nelson Province.
22 Set up by the South Australian (Foundation) Act 1834.
23 This company was the result of an amalgamation of a number of individual interests in the New Zealand Land and Colonisation Company, the 1825 New Zealand Company and the New Zealand Association of 1837–1838.
24 Burns, op cit, 1989, pp 16–17.
25 McIntyre and Gardner, op cit, 1979, pp. 21–23.
26 This was normal practice in the drawing of lotteries in the 19th century. For example, until the National Lottery was finally abandoned in 1828, as a result of multifarious irregularities, it was the custom to engage students of Charterhouse School to draw winning tickets from the wheels. Despite a number of proofs to the contrary, it was maintained to the very end that children were less open to dishonesty than adults. For descriptions of the conduct of 18th and early 19th century lotteries see John Ashton: *A History of English Lotteries: Now for the First Time Written*, London, The Leadenhall Press, 1893; C L'Estrange Ewen: *Lotteries and Sweepstakes: An Historical, Legal and Ethical Survey of their Introduction, Suppression and Re-establishment*, New York, Benjamin Blom, 1972; James Raven: "The Abolition of the English State Lotteries", *The Historical Journal*, Vol 34 (1991), No 2, pp 371–389; Penny Williams: "Lotteries and Government Finance in England", *History Today*, Vol 6 (1956), No 8, August, pp. 557–561; and Robert Woodhall: "The British State Lotteries", *History Today*, Vol 14 (1964), No 7, July, pp. 497–504.
27 Presumably the equivalent of Suburban Land.
28 In the case of South Australia claims for selection were also sold to investors in London. They were called Preliminary Land Orders. Each Preliminary Land Order entitled its holder to make a selection of previously surveyed land consisting of one town acre in Adelaide plus a 134 acre Country Section. The first ballot to decide the order of selection was held among 437 purchasers of Preliminary Land Orders was held in London on 28 March 1838. It is not known if it involved the complex ritual employed by the New Zealand Company. See John Tregenza: "Colonel Light's 'Theberton Cottage' and his Legacy to Maria Gandy; A Reconstruct ion of the Evidence", pp. 1–21 in Glen Ralph (ed): *Theberton Cottage: The Home of Colonel William Light and the Great Controversy Surrounding It*, Lockleys, Wilmar Library, April 1997.
29 In the "Daily Register of Notices of Transfers of Land Orders, August 1839 to 21 December 1858" (hereafter Daily Register 1839–1858) of the New Zealand Company one exception to this is recorded. Four non-transferable Land Orders were issued to Alexander Currie on 19 April 1842 and were converted into transferable ones on the same day. I have been unable to discount the reasons behind this entry in the register. See nzpictures.co.nz/nzc33.pdf.
30 For example, John Stuart Mill purchased a Land Order for land near Takaka in Golden Bay. After the passage of the Land Orders and Scrip Act 1856, to bring some order to the demise of the New Zealand Company, he was offered scrip in return for his Land Order which he had still not exercised.
31 *Daily Register*, op cit, 1839–1858. Some Land Orders were transferred many times between different parties.

32 Sue Middleton: "Labourers' letter from Wellington to Surrey, 1840–1845: Lefebvre, Bernstein and pedagogies of appropriation", *History of Education*, Vol 39, No 4, July 2010, pp. 459–479.
33 Donald Sinclair was Algernon Tollemache's nephew conducting some business for his uncle who remained an absentee landlord and financier until his death.
34 Presumably, these were the same selection options which Sinclair and Tollemache purchased in July 1839 at a sale conducted by the New Zealand Company in London.
35 In these cases, the ownership of ecclesiastical sites located in Auckland Province was decided by lot in direct contravention of Section I.3 of the Waste Lands Act 1858 which stated: "The priority of choice shall in no case whatever be decided by lot…".
36 Brodie, op cit, 1845/1997, pp 117–118.
37 Ibid, p. 118.
38 Sharp ed, op cit, 1954, p. 19.
39 For example, Hon. Algernon Tollemache was a close friend of Donald McLean. He supplied McLean with mortgages for land purchase and leases in the Hawkes Bay.
40 The Company had already been provided with a crown grant over the land it put up for sale.
41 Burns, op cit, 1989, p 250 provides a facsimile of the terms and conditions published by public notice.
42 It seems very likely that, at this time, the Directors of the Company were allowing operations to continue despite the Company's being insolvent. However, such were the accounting standards of the age, the extent of puffery by the Company and the political influence its sponsors could command, public recognition of this reality was postponed for a further seven years. Thus, it was not until mid-July 1850 that the Directors proposed to the Government that they would relinquish the Company's charters, ibid, pp. 298–299.
43 Ibid, pp 252–254.
44 In 1846, the New Zealand Company demanded compensation from the British Government for land which it had purchased but for which it had not received legal title. It claimed direct losses of £190,000 and an additional £35,000 in accrued interest. Lord Grey responded by offering the Company the sole right to dispose of native lands in the "Southern Government" of New Zealand for three years. He further proposed an advance of £236,000 which would become repayable after three years if the Company were then in a position to continue operations. If, by contrast, the Company could not continue all advances received would be remitted and it would be reimbursed for its expenditure on land in New Zealand at the rate of 5/ – per acre up to a maximum of £268,000. The costs of this agreement would fall upon the budget of the colony. The Company accepted this proposal on 14 May 1847. See ibid, pp 292–294. So far as is known, little or no consultation took place within New Zealand about this matter.
45 Canterbury Provincial Government: "Land Regulations of the Province of Canterbury, New Zealand; As Amended", Lyttleton, *Lyttleton Times*, 1857.
46 Ibid
47 Ibid, Regulation 32.
48 Ibid, Regulations 37 and 38 allow certain exceptions to this general requirement.
49 Ibid, Regulation 36 NOTE states: "A frontage line shall be taken to mean the boundary of a road, river or public reserve, or any stream or watercourse which shall have been declared by notification in the Government Gazette to constitute a frontage for the purpose of selection."
50 A license to occupy conveys the same rights to occupy as a lodger in a family household or an occupant of a modern-day rest home.
51 Samuel Butler, op cit, 1964, pp 95 ff describes a race to Christchurch to ensure that his name is entered into the Application Book held by the Waste Lands Board before a competitor, John Henry Caton, so that he could obtain the right to purchase the right to occupy Erewhon station.
52 A pasturage license covering 5,000 acres cost £25 per annum, while one containing 100,000 acres cost between £104 and £105 per annum.
53 Holders of Licenses to Occupy were required to provide, on receipt of a written request from the

Waste Lands Board with an annual return on the quantity of stock for the run. This appears to be the only source of such information available to the Board.

54 Canterbury Provincial Government, op cit, 1857, Regulation 53.

55 The identity, backgrounds and financing of these license holders does not seem to have been the subject of systematic study. However, McAloon, op cit, 2003, using data on registered mortgages, has pioneered the study of some aspects of the financing of lessees of Canterbury sheep-runs.

56 Ibid, Regulation 60.

57 By such tactics, pastoralists were able to occupy large acreages without needed to find the purchase price. They included the exploitation of pre-emptive rights, "gridironong" and " spotting". Any building, no matter how crude, and every thirty eight and a half chains (847 yards or 774.5 metres) of fencing carried with them a pre-emptive right to purchase 50 acres which led to the strategic siting of shepherd's huts and the fencing of water courses. Gridironing was possible because every parcel of 20 acres or more had to be sold at auction so runholders bought a series of 20 acre sections leaving smaller areas un bought in between which were left to the runholder to use. "Spotting" involved the purchase of blocks of 20 to 100 acres which included all available water while the remaining land was left un-surveyed and so went unbought. See Sutch, op cit, 1966, pp. 36–37.

58 Reprinted in Government of the Province of Wellington: "Acts of the Province of Wellington Session I, 1853 to Session XL 1864", Wellington, Province of Wellington Government Printer, 1865, pp. vi-xx

59 The regulations provide for their commencement 15 days after a copy of the regulations is received in each Province. Thus, for example, the regulations did not become widely known in Nelson until 9 April 1853 when a copy of them was published in *The Nelson Examiner and New Zealand Chronicle* by which time they had already been put in place in Wellington for some weeks.

60 The Governor could divide waste lands of the Province of Otago into Hundreds. A Hundred was supposed to be sufficient land to support 100 families although the actual areas involved varied. The aim of the subdivision was to encourage closer settlement of useful agricultural land which could be purchased or leased by its occupiers. Each Hundred was managed by a Board of Wardens elected from among those holding licenses to occupy land in the Hundred. In 1861, about 6.6% of Otago was administered in this way.

61 14 separate measures are listed in the Schedule. For Auckland 2, New Plymouth 1, Wellington 2, Nelson 2, Canterbury 4 and Otago 3.

62 Waste Lands Act 1858, Section I.

63 Section IX , The Nelson Waste Lands Act 1863.

64 Section X, The Nelson Waste Lands Act 1863.

65 Section 7, Auckland Waste Land Act 1858

66 Unlike some other provinces, there were apparently no gender or racial qualifications attached to the Auckland legislation.

67 The whole estate of Credit Land was limited to 200,000 acres in total by Section 7 of Auckland Waste Land Act, 1858.

68 Section 43, Auckland Waste Land Act 1858.

69 Sections 48, 49 and 50, Auckland Waste Land Act 1858.,

70 Section 3, Auckland Waste Land Act 1858.

71 Ann Parsonen, pp 140–167 in Oliver and Williams, (eds) op. cit, 1981. At p. 153 Parsonen states: "A short-lived Government scheme of the mid-1850s to allow Māori sellers to buy back part of their land as individual crown-granted sections, as in the Hua (or Bell) Block near New Plymouth, was wildly popular." Cowan, however, is less complimentary about this procedure. See James Cowan: *Sir Donald McLean: The Story of a New Zealand Statesman*, Dunedin, AH and AW Reed, 1941, pp 67–68.

72 Provincial Government of Wellington, op cit 1865, pp. xxi-xxiv.

73 Ibid, pp xxiv–xxix.
74 Prominent Wellington politicians were significant owners of pasturage in the Manawatu and the Wairarapa which they could hold without the burden of fully stocking.
75 Section V, The Nelson Waste Lands Act 1863.
76 The first railway in New Zealand, the Dun Mountain Railway, opened on 3 February 1862. It was a local horse-drawn, narrow-gauge (3 feet) railway running between a chromate mine (called the Duppa Lode after the pastoralist upon whose holding it was found) 10 miles to the south east of Nelson and the port. When the mine became uneconomic in the 1860s the lower part of the railway continued to operate as a passenger service within Nelson until its closure on 30 May 1901.
77 Fox describes this as follows: "Nelson owes its success entirely to itself; it has never participated in the immense sums of money expended at Auckland and Wellington, but has patiently dug its own maintenance out of the ground." William Fox: *The Six Colonies of New Zealand*, London, John Parker and Son, 1851 reprinted by London, Forgotten Books, 2017, p. 26.
78 Section XXIV, The Nelson Waste Lands Act 1863.
79 Section XXVI, The Nelson Waste Lands Act 1863.
80 Section XXVII, The Nelson Waste Lands Act 1863.
81 Section 38, Nelson Waste Lands Bill 1858.
82 Section XXXIII, The Nelson Waste Lands Act 1863.
83 For example W H Oliver *The Story of New Zealand*, London, Faber and Faber, 1960, has no index entry for the 1856 Compact and does not discuss the contents of the agreement; Keith Sinclair *A History of New Zealand*, New Edition, Auckland, Penguin, 1991 also has no separate index entry for the 1856 Compact and only mentions part of its contents in high level summary; James Bellich *Making Peoples, A History of the New Zealanders From Polynesian Settlement to the End of the Nineteenth Century*, Auckland, Allen Lane, 1996 has no index reference to the 1856 Compact and Provinces and contains no discussion of the provisions of the Compact; Michael King *The Penguin History of New Zealand*, Auckland, Penguin, 2003 makes no mention of the 1856 Compact but does have an index entry for provincial government.
84 McIntyre and Gardner, op cit, 1979, pp. 99–105.
85 Ibid, pp. 91–92. The despatch from the Secretary of State for War and the Colonies to Major Wynyard, officer administering the government, was dated 8 December 1854 and received in Wellington on 30 March 1855. It states: "… Her Majesty's Government have no objection whatever to offer to the establishment of the system known as 'responsible government', in New Zealand".
86 The so-called New Zealand Company's fourth. See Morrell, op cit, 1964, p. 74. This meant that the remaining debt to the New Zealand Company would become a charge against the Land Fund.
87 Summarised from McIntyre and Gardner, op cit, 1979, pp. 102–105.
88 Stafford speaking in reply to Fox's Motion of Want of Confidence on 15 June 1869 said: "… I was party to the arrangement. I was so, because I believed it was really the proper thing to do, to allocate the land revenue as much as possible to those districts where it was raised. If I could have contemplated at the time that the land revenue would have been so unwisely applied, and so little expended in the districts in which it was raised, I should have gone further than the arrangement which my Government affected, and allocated it to the districts instead of the Provinces." Hansard, 15 June 1869, pp 115–116. Downloaded, 22 October 2020, from babel. hathitrust.org/ogi/pt?id=uc1.32106019740270&view=1up&seq=140.
89 For example Sinclair, op cit, 1991, p. 108 states: "The North Island had made a bad bargain…" and "The South Island Provinces were enabled to advance with little regard for the country as a whole."
90 William Gisborne: *New Zealand Rulers and Statesmen 1840 to 1885*, London, Samson Low, Marston, Searle and Rivington, 1886, p. 160 stated: "It is true that Province loans were raised on

the credit of the whole colony for the purchase of native lands; but these loans were but a poor equivalent for the relinquishment of the legal right to common property in the whole land fund of New Zealand; and native disturbances soon made these loans for the most part practically valueless." This view has been often repeated down the years and remains the most frequently-made judgement about the 1856 Compact.

91 See McIntyre and Gardner, op cit, 1979, Map 5, p. 74. Auckland, New Plymouth (renamed Taranaki 1 January 1859), Wellington, Nelson, Canterbury and Otago were proclaimed on 17 January 1853 and their boundaries were gazetted on 28 February 1853. Hawkes Bay and Marlborough were formed on 1 November 1859, Westland became an independent county on 1 January 1868 and a Province on 1 December 1873 and Southland became a Province on 25 March 1861 but was re-united with Otago on 5 October 1870.

92 This is the story commonly told. However, I have been made aware that Michael Reddel, an ex-Treasury official, has reported in his blog "Croaking Cassandra" that in 1933 the Government of New Zealand defaulted on a debt of "$24.1 million" to the British Treasury incurred during World War I. He also stated that at least two New Zealand local authorities defaulted on loans contracted in London. Only a full investigation of these claims can decide the truth or otherwise of these assertions.

INDEX

Antipodes, ix
Auckland, 127
Auckland Savings Bank, 183
Australasia, ix
Australia, ix

Ballara, Angela, 133–4, 136
Bank Charter Act, 1826 188
Bank Charter Act, 1844 95, 179–80, 187–9, 195
Bank Charter Act, 1851 188–9
Bank Lending, 95
Bank of Australasia, 96, 155, 159, 190, 191
Bank of Australia, 94, 155, 190
Bank of England, 91, 93, 97–99, 151, 179–184, 195
Bank of New South Wales, 85, 90–93, 154–8, 162, 190–91, 195
Bank of New Zealand, 96, 99, 180
Bank of Van Diemen's Land, 94, 154, 183
Baring Crisis, 99
Baring, Hon Francis, 187
Basset, Michael, 126
Bathurst, Lord, 52, 92
Beauchamp Committee, 1785 19, 20
Bentham, Jeremy 27, 136
Bigge, John Thomas, 24, 52–3
Bills of Exchange, 83, 93–4
Black Band, 58
Blackstone, Sir William, 9, 110
Blainey, Geoffrey, 48
Bligh, Gov William, 88
Board of Enquiry into Native Affairs 1856, 131

Bourke, Gov Richard, 58
Brisbane, Gov Thomas, 53, 94, 154
Brodie, Walter, 137, 210
Bullionist Analysis, 90
Bunbury Committee on Transportation, 19
Busby, James, 24, 65, 67

Clapham Sect, 27
Coke, Sir Edward, 12
Colonial Bank of Issue, 169, 188–189
Colonial Land and Emigration Commissioners, 115, 116, 127
Commercial Bank of Sydney, 155, 191
Commissariat, 13, 20, 48, 83–86, 104, 168, 184, 191
Common Law, 109–110
Compact of 1856, 218, 222–226
Constitution Act 1852, 125, 211
Cook, Captain James, 8, 117
Country Bankers Act, 1826 93, 96, 182–183
Credit Creation, 88
Crown Grants in NSW, 52
Crown Pre-emption, 61–71, 129, 207–210
Currency, 81, 82, 87

Darling, Gov Ralph, 54, 57
Durham Report, 207
Durie CJ, Sir Eddie, 120

Easton, Brian, 81
Eureka, Victoria, 211

Face Value, 88

Fatal Necessity, 7, 14, 15–17
Fenton CJ, Francis Dart, 122, 132, 133
First Fleet, 45
Firth, Raymond, 86, 87, 134
Fitzroy, Gov Robert, 70, 128, 131, 167, 184–5, 193–4, 207
Free Settlers, 49

Gipps, Gov George, 58, 61, 69, 115, 117
Glenelg, Lord, 10, 58
Gold, 70, 94, 98–9, 178ff
Gore-Browne, Gov Thomas, 134
Grand Bargain 5, 5ff, 55
Gregory, Augustus 117
Grey, Earl 66–7, 124, 136–7, 164, 168, 187, 203–5
Grey, Gov George 66, 68, 70, 112, 120, 124, 203–5, 218
Griffiths Case 117–18
Grose, Acting Gov Francis 13, 49, 83

Hobson, Governor 10, 61–5, 126–8, 165, 194
Hughes, Robert 50

Jacobinism, 17
James, Carwyn 132

Kemp, Henry Tacy, 205
King, Gov Philip Gidley 85, 86, 88
King's Peace 6, 12, 24
Kingi, Wiremu, 134
Kith and Kin, 10–13
Kwaymullina, Ambelin, 114

Land, 51, 111–12, 123
Land Leagues, 205, 209–10
Land Markets, 50, 53, 63,123
Land Orders, 185–7, 193, 209, 213–14, 219
Land Purchase Department, 207, 210
Land Question, 60
Limited Liability, 154
Locke, John, 67, 68, 136
London Funds, 97, 197
London Markets, 93, 94, 182
Long Nineteenth Century, ix

Macarthur, Elizabeth, 84
Macarthur, James, 49, 51–52
Macquarie, Gov Lachlan, 13, 26, 52, 86–8, 90–93, 152, 154
Manifest Destiny, 7–10
Māori Land Proprietorship, 122
Market Making, 89
Marsden, Bishop Samuel, 24
Marshall CJ, John, 137
Mathew, Felton, 126
Matra, James, 19
McLean, Sir Donald, 133–6, 163–6, 204–5, 208, 210, 220
Melbourne Banking Co, 156
Mercantile Bank of Sydney, 156
Money-Go-Round, 14
Moorhead, Alan, 113, 114
Morton's Hints, 8
Myall Creek Massacre, 58

National Bank of New Zealand, 96, 157
New South Wales Corps, 11, 49, 85
New South Wales Legislative Council, 57–59 62
New Zealand Co, 56, 125, 128, 187, 193, 208–16, 218, 223–4
New Zealand Declaration of Independence, 24
New Zealand, ix
New Zealand Land, 62–7
New Zealand Strategic Importance, 16
Nineteen Counties, 10, 13
Normanby, Lord, 62, 68, 195

Oriental Bank, 170, 189, 190
Overend Gurney & Co, 98, 161, 170, 182–3

Parliamentary Select Committee on Aboriginal Tribes, 10
Pastoral Association (NSW), 59–60
Peel, Sir Rober,t 180
Phillip, Gov Arthur, 20, 21, 47, 48, 53, 83, 112
Pilbara Strike, 118
Promissory Notes, 87–9, 186

Resumption of Cash Payments Act 1819, 97
Richmond, Captain Matthew, 123
Ripon's Rules, 50, 126, 183, 214
Robertson Acts, 60–61
Rose, Thomas, 49
Royal Prerogative, 110, 154–8
Russell, Lord John, 63–6, 126

Seeley, John, 7–8
Select Committee on the High Price of Bullion, 90
Shortland, Acting Gov Willoughby, 126–8, 133
Shortland, Edward, 133, 165, 194
Silver Dollars, 84, 90
Sinclair, Keith, 96
Slavery, 182
South Australia Co, 208, 212
Squatting, 57–61
Stafford, Sir Edward, 168, 214, 219–24
Stanley, Lord, 128, 129
Starvation Years, 48–9
Stephen, Sir James, 10, 11–12
Stevenson, George, 10
Stock and station agents, 100
Stone, Russell C J, 126

Taranaki War, 205
Te Rauparaha, 187, 205
Te Teira Manuka, 134
Te Tiriti O Waitangi, 61–62
Terra nullius, 21, 22
Thermal Region of Rotorua, 119
Thomson, E Deas, 125
Title to Land, 124
Tollemarche, Hon Algernon, 164, 166, 215
Transportation, 18, 83
Treaty of Paris 1783, 18
Treaty of Waitangi, 61–2
Tyranny of Distance, 7

Union Bank of Australia, 96, 129, 169–70, 184–9, 190–94, 210, 214
Unsigned Treaty, 69

Wage Orders, 59, 185

Waitangi Tribunal, 135
Waikaremoana, Lake, 119
Wakefield, Edward Gibbon, 24–6, 54–6, 164, 208
Wave Hill Strike, 118
Wentworth, William, 52, 59
Whanganui River, 119
Wiremu Tamihana Tarapipipi, 210

Zealandia, ix

www.ingramcontent.com/pod-product-compliance
Lightning Source LLC
Chambersburg PA
CBHW080729230426
43665CB00020B/2680